The Journals of
Denton Welch

Books by Denton Welch

Brave and Cruel and Other Stories
(Hamish Hamilton, 1949)

Denton Welch. A Selection from His Published Works,
ed. Jocelyn Brooke (Chapman & Hall, 1963)

Dumb Instrument,
ed. Jean-Louis Chevalier (Enitharmon Press, 1976)

I Left My Grandfather's House
(Lion & Unicorn Press, 1958; Allison & Busby, 1984)

In Youth Is Pleasure
(Routledge, 1945; E. P. Dutton, 1985)

The Journals of Denton Welch,
ed. Michael De-la-Noy (E. P. Dutton, 1984).
Unabridged version, edited by Jocelyn Brooke,
was published by Hamish Hamilton (U.K.) in 1976.

A Last Sheaf
(John Lehmann, 1951)

Maiden Voyage
(Routledge, 1943; E. P. Dutton, 1984)

The Stories of Denton Welch,
ed. Robert Phillips (E. P. Dutton, 1986)

A Voice Through a Cloud
(John Lehmann, 1950; E. P. Dutton, 1984)

The Journals of

Denton Welch

Edited by Michael De-la-Noy

A Dutton Obelisk Paperback

E. P. DUTTON / NEW YORK

CONTENTS

This edition for Eric Oliver

INTRODUCTION

Maurice Denton Welch — he was baptized Denton after his American maternal grandmother, Katherine Denton — was born on 29 March 1915 in Shanghai, where both his grandfathers had settled to earn their fortunes, his maternal grandfather, Thomas Bassett (born in Boston, Massachusetts), in shipping, his paternal grandfather, Joseph Welch, as a tea merchant. All four of Joseph's children, including Denton's father, were born in Shanghai, as were all three of Denton's brothers. The eldest of Arthur and Rosalind Welch's sons, Bill, was seven years older than Denton; a second boy, Tommy, died in childhood; and Paul, Denton's favourite brother, was nineteen months his senior. Their father, a taciturn, undemonstrative man, related most closely to Bill; the most overwhelming influence on Denton's childhood, perhaps on his life, was his mother. Beautiful and possessive, she died at the age of forty-one from nephritis, a disease of the kidneys, when Denton was only eleven.

Denton's early childhood was one unsettled holiday, travelling with his mother between China and England, visiting Korea and Canada, staying in expensive hotels and rented houses, and his formal education was almost entirely neglected. At nine, the year he was sent to a girls' school in London, he still could not read. At the age of eleven, he progressed to an eccentric preparatory school, St Michael's at Uckfield in Sussex. His mother was a Christian Scientist and the school especially welcomed boys whose parents believed in the doctrines of Mrs Mary Baker Eddy. Although in adult life Denton was to reject Christian Science on intellectual grounds, he retained a natural distrust of doctors, and his mother's religious faith coloured and to some extent clouded his childhood.

Following his mother's death, Denton spent his school holidays in Henfield, Sussex, at a house called Whaphams, where his grandfather, Joseph Welch, had retired in 1910, and where his father's unmarried sister, Dorothy, kept house. At fourteen he joined Paul at Repton, but after two years he could endure the restrictive atmosphere of a public school no longer, and ran away. His family persuaded him to return for one last term. Then his father unexpectedly suggested a holiday in Shanghai. Repton, and the year spent in China with his father and Paul, were to provide the material for his first novel, *Maiden Voyage*.

On Denton's return to England in 1933 he enrolled, when still only seventeen, as a student at the Goldsmith School of Art in New Cross. When he was eighteen he discovered lodgings at 34 Croom's Hill, Greenwich, with Miss Evelyn Sinclair, whom Denton was destined to know for the rest of his life. And on 7 June 1935, when he was twenty, the course of his life was changed for ever. On his way to stay the weekend with an aunt and uncle at

Leigh in Surrey he was involved in a disastrous accident. A motorist knocked him off his bicycle. His spine was fractured, which led to inflammation of the bladder and kidney failure. Partial impotence resulted, he had to wear a catheter, haemorrhaging eventually developed, along with tuberculosis of the spine, and towards the end of his life he became subject to frequent and severe attacks of feverish headaches, high temperatures and pain.

The result of Denton's accident was to compel him to live an increasingly cloistered life; in spite of astonishing periods of respite, when he would walk, drive a car and again ride a bicycle, ill-health did mean long periods in bed, and a drastically curtailed social life. He became heavily dependent for human contact on letter-writing, and as his physical world closed in around him, confined as he eventually was for weeks at a time to his bedroom, he came to rely for literary inspiration to a very large extent on his memories of childhood and on people and places he had known as a young man before his health was ruined.

Even for a writer, Denton was lucky to possess an exceptionally retentive memory, and an astonishing ear for dialogue. His literary career was launched in 1942 with the publication in *Horizon* of an article recalling a visit to Walter Sickert, yet that visit had taken place six years before, while Denton was recuperating at a nursing home in Broadstairs. It was in 1942 as well that Denton began to keep his *Journals*, writing, as always, in longhand, in nineteen school exercise books, sometimes turning the books round and starting again at the other end. He illustrated each cover, and in his life-time provided the illustrations too for *Maiden Voyage* and *In Youth is Pleasure*, his first two novels, and for the jacket of *Brave and Cruel*, his first collection of short stories. No difficulty was experienced in discovering among his papers suitable illustrations for *A Voice Through a Cloud, A Last Sheaf, I Left My Grandfather's House* and *Dumb Instrument*, all published posthumously. Indeed, as an illustrator (he did work for *Vogue*) Denton might well have reached the top flight, and as an artist he progressed steadily from ineffectual student work to paintings of outstanding originality and often startling beauty. But it was in the last eight years of his life that he was to discover, and most probably exhaust, the material that went into his three novels and two collections of short stories which, together with the *Journals*, remain his limited, idiosyncratic and frequently brilliant contribution to autobiographical literature.

Although Denton occasionally juggled with events for dramatic purposes, every occasion about which he wrote and every character he wrote about was taken from real life. It was his power to recreate in fascinating detail the minutiae of life, as well as the sweep of sometimes terrifying, and often very funny, events, together with his belief in the relevance of unconsummated, even unaccomplished experiences that stands out as the hallmark of his work. He was, as Edith Sitwell never tired of telling him, a born writer, and everything he wrote was written after he had been condemned to death.

When he had recovered sufficiently from his accident to leave the Southcourt Nursing Home in Broadstairs, about which he was to write, without identifying it, in *A Voice Through a Cloud*, Denton moved in 1936 to a flat at 54 Hadlow Road, Tonbridge, taking as his housekeeper Evie Sinclair. In January 1940 they moved to another house in Kent, at St Mary's Platt, which he called the Hop Garden, where two disasters occurred. A bomb landed in the garden, and then a fire rendered the house uninhabitable. As a result, the beginning of literary success coincided, in the summer of 1942, with a move to rooms above a garage at a house called Pitt's Folly in Hadlow — again in Kent. Here Denton lived, in cramped and damp conditions, for four years, writing, painting, and whenever he could paying visits to antique shops, country houses and village churches, and it was here, in 1943, that he was introduced to Eric Oliver, whose friendship, after a stormy start, was to bring unexpected happiness and peace of mind to Denton's last years.

Denton began work on his first novel (a travel book, really), *Maiden Voyage*, late in 1940, after he had abandoned work on a more conventional style of autobiography, and it was published in May 1943; dedicated to Edith Sitwell, and carrying a Foreword by her, the first edition, now extremely valuable, sold out before publication. Miss Sitwell was not alone in recognizing Denton's gifts. Other distinguished writers and critics who praised Denton in his lifetime or encouraged him in one way or another included James Agate, W. H. Auden, Lord Berners, Elizabeth Bowen, Alex Comfort, Cyril Connolly, Maurice Cranston, C. Day Lewis, E. M. Forster, John Lehmann, Rose Macaulay, Harold Nicolson, Peter Quennell, Herbert Read, Vita Sackville-West, Frank Swinnerton, Tambimuttu, Henry Treece, W. J. Turner, Edmund Wilson and Woodrow Wyatt — by any standards an impressive roll-call of Denton's contemporary literati.

Denton's second novel, *In Youth is Pleasure*, recalling a holiday spent in England when he was fifteen, was published in 1945, to renewed critical acclaim. And in January 1944 Denton had already begun work on the third of his novels, *A Voice Through a Cloud*, arguably his finest achievement; it tells the story of the accident and its immediate aftermath, and proved, perhaps understandably, the hardest book he undertook. At one stage he laid it aside for twelve months and, all told, it took four years to write; in fact, it was not quite finished when Denton died, and like a number of his short stories it was published posthumously. The third book Denton actually saw to press, checking the proofs with Eric Oliver's assistance in August 1948, when he was by then quite desperately ill, was *Brave and Cruel*, his first collection of short stories, published on 7 January 1949, two days after his funeral. In 1951 John Lehmann, who had published Denton's work in *Penguin New Writing* and had undertaken the first edition of *A*

Voice Through a Cloud, gathered together a second collection of short stories, fragments and poems under the title *A Last Sheaf*. A further collection of Denton's poems, *Dumb Instrument*, edited by Jean-Louis Chevalier, appeared in 1976.

The circumstances of Denton's circumscribed life, in particular his lack of contact with other writers, made him peculiarly dependent on friendships with neighbours, with many of whom he enjoyed somewhat ambivalent relationships. One such was the painter Noël Adeney, whose holiday home in Kent, Middle Orchard at Crouch, Denton came to covet. Mrs Adeney declined to sell the property, but Denton did at last manage to persuade her to rent him the house, and it was here that he spent the last three years of his life, marred as they were by increasingly precarious health. And it was at Middle Orchard that Denton died, on 30 December 1948, aged thirty-three.

Denton Welch's *Journals* were so named by himself, for he never intended keeping a conventionally conceived and chronological diary. While it is true that many of the events recorded were written-up as they occurred — in bed, on picnics (which Denton adored), in churches, and sometimes while he was extremely ill — Denton also made deliberate use of the *Journals* to remind himself (and us, for without a doubt the *Journals* were intended for publication) of past events, often having his memory jogged by the arrival of an anniversary. Thus the *Journals* tend to shift around in time. Denton also used the exercise books in which they were written to draft stories and to jot down poems. The longest section omitted by Jocelyn Brooke in a heavily abridged edition of the *Journals* published in 1952 related to a walking tour Denton made when he was eighteen, and this was published separately in 1958 as *I Left My Grandfather's House*. Although at present the limited editions of this work remain collectors' items, an inexpensive reprint is due out from Allison & Busby in 1984, and for the sake of continuity and of space — the account runs to about 35,000 words — I, too, have omitted this long narrative section. I have also deleted the poems. They seem not to relate to the *Journals* proper any more than would a shopping list; sixty-seven of Denton's poems have already been published in *A Last Sheaf* and fifty-eight in *Dumb Instrument*, and with the greatest respect to Denton's poetic efforts, more than ample justice has been done to the least successful aspect of his literary output.

I have made two very minor cuts on grounds of libel, and a further minor excision on the entirely subjective grounds that I thought it a piece of gratuitous gossip likely to cause unjustifiable distress. Denton never revised the *Journals*, nor of course prepared them for publication, and I have taken the opportunity, here and there, of tidying up his punctuation, but not so as to alter in any way his sense or style. Every dash in the 1952 edition has been replaced by the name omitted, and at least 75,000 words of Denton's original manuscript appear in this edition for the first time. Most of

Brooke's major deletions were made presumably on grounds of space; it seems inconceivable that they were all made (although some were) because Brooke thought them boring, irrelevant or repetitious, and indeed some, like the occasion when Denton returns to Repton for an Old Boys' Dinner, or he meets Lady Ottoline Morrell's daughter, are among the most entertaining entries he wrote.

There is no guarantee that all the entry dates are accurate. On some occasions Denton merely wrote a date, on others both a date and a day. Sometimes, when he followed the later course, the date fails to tally with that of a previous entry. For example, in 1943 Monday, 21 February is followed by Tuesday, 23 February; in 1944 Saturday, 1 July is followed by Saturday, 7 July. There is no way of checking for certain whether he slipped up on the date or the day. He was often hazy about dates, sometimes failing to date letters at all, and once mis-dating a letter by two years! For the sake of simplicity I have deleted all the days, and it can reasonably be assumed that the majority of dates are correct.

In preparing this edition of *The Journals of Denton Welch* much of the help I earlier received while writing my biography of Welch has proved a boon a second time round. In particular I would like to record again a special debt of gratitude to Denton's cousin, the late Miss Beatrice Kane, who enabled me to fill in much family background; to Mr Eric Oliver, Denton's literary executor, who has continued until the bitter end to answer innumerable queries with inexhaustable good humour and patience; and to Mr Benjamin Whitrow, without whose initial fieldwork I doubt whether I should ever have edited the *Journals* at all. His discovery in England of a typescript of the expurgated portions of the *Journals* before I had researched at the University of Texas set the whole project in motion, and his careful identification and incorporation of previously omitted sections has saved me hours of routine work.

Because Denton Welch was an exclusively autobiographical writer, sometimes obsessed with an incident to the extent that he would write about it in a short story, again in his journal and yet again in letters to friends, the *Journals* do to some extent repay reading in conjunction with his other books and, if I may be permitted to say so without undue immodesty, his biography, for the thread of his life runs so closely entwined with that of his work. It is simply a question of fitting together a complete jigsaw, and not all the pieces lie in the same box. But the *Journals* still make compelling reading on their own, and deserve to rate with the journals or diaries of almost any other writer of genius, for they reveal the mind of the author with the kind of clarity only achieved through intellectual honesty and courage — in Denton's case, physical courage as well as moral. He has been thought by some too restricted or too precious, and by others too fruitful a field for pseudo-psychological dissection. Denton knew his own limitations, and never stepped outside them; he had enough self-knowledge to know he was in danger of offending against literary taste and almost always guarded against it; and his consistent honesty about himself leaves any necessity for psychoanalysis mercifully superfluous. For some readers, however, Denton may go on at excessive length in the *Journals* about visits to churches or repairing his dolls' house, but it needs to be remembered that in his novels and short stories he was among the most fastidious and self-disciplined of writers, and that to some extent the *Journals* were a perfectly justified self-indulgence. In any event, journals and diaries are written and published to be dipped into, and the reader is free to a large extent to act as editor, skipping the bits that do not interest him or her. At the end of the day, I believe the *Journals* deserve to be published, read and judged warts and all, not because they pretend to represent a polished example of Denton's neatest literary style or most cleverly condensed subject matter, but because they stand as a testament to his astonishingly rapid maturity as an author, as an invaluable record of a tragic and often heroic life, and as part of a permanent memorial to a unique and above all intensely interesting writer who achieved, under appallingly adverse conditions, precisely and immaculately what he set out to accomplish.

Michael De-la-Noy
London NW1
1984

In Gide's Journal I have just read again how he does not wish to write its pages slowly as he would the pages of a novel. He wants to train himself to rapid writing in it. It is just what I have always felt about this journal of mine. Don't ponder, don't grope — just plunge something down, and perhaps more clearness and quickness will come with practice.

Denton Welch, 27 February 1948, ten months before he died.

1942

AND THEN we all met at Penshurst; I and Maurice and Filthy Freddie, R.A.F.[1] And first we had tea (I found them waiting for me with the scones and butter on the table, when I came in from the rain). I played hostess and poured out and we talked of Freddie's R.A.F. adventures and the male qualities of the many women who passed by us in trousers. Not Leicester Arms but Lesbian Arms we called it for the hundredth time.

We talked of my Sickert article being accepted, and I showed with joy Connolly's rude little note asking if my unnamed man who couldn't pass water for six days were George Moore. I told them how I had written back to say that poor George Moore had died of his stricture long before my tea-party with Sickert.[2]

O how I want to be great!
Delusion of grandeur's my fate.

Then Freddie's girl, Molly, arrived. I had been warned that her face was scarred with impetigo. I steeled myself for sights and decided to keep far away, but when she came she was just the same, with pale, smooth, slightly blotched skin and pale quite lifeless hair. They twined hands lovingly and we all tried to order lemon gins again but the woman said, "Only one gin each", and so we all had shandy, two lemonade and two ginger.

21 July

Today I walked by the river and saw a man and boy working in the cornfield at the water's edge. They had taken their shirts off and their skin was beautiful and pale, like nacre, in the sunlight. Their brown throats and arms, grafted to their pearly bodies, were surprising.

I spoke to them shyly, asking where I could bathe. The man answered me. I saw that he had something blue and green tattooed on his arm. He said,

---

1 Maurice Cranston, later author and professor of political science. He and Denton met in Tunbridge Wells when Denton was twenty-three and Cranston eighteen. He appears as Markham in an untitled short story published posthumously in *Chance* in 1953. "Filthy Freddie" was Freddie Beale.

2 In 1936, while convalescing in Broadstairs from a road accident, Denton had been invited to tea by Walter Sickert. He recorded the occasion in "Sickert at St Peter's", published by Cyril Connolly in *Horizon*, August 1942, and reprinted in *A Last Sheaf*.

3

"Don't go in here because there's a whirlpool!" It looked as calm as ice. The boy looked into me with that deep, sulky, suspicious, adolescent look. His biceps and shoulders were like silky balls melting together. How I longed to be strong and lusty, not ill![3]

And being ill made me think of being great and famous. They are always linked together in my mind. I must not be so ill that I cannot be famous.

I walked on down the river with the hot sun on my shoulders, thinking of my first proof-reading which took place yesterday. When I tore open the envelope marked "Immediate" and saw the long roll lying like a Chinese scroll in front of me, I just had a feeling of easy confidence, almost indifference, which is quite alien to me. I saw that my name (in such large letters at the head of the article) had been spelt wrong. Then I had a flood of excitement and called to Eve to come and see.[4] All that morning we read and re-read, although there were only two mistakes.[5]

There was also a letter from Sacheverell Sitwell thanking me for the photograph of my Berners picture which I had sent him.[6] He had addressed the envelope to Mr Denton Welch. I wondered why; and also why I should mind.

24 July,

How I long, how I search for them when I pass. When I see them standing there, the sailor, the fat woman, the dirty little man with the pipe, I wonder what they will do when they break up and go home. They will think of the pub they have left, the road will be lonely to the cottage, they will know that

---

3 Denton's illness referred to throughout the *Journals* was caused initially by his road accident; on 7 June 1935, when he was twenty, he was knocked off his bicycle by a motorist. His spine was fractured, his bladder became infected, his kidneys failed, partial impotence resulted, he had to wear a catheter, and haemorrhaging, prolonged feverish attacks and eventually tuberculosis of the spine developed. It was against this background of appalling ill-health that everything he wrote, including the *Journals*, was achieved.

4 Evelyn Sinclair, twenty-two years older than Denton, who was his landlady from 1933-5 when he had lodgings as an art student at 34 Croom's Hill, Greenwich. When Denton left the Southcourt Nursing Home in Broadstairs to live in a flat at 54 Hadlow Road, Tonbridge, Miss Sinclair went with him as his housekeeper, and except for two short periods she remained with him until he died. He called her Eve or Evie, nicknamed her Lydia, and libelled her in letters as the Harlot and the Whore. She called him Puss. She appears as Miss Hellier in *A Voice Through a Cloud*, as Mrs Legatt in "The Fire in the Wood", published in *Brave and Cruel*, and as Miss Middlesborough in "A Novel Fragment", published posthumously in *A Last Sheaf*.

5 These were the proofs of the *Horizon* article on Sickert, the article that launched Denton's literary career (see 1942, note 2 above). His name had been misspelt Welsh.

6 *Portrait of Lord Berners as a Child, Dressed up as Robinson Crusoe.* This was a conversation piece inspired by a photograph of Lord Berners at the age of eight in the first volume of his autobiography, *First Childhood.* Denton began work on the painting at the Hop Garden, St

they will always be all alone in the world. The sailor will undo his trousers. The fat woman will think of her illness and the dirty little man will burst out crying.

20 August

And as I walked by the river today all the corn had been cut, and there were no barges left where the soldiers would work like slaves to get them in and out of the water while the officer sat on the bank, not even watching, but paring his nails. The soldiers were dressed in flimsy football shirts and dirty singlets or nothing, but the officer had on his neat uniform and a white jersey which he must once have had for school sports.

Now those barges were not there. They and the men must have crossed the channel to take part in the great battle the day before yesterday. Each barge would hold a tank so snugly and the men would sweat and strain just as they did here, only now it would be to get the monsters on to a French beach, and overhead there would be bombers and gusts of machine-gun fire.

Then there is death and dying over there still and agony all night for some. The five labourers forking the corn into the lorry see me by the river's brim and shout. I think one waves. It is so far away that I dare not answer for fear of a mistake or insults. I just watch the rhythm of the blue shirted and the white shirted ones playing to each other with their movements like flute and oboe. I think that being still by the river with prunes and biscuits and coffee and precious chocolate is almost to be easy. To take your shirt off and lie back against the spiky satin grass! To feel the first heavy drops of rain on your skin and to know that no one will come near you. Yet how I loathe nature lovers! My thoughts are never on nature though I go out to roam for hours in the fields every day. My thoughts always go to history, to what has happened century after century on each spot of earth. To lovers lying on the banks, young men that are dead.

On a torn piece of note-paper that I found was an eagle coming out of a circle on which was written Per Ardua ad Astra, then in washed-away ink an address of some aircraftman. And I remembered how a month ago I had found the same piece of paper, only then I could read his address. Now I couldn't. What was the letter about?

Mary's Platt, Kent, in 1941, where it nearly perished in a fire. Denton failed to persuade Lord Berners either to buy the painting or accept it as a gift, and after failing to sell it at the Leicester Galleries for £40 he gave it to the painter Helen Roeder, whom he had met as a student at the Goldsmith School of Art. Lord Berners had viewed the picture at the Randolph Hotel, Oxford, and Denton's account of his meeting with Berners, "A Morning With the Versatile Peer Lord Berners in the Ancient Seat of Learning", was published in *Time and Tide* shortly after Denton's death.

22 *August*

And as we sat there in the wood marked "Strictly Private" Noel Cousins and Frida and myself, we talked on gossip, and Noel was censorious.[7] How stupid the talk was! And how willing we each were really to do evil to one another! In years, in many years to come, thinking back to the far afternoon in the wood, what will I think but flat waste and desert feeling?

And now late at night they are playing *Pinafore. Pinafore* over the wireless, wafting me back to that first Christmas at St Michael's when I was so tense with life and unhappy that I can remember every flavour of those trivial, tuneful songs.[8] And I am amazed that the actors are singing so glibly, so lightly, not with all the fear, sorrow, hope and beauty that I felt. They are singing it for what it is — silly stuff that perfectly expresses late Victorian England, and I am singing it to myself as the language of all my life as a boy of eleven. It spells out now how I was afraid of what life could do to me; how I was alone among wild animals.

And now I see myself as I was then, running up to the cold dormitory, hiding myself in the bedclothes, imagining my cubicle transformed with precious stones and woods. Praying, always praying for freedom and loveliness.

Hearing the masters laughing downstairs and thinking of their horse-play.

Then I would sing:

"O joy O rapture unforeseen,
For now the skies are all serene,
The God of joy, the orb of love
Has set his standard high above,
The sky is all ablaze",

until I wanted to cry at the heartless wicked words.

Now that is all gone. Broken away, lost and forgotten. All that agony was poured out for nothing and I am still here fighting; with these four inept remarks still ringing in my ears. All said today by friends:

"That's where genius counts — I don't mean that you're a genius, but I think you're very talented."

But I won't recount the others, for they are silly, nor do I wish to remember them, for fear they might hurt when I read again.

---

7 Frida Easdale, married first to Brian Easdale, secondly to Noel Cousins. Friends and neighbours. Brian Easdale was a nephew of Noël Adeney, the painter, whose holiday home, Middle Orchard at Crouch in Kent, Denton rented for the last three years of his life.

8 St Michael's Preparatory School at Uckfield in Sussex, where Denton was sent as a boarder from the age of eleven until he went to Repton at fourteen. It catered largely for the sons of Christian Scientists, although the headmaster, the Reverend Harold Hibbert Herbert

30 August

To think of yesterday — along the river front at Chiswick, watching the silent baby and the young father in shorts and with a pipe.[9] Watching the baby swinging on the railing and the father gazing on it lovingly and treating it as if it were almost grown up. Then hearty, crude, deep shouts and singing, and seeing two nearly naked boys appearing over the top of the mud flats, paddling through the slime, cat-calling, gutturally crooning and splashing in the deeper pools, running their hands harshly all over their bodies to scrape off the mud. Then seeing them jump on to the road and getting set to run a race. One was much bigger than the other, with body almost formed, square, hard, swaying lightly, laughing with self-consciousness and swagger, pulling his trunks up, tossing his head to shake back his inert hair.

He ran with an amazing unmovement of the top of his body, holding his arms against him and flapping his hands loosely as if they had been ornamental fins. The younger boy, running with all his might, cannot contend for long; slowly the other, inch by inch, is carried beyond him. They disappear, laughing, shouting, tossing back their hair, down the squalid side-street.

Helen and I walk on past A. P. Herbert's house until we come to Lord Burlington's villa at Chiswick. An old Italian looking exactly like an English Cockney is selling ice creams at the gate. Helen insists on having one. "No pies, no pies," he says, "only corny-eets, only corny-eets!" Said like this with the long "e" and suggestion of "y" the word is so pretty and strange.

I must remember that before we got to the villa we passed through the churchyard. The service was on, we could hear the intoning, and as we passed the open door, to reach Hogarth's tomb, a breath of incense came out and surrounded us. The hot sun melted the resinous smell, it floated away through the dry grass, and Helen and I stood reading David Garrick's epitaph aloud, but in a whisper because of the service.

And so on to the gates of the villa. When at last we came in sight of the building we saw that it was defaced by everything from posters for dances, firemen's hoses, sandbags, firemen in shirt-sleeves (one had his shirt open to his belt showing a froth of black hair on his chest and a little, bright red identity disc on a greasy string winking through it) to sheer neglect.

We skirted the building, hating its degradation, wondering why no one

Hockey, was an Anglican clergyman. The school, which no longer exists, has been described by Michael Astor, a contemporary of Denton Welch, in *Tribal Feeling* (John Murray, 1963) and, disguised as St Ethelbert's, by another former pupil, Jocelyn Brooke, in *The Military Orchid* (the Bodley Head, 1948; reissued in 1981 by Secker and Warburg and Penguin Books in *The Orchid Trilogy*).

9 Denton had been staying the weekend in London with Helen Roeder (see 1942, note 6 above).

cared for its beauty. When we reached the other side we saw spreading in front of us a vista of old cedars, urns and sphinxes, with a semicircle of philosophers guarded by two lions at the end. A squat round of yellow privet had been planted, half hiding the philosophers. Everything was coarsened, neglected. But there was a mournful, sinister beauty about the whole wide garden which I think must have been intended. I thought that it was not the place to have been used for a lunatic asylum.

Winking through the evergreen oaks and other lovely trees were exquisite classical monuments; a tiny temple with an obelisk set in the middle of a lily pond, a terribly neglected bridge, delicate as ivory-work, a column with something set on the top that I could not distinguish. I thought that this lovely romantic patch could be made into the most beautiful garden in all England, but instead of that it is allowed to go to ruin, while the town worthies spend all their money on silly, gaudy "beds" and gaunt greenhouses.

The house is the least thought of thing of all.

Helen and I gnashed our teeth and then went back by bus. And as I sat after lunch I thought of the night before, Saturday night in Soho. Everyone gay and ready to be drunk. A negro in the bar, much in demand, shouting loud, good-natured threats at a just entered soldier. Sailors hot and sweaty, but looking "so fresh" as old ladies say of them. Little blondies talking to strange women and stranger men. In spite of what is on the surface, it is difficult, almost impossible to know the connection between any of these people. Then afterwards in the Chinese restaurant with the insolent little monkey waiter who told us that the table was too small to sit side by si ' who smiled at us contemptuously and brought us chicken, pineapple and noodles and rice.

While we sat there in the sweltering heat the rain beat down outside so that when we had finished and pushed back the whorish, dirty red satin curtain we found the porch full of sheltering people all laughing softly, whispering, giggling, fumbling with each other.

Helen and I waited a moment, then ran. Curious flares suddenly lit up the sky. "It's guns," I said. "It's the Underground," Helen said. Then we both realized that it was God's lightning and nothing to do with human beings.

We travelled fantastically through the bowels of the earth with all the others. They were thronging, laughing, lusting, looking sad. We saw strange old women sleeping in the bunks that lined the wall. "They have to sleep in their bunks," Helen said, "to keep their claim on them if the raids begin again." One bunk was draped in sacking, but I could just see sticking out a delicate child's leg.

Once home again, while Helen bathed I walked in the streets round Notting Hill Gate. It was getting late, after midnight. I went in at a door marked "Gentlemen" and found it thronged with stationary people. They were not going or coming, just standing in a sort of sinister trance. I fled

8

without more ado, feeling that I had intruded in some way. I wondered if people were all night in there, standing together in silence.

On Sunday afternoon we went to the Palace, past the lovely brick orangery and up the broad oak stairs into the chain of sober-panelled, delicious rooms with their thick barred windows and broad low window seats.[10]

One could sit there all day with a book and every now and then a glance at the huge pond, the children, the dogs, playing what seems so far away. Playing in another century, while you sit on, safe, encased, dreaming in a perfumed oaken box.

Helen had helped K. Clark to hang the pictures.[11] She showed me the wall she had done. We looked at all the topographical ones of London in the nineteenth century.

17 September

Yesterday was the day of miracles. I had four letters.

One was to say that C.E.M.A. wanted to hire a picture for £5 a year to send round the countryside in a travelling exhibition. One was to say that Mr J. Middleton Murry wanted to publish poems in the *Adelphi*. One was to ask me to correct my proof of a poem which Mr W. J. Turner had chosen for the *Spectator*.[12]

And last final plum, jewel, diadem and knock-out was a four-page letter from Edith Sitwell, telling me how much she and her brother Osbert enjoyed my Sickert article. How they "laughed till they cried". How one thing was clear, and that was that I was a *born writer*! She said twice how they had both *admired* the *writing* of it.[13]

It was such a beautiful, generous, deliriously exciting letter. I was childish with vanity, and still am, from its effects. It took all the bitterness from Lady Oxford's cold, almost coroneted objections to the Americanism "sensed" and the mention of W.C.s![14]

It is so thrilling to have such warm-hearted praise from a great genius. It was so utterly unexpected. It appears that Osbert was going to write to tell

---

10 Kensington Palace.
11 Sir Kenneth Clark, later Lord Clark. Helen Roeder worked at the National Gallery, where Clark had been appointed director in 1934, at the age of thirty-one.
12 "My House", published 27 November 1942 and reprinted in *A Last Sheaf*.
13 Realizing that Edith Sitwell, who was prone to champion new young writers, was bound to read *Horizon*, he had sent her, just before publication of his article on Sickert, a copy of her book *Street Songs* asking for her autograph.
14 The Countess of Oxford and Asquith, widow of the prime minister Herbert Asquith; Denton had written praising her autobiography. When he sent her a copy of his *Horizon* article on Sickert she told him she thought it "an error of taste to write of 'W.C.s'." Denton never forgave her.

Connolly how much they "admired" it. That delicious word! Of course one would give all the screams of praise that Lady Oxford has ever uttered just for one word from Edith Sitwell. And I have four pages to salve all the wounds that may have been inflicted.

It makes me fearful though, gives one the silly feeling that what one did cannot be repeated.

It is very intoxicating when a great person takes up a thing exactly as you intended when you wrote it — shows you by their remarks that nothing has misfired. One quickly gets the megalomaniac's outlook — that all who pick holes are swine, and that in future you will only keep your pearls for the great because they have minds like your own and do not tediously misunderstand you. It is fatal I see. O I have fed on her letter all day. It is perhaps what I live for, this sort of appreciation. I can never hope again to get quite such a generous dose, sent straight from the blue sky.

I was all day answering it, lying in the fields, by the lake and the stone camel bridge. Glittering Oxon Hoath over the choppy water looked wicked and wise, flashing its panes to the sun, anchored there in the middle of the green fields as it has been for a hundred years.[15]

26 September

That portrait of Gerard Hopkins in the [Times] Lit. Sup., so quiet, so thoughtful, so almost prettily devout. Strange to think that many, many years ago he actually sat exactly in that position, with folded hands (although they are not there), with secret, slightly hooded eyes, with gentle, posed mouth and soft tongues of hair lying on his forehead, licking sleekly down beside his ear.

Then the verbose article that tells one nothing — nothing of the secret from which his genius sprung. It is an insult to hide his secret — to pretend that he was "normal", in other words ordinary.

My letter from Herbert Read in his own hand that I had yesterday. It was hopeful and encouraging. May lunch on Monday be successful and delicious. May he like me, may I like him. May the book be published with success. May I be paid and famous. My book is almost lovely. I know it. But for the cloud which is me in it, as well as the loveliness which is me in it. Miss Sitwell has taken it for her present. I would write something fulsome and beautiful and florid at the beginning for her, but I may not dare.[16]

I cannot think how I shall lunch alone with him! Will I be asked to eat chops? O that they had entirely abolished the meat ration! It is dirty and

---

15 A local manor house, owned by Sir William Geary.
16 Herbert Read, the poet, was a director of Routledge and had recommended publication of Denton's first book, Maiden Voyage, after it had been rejected by Jonathan Cape, Chapman & Hall, the Fortune Press and the Bodley Head. Denton had asked permission to dedicate Maiden Voyage to Edith Sitwell before it had even been accepted.

villainous. Only devils should eat meat.[17]

There is new demonology afoot. Stupid of people to titillate themselves in this atavistic way.

Talking under the moon to the "superior"-voiced soldier who said, "Oh, I say, can I help?" when I exclaimed that my tyre was punctured. I thought, I like you, yet I hate you being almost educated. I cannot admire you as I would if you were a clod. This is a terribly muddled state to be in. It shows that I can never be true friends with anyone except distant women — far away. For I wish for communion with the inarticulate and can only fray and fritter with the quick. I would tinsel, tinsel all the day if I were so placed. Yet I love myself and my company so much that I would not even ask the soldier to come in for fear of his becoming a regular visitor. I even feel that people pollute my house who come into it.

28 September

Such full hours! Tea with the Graham Sutherlands yesterday (at C.C.'s).[18] She in black fish-net stockings, quite scarlet dress and bus conductor's satchel for a bag. He in good spirits and a curious shrimp-pink shirt and tie with what looked like little surréaliste spiders all over it. Talk lapsing to chichi quickly and then righting itself in periods of silence. But a success, really a great success, for they were kindness and sweetness to C.C. Mrs Sutherland taking my address and telephone number gave me the pleasant feeling that she thought me worth keeping an eye on. It is strange how even the slightest success will make ears prick up! How repulsive this sounds, now that I have written it!

Then today, in the crowded first-class carriage, to see Fay Compton and Someone squashed together on the seat opposite! At first I didn't think the large fine opal or the cabochon saphire real, because of the large and bulging satchel of imitation "hog". The snaky green bandeau round the red-gold hair; and there was an unpleasing and, I should imagine, fortuitous combination of brown and navy-blue clothing. But the moment she got her book of words out and Someone began hearing her part, I could no longer doubt who she was. It was all carried on in an undertone except suddenly when Someone went gay and piped, "Oo's my mummy!" in a piercing falsetto. They both collapsed and my *New Statesman* rose higher and higher so that I could grimace in privacy.

I had forgot to say that when I entered the carriage, Fay Compton stared at me, and then ever so slightly smiled as she looked at Someone who also

17 Despite this remark, Denton was not a vegetarian.
18 Cecilia Carpmael, a wealthy friend of Denton's mother, often known as Cecil. She was a painter, with a studio in Cheyne Walk, but the tea party would have taken place at her house in Trottiscliffe, Kent, where the Sutherlands also lived.

stared at me and ever so slightly smiled as he looked at her. The smiles met and evaporated in a moment.

My first, rather piqued, thought was, "What are those tinselly creatures interested in, and why does the man wear that ring on his *fourth* finger?" Then I quietened myself down and told myself not to be touchy; that they were probably thinking quite nice things about me. I now think this to be highly unlikely. Unless, of course, they weren't thinking about me at all. But is this nice either?

The part-reading went on until Fay brought out a benzedrine inhaler, heartily pushed it up her nose and then blew noisily. There was hand patting at the end of the hearing, much and loving hand patting, then a cigarette was unwisely offered to the Air Force man next to me. Fay's own somehow got too far into her mouth and she pulled it out, covered in lipstick.

The Air Force man said archly, "Another thing that's not so good."

"What?" said Fay, bewildered.

"It comes off!" he exclaimed.

"Oh," Someone and Fay said, as if this had been a gaucherie.

"Serves us right for using it," Fay remarked severely.

"Well, you've *got to*, more or less," the Air Force man returned with conviction and understanding.

There was no more conversation after this.

Then when I got to London I waited in the National Gallery refuge, supplier of food and W.C. I took advantage of both services. The Giotto is tiny and pretty and would be lovely to have for one's own. Something truly precious and magic.

When it was nearer lunch time I made my way into the city by bus. I found Carter Lane and stood under an arch, for it was raining hard. I wiped my face and looked at it in the top of my cigarette case. It looked strange. A gold face that moved about in strange wriggles and shiftings, but gold, gold like the sky in the Giotto. I thought that people with gold-coloured faces would be nicer and warmer.

I had no time to wait when I did go into Routledge's.

Herbert Read came out quickly and said, "I'm glad you're early because we'll get there before all the food's gone."

We went, without much talking, out of the building into Ludgate Circus to catch a bus. We had to separate then and I did not know where we were going yet.

Just before we got out he said, "I went to the Logar to see William Scott's picture, after I had read what Clive Bell said in the *New Statesman*."

"Aren't they frightful?" I said.

"Awful," he agreed. "There wasn't one you couldn't put a name to that wasn't William Scott's. As derivative as they could be."

"Why do you think C.B. writes that nonsense then?" I asked.

"I think Clive gets desperate," he answered, "and feels that he must discover someone or bust."

We laughed and walked on. I still did not know where we were going. I thought perhaps the Athenaeum. I was almost guiding his footsteps in that direction until he veered down Pall Mall.

"Up here," he said suddenly.

I climbed the stairs and entered the sober, ponderously rich hall with its marble balustraded gallery and its clear-cut anachronism of atmosphere. The late thirties and the forties of last century preserved like a mammoth in ice. Portraits framed in arched panels.

I still did not know where I was. While Herbert Read went to wash I sat on the button-tufted leather sofa to wait. It was in perfect keeping, breathing out a soft, faded tobacco scent, and almost one felt the stringent smell of some military hairpomade, though this was, no doubt, pure association and fantasy, playing tricks.

A thin, lame young man stiffly mounted the stairs, everything held tautly and erect, out of compliment it seemed to his unbendable leg.

"Ah, there you are," he said jauntily, abruptly, to another waiting figure. "How long have you been waiting?"

The question sounded rude because it was almost gracious. Immediately the friend fell into the opposite rôle.

"About a minute," he said, jokingly, humbly. Toadyingly is too strong, too clumsy and perhaps too non-existent a word.

They walked away together to the cloak-room. Stiff leg and rubber-ferruled stick leading, ordering, holding himself stiffly, making a hard shell to help him through each moment.

I thought of that melodrama *Rope* that is embedded in my childhood, and of how the arrogance which goes with injury pierces deep into one and melts one as no other thing can. It is probably no "good" feeling, just something unbearably poetic and picturesque.

I jumped up with a sudden brainwave and rushed to the notices and dangling bits of paper which always strike me as so repellent, I suppose because they remind me of the board in the House, on which all the horrible things one had to do at school were pinned.[19] Where one had to sleep, where play games, where have one's study.

"The Reform Club" in large letters met my eyes. "Thank God the conspiracy of silence is carried no further," I thought.

Herbert Read came back to me and ushered me before him into the dining-room. The clattering, newly imported waitresses did not go with the ponderous Corinthian pillars. One felt that it was not quite nice for them to be there, neither for the men, nor for themselves. They seemed excessively female, almost exuding a smell. And the men in their turn it seemed were

19 Brook House at Repton.

not exactly masculine (since this word inevitably conjures up a certain nobility, however fictional) but porkier, more obtuse, more neglectful and dead to any sort of attempt to make themselves either beautiful, attractive or even clean. I think one can only have this sensation (which is essentially a private thing and not an absolute reality) in English clubs now, apart from lunatic asylums, H.M. Forces, the Public Schools and other such dreadful institutions of course.

Herbert Read led me to a table in a corner on the left of the fire-place at one end of the long room.

"This used to be Henry James's table," he said.

I thought of my behind imprinting itself, just where that other behind had been, and the idea did not please me. But I was pleased romantically, apart from this physical association which was unhappy.

I thought of snobbery, of sensibility, of American idealism which roots about and climbs until it gets to the "best". I thought in fact about all the things that a not very well-informed person would think about when Henry James was mentioned. I thought of long, long sentences that wound to an end like the graceful coilings of a dying snake. I thought of Italy and my mother and my idea of the 'eighties and *principes*. Camellia-skinned American girls pursuing *principes* through the endlessly communicating state-rooms of a baroque palace.

How far I wandered from Henry James, into my own fantasies, remaking him in my own image.

"One has to keep one's meal under five shillings," Herbert Read said, busily beginning to write on a little slip of paper.

I chose duck soup; so did Herbert Read.

I chose plaice and sauce tartare and mashed potato; so did he.

I chose Apple Bouilliardoue (I have made this up, for the name is not properly remembered). So did he.

"Will you have half a pint?" he asked.

"I don't think I could manage it," I answered, as if it were some sort of "black draught" or nauseous medicine, which it is of course to me. "I'll just have water if I may."

And he had water too.

Was this following my lead, true politeness, lack of energy or love of simplicity, or even kindness for the waitress?

My book had not even been touched on yet. He told me an amusing and characteristic story of Queen Mary and a Wedgwood plaque. It appears that not even Queen Mary can change the identity of a sitter dead for a hundred and fifty years. She would have it that the portrait was of Princess Blank but unfortunately the original catalogue refused to adapt itself to this new theory. There was much displeasure for the keeper of the department for not agreeing with her and, I judge, for the original catalogue not confirming her.

He told me how when he told T. S. Eliot that he was thinking of resigning from the Reform, T. S. Eliot replied in shocked tones, "But don't you think you *ought* to go on supporting it?"

"I had never thought of a club as anything but something to use," Herbert Read said. "But Eliot is so much of a conservative in the true sense of the word that he feels it his duty and mine to go on supporting them even if we can't afford it.

"I've never known a man with less plastic sense," he said flatly, in answer to a question of mine on this point. "I've only heard him mention about three old masters all the twenty years I've known him."

Our apples with their little pastry boats and custard hats had been broken and eaten now. So I rose and left the seat of Henry James and went to wait by the door while Herbert Read paid the bill. Then we climbed the stairs and sat on the ponderous balcony, close to the cheese-yellow marble balustrade, under a little reading lamp, with an almost religious taper burning in a saucer between us. This was to light cigarettes from. I promptly picked it up, and in holding it out to him managed to put it out!

I brought out my Edith Sitwell letters to show him. After a moment of shy silence he said very stilly, with a smile, "I used to know her very well. I used to make omelettes for her."

Then he told me how she was good to him when he was young and provincial, but how there grew up a coldness, because he did not tell her that he was engaged.

"There was no reason why I should have told her; or Osbert," he said. "My future wife was quite unknown to them and not literary."

Long after this there was trouble again because of Geoffrey Grigson's article in which he said that Edith Sitwell had plagiarized some remarks on poetry in a book by Herbert Read.

"I can't go on saying that I don't believe a word of what Grigson wrote," he said. "You know what these things are. One can never put them right it seems — especially with the Sitwells."

After a pause: "Conceit isn't the word to describe their attitude," he said. "It's a sort of arrogance due, I think, to their loveless childhood. Their old father may be a genius in his way, his books on inner Mongolia and the history of the knife and fork" (a giggle here) "are masterpieces in their way, but he is completely eccentric, and their mother, of course, was locked up in prison, so the three children were thrown together and defended themselves from all about them in an almost fanatical way."

After this he said nothing for a moment; then, "Now let's talk about your book."

I waited anxiously.

"Some people might call it precious," he said, pausing.

I could bear it no longer.

"But then I suppose that's my personality," I croaked.

"Exactly," he agreed. "It struck me in some odd way as very contemporary, or of your generation."

"How strange that you should say that," I broke in, "when other people have told me exactly the opposite!"

"Ah, that's because it isn't full of politics and ideologies," he answered. "But I'm talking of its spirit, not its trimmings."

He went on, "I'm not quite sure whether this is the best time to publish such a book, though; on the other hand there may be a feeling in that direction, a boredom with war and horrors."

He then told me that I might take it that it was accepted, if the libel lawyer vetted it and passed it.

"Two of the directors, including myself, liked it very much. The other two couldn't *see* what *we* saw in it. I've had to explain rather patiently the merit I saw in it. What I've really been sent to find out is *terms*."

"I know nothing about terms," I said.

"What a good thing I'm a poet as well as a publisher," he smiled.

He asked me if I thought an advance of £50 all right. This was the most I had expected.[20]

We went on to talk about the jacket and the title page.

"Would you like to do them?" he asked. "Something rather elaborate and ornamental, don't you think?"

This strange, from the lips of Herbert Read.

We went on talking for a little. He took me into the rather beautiful library where bodies lay almost flat in cold-looking leather chairs. One gave us a queer incurious gaze, like an invalid or a mummy, or a weary old watchdog. No talking was allowed, so we whispered about the prospective size, shape and binding of the book.

Then he took me downstairs and I retrieved my disgusting old mackintosh.

"Do you think the title's good?" I asked.

"Yes, very, really."

"I'm glad," I answered. "I wasn't sure whether it was silly."

He took me to the front door.

"Good-bye," I said.

"Good-bye. You can take it that if there is no hitch it will be out in February."[21]

"I will send you my designs when done."

I walked quickly down the steps, thinking that it was a good lunch, a good day.

20 The advance was later reduced to £30.
21 *Maiden Voyage* was not in fact published until 7 May 1943.

28 *October*

Edith Sitwell.

I have just read your lovely letter.[22] I knew your writing and the notepaper at once, but did not open it for some time, waiting, wondering, almost afraid to. Then I slit it with the handle of my spoon (for I was eating breakfast), which is old and worn down to the thinness of a knife. I wanted to keep the envelope perfect as well as the letter.

Now with the tray still on my lap I write to thank you for it. It is too good of you to write when you are ill, especially as I did not expect it and told you that you must not.

I sent the book off to you last Friday and I expect you have it by now. You must not bother with it at all until you feel better. That copy may be kept as long as you like.

Yesterday I went up to London again to see Mr Read. Rather too short an interview to say everthing I had to say, as he had to go out to lunch, but still most things were settled, and I have my agreement to sign. It is for an advance of thirty pounds and ten per cent up to two thousand copies; after that, twelve and a half per cent. I suppose this is all as it should be. The only thing I am not quite certain about is the fact that I am to get nothing for the decorations I am doing. I think I must ask Mr Read about this, for although I am quite willing to do them for nothing, yet I would prefer to have them recognized in some way — even by a nominal payment.[23]

It was strange that when I got your letter I was re-reading pieces in your *Pleasures of Poetry* as I ate my toast and jam. I had arrived at the passage about Blake's "Tyger! Tyger! burning bright"

How I loved that poem when my plump cousin aged 12½ first recited it to me![24] She went on with, "Oh rose thou art sick", and I thought how sad it was that my own form-master would make us learn only Kipling, sometimes Sir Henry Newbolt and *once* Byron — "The Assyrian came down". This was in the whole *two* years that I was at Repton. I have omitted Shakespeare, for he came into another "class", not "repetition" as the learning of poetry was called.

Surely this is a terrible state of affairs — and it is only eight or nine years ago!

I realize how terribly my education has been neglected, firstly by

22 Denton occasionally transcribed in his *Journal* letters received. The following entry is presumably a transcription of the reply he sent to Edith Sitwell in response to a letter she had written him on 25 October, saying how delighted she was to hear that *Maiden Voyage* had been accepted by Routledge. When Denton says he had sent "the book" to Edith Sitwell, he meant a typescript.

23 On 17 May 1943, ten days after publication of *Maiden Voyage*, Denton heard he was to be paid for his decorations; the fact had earlier been "omitted in error".

24 Lois Marson, the youngest of nine children of the Reverend Thomas Kane and Edith Welch, elder sister of Denton's father.

submitting to orthodox, traditional schooling; then by rebelling against it and spending all my energy in trying to escape — ties and obligations of every sort. I am almost resigned to being nearly illiterate, but sometimes I have a sharp regret that nearly all my school days were wasted days!

31 October

Another precious letter from Edith Sitwell.[25] I realize that I almost begin to live for these. It is so funny, so winey, so toxic, always to be hearing fine things about one's attempts from someone famous. How much she says with no fear of using words full of feeling. There is beauty in someone being generous even if it should lead to difficulties of misunderstanding and withdrawal. No aftermath need spoil the pleasure she has given me; it is accomplished, done, set in time as history.

Miss Sitwell, your letter makes me ashamed of what I am not able to do. Your praise fills me with anxiety. Tell me, tell me the most glaring faults of my book, for if you don't I shall go on indefinitely reproducing them and then shall forfeit even your coolest interest.

How much I treasure the fact that you think my book moving! I, quite simply, want to cry about my book, but I know that I have not been able to dig deep, deep down and show myself and everyone else as we are, so striving after everything so looking, looking.

6 November

The Red Lacquer Screen in the gloaming.[26]

I think I have been told that such a scene is the celebration of the birthday of a grandfather; that the boys with the dragon kite are his grandchildren, arabesquing for his benefit.

Through the gateway, what is happening in the other pavilion — the one in front of which the boys turn cartwheels, playing strange antics, flinging their bodies in naughty positions, making fantastic, grotesque faces while the lovers in the gateway look on and are sad, full of passion and sadness for the extreme youth of the boys?

The evening, turning the red to dark blood, gathering in the corners of the angular design, gives it a wicked mystery, a murderous quality of guilt and beauty. In the daytime all is red, is gaudy with the blowsy, blooming peonies

---

25 Sent by registered post, acknowledging receipt of the typescript of *Maiden Voyage*. "You are most certainly a born writer," she told Denton. "Touch after touch, flash after flash, proves it."

26 The screen stood in Denton's room at Pitt's Folly Cottage, rooms above a garage at Pitt's Folly, Hadlow, Kent, into which Denton and Evie Sinclair had moved in June 1942 after the Hop Garden had been damaged by fire in December 1941.

in elegant vases flaunting their heads in a ceremonious row beneath the mountebank scene of gaiety.

Now in the furry shadows linger my secrets and yours; our terrors crystallize behind the bland old man so set out for his seventieth birthday. And what of the rabbit kites, the bird kites, the lotus leaves and clouds? All floating together in mingled jerking lines, it fades away as even does my paper where I write.

13 November

Now I hear that Freddie has been killed in action. Freddie was always dirty and, one felt, faintly slippery all over, with brown polished skin and a mind which leapt about and coloured itself according to the company. All things seemed almost equal to him. Broad, narrow, high, low, fat, thin; all were inquired into, laughed about. There was no sort of restraint or selection at all. Everything was made to be enjoyed as much as possible.

Only in the summer we had that lemon gin at Penshurst and I told them of my *Horizon* acceptance. Now with the notice of his death comes another fabulous letter from Edith Sitwell, praising my book with such a wealth of careful thought and expression. It is lovely and blossoming and budding and it comes with Freddie's death note. In an aeroplane in a blinding flash with burning hate and sights too horrible to dream of he must have died. He never meant anything to me, he was only someone who seemed miraculously unfettered by his sordid upbringing and by fear.

Three years ago when we went hunting for his ancestors' tombs in my little red car, to Biddenden, to Benenden, to the farms and other houses, picking up lean fragments about [Freddie's family], it was strange to imagine any sort of settled background with Freddie, any worthy burghers, prosperous farmers, gone-off squires. Yet his family was supposed to have a sort of trashy romance about it. They had lived for centuries in this part until they rotted away to Freddie's father who was always away from home "on the booze", a mysterious figure whom nobody ever met. And his mother? Well, she, it was said, would come to the door and then divest himself of her clothes as the visitor waited. There was obviously madness and instability on both sides.

Freddie saying aloud with childish fervour, "I want to be able to play Bach and Chopin better than anyone else in the world."

What must I write to Edith Sitwell? What must I tell her that I feel about her generosity? Somehow to accept it all is conceited, and yet to imply that she does not really mean it is insulting. What should one do but only be grateful. When someone who is able to judge so well only gives you praise and respect one feels *manqué*, lacking to such a degree that one is almost angry. Angry for praise, angry with God for not giving more gifts, angry for the talents that are wasted. With encouragement one feels pressed down, weighted, unworthy. Without it one feels left, deserted, kicked about, aggressive, hopeful (as nothing could be worse), and striving, striving, not bothering who one offends.

But with appreciation comes a little restraint, and fear that one will not again come up to expectation.

Everything jumps now in my mind back to the disasters at the Hop Garden.[27] The bomb first, on 15 August 1940, then the fire on 3 December 1941. There was something that was violent that would drive me from that house.

The day of the bomb I was in Tonbridge with May[28] at Peggy Mundy Castle's[29]. We heard the sirens go and ran about the house trying to see sights. Then as the guns began to go off we all gathered in the cellar. It was our first raid. The charwoman, who was still in the attic, shrieked out, "One's gone down over there, or is it a bomb?" We all ran to look and saw a wicked spiral of smoke from the direction of Platt. I said gaily, "I expect it's the Hop Garden."

Then I told lies to get away from them all, saying that I had to attend a gas-lecture.

I jumped into the car and went to the Angel, where I fraternized with three cadets.[30] One wore on his arm a little silver bracelet with the name Duveen inscribed on it. They talked about their schools and were still really prefects in mind. The other two chaffed Duveen about his identity disc, saying that he should wear it round his neck, not on his wrist. He said, "I know, but my girlfriend gave it to me and nobody will see it round my neck."

I left them late at night and drove through the darkness to Platt. Just as I put the car into the garage a most extraordinary explosion shook the place. I trembled, not knowing what it could be; there were no 'planes about. (Later I learned that it was a time-bomb, the last of the stick to be dropped on Platt.)

I walked up to the house in the veiled clouded moonlight. Nothing could clearly be seen. Then Evie met me and said, in a curious, frightening voice, "Don't be frightened. A bomb has landed in the garden but none of your treasures are hurt."

---

27 After living for four years at 54 Hadlow Road, Tonbridge, Denton had moved to a house at St Mary's Platt he called the Hop Garden in January 1940, leaving, because of the fire, on 3 December 1941.

28 May Walbrand-Evans, widow of the Vicar of Hawkhurst in Kent, whom Denton first met in 1938. She lived in a converted Georgian inn called the Brown Jug, at the entrance to Pitt's Folly. A painter and former "Edwardian beauty", she appears as Julia Bellingly in the title story "Brave and Cruel".

29 A neighbour.

30 The Angel Hotel, Tonbridge, since demolished.

I went round the corner of the wall and saw a huge mound of earth by the outside-staircase, the fir tree uprooted and tossed away, a hole like a burst blister dug deep into the large bed. Everywhere was earth, on the veranda, on the roof, and glass in huge knives and spears sticking into everything.

I went into the drawing-room, smothered inches deep in débris. But by a miracle nothing broken. Not even the glass lustres standing on the marble chess-table. Little digs and gashes showed on the walnut of the harpsichord; nothing more.

I went to bed in wonder and excitement and annoyance. How the room had been polished and beautified only the day before! So that all my things looked loved and cared for; the twelve and sixpenny ancestress, the Louis Seize bureau, the black and gold chess-table, the scarlet Coromandel screen, the Etruscan head, the fifteenth-century Nativity, the Empire bit of nonsense, so beautiful with Apollo's golden head and the wicked crystal spikes radiating from it.

Next day, from early morning, when workmen came, we had a constant stream of visitors. Unshaven, I showed them the hole. After ten days or a week the glass had all been replaced and the hole filled up, but the tree was dead.

Now to the other catastrophe.

Paul had arrived that afternoon and we sat by the stove talking of my buying the house[31] . We considered it as a good investment. I was going to write to Lucas about it.

After supper that night we went to Frida Easdale's and sat there drinking coffee and listening to her playing Chopin mazurkas. Suddenly, about quarter past ten, the telephone bell rang. Frida ran to it and we waited for her. There was something curious in her tone. I heard her say, "Oh, I see — I'll break it to him gently." I could not think what had happened. I wondered if a friend or a relation had suddenly been killed or had died.

Frida came back into the room and said rapidly, "Denton, don't be too alarmed, but I must tell you that your house is on fire."

I jumped up utterly surprised, not understanding how a ferro-concrete house could be on fire. I immediately thought that it must be a very small fire. Paul and I ran to the car and started to drive. "Not so fast," he said placidly. We scanned the sky for signs of the fire. I expected a glow on the clouds but there was nothing.

As we turned into the drive I saw the long thick hose like a fat worm. I ran up the path to find the house alive with people. Squirt and hiss of water and flame in the kitchen, and trampling feet and pools of swimming water in the drawing-room. I ran to take the Nativity from the wall. It was hot! And I felt a sort of sweat on it. I ran with it into the garden, then I went back for the

31 Denton's second brother (1913-54). He served in Italy and Tunisia with the North Irish Horse, and won a Military Cross.

Etruscan head and great-great-grandfather's sword.[32] This last was floating in its box on the black water which swilled over the floor. I held on to the arm of Amos the policeman as he helped me over the armchair and the rolled-up carpet. I could not bear to look at my things. Curls of burning paper had fallen from the ceiling and stuck to the covers and carpets.

I remembered my picture of Lord Berners which had to go to the Leicester Galleries in a few weeks' time. I almost fought my way up the stairs. People stood on every step laughing and talking excitedly. Soldiers, villagers, firemen, A.R.P. wardens, all had come as if to a victory celebration.

At the top of the stairs was blinding, choking smoke collected in a heavy blanket. Through the smoke I heard Evie say, "Oh, this is awful." I was nearly choking myself and felt my head reeling. I pulled her quickly to the sleeping-porch doors, which at first I could not open. Then I drew them wide and stood there gasping horribly and swallowing as much night air as I could.

When I had recovered I ran back again, keeping my eyes half shut. I twiddled the screws of the easel and pulled the picture away. It too was warm and the new paint had been made sticky. I was terrified to look at it for fear that my work of all the summer had been spoilt. I still clung to the idea that only the things in the kitchen had been lost.

Gradually the crowd dispersed, but not before a playful fireman had squirted me from an upstairs window! Captain Turner took Evie back to his house. She had burnt her head and still seemed dazed and lost.

Paul and I lit candles and went up into the studio. We made some sort of bed for him on the floor and he lay down. Then I remembered the silver basket in the kitchen! I ran down and searched under the wreck of the burnt trolley; the black wet mess was still hot. I raked it over with a stick. There was what remained of my mother's family's silver. Whole "nests" of spoons and forks had melted together. What had not lost its shape was burnt black and terra-cotta red.

This was the final thing. I had always longed for this silver, and nine years ago had actually got possession of it.[33] Now it was burnt and melted and twisted. I gave out a cry to Paul and he said, "So awfully sorry, Punky."

I thought of the people in Boston or New Bedford who had ordered the spoons and forks, who had decorated them with their initials; then I thought of them being taken to Shanghai by my grandmother and how we had used them ever since. Some had been made for Russells and some for

---

32 Presented to John Welch in 1808 for his work in the East Maylour Volunteers.
33 While staying from 1932-3 with his father in Shanghai, the city where Denton had been born and his father was in business.

Dentons and some for Randalls.[34] Now most of them had disappeared as their first owners had. I searched with my bicycle torch for all I could find; then I went up to my bed and lay down. My night was terrible, full of dreams coloured by the brilliant tossing fears in my brain.

When morning came, Paul gave one look at everything and said, "I'm going! I'll spoil my uniform!" He went off hurriedly and I was left to fight with the wreckage and salvage what I could. It seemed the end of everything. I did not know where to begin. I threw on my trousers and a thick sweater and went downstairs. Only then in the light of day could I see the damage.

[*The following extract was written on 24 November. It is clearly a continuation of Denton's recollection of the fire, and has been transposed here for the sake of continuity.*]

All the green velvet curtains were singed three feet from the ceiling down. The twelve-and-sixpenny ancestress had a gaping black hole for a face and terrible blisters all over her low bosom and satin dress. The carpets were scarred and pitted and soaking wet. Everything was in ruin and filth.

We started to salvage as much of the silver, china and glass as we could. Nearly all the sprigged dessert service was gone and most of the charming old tea-set which had been bought for twenty-five shillings. The pieces that had escaped being cracked to pieces were covered with a thick, black, baked-on crust. Slowly and mournfully we began to pack up what we could save. The most valuable things — except for the silver — had been saved.

We did not know where we could go that night, what we would do, for the house was made quite uninhabitable. The kitchen was gutted absolutely, with walls eaten into by flames, the metal frame of the window all twisted, the electric cooker a grotesque, disreputable affair of twisted wire and crazy gadgets. The thick sink lay in two broken egg-like parts on top of the pile of soaked wreckage, and the fitted cupboard had fallen apart, but some of its tinned lined drawers were stuck together and could not be opened.

I found a few more spoons and forks, some whole, some melted. I gathered all the remains up.

All the light wires and water pipes were made useless, many of the windows smashed or cracked. The fire had spread from the kitchen upstairs, not through the floor, because it was of concrete, but by looking out of the window above and catching the wall and ceiling "Gelotex" there. In this way the upstairs had been badly messed up too.

The whole thing was horrible, wasteful and stupid, and the pity of having interesting old things burnt is not to be thought of. It all came about because

---

34 Denton's maternal grandfather, Thomas Bassett, had settled in Shanghai from Boston, Massachusetts, and Denton had been baptized Denton after his American maternal grandmother, Katherine Denton. Elizabeth Randall and Kezia Russell were two of Denton's great-grandmothers.

of some fault in the construction of the flue of the kitchen boiler. It had happened once before in that house, before I went to live there. Now many of my things were sacrificed to it on this second time.

If only Paul and I had been in, we could have saved so much more and arrested it much sooner.

Evie explained that she had gone up to her bath, leaving the kitchen window wide open, because she noticed some curious smell which she thought I would not like. This, of course, was the first warning of the fire. As she lay in her bath she heard strange bangs (the bolts of the boiler bursting); then she saw a bright light playing on the trees in the garden and thought that we had come back and been careless about drawing the curtains. At last she rushed down, opened the kitchen door and saw the flames playing over the walls.

She lost her head and ran in to save the first thing she saw gleaming. It was the electric kettle! In doing this she burnt her head. She ran back again and rescued the old pyjamas and socks on the towel horse! Meanwhile the old silver, the lovely tea-set, the dessert set, the lovely Georgian square-based glasses were left to perish. (Later that night she remembered all these things and gnashed her teeth movingly.)

The fire by this time had spread to the hall. She whipped out the classical pedestal which had already caught at one corner.

The telephone seemed to go out of order as she touched it. She ran from the house to the workshop studios and got Mrs Galpin to telephone the Fire Brigade and me. Then everyone began to arrive. The flames were roaring as they poured on water. The soldiers nearby first made a line of buckets. How glad I am that I was not there to see all this horror. My things licked up.   Things people had loved and used for a hundred and fifty years.

Filthily black and utterly weary, we finished that evening by locking the most precious things in the bathroom (the only complete room); then we drove to May Walbrand-Evans who was going to put us up for the night. When she opened the door her face went quite blank with surprise and horror at our appearance. (We must have looked terrible with black faces and the burn in Evie's hair.)

Everything was spoilt of that home. Gradually, day by day we drove over to that "Hop Garden" and collected and packed all that we could save. [Jane] Gardener offered to let me the front rooms of Pond Farm, East Peckham. After the first appalling thought of close proximity, I steeled myself and accepted, for there was not a house to be had anywhere.

On 10 December we removed all my remaining stuff into the two bleak, dark front rooms. They looked unhappy, lost and cold, but I hung up the Louis Quinze cartoon to decorate the bareness; it looked rather fine all across one wall. We borrowed what china and cutlery we had not got and tried to settle down in this Pond Farm.

14 November

Sometimes I think of when we shall be quaint, be ancient history — like 1840 and gas lamps in the street or like De Quincey and his Anne in Soho Square, in the doorway with the port and the spices which saved his life. When we shall be like ivories or wax figures seen against a flat background. Something after us as well as before. Our future laid out as the nearer past of the people gazing back at us.

How fascinating to think of points in history when one passes the very places where the events took place. And how piercingly sad it is to know of all the agony that has washed down the city's walls.

24 November

Now I am ill in bed, but much better than yesterday when I could only think of things for a second before my mind switched in a painful dance to something else. All the time moving, jumping, thumping, aching; and strange visions of food that I could not rid myself of, sometimes making me feel sick and sometimes tantalizing me.

In this state, shut away from everyone, I think of ancient houses shut in by trees and garden walls, where conversation-pieces come to life. People moving in wide-panelled rooms, across the broad waxed boards, carrying their harsh clothes stiffly, holding their heads as high as possible as they sit in the high-backed chairs.

I am a little boy wandering down ever-lengthening picture galleries where the pictures lean out from the wall at a sharp angle, with their worn and dirt-encrusted gilt weakly gleaming in the late afternoon light. I am alone by the great high feather-crested bed, rubbing my cheek on the darned and brittle silver-thread hangings, running my finger along the tortoise-shell and ebony cabinet which has cockled in the damp. I am by the withered oak of the window-sill where the rust of the latch seems to grow like an orange lichen. Out over the mist-drenched garden goes my breath in a plume as I push open the shaking, faintly smoky-purple panes.

I am alone in some great house with the silver fire-dogs and the pot-pourri in the cracked Kang-shi jars. Rose-leaves thin and dry as flies' wings fall through my fingers, and send up the forest-spiced dust. At the bottom of the jar lies the scent of the rose dead for two hundred years. Layer upon layer lie the roses of each summer since then.

I conjure up the tea by the firelight, the Zoffany group round the simmering silver urn with the delicate plume of steam issuing from the delicate spout, the ivory knob carved like a pineapple; and the master of the house, bored with good living and no work, leans over the brocade sofa to his wife, searching her with his glassy, animal eyes. Those quaint, grotesque children playing with their rocking-horse in the shadows, with their wide cheery smiles which make their mouths look like slashed pomegranates, their tiny teeth appearing like the seeds; those children have died in old age a hundred and thirty years ago, yet I see them now as they keep away from Mamma who is undemonstrative and Papa who is downright harsh.

There, on the window tap the feathered trees and drip with the stored-up moisture of the air.

In the great house the family drinks its tea and the servants quarrel and make love.

2 December

Today I found, or think I found, three pure white hairs. They seemed to be shining like silver, but as there is gold in my hair they were difficult to track down and I am still not absolutely certain.[35]

When I had them all plucked out and in the palm of my hand a curious thrill of horror and pleasure ran through me. I had a resurgence of my longing for death which obsessed me so four years ago. Then I was twenty-three, now I am twenty-seven, and it comes back vividly how I longed and prayed to die before I was twenty-four.

I remember that terrible afternoon when Francis took me to the thirty-year-old religious film in the parish hall.[36] The flickering and the spitting and the starring of the reel gave the picture an unbearable nostalgia and depression. The camels, the robes, the city gates and the hats of the parishioners and the smell of their clothes hemmed one in and stifled me. I was seized in the panic of not being able to breathe or escape.

Roughly, I pushed past the others, disarranging the row of van-wood chairs. Francis said, "Where are you going?"

I did not answer but ran out into the air.

I wandered in the street; the light was failing.

I passed down the High Street and climbed the hill inevitably to J.E.'s house.[37] I spied through the hedge but could see nothing; the curtains were tightly drawn. Then I slunk into the garden and flattened my face against the

---

35 In a poem, "Will it twine at last", published in *A Last Sheaf*, Denton described the colour of his hair as "gingerbread".

36 Francis Streeten, whom Denton first met at the Angel Hotel, Tonbridge, in 1937. Nine years older than Denton, it was he who introduced Denton to Maurice Cranston, and later to Eric Oliver, with whom Denton was to live for the last four years of his life. Streeten appears as Danny Touchett in "A Fragment of a Life Story", published posthumously in *A Last Sheaf*, again as Touchett in *Chance* (see 1942, note 1 above) and as Danny Whittome in "A Picture in the Snow" (also published posthumously in *A Last Sheaf*). The account that follows was a first draft of "A Fragment of a Life Story".

37 42 Pembury Road, Tonbridge, the home from 1936 of Dr John Easton, always known as Jack. While convalescing at the Southcourt Nursing Home in Broadstairs, where Dr Easton

pane of the living room window. The warm lamp was shining, and through a crack in the living room curtains I could see the corner of a bookshelf and the cream paint of the wainscot. Once the little black Aberdeen ran across my line of vision, then there was nothing.

I took my face away in despair and utter hopelessness. It was then that I had the idea to kill myself. "These things are cumulative," I remembered reading. "If you go on trying, you'll one day succeed."

Alertly, and with more vigour, I threaded my way back through the town. I knew now that there was something I could try. When I got back to the flat Francis was waiting for me, wanting to know why I had run away. Supper was nearly ready too. I could smell the soup.

I was in a sort of drunken state with the hard stone in my heart and stomach. I went into my bedroom "to change my shoes", as I told Francis. I sat down on the bed and looked out the little black-and-white box of Prontosil tablets. I looked at them long, nestling in the puce lining of the box. I counted them. There were sixteen. I had been ordered three or four a day and was always asked rather anxiously if they made me feel depressed. I thought from this that they must be poisonous.

Sixteen, I felt, would be decisive, or at least enough to make me extremely ill.

Getting some water in a glass, I sat with the water and tablets before me; then I began systematically to swallow the tablets until they were all gone.

I stood up desperate and happy, wondering when I should feel the effects. I ran back into the other room where the soup was already steaming in two bowls. I felt that I must enjoy my last moments to the full. I laughed and shouted.

"Have some soup, Francis, some lovely, steaming, soothing soup."

I caught hold of the sherry bottle and poured out two glasses. I drank mine quickly, taking some more. I poured sherry into the soup and spread my toast with butter.

"I must die happy and contented," I thought.

Suddenly I burst out with what I had done. I became terrified and ecstatic because I felt a creeping tingling and swimming in my head.

"I've just swallowed sixteen Prontosil tablets," I shrieked.

At first Francis did not believe me, then he jumped to his feet nervously. "Are you all right?" he asked. "Why did you do that?"

I tried to calm him.

"Don't be so stupid. Don't be so stupid. I only feel a little queer."

I seized the sherry bottle again and poured more out, slopping it on the

was a visiting physician, Denton had become obsessed with him; he appears as Dr Farley in *A Voice Through a Cloud*. He also appears, unnamed, in "A Fragment of a Life Story" (see 1942, note 36 above), and as Jack in "Alex Fairburn" (*Texas Quarterly*). It was Dr Easton's decision to move to a practice in Tonbridge that prompted Denton to live in the town, where he proceeded to make a considerable nuisance of himself.

tray and feeling sorry at the mess and the waste. I suddenly realized that it would not matter how much I spoilt and degraded the things I loved, for I was going to die. I almost knew it, yet I could not quite believe it. When I said, "These are your last moments; look long, bore down with those eyes which will soon never be able to see anything again", when I said, "Taste this last bowl of soup which will never pass those lips," I wanted to cry and laugh and smack myself and wake up to find that I was still a small boy of nine or ten whose mother loved him and had a warm place by the library fire at night where his father would sit reading some old, leathery, upholstered, comforting fustian. Something about Maria who lived in Genoa which was the great and wicked rival of Venice where the winged lion, so wonderful and fierce, swam against the sky in the square of St Mark's.

I opened my eyes again to see Francis still sitting there awkwardly, feverishly fiddling with his cigarette, and giving me short, sharp furtive glances. He was clearly about to jump up and leave me.

"Those nicotined fingers," I thought, "and those dirty nails; those unspeakable teeth and your agile diverting mind, you are a wreck at thirty-four. You're craven and you'll one day be a lunatic."

I stretched out my hands and said, "Don't go." I had a sudden horror of being left to die alone.

"You can't go and leave me. Look at the state I'm in."

He lurched to his feet like a frightened bullock.

"You go to bed," he urged. "Or get the doctor."

The drumming was rising to a crescendo in my ears. I could not tell now whether I was drunk or whether it was the Prontosil in action.

As he pushed his way clumsily to the front door I followed, snatching up a stick in the hall. We walked rapidly in the direction of his house.

My legs were getting curiously heavy but I was still able to move them. I laughed and sang, cracking stupid jokes and saying how disgusting it was to leave someone who was dying. When we got to the fork at the Star and Garter I shouted again: "You can't go. You can't go. What's going to happen to me? I can't be abandoned like this. It is shameful, you're a monster."

Anyone seeing us would think we were acting. It was midnight, the lights were still burning in the silence. Nothing moved.

"Shall I take you to the doctor's?" he asked, half-heartedly.

"Yes, if I can walk that far," I answered.

Then I saw the craven, lazy light come into his eyes again and he veered away rapidly, saying, "Good-night. Go back to bed quickly."

I screamed oaths and blasphemy after him, half in fun, then, alone, beginning to be frightened, I wondered whether to go on to the doctor's house or home.

I decided on home and dragged myself there somehow. The fire was still burning in the sitting-room. I told myself that there were things that must be burnt before I lost consciousness.

I threw them on to the fire so that great flames licked out and roared up the chimney. The paint on the mantle piece blistered. I got alarmed, ran for water and E. came in excitedly.[38]

Gradually the blaze subsided. Then I lay down and thought that my hour was nearly come. My head was splitting. Everything in me seemed to be burning. I was in some way losing all the salt and virtue of my senses; all was dumb, muffled, distorted, terrifying.

I told E. to ring the doctor. I dreaded calling him so late, but I felt that I could not be left in ignorance like this.

I waited, wriggling and lashing about on the bed, with the dull stone heated to red heat now in my stomach or my heart.

He came and saw me on the bed. There was an unbearable moment of self-consciousness. He roughly turned me towards him and said, "What's this?" like a school prefect coldly, disdainfully.

I faltered out something about the Prontosil and more about my unhappiness. His manner suddenly changed to one of businesslike gaiety.

"I think first of all we'd better try and make you sick," he said.

I smiled and laughed in spite of everything.

He went for the mustard, the hot water, the spoon.

I drank the yellow stuff in great gulps, and waited. Nothing happened. He looked at me rather anxiously.

"Nothing doing?" he asked.

"I don't think so," I said.

Then, because my head seemed about to boil and crack, I added, "Can you give me anything for my head or to make me sleep?"

"It would be very much better for you if you didn't," he said. "You've taken quite enough drugs for one night."

He laughed and joked and I began to be grateful to him.

He had driven away the nightmare, if only for the moment.

At last he left me. He came forward saying ceremoniously, like a schoolboy again, "Let's shake hands."

I sat up in bed and held mine out. It was not silly, although it was self-conscious.

"I'll come and see you tomorrow," he said. "Try to sleep and be as calm as possible. Although you'll have a hell of a night. It's much better that you shouldn't take anything else. You've got to work all that stuff out of you."

I lay back in the dark room, thankful to him and grateful but just a little resentful about his seeming unconcern about the effects of prontosil. I'm sure it will be more serious than he makes out, I thought. If only there had been more tablets I would have swallowed them all. I am fond of him for being

---

38 Evie Sinclair (see 1942, note 4 above), called by her nickname Lydia in the final version. The doctor for whom she telephones in Francis Streeten's doctor, not Dr Easton.

nice. He is young and lusty and quite different from me and those people are only nice when everything else is stripped away, and they see someone else left quite hopeless and "dished". In ordinary circumstances they are bound up and encased in all their funny little fetishes and taboos.

Towards early morning I fell into a short sleep, and on waking, the fantastic memories of the night seemed to hover above my head, out of reach; then they came down like a shirt enveloping me, lapping me round, submerging me.

4 December

Nine years ago, in November 1933, I went back to Repton for an Old Boys' Celebration Day or whatever it may be called. It seems perhaps a curious thing for me to have done, and yet not curious at all. Although I ran away and hated it so much, my eyes and my heart often look that way. At any moment of the day a picture may flick up in my mind of the street outside Brook House with the high wall of the games yard and the little gate piercing it. The high wall looks like a prison wall and the little gate is wicked too, yet they still hold their sort of frightening glamour.

At the art school on the Friday evening I told Johnny Lewis that I was going and asked him anxiously if he thought that my blue checked shirt was too conspicuous.[39] He hesitated for a moment and then said gently, "I think perhaps it is a little."

This determined me to wear it, although I had misgivings. I was always defiant, feeling it cowardly not to persist, if surprise was expressed at my clothes.

I got into the train at St Pancras and sat with two men from the Midlands. They were strangers to each other but soon got into conversation. It seemed to be a curious mixture of business, food and betting. I heard remarks about hardware and goods and rice and form.

I sat gazing out of the window as the passing landscape gradually lost its colour. Soon it was quite dark and I could no longer say the names of the different counties to myself, trying to discover differences.

Changing into the little Willington train at Derby, I found myself in a compartment with two older men. I soon learnt that they were also Reptonians, but of an earlier vintage. They did not speak to me, only to each other, but I listened carefully to every word.

The most interesting and the most diffident one began by talking rather pretentiously. There were questions about Paris and other places, which he could answer far better than his companion, one felt. In spite of this, the rather boorish companion still seemed to have the upper hand. He

39 The Goldsmith School of Art at New Cross. He enrolled in 1933, when he was still seventeen.

occasionally grunted or said a word or two; and I felt sorry for the other one who was obviously the more intelligent and yet was showing up to so little advantage.

I lost them on the platform at Willington and did not see them again. I drove to Brook House and let myself in to the boys' part. It was not quite two years since I had left and gone to China with Paul. It seemed far longer than that, of course, and yet, when I smelt that mixture of scrubbed wood, sweaty football socks and shirts from the "Dryer", and hair oil and toast, I was back again in a moment, dressed in an Eton suit, frightened, stifled, full of revolt, feeling that I would never be young and happy again.

Now the remembrance of my pain gave a sort of fillip to everything I did and saw. "Green" Anderson was the Head of the House now and he came and rescued me before I could feel embarrassed by the eyes of unknown, younger boys.

He took me to his study and I tasted the privilege which had been denied me as a schoolboy. He told his fag to make me two pieces of buttered toast for tea and I remembered how I had had to do this every night.

Now, whenever I see toast I judge it by those rigorous standards of my study-holder. It must not be burned even in the minutest degree. It must be golden, honey, amber brown all over, but not hard-crisp with a fluffy centre. The butter must be smoothly spread and gently sizzling as you rush it into the dining-room.

Oh, the agony of producing this dainty every night on a difficult fire for someone you would gladly choke if you could!

I felt as guilty as the poor boy settled again at the fire. His face was crimson from the heat. And he looked curiously pleasant and attractive, because, although he seemed strong and sensible, yet he was submissive. This is always flattering. He did not mind making toast for the old boy; he even seemed pleased. Anyhow it was his duty to do what he was told and he did it without question.

It is difficult for anyone who has not experienced it to realize the cast-iron convention of submission in English schools. If you do not bow the knee willingly and with good grace you are an outcast and a cad. In some subtle way, independance is made to appear low, "canaille". Hence, if you are a prefect (or an old boy down for the day) you have the extraordinary and rather wicked pleasure of being waited on by boys who are in every way your "equal" except for the number of years they have lived. Their deference must make after life seem flat and rough to the person who has been successful at school.

I was so filled with pleasure and the sense of comfort that I jumped up and said that I was going across to Taylor's to buy something for tea. Other people who knew me had collected by now and I asked them what they would like.

"Pilchards!" they said, and a thrill went through me that I could buy lovely pilchards in tomato sauce for my school fellows who liked me now and treated me with affection and respect because I was "grown up" and free.

I ran across the road and smiled at the girl. She knew me but I did not dare talk to her for long, for fear that she would muddle me with someone else and so hurt my pride.

The sleek oval tins and the Bourbon biscuits seemed to hold more pleasure in store than was decent.

"Oh, I'm so happy," I thought. "Don't spoil it, God, don't spoil it, by letting me think of other terrible things."

We had the pilchards heated and put on to our delicious pieces of toast. I sat at the high table with the prefects and felt utterly satisfied. I was treated with that mixture of respect and comradeship which is so soothing. Their gratefulness for the pilchards and the chocolate biscuits was touching. I had made a little feast, an occasion, by providing them.

Afterwards I trudged up to the San', where I was supposed to be staying. I would soon have to change into my dinner-jacket for the Old Boys' Dinner in the gymnasium.

"Spooney" Walker had been put into the same dormitory as myself. He was already changing by his bed. He gave me a studied, casual greeting as if we had seen each other every day for years. He was now up at New College and was going to be a doctor.

I asked him to tie my tie. I was still very incompetent at this.[40] He fiddled about with it and produced some sort of bow.

We walked together through the cold street to the Gymnasium. I was so pleased that I had found someone to give me moral support.

The room was already fairly full and dinner soon began. We sat at a table near the door. There seemed to be some arrangement by which one went to fetch one's own drinks from a bar. At the end of the meal Spooney kept on leaving me to fetch glasses of port. I refused them and drank nothing, so he drank for two.

I was thinking of the Gym on punishment drill days when one sweated round with dumb-bells, and of the days when I would let myself in and would swing alone on the ropes, climbing higher and higher until I nearly touched the beams, when a climax of fear and pleasure would pass through me.

Christie, the new headmaster, stood up and said something about a concert.[41] Then there was half-hearted singing and a lot more drinking.

---

40 A reference to the scene in "When I Was Thirteen", first published in *Horizon*, April 1944, and reprinted in *Brave and Cruel*, in which Archer helps Denton to tie his bow tie before dinner.

41 Denton's headmaster at Repton had been the Reverend Geoffrey Fisher, later Bishop of Chester, Bishop of London and Archbishop of Canterbury.

Indeed the behaviour was getting quite childish and skittish. People chased each other, and there were skirmishes and collisions. Christie looked on and smiled with a sort of pained and understanding expression — very insulting. I hated to be included in such a smile.

"Let's go," I said to Spooney.

"My dear young Welch," he answered, "by all means, if I can stand up. Will you give me a little inconspicuous support?"

"Don't be silly, Spooney," I said, "you're not as drunk as that."

But I linked my arm through his as carelessly as possible and we moved to the door. He lurched a little and leaned on me, but I thought that he was probably acting. Outside in the cold he turned away from me for a moment and, when he had finished, we passed on up the village street, leaving the chapel, the arch, the music schools behind.

"Let's go for a walk," I said. "It'll sober you up."

"All right, but you must guide me. Where shall we go?"

"Crew's Ferry," I decided at once. "You can lean on me as much as you like. Is that all right?"

He was so much taller that I seemed to fit into the niche under his arm, and in this way I also gained support.

Soon we were out of the village, between the fields. It was so still and serene and wet and misty that we began to sing. We both sang in hoarse, croaky altos, pretending that we were little choir boys. Spooney told me about Oxford, and I told him about the art school.

When we got to the Crew's pond we leant over the stone balustrade of the bridge and spat into the misty, woolly surface of the water. It looked thick and pearly, like paste.

We came back by the footpath which follows the stream through the fields. The trees dripped and the clots of autumn leaves stuck to our thin patent leather shoes. Spooney's black silk scarf waved about, and I wound it round both our necks to tie us together more securely.

We were coming to a dangerous bit where the ground shelved steeply to the little stream.

"Lean on me and be careful, Spooney, else we'll both overbalance in the water," I said.

"Oh, why did I drink so much?" he asked, and with a specially manoeuvred lurch brought us down.

We rolled in a heap to the edge of the water where we lay. One of my feet went under the water.

"You devil!" I hit out, laughing, dragging myself up, and trying to drag him up with me. But his large bulk was too heavy and he sat there trying to defend his head with his arms.

I pulled at him again and he staggered up and clung on to me. "You did it on purpose," I said, "and you've ruined our clothes."

We walked on, not minding now whether we stood or fell as we were already covered in mud.

What fun it was to sing and bawl through the streets where we had lately had to behave so dully and correctly!

Back in the Sanatorium, the dormitories were buzzing with an extraordinary glamour. The Old Boys, rather the worse for wear, were indulging in horse-play. Very exuberant and rather peculiar in some cases. Spooney and I were some of the youngest there. I think I was quite the youngest.[42]

For some reason our appearance caused a diversion. A plump drunk came up to me and made a curious suggestion in mockery and fun. I was extremely non-plussed and flustered. Everyone laughed and shouted, and two sporting-looking creatures, with flattened noses and straw coloured hair, began to roll the white chambers down the long corridors.

"Can't we shut ourselves into our own dormitories?" I asked Spooney.

We went in and shut the door firmly. When I turned round who should I find but Riley undressing by his bed on the other side of the room. Riley, who had in some ways been the evil genius of my schooldays.

He gave me a superior smirk and said, "Still exactly the same young Welch."

I remembered the last day of my first term when he had dragged me on to his knee and I had burst into tears, which seemed to please him all the more. I remembered the awful nights in the dormitory when he ordered me to come and stand by his bed after I had come up from practising for the House singing competition. I would stand by his head and he would reach out his rather "hungry" hand and grip hold of me. How I disliked him! Not so much because of his acts, which were bad enough, but because of his body and face. He was well built, but his skin had a repulsive tone and touch and all the features of his face seemed thickened, like those coarse black-eyed portraits on Alexandrine mummy-case lids.

Now, as I gazed at him in his shirt and pants, he had the strange sort of fascination frightening things have. I laughed and joked with him a little too much, with too much emphasis on words and gestures. He did little to veil his eyes, which wore the viper-glare that Francis Bacon's were supposed to have. Indeed, take away the intellectuality and blunt the features and you have something of Riley in Bacon's pictures.

We turned out the lights at last and soon Spooney was snoring almost inaudibly. I could still feel the alertness of Riley in his bed. He turned and let out sighs of breath. I waited with dread for what might happen. Everything was wiped away of the last two years and I, now at his mercy again, a fag in the dormitory of which he was head.

Suddenly the door flew open and someone fell on the floor in a heap.

42 Having absconded, Denton had been allowed to leave Repton at sixteen, and on his return for the Old Boys' Dinner he was still only the age of the senior boys at school.

the light in the passage I could see that his evening clothes were "tousled", to say the least.

He picked himself up, cursing, and started to chant like a priest; then he went over to the fire, which was burning brightly, and spat into it.

"Bloody thing's going out," he grumbled, and spying the coal box, picked it up bodily and threw almost the entire contents on to the flames. The lumps of coal cascaded on to the floor in an avalanche. Spooney woke up and asked, "What's happened?"

Riley became testy and sergeant-majorish. The drunk Old Boy, who was senior to all of us by many years, switched on the light, and staring round said, "I don't know any of you."

We gathered round the fire and began to pick the coals off and to gather them up from the floor.

"There's quite enough on already," we explained, and suggested that he should go to bed.

As soon as we had put all the coal back in the scuttle, he picked it up again and threw it on the fire. This happened several times and we were in despair, fearing that the place might catch fire.

At last the drunk fell into bed, but the rest of us did not dare to sleep for some time, in case he should wake and start his tricks again.

In the early hours, I heard Riley tiptoe across to me and say, "Let's go to the bathroom before the others wake up; there'll be a terrible crush."

I was most unwilling to do this, but I had to be amiable.

"Shall I go first," I said firmly, "or will you?"

This was clearly not his idea, but he appeared to fall in with it.

"All right, you go first, if you're quick."

I got up hastily, taking my clothes with me to the bathroom.

As I stood up in the bath naked (for the water had not yet warmed the cold enamel) I heard the door being tried.

"Let me in, let me in," Riley said, "I want to get some water for shaving, while you're bathing."

I turned the key reluctantly and jumped back into the bath. He came in, muffled up in his dark camel-hair dressing-gown, and bent over the can as he held it under the tap. Something was going on within him and he would not talk, but seemed to be fuming and fretting. He spent far too long over filling the can and still would not go. At last the situation petered out in complete anticlimax. Something went quite hard and stern and loathing within me. I would not even look at him until he gradually, weakly withdrew from the room.

Then I became quite sorry for poor Riley, who must be hated quite as much, now that he was at Sandhurst, as he had been at Repton.

We all had breakfast that morning at the Bull. It seemed such a small pub to hold so many people. I sat next to someone who I remembered as a dark person with thick red cheeks. The dark hair and the red cheeks were still there, but something had happened to his face. Some dreadful operation had been performed and now there was a huge dent in his forehead and the skin was pulled away from his eye. One of the red cheeks went in instead of out.

It was difficult to eat my breakfast while looking at him, yet I could not look away.

7 December

I have just heard that my father is dead. He died on 9 November, I don't know where. I suppose in Shanghai.[43]

I said, "Oh Lord," and 9 November seemed to leave the paper and enlarge as it came towards me, but it was really only the slightest shock and there was hardly any grief with it at all.

I thought of the happiest times; when I had been a little boy, sitting by the library fire in my thick, quilted kimono, eating bread and butter and drinking hot milk, while he read to me, as I have described before.[44]

I thought of his dull life dedicated to making money; and the thought of money made something churn and stir inside me. What would happen? Would I be richer or poorer? Would all sources of supply be cut off, at least for the time being, because of the war with Japan? Would the London office cease paying me his allowance because my father was dead and consequently no longer a director of their company? What was my step-mother going to do — and my eldest brother? Were they all seizing as much money as possible?[45]

I had always looked upon my father as a rich man and a bulwark in some measure between me and the future. And now I wished that if he had to die he had died in England or America, not in far away China.

I am asking myself all these questions still. I cannot help it if they are nearly all to do with money. All that is left of my father is what he has left.

Will my step-mother Ada ever send me, or be able to send me, anything of his — a cigarette case, cuff-links or a watch? I should like them chiefly for what they are and only a very little because they were his.

In the evening.

I have heard three shapes of music tonight: (1) "Je cherche, je cherche

---

43 Arthur Welch had died in Shanghai from lung cancer at the age of sixty-two, a few days after being interned by the Japanese.

44 The last paragraph of "Sickert at St Peter's" (see 1942, note 2 above).

45 After Denton's accident his father had made him an allowance of £300 a year. This now ceased. His stepmother, Ada Henderson, who married Arthur Welch in 1937, had made her escape to America; she was, like Denton's mother, American. Denton's eldest brother was William (1908-65), always known as Bill.

Titina'', (2) something to do with ''amour'' and ''Martini'', I think, and (3) Beethoven's Fifth Symphony. ''Je cherche Titina'' takes me straight back to the Van Dyck Hotel drawing-room in the autumn of 1924.[46]

The room looks on to the Natural History Gardens. I am nine years old and am sitting with a sort of friend who is poor and so is acting as a sort of playfellow-companion to me. This arrangement is chiefly made, I think, because my mother wants to help her friend, but I have the sneaking fear that it may also be because my mother is bored with me. This makes me a little resentful and wilful with Molly, although I am really fond of her. Although she is middle-aged, I am told to call her Molly — just like that — nothing before or after. It strikes me as daring and rather nice, but a little embarrassing. I always have to say it very quickly and quietly. On the other hand, I would be disgusted if told to call her Aunt Molly, or worse still Auntie Molly. This strikes me as peculiarly middle class and plebeian. I have very queer snobbish taboos. One is to do with ''Auntie'', and the other, an even earlier one, is to do with the tonic-solfa scale. If anyone should sing or say ''Do, Re, Mi, Fa, So, La, Ti, Do'' I would yell out or say to myself vehemently, ''Don't sing that vulgar song. Stop it! Stop it!''

I can remember belabouring my eldest brother's legs while he stood on a chair and sang these words. This must have been early in 1919 or perhaps it was in 1918 when I was only three years old. I shall never know what caused me to think these words so ''vulgar'', or what caused me to dislike a person for calling an inanimate object, like a boat or a car, ''she''.

To go back to the Van Dyck drawing-room. Molly is reading to me, *Stalky & Co.* (chosen by her, of course, as suitable literature). But at the other end of the room, beyond the lace-backed sofas with their chintz frills, sits an old lady in an upright chair. She is fat, rather shapeless, with two little black currants pressed into the dough of her face.

The black currants keep swivelling in our direction until, at last, she says, ''Excuse me but would you mind—?'' She does not finish her sentence, but leaves it in mid-air.

Molly turns to her and asks, ''Are we disturbing you?''

''Reading aloud in the public drawing-room is a little— don't you think?'' says the old lady with an apologetic smile.

I am thoroughly exasperated by her objection. This is what being fussy means, I think. Then up through the closed windows comes the crazy, tinkling churning of a barrel-organ — ''Je cherche, je cherche Titina, Titina, Oh Titina!''

The music is so beautiful, and bringing with it that awful and all-enveloping depression of popular tunes. The gayer and more sprightly they are, the more evocative they seem to be of gloom and despair. I listen as the song grates out

---

46 Where Denton's mother, Rosalind Bassett, was staying at a period when he was boarding with a family while attending a school in Queen's Gate, London from the age of nine to eleven.

of the machine. The notes seem to be dancing on rusty metal feet, awkwardly, and yet with such perfect timing that they make or dance their sound just in the nick of time. I wait nervously, fearing that the "teeth" of the machine will be caught and the music broken.

Molly turns to me and says, "Come on, Denton, we'll go on reading upstairs."

I come out of my trance of listening and follow her upstairs. "What a troublesome old thing!" she says playfully, and I do not like her for criticizing the old lady, although I quite agree in my heart.

We shut the door of the bedroom, turn on the gas-fire and Molly sits down in the armchair while I settle at her feet on the "pouf". It is altogether cosier up here and I am pleased that we left the drawing-room. We have come to the bit in the story where the dead rat is under the dormitory floor, or ceiling. I suddenly have the awful realization that I may one day have to live with such barbarians in some such slum called a public school. The looming horror is too much for me. I turn away and jump up. Molly says, "What's the matter, Denton? Are you tired of it?" But before I can answer, the door opens and my mother comes in. Her cheeks are red and some of her curly hair has blown out from under her hat.

"Hullo Molly, hullo darling," she says gaily, kissing us both. She takes off her fur coat and her little embroidered hat and I see that she is wearing her favourite agate brooch which always reminds me of a square of solidified beef-tea.

She sits down on the bed and we all talk for a little; then Molly gets up to go. I follow her down and say good-bye at the front door. People sit about in the lounge as if their behinds were striking roots into the cushions and they were keeping perfectly still so as not to disturb the operation. I climb up the stairs again and pass along the white-doored corridor. I go into our room and find my mother lying on the bed in the half-light. I go up to her and see that she is clearly not well, for her face is buried in the pillows and I think that she has been crying.

"Love me, darling," she says, turning towards me. "Love me, love me, and I shall be all right."

I am terribly disturbed. Tears start to run down my cheeks and my mother sees them shining on my face.

"Don't cry, darling; I didn't say cry." My mother laughs and teases me so that it is unbearably sad.

"Sing to me," she says. "Sing 'O Gentle Presence, Peace and Joy and Power' or 'Saw ye my Saviour? Heard ye the glad sound?' "

I try to sing the Christian Science hymns, but break down completely and hug my mother fiercely. Gradually she seems to get better. At last she sits up and says laughingly, "How silly to behave like that! It's only Error trying to get hold of me!"

Now when I think of this — the beginning of my mother's death — the first faint inkling of what was coming — I remember my father's death again. It means nothing like this and never will do to me.[47]

(2) The tune about "amour" and "Martini" conjures up something in me but I cannot pin it down. I cannot even remember the tune — I have forgotten it already — so soon after hearing it. It must be linked with something that was once significant. It comes and goes through my life like a water-logged ball, just rising to the surface when the water stirs.

(3) Beethoven's "Fifth" flicks me straight back to the Saunders' Edwardian Gothic hall in Shanghai, 1932. The records are being changed one after another by Jane, the simple-minded daughter. She does it laboriously and lovingly, breathing hard through her Mongolian nose. Pocotta and Enid and I listen religiously.[48] And at the stirring parts I stir and want to fight, and break down everything that hampers me, I want to be free of everyone and great. I am seventeen and have no direction. I stifle because nobody believes in me at all. This is quite the worst feeling, because it makes me not believe in myself.

Fighting and clawing at the rocks and cages — I seem to see people doing this. Beethoven and I are doing it. We are like figures in Blake's drawings and the rocks and chains are like Blake's. We are in a fiery hell that is all a white-hot and white-cold picture. The fiery icicles are nothing but a picture. Everything is a picture and nothing is "real".

The music stops. We sigh and smile and eat large slices of Bianchi's cream cake for our tea.

14 December

Suddenly I remember that afternoon by the river near Henfield. It must have been in the summer of 1933 when I was in a sort of disgrace with my aunt and grandfather because I had left China to go to an art school and *would not* "settle down".[49] My aunt had said, "If you want to study art, why

---

47 Denton's mother died from nephritis, a disease of the kidneys, on 3 March 1927, aged forty-one. Denton left his most comprehensive account of his relationship with his mother in "At Sea", first published in *English Story* in 1944 and reprinted in *Brave and Cruel*.

48 The Saunders and their three daughters were a family Denton met in Shanghai in 1932. In *Maiden Voyage* he called them the Fieldings, and named the three girls Ruth, Vesta and Elaine.

49 Aunt Dorothy, known as Dolly, the unmarried younger sister of Denton's father, who kept house for their widowed father, Joseph Welch, at Whaphams, Henfield, in Sussex. It was here that Denton spent his school holidays after his mother's death. The following incident was re-written in March 1943 as the concluding episode of a lengthy narrative relating to a walking tour in the west country undertaken in 1933, and some interesting and seemingly inexplicable contradictions can be discovered by comparing the *Journal* entry with the later narrative, published as *I Left My Grandfather's House* (Lion and Unicorn Press, limited edition, 1958; reissued by Allison and Busby, 1984).

don't you do some work? You should be sketching every day; instead of that, you wander in the fields doing nothing at all from morning till night."

I left the house and wandered again as she had described, only this time I wandered on my bicycle and got as far as the river. It is a forgotten place, because the road-bridge was washed away a hundred years ago and now there is only a footbridge and a track across the fields.

I threw my bicycle into the hedge and started off across the tufty grass. In the winter, I thought, this will all be flooded. Now it was hot and heavenly with the scented, dried-up grass and a loneliness almost piercing.

I sat down on the bank where I had sometimes seen small boys bathing. The river was wider and deeper there and one could dive from the bridge.

I sat there nursing my solitude yet longing for somebody to talk to. And as I longed, I saw approaching from the old farmhouse on the opposite bank a brown figure — almost the colour of the landscape; that sort of worn, lichen, olive green-brown.

It crossed the bridge and walked along the bank in my direction. When he was still some way off I saw that his hair was of that pale "washed" gold, because it suddenly glinted in the sun as if it were metal.

He came up to me coolly, with the loose, bent-kneed stride of someone used to walking over rough fields.

"Thinking of going in?" he said pleasantly and in an unexpectedly "educated" voice.

I was so pleased at his sudden appearance and so curious that I looked him straight in the face and smiled. He smiled back.

I saw the gold hair, untidy and rough, gold eyebrows too, sunburnt chestnut skin and the vivid brick-dust cheeks and lips which framed the almond-white teeth. Not distinguished or handsome — the ears were thick, the nose was short and thick, the lips were thick, all the details unfinished, yet the skin, the teeth, the eyes, the hair had that wonderful, shorter-than-springtime, polished, shining look as of some liquid or varnish of life spread over the whole body. The shirt and the breeches were the colour of the mud and the cow-dung caked on them. By their dullness and drabness they stimulated one's imagination so that one could almost feel the tingling fire and coolness of the body they sheathed.

"Lusty" and "rough" were the words that flooded through me as I looked at him. In their right sense they fitted him perfectly. As you can see I was extremely impressed by him. He must have been a few years older than I was and my capacity for hero-worship was enormous at that time. It still is. He was all that I was not — stalwart, confident and settled into a "manly" life.

The only thing I could not quite understand was the "educated" voice. It struck a slightly jarring note, yet made communication much easier and more "natural". I started the eternal game of placing people and fitting them into their right pigeon-holes. He could not be ordinary "gentry". Nobody would wear quite such dirty clothes or such hob-nailed boots unless they were *really* working. Besides, he had come, as if from home, from that ancient farmhouse, which, by its untouched appearance where no single beam was exposed, proved that no "improver" had been near it since the eighteenth century.

On the other hand he could not be an ordinary farm hand. I was just deciding that perhaps he was the farmer's ambitiously educated son when he stopped all my dreary surmises by saying that he was down here learning farming — at least I think he said this, but I am not absolutely sure for at that moment he started undressing.

With the words, "If there are any women round here they'll get an eyeful!" he started to pull his shirt over his head. I was shocked at the whiteness of the skin on his chest and upper arms when he stood up in only his trousers. They were junket-white, but matt, as if powdered with oatmeal. The long gloves of his burnt arms and hands and the bronze helmet of his face and neck joining this whiteness did something curious to me. I could only gape and wonder as he stripped his wonderful body. He unlaced his boots and kicked them off, then peeled down his thick and sweat-sticky stockings. The breeches he pulled off roughly, and stood revealed with the gold hair glinting on his body as well as on his head.

As I say, I could only watch. This was not just an ordinary man taking off his clothes for a swim — and yet it was. It was this prosaic, mundane quality and the bubbling-up spring of some poetry which held me enthralled.

He flung back his hair with the gesture which is considered girlish when used by effeminate men. (When used by others it has, of course, a quite different effect.) Then he dived into the muddy water and came up spitting and laughing. "Bloody filthy water," he shouted and spluttered, "bloody filthy water, but it's lovely."

He stood up near the bank, so that the water gartered his legs round the middle of his calves. The hairs on his body and legs dripped like sparkles of water. He looked like a truncated statue fixed to a base in the bowl of a fountain.

He whirled his arms round, dived, and swam about for some time; then he crawled up the bank and lay down beside me on the grass. As he lay with his face to the sky and his eyes shut I watched the rivulets coursing off his body. The main stream flowed down his chest, between the hard pectorals, over the mushroom-smooth belly, to be lost in curly gold hair. I could just descry the quicksilver drops weaving a painful way through the golden bush.

He opened his eyes and saw me staring at him; he didn't seem to mind. He sat up and started to rub his arms and chest brutally with a dirty towel.

"I'm working down here at the moment. What do you do?" he asked, abruptly but without giving offence.

"I, I'm at an art school," I got out with difficulty. The shame and fear of sinking in his estimation were very real.

"Oh — my sister's a very clever artist, too," he said confidently. "She's been studying for some time and has got a scholarship. She's going abroad."

He continued talking about his sister and his family. I got the impression, perhaps wrongly, that he was a little in disgrace too. This thrilled me. I felt I had found a brother. When he talked of being drunk and brawling, I was tremendously impressed and horrified — to be so cool and casual about it all! Then I had the fear that the beer would decay his teeth or that they would be knocked out in the fights. This caused me the sort of pain one feels when some beautifully-made and intricate thing is threatened.

He asked me what I had been doing all my holidays and I told him that I had been for one walking tour down to Devonshire and would soon be going for another, as my aunt obviously did not want me at my grandfather's.

"I'd like to do that too," he said decisively. "I'd like to go abroad, walking and paying my way wherever I went. My parents wouldn't give me anything, you see," he added in explanation.

"I wouldn't like to go alone though," he mused.

Thoughts, hopes, fears were all seething together in my head. The idea was too exciting to be considered seriously. Here, I longed to step in and say that I would go with him whenever he wanted to go, but I was much too clear-sighted not to see the difficulties of money and also of temperament. I felt that I would fall short of his daring and careless sense of power. When I would be tired or timid, he would be vigorous and scornful, and when he would be drunken and brawling I would be frankly alarmed and irritated.

"I'd like to do that too," I said. "Fine if we could go together some time," I added boldly.

If there had been the slightest reluctance I would have been ashamed, but he took me perfectly seriously, saying, "I wonder if we could ever fix it up."

We exchanged names. He pulled on his khaki shirt and caked breeches and lost some of his magic, thus becoming more comfortable.

I knew that I would never go with him. I felt cowardly for not *making* it happen in some way.

He held out his hand and I shook it, wondering as I felt the horn on his palm.

"You can always get hold of me there," he said, pointing to the farmhouse. Then he turned and walked back along the banks.

I watched him the whole way. The legs and the shoulders and the dirty towel swung in rhythm until he passed through the little gate into the garden.

At the last sight of him I felt unbearably angry and frustrated. I jumped up and ran over the tussocks. I jerked my bicycle out of the hedge and pedalled viciously, cursing God and everybody, pouring scorn and pity in a deluge all over myself.

Now stranger, whose name I have quite forgotten — where are you now? Even if you are not dead in battle, that "You" is dead and nowhere, for at most it could only have lasted a year or two — that animal magic.

31 *December (10 to 11)*

O God, to have all those old thoughts back in a torturing flood! To be swept over again by those demon wings!

The very noise and scream of their jealousy is *meaningless*, which makes the stabbing so much worse. To be jealous and driven down by something which you know to be petty, minor, nothing!

But very gently to fight it with buoyancy is the only thing. To fight it with what the religious would call Good. Good, I suppose, is always something constructive but with no "fight". (The word is quite wrong that I have used before.)

It is an utter change of front. No surrender but a turning of the back and a shutting of the nostrils to the stink and the filthiness.

Our hearts, into which something has eaten once when we were ill or weak, must be mended and patched so that that terrible pettiness and fear of being overlooked may be wiped out for ever. Not to worry about how one stands with people. Only to worry about real things.

And all this triteness, because my pride, which was once so terribly hurt, has been reminded of its wound. It was terribly battered when most susceptible.

It has been damnable, on top of all my difficulties of temperament, to have that obscene accident. And I have been tortured enough. Something screams out in me that all is filth and devil-worship.

Betty Swanwick has been today — who has that "something" in her still, but she is not competing, which is strength and weakness.[50] Better than many artists, she has never yet shown in any private gallery. Her *naïveté* is real and assumed and the blend is strange. Something shoots through but one feels too that she might be content gradually to do less and less.

Now this year ends and I look back to the things that have happened to me. In painting not very much, but more than before — my Berners picture was illustrated in *Vogue*, and Jan Gordon mentioned another picture in the *Observer*.

But the chief thing is in writing.

My Sickert article was taken by *Horizon* and then I had the amazing letter

---

50 A student with Denton at the Goldsmith School of Art, now a Royal Academician. She appears as Fat Bertha Swan in "A Party", published posthumously in *A Last Sheaf*. She was also one of the two art students who went to see Denton in Lewisham Hospital, as recorded (although the hospital was not identified) in *A Voice Through a Cloud*.

from Edith Sitwell. I got in touch with Alex Comfort who cracked my book up.[51] Then Herbert Read took it and now it will soon be out. W. J. Turner took a poem, and Middleton Murry two others. Henry Treece used one in *Kingdom Come* and others in *Decachord*. [And there was one in] *Abinger Chronicle*.[52]

Tambimuttu says he is going to use one in *Poetry* too.[53]

This all may be only a beginning but it means something and I must go on and on and on.

---

51 Alex Comfort, poet and novelist, had recommended *Maiden Voyage* to Arthur Waugh of Chapman & Hall (unsuccessfully) and then to Herbert Read of Routledge.
52 "Jane Allen", first published in *Abinger Chronicle* in 1941 (not 1942), and reprinted first in *Kingdom Come* and then in *A Last Sheaf*.
53 Born in Ceylon, the same year as Denton. Editor from 1939-47 of *Poetry London*, in which he also published George Barker, David Gascoigne, Louis MacNeice, Kathleen Raine, Stephen Spender and Dylan Thomas.

JOURNAL

III

1943

28 January

ON MONDAY — to meet someone who just takes you as you are — charming!
— no fuss! We just walked on and on through the rain, down the muddy
cow-smelling lane. The elms swayed and speared the misty wetness with
their scarecrow fingers. We linked arms, walking tightly and neatly
together. It was comfort and pleasure to walk in that tidy rhythm and to talk
loudly and gaily about the blitz days.

I heard stories thrilling and gruesome about Portsmouth in those fires.
My new friend said, "I was in Civvy Street then. One morning I had just
climbed over a huge pile of rubble (to get across to a shop, you see) when
just behind me a terrible explosion took place. I was thrown on to my face
and stunned, but when I came to I was only bruised. It was a time bomb, just
across the street from me. Then there was the time when I came back from
work and found the road near the aerodrome lined with fire engines. Three
hundred and sixty five I counted. Three hundred and sixty five! Can you
imagine it? I began to get the wind up. I hared home and had my tea, when,
just as I'd put the last cup to my lips there was a terrible bang and tea went all
over the floor. I ran to the front door and saw the sky all red, right across. It
was just like a long sausage of lit-up sky.

"That night thousands of people were killed. One landmine did for two
thousand in some shelters. But do you think the Government would tell the
people beforehand that there was going to be a large scale raid? Not on your
life! They knew about it, as was proved by all those fire engines down from
London and God knows where. But they don't dare tell the people about
the damage at Portsmouth. Talk about the people going out into the hills at
night! Can you blame them? Hundreds of thousands went to the hillside
nearby, then a landmine came down and blows most of them skyhigh. Can
you beat it?"

We walked on, cosily talking of these horrors. It was so warming. We
railed against the war and the blood spilt out. The rain came down thicker.

"Do you think there's any shelter here?" the soldier said.

"There might be a cattle byre or whatever you call it. Let's go on a little
further and look."

But there was nothing, so we sat on a fence under some trees and told each
other our ages and what we could remember as small children. A car passed,
a bicycle, and then another bicycle. Why can't we do this with strangers
more often? Why can't we just talk and amuse each other a little without

any necessity for intricate or lasting understanding? Why can't we just go for walks in the rain and come back pleased?

4 February

I love to read of dignified surrenders, of the victors coming into the cellar and finding the gloomy general with his staff, of snow on the fields and someone walking forward with his sword and giving it in silence. It is not the theatre of it that I love only, but the glorious return to sanity, the turning of the back at last on force, and the triumph of reason and the arts. For it is all arts and graces, miming and stage to surrender yourself, or to accept surrender. The animal is hidden and the people comfort themselves again. There is no more of this stinking war, but forms and ceremonies and gentlemanly behaviour. For once the gentleman's code is glorious — if still slightly rediculous — yet on these occasions one's heart melts for the gentleness and peace whatever hate lies hidden underneath.

And this all swings into my mind because Paulus has been found unshaven in a cellar by the Russians.

12 February

As I lie in bed here, now, this morning, and watch the crystal glitters of the candlesticks, the white iron twisting table, the yellow satin chair, the grey morning light on the crusty bark of the trees; as I watch the patiently silent harpsichord and the scarlet lacquer screen behind it, and the four miniatures of people long since dead, I think of myself as dead. I think of the years and years to come, when the sun will rise and I shall be nothing but a burnt up cinder. I think of myself as two eyes looking down on my empty room, on my silent velvet bed, on all my pretty things, and knowing that I shall never use them again. I think of them floating into other people's homes and being used for a hundred years from hence. I think of wars and torture and the blackest sins of power. I think of babies and all the screaming life of eternity.

This is the horrible, beautiful immortality that we've been looking for. The never-ending of our race on earth. How it pierces down and seems to light everything with a lurid glow — this knowledge of what is in store. And all the ideas of behaviour of Jane Austen and our town, all our delightful and nasty little snobbisms and aspirations, all our fears of offending — how exciting, how sad and heart-rendering they become when we think of them under the heavy layers of dust and earth, under the dripping trees in the churchyard, under the down-pressing sagging-with-rain sky. O think of feather boas and reticules and white kid gloves that have been buried for a hundred years.

18 February

Over to Trottiscliffe on my bicycle, starting early, after seeing the doctor. He was stupid, and no use, but the day was lovely, just emerging out of mist, and in Oxon Heath Park the cattle looked soft and lovable and warm. I had taken off my glasses, so when I was in the Cedar Walk I could not recognize the person bending down with the wooden rake until I was near her. She looked at me and said, "It's Mr Welch, isn't it?" and I saw that it was Miss Heywood. She was dressed in strange dungarees and wore a riding-hood of knitted wool. She looked strange and grisly and gnome like.

"I'm the land-girl here," she said with the warmest smile. "I'm looking after the garden here."

We talked for a little constrainedly; then I pushed up to the hill, getting hotter but feeling fairly strong. Someone was in the garden of Tom's cottage, but I did not stop.[1] The misty landscape was lovely. I only gazed at it with half my eyes, and went down the road through the Hurst Woods. I could hear the woodmen in the distance but only caught the glimpse of a blue scarf. Once I thought I saw one naked to the waist and marvelled that it could be so in February, but then I looked again and saw that it was the tawny orange of a split and gale-torn-up-tree.

Further on, sitting alone on a tree trunk, I came upon Charlotte Adeney![2] She had evidently slunk away to be solitary in the woods. She hates life at nineteen as so many of us do. I talked a little too gaily, then bustled on again. At the Hop Garden I saw that it was all being done up. I went up to the man who was working, and after talking I gathered that he had brought it and was renovating it himself. I told him I had lived there until the fire last year.

I thought of it now so strangely and unpleasantly transformed. The high hedge cut down, the paintwork a treacle green and the kitchen window half bricked up. It was degraded, a poor house, and it will never know me again. I made it something for two years; and when we lay in the sun naked or got close to the stoves in the winter, behind the velvet curtains, a sort of interest lived in it. All that is washed and burnt away now.

At Treasley, Carmael was out and Miss Brown and Piffard.[3] I found Johnson the gardener, who let me in. I freely looked at things, opening

---

1 Tom was a woodman from Yorkshire whom Denton first met in 1940, inviting him back to the Hop Garden to be painted, and with whom he had what he described in a letter dated June 1941 to Marcus Oliver (a friend with whom Denton had corresponded since 1937), as a "romantic affair". He appears as Jim in "The Fire in the Wood" (see 1942, note 4 above), a story in which Denton disguised himself as Mary.

2 The daughter of Bernard and Noël Adeney.

3 Miss Brown was Cecilia Carpmael's companion, who took care of her mentally disturbed sister, Connie Piffard. Denton was on a visit to Mrs Carpmael's home in the High Street, Trottiscliffe, Kent. "Treasley" was Denton's phonetic spelling for Trottiscliffe, based on local pronunciation.

cabinets and feeling the china. Then I read a page or two of some book and after that I tried playing Schumann from an old book.

C. suddenly came in from London and made tea. We talked about my book and I told the story of my father's death and my disinheritance. I suddenly thought that I had made a little too much of it and that she had the idea that I was about to make her feel guilty about being richer. Of course I would like her to leave me any money she can, but I should never expect this. How dull it is to sit with someone with very little mind! We looked at her pictures afterwards and I was allowed to pick a bunch of violets. I stared at the Graham Sutherlands' house as I passed but no-one was about.

I wanted to have some sort of adventure on the way home. But nothing happened. The sun set gloriously into the thick matted woods and an enormous yellow moon began to gain strength. It was all set for something but nothing happened.

Now, just before eleven at night, the soldiers have arrived at Greentrees in a lorry and are shouting and singing lustily and drunkenly — quite in the approved manner. It must be gay to be drunk under this wonderful moon, although it is this stinking war year still. No more news of my book. Soon, soon it's going to appear.

21 *February*

Here is my breakfast tray laid out for me with silver pots and Georgian glass salt-cellar filled with jam. It is shaped like an urn and is a bluish colour which would make the dealers call it Waterford. And Waterford makes me think of Ireland of course. And at this moment I have just come to the Irish part in Siegfried Sassoon's *Sherston's Progress*. This is a queer book, full of dullness in the active war parts and then holding the penetrating when he writes of peace and leisure and thinking. Perhaps it proves that one should never keep a diary if one wants to write a book about one's past. If he had had no diary, could he remember all those things which bore one so? Wouldn't just the bare essentials of his experience emerge? (Not necessarily facts at all.)

O, but writing seems such a fantastically clumsy and blunted instrument. Now I want to tell how I lie here in bed in my cold room with the morning light coming in at the three windows, and with the breakfast tray in front of me, but it all sounds too drab for words, not a bit like the reality.

And all my thoughts — what are they like, when I fish them out? Thoughts of Ireland, thoughts of eighteenth century, of mists blowing up and enveloping the hills, of [*sentence unfinished*]

23 *February*

It must have taken place on the Speech Day of 1930, I think.

I remember standing rather forlornly by the school shop (for no one had come down to see me) and wondering whether to go on staring at the cricket match or to slip away and hide myself either in the library or the fields.

As I stood there, I suddenly realized that I was being watched. Two prefects from another house and two recent Old Boys were gazing at me and talking in subdued voices. My embarrassment became acute; I felt that I must have transgressed some unwritten rule or behaved in some horribly gauche way.

After several minutes' deliberation one of the Old Boys came up to me rather hurriedly and nervously. I could remember his face; he had only left the term before.

"Are you at a loose end?" he asked as casually as he was able. "Would you like to go for a drive with us? We've got a car."

The honour, the unusualness, the general dreamlike quality of the whole episode, tinged as it was with something hidden and urgent, made my head swim. I think my chief feeling, apart from flattered vanity, was one of surprise, almost of alarm, that I should have been approached in broad daylight. Anyone might see them talking to me, I said to myself.

Of course, I never thought of doing anything but accepting. Although I was filled with trepidation and fear, I knew I must accept. To refuse would be utterly boorish when these great people had so honoured me. Also I knew that I would be haunted by my cowardice and the thought of what peasures I might have missed.

"Thanks awfully," I said gruffly.

"Oh great!" he said lightly; but I could tell how relieved he was that I had accepted his suggestion with no gapings and wonderings. "The car's outside."

He led me hurriedly through the "Hole in the Wall" and the others followed.

"We'll sit in the back," he said, bundling me into the old-fashioned limousine. The other Old Boy took the wheel, and the two prefects squashed in beside him.

My alarm and unsteadiness were increasing. As the car bowled along I felt my inadequacy acutely. I knew nothing of their world. I did not drink or smoke. They would discover how dull I was. How little I swore. How I knew nothing of women at all. How impossibly bad I was at games.

The Old Boy sat beside me rather stiffly, not saying anything. The two prefects opened the divided glass window and shouted pleasantries to him. Me they good-naturedly ignored. It was undoubtedly the kindest treatment, but it did not help me to feel easier. I felt that for once they had lifted the taboo on younger boys talking to older ones, but they had only done it because they were tolerant and because it was Speech Day and because they wanted to please this particular Old Boy, who had been an athlete and was rather dashing in his way.

Now that we were in the country our driver was rattling along recklessly, giving whoops of delight if we went over a hump-backed bridge or narrowly missed some other vehicle.

I was frankly terrified and must have shown it, for my companion said gravely, " Don't be frightened. He's all right." He put his arm round my shoulders loosely and I felt it to be perfectly natural, until the others, looking through the partition shouted, "Oogh, Oogh," gleefully and derisively and then slammed the window shut.

We sat there uncomfortably, in that aromatic, leathery stuffiness, until we found ourselves shooting through an open gate into a rough-grass field. The car lurched about madly over the tussocks. We were thrown up to the ceiling and then on to the floor. The others in the front shrieked joyfully till the car came to a standstill at the bottom of the field against a wood.

My companion swore at his friend with playful roughness, giving him quite a considerable punch on the body. The others disappeared in a knot of three, leaving us alone.

We walked into the wood constrainedly. I did not know what was going to happen. I felt again horribly inadequate.

The Old Boy sat down on a tree-stump and said awkwardly, "There doesn't seem to be anywhere else, you'd better sit here." He smiled shamefacedly and patted his knee.

I held my breath and sat down. He held me very gingerly, as if I were a ventriloquist's doll. My body was taut. I could not relax. I didn't know what it was all about. I didn't want to be a prig. I wanted to be nice; but I also wanted to escape.

The Old Boy, in a funny gulpy voice, started talking about the European situation. I could not listen. I was nervously fluttering my eyelids. He saw this, and putting his face close to mine he said, "Don't be frightened of me, dearest." The endearment shocked and thrilled me. I could feel his eyelashes tickling my face and the extraordinary damp warmth of his cheek (it was a very hot day). This humid warmth is with me still, I can feel it as I write. (That — and the feathery spidery touch of the eyelashes — seemed amazing, and still seems so to me.)

My one thought was to behave properly, not to give myself away in this fantastically difficult situation. I was like wood or stone — utterly unmoving.

Gradually he saw my complete ignorance. He sighed and got up, lifting me with him.

"Time to go back, I expect," he said, "We'll go and find the others."

We walked arm in arm out of the wood; the others joined us in a moment. As they walked in front, laughing and hitting about with their sticks, my companion held me back until several yards were between us; then, still holding my arm, he started to walk again.

There seemed to be now a curious, everlasting sort of silence about him.

He sighed again, and so powerful was his hold that he seemed to be more or less completely supporting me.

"What would the Headmaster do if he could see us now?" he asked. "He'd beat you like hell I expect, and God knows what would happen to me."

For some reason I was not bit alarmed at the idea. You see, I had not entirely got the shallow import of the wood, only the deeper one.

"Oh, he wouldn't do anything, why should he mind?" I said with assurance. "Aren't you allowed to take me out if you like?"

And in this way we made our way back to the car, through the corn and potato crop. I thought once, as I looked up at the hugh white clouds in the blue sky, "I will remember this day always." And I have.

A week afterwards I had a letter from this old boy, quite elaborately romantic, the sort of letter that only generous unwise people write. Through it ran a nostalgia to be back at school; to have a job in a rich friend-of-the-family's brewery seemed a degradation. And he had no games. I saw in a flash that leaving school was not freedom for this sort of person.

In the mid-morning break, as we stood round the "Hole in the Wall", waiting to get at the counter of the Grubber, I had a desire to look at my letter again. I took it out of my breast pocket and started to read, saying the extravagent words and phrases to myself with pleasure.

Of course it was stupid, but I think I almost half wanted to be questioned about the letter. As Geoffrey approached I held the letter down, against me, quickly.[4]

"What are you so engrossed in?" he jeered, rolling the "r" stagily. "A tart-note I bet. You've had a tart-note."

He snatched the piece of paper and read it avidly. He had not expected anything like it. He seemed hardly able to believe it.

"Christ, what an absolute marvel," he said, handing it back to me. "But the only trouble is that now you'll think you're Cleopatra, or the Face that Launched a Thousand Ships or something. There'll be no holding you." He gave my ankles a vicious little kick to quell my pride in advance.

Swiftly I tucked the letter away; but it must soon have lost its significance for me or caused me too much anxiety, for I know tore it up within the week.

3 March

It is 1924 and the winter. I and my mother have been asked into the country for the weekend. I race into the great murky station, tugging at my

---

4 He appears in *Maiden Voyage*; Geoffrey Lumsden, later an actor.

mother's hand. I am joyful and excited, but also terrified that we may miss the train.

I have forgotten where we went, that is, the name of the place; everything else is in a series of charming, sharp pictures.

I know that we took an ancient taxi at the station. It belonged to the only sort of car that I really love, the sort that is tremendously high and old-fashioned, with musty elaborate upholstery inside, little cut-glass flower vases, straps, mirrors, and a sliding glass screen between the passenger and the driver.

We must have driven in the gathering darkness for some time, for I had the feeling that we had pierced into the very heart of the country. I talked to my mother excitedly and held her gloved hand, sampling the new feel of the suede leather warmed from within. She was happy too and I knew she was smiling, although I could not see.

At last we entered some park gates and bowled along the curving drive until we branched off into a narrower road. I felt that we might continue our journey for ever, on ever-narrowing roads.

At last the car stopped on what seemed to be completely bare and desolate fields; but then I saw in front of us a low house, obviously old because of its irregular outline against the sky. Warm orange lights were showing, and my excitement suddenly rose to fever pitch.

"We're here, Mummy, we're here," I shrieked.

I remember looking across the mistry wet fields to the lightest patch of sky beyond some hills. I think there was some sort of pink in the collecting darkness. It must have hung in the air for a few moments before the thick grey night clouds rolled up. I knew that the setting for the black house with the orange lights seemed wonderfully lurid and romantic to me. It was mournful too, and this I loved most of all.

My mother paid the taxi man and we both walked up to the jutting-out porch. The door flew open and my mother's friend stood there with her hands out to welcome us. She was a short, dumpy little birdlike woman called Mrs Aldridge (later in her life to be nicknamed Quail).

She kissed my mother and was boisterous with me, treating all boys in exactly the same way. Her big, ungainly husband in rough, hairy plus-fours hovered behind her and smiled at us. I remember thinking the purply-red colour of his face very ugly.

Mrs Aldridge led us down the side passage into the drawing-room, which was long and low and must have had, I think, early Victorian rosewood furniture and things of that period. Everything seemed brilliantly polished and clean; there was an aromatic whiff in the air, perhaps the combination of logs on the fire, the furniture polish and the ghost of some pot-pourri or lavender and leather.

"This is the dower house," Mrs Aldridge was saying to my mother. "Don't you love it? We were so pleased we were able to rent it. It's in very good order, but it hasn't been altered for years. The water has to be pumped and we only have lamps, but aren't they lovely lamps! They're all solid silver."

I looked at the lamps while Mrs Aldridge went on talking about the dower house and the estate to which it belonged. The lamps were made in the shape of heavy Corinthian pillars with cut-glass bowls for the oil at the top. They had warm pink-silk "party-looking" shades.

"They're really solid silver," I thought. I was impressed.

But there were other delights for me upstairs. When we were led up to our room with much chattering from Mrs Aldridge and shy silence from her daughter, who had now joined us, I saw with a thrill of delight that it was entirely lit with candles in brass sconces. I counted eight round the wall.

"But Mummy," I cried, bubbling over with excitement, "it's like hundreds of years ago. Our room's lit only with candles! There's nothing else. Oh, isn't it marvellous."

Mrs Aldridge laughed as I jumped about, and my mother said, too, how lovely it looked.

The daughter, Ba, who had joined us, was a shy girl of about fifteen. Of course being twice my age she seemed almost grown up to me. I thought her rather pretty, in a white, delicate, fragile way. She seemed just a little conceited in her quite shyness, too.

I think I must have been allowed to stay up to supper that night, for I seem to remember Mr Aldridge pottering around the sideboard as if he were carving there, or drawing the corks from bottles. I think the dining-room must have had light Sheraton mahogany furniture, an old green silk curtain hanging from a brass rail behind the sideboard, and steeple-chasing prints with romantic men in side whiskers and night caps.

I remember one of the heavy silver lamps being carried back with us to the drawing room.

That night, as I undressed and my mother unpacked, all the candles would waver, and then right themselves as secret draughts, like invisible ghosts, struck them.

Mrs Aldridge said to my mother, "Rosalind, when you bath Denton, will you only take six inches of water? As otherwise the man will have to pump for hours in the morning."

My mother went into the dark bathroom, each carrying a candle. It seemed, at first, grim and sinister in there. I saw the little illumination notice on the wall about not using too much water.

I turned on the tap. The water was beautifully hot and comforting. I undressed and splashed about in it. My mother and I laughed and talked about the charming house; then she wrapped me in the big warm towel and I rubbed myself fiercely.

I lay awake in my bed, near my mother, thinking still of the house. I was longing to see it in the morning. I thought I would get up early before breakfast and explore.

I did wake up early, so I dressed quietly and went on to the landing; a tiny gallery surrounding a well where the staircase lead down. I could hear the man pumping the water with metallic squeak and groan.

I ran down the stairs and went into the drawing-room. The servants had tidied it and a fire was just beginning to burn. I was filled with delight and joy. I ran to the French window and pushed it open. The warm, damp winter feeling struck me from the grass and the sky. I could see nothing over the gently curved hill, but I knew the big house brooded on the other side. I imagined it all stone battlements and huge library windows. I saw scarlet geraniums in huge urns on a balustrade (imagination does not confine itself only to one season of the year). I know I identified the whole scene with little Lord Fauntleroy too, which an old-fashioned governess had lately read to me. The scene was absolutely right and perfect. The great house was there for the old Earl, and this perfect "dower house" for "Dearest".

I walked about in the garden, looking up at the eves or out across the fields. I began to feel hungry. I went back into the drawing-room and found Barbara by the fire. I ran to fetch my tiny pot of marmalade and minute *Times* which I had got when I went to see the Queen's dolls' house at Wembley.[5] She did not seem quite as interested as I had hoped.

"It's real marmalade," I said, "and you can really read the *Times* with a magnifying glass."

She was polite but a little lethargic; the sort of child who is always considered a little ill by its mother.

My mother came in and complimented Ba on her checked skirt.

"I've got stockings that almost match it, but Mummy says there are too many squares if I wear them all together," said Ba. We, all laughed, and Mrs Aldridge led us in to breakfast.

After breakfast we sat and talked. I remember Mrs Aldridge saying that she made charming flesh-coloured stockings for Ba by dyeing them in water tinted with a few drops of red ink and some coffee. Then she turned to Wycome Abbey, where Ba was at school, and said, wasn't it disgraceful, she had paid for Ba to have extra coaching and she'd had none at all.

I wondered what extra coaching was. I felt it must have something to do with learning to drive a coach; but I was doubtful, because this seemed such an extraordinary subject to teach at a girls' school. It seemed *important*. I said the words "extra coaching" over to myself several times. I even imagined Ba tearing round the countryside in a rakish carriage. I knew she would be terrified. She must be glad, I thought, that her extra coaching had fallen through.

---

5 The dolls' house designed by Sir Edwin Lutyens for Queen Mary, exhibited at the British Empire Exhibition at Wembley in 1924 and now on view at Windsor Castle.

Mrs Aldridge told my mother how unhappy Ba was at school, and how she'd like to take her away, but didn't know where else to send her.

"It's supposed to be the best school," she said.

Ba said nothing until spoken to, but she did not seem to mind them talking about her as she sat there.

I think that I must soon have gone off to wander by myself. I can remember no more.

All I know is that when we left the next day, I felt that I had had a wonderfully romantic and exciting time; and I have remembered it ever since. Really, the whole adventure, I suppose, boils down to the excitement of the arrival at the unexpectedly charming and old-fashioned house, lost in the darkness and the wintry fields.

As the taxi bore us away I am sure that I felt a great sadness. Now I should like to be able to know where that house was and whether I could ever see it again.

5 March

[*The extract dated 5 March is headed Book I and was evidently intended by Denton to represent a literary exercise quite separate from the* Journals. *It was in fact his account of a walking tour in the west country, already referred to, and published in* 1958 *as* I Left My Grandfather's House.]

16 March

I was suddenly fired by restlessness to go out into the moonlight at a quarter to ten tonight. I had already begun to undress, but I put my jacket on again without my jersey or my tie. I suddenly delighted to think I would go out drab and workmanlike, with no tie, my clothes not considered or thought out.

Out in the drive I felt the cold air on my throat. I knew the ring of my vest would be showing white in the dark. I delighted in the slovenliness, but wondered if I should be ill again, just having recovered from pneumonia 'flu. My teeth were chattering now.

As I passed May's house at the end of the drive I wondered if she was going to bed and at the window, drawing the curtains. She would look down and see me, and say nothing, but wonder what I was doing. I cursed her to myself, and stood specially at the end of the drive, so that her inquisitiveness could see me.

I waited for footsteps under the light of the moon. I could hear nothing but trains, and sheep furtively munching green cabbages in the nearby field. I was getting colder and colder.

I began to walk up the road past May's house and then I did hear footsteps. I stood at the side of the road, and as the figure came up he must have thought I was peepeeing, for he gave me a cheery call and said, "How is it?" I laughed and started to walk at his side. He must have been Canadian. He was not very tall, with dark hair and a small moustache — glistening, like Ramon Novarro of my childhood.

We walked along and he said chaffingly, "Did it get frost-bitten?" Then he told me of his leave and how he did "it" twice a night. "That's twenty times in ten days!" He laughed, showing all his teeth. He talked of girls and asked me where mine was and where I lived.

"Have you got a nice bed to go back to?" he asked. "That's the main thing."

He asked me more questions and I became uneasy. How I hate to answer questions! He went on saying that he was well set up for three weeks. He looked an extraordinarily vital, compact little man with his showy, handsome head, under the moon.

Everything was wrong. He wanted to find out about me and he wanted to talk about his women. Probing and bragging.

"Taking precautions is like paddling in your socks," he said in a business-like voice. He spoke of flesh touching flesh — it was all so gruesome and brotherly.

I left him, turning off the road and walking down a lane some way to shake him off. I had the fear that he was waiting to see if I would return again.

At last I came back and longed for him, for everything, to be different in the world; and for my poems to be good, not smeary as his love affairs were smeary.

17 March

Time's passing; time's passing. Horace Walpole said, even while one thinks of one's pain one can know that it is passing. And I know it now, that every moment passing is washing out its pain and happiness, and will leave me a blank state at last. What happiness this gives — to know that one can lay plans and be busy because the labour will not go on for ever. How is it that we are born with this fixed idea that we shall live for ever? It poisons and perverts us. It is the chief reason for our hopeless lethargy.

Now as I lie in bed at quarter to eleven and hear the drunk soldiers sing and shout as they crawl back to their billet I am filled with satisfaction, for it is all passing, which is the only reason for wanting to preserve it.

24 March. Eleven o'clock at night.

This afternoon I went out early, after having written all morning in bed.

I bicycled through Hadlow, past Mereworth, where I thought of Horace Walpole's remarks about the church and the castle, because I had read the accounts in the Letters this very morning.

I thought of us all passing, repassing these monuments through the centuries. Somehow the steeples still stand, and the painted ceilings still hold up, in spite of soldiers billeted, bombs, neglect and wantonness.

I climbed gently up to West Malling and tried to get into the ruined tower again, but as usual could find no one at the Stone Cottage.

West Malling seemed empty except for a policeman and a knot of girls. I passed through the town and saw a notice on the big grey house just before the London Road.

"By order of the executors of Miss Nevill." Then a list of household things for sale.

I had always seen the Nevill arms and motto over the door of the ugly covered-way. I thought of an old lady lying dead in the big grey house, which wasn't really a grey house at all but a Queen Anne brick one, daubed all over, turreted, conservatoried, porte-cochered in the sixties or seventies of last century.

I pedalled on to the main road past Addington, which is almost stripped of trees now, and ended up at the Sandy Lane Tea Rooms or some such name. At one point a whole school of army motor-bicyclists passed me, all with L's painted on their archaic-looking crash helmets.

I went into the tea room and ordered tea and biscuits and cake. No one else was in there. I looked in vain on all the Windsor chairs and gate-legged tables for a book or magazine, but there was nothing.

I studied the appalling ingle-nook, ply-board panelling, and the row of china plates and ornaments above it.

My tea came, and it tasted so nice and strong and unlike home tea — in fact the sort of tea I really hate. Only the change was nice.

I started on a cake, but it was so heavy that I picked all the fat currants out of it and dropped the dough-part in my pocket. I ate the raisins and the biscuits and then began to smoke a cigarette. I liked my old snuff-box and my amber holder. I liked to use them and admire them in a new place.

Three people arrived from a Morris car. One of the two women seemed to be just up after a long illness, she walked very slowly and stiffly.

The man made facetious remarks about ordering strawberries and cream and ham.

Before I left I heard one of the women say, "We once stayed in a farm in the Mendip Hills, you know, and they had a fireplace like that, only a real one, you know. It was bigger too, and it was such a lovely farmhouse, with a flagged floor in the kitchen."

I got on my bike again and pedalled to Borough Green. There I went into the church. All the images were shrouded in rich plum-coloured cloth for Lent, the Virgin Mary alone excepted.

I went up to her. She was much the biggest statue and she had a stand for candles in front of her.

I always love to light candles, so I put two pennies and a halfpenny into the box, which was so full that my money rested on top, half out of the chink. I pressed it down and then lit the candle. I wondered if they ever fell on the floor and burnt holes there.

I thought of the Christmas and Midnight Masses I had been to in that church. At the door, just as I was going out, I had the impulse to make strange gestures and faces.

I went on till I came to the chemist's where I saw blackcurrant purée in the window. I wanted some, but of course the door was locked for early closing.

As I stood by the kerb a strange sort of tractor-farm-implement passed me, driven by an arrestingly dirty and handsome man with the smallest beret jammed down on his shining yellow hair. He seemed to be dressed in very dirty, oily battledress, which I could not understand, for he was with an older labourer in civilian clothes, and they seemed both just to have come off the fields.

I saw four girls turn round to look at the man. The first couple, with handkerchiefs over their heads, were laughing and smiling shamefacedly when they turned back from staring. I wondered what they were saying — what excuses they were making to each other for turning round. The other two were franker; they just gaped and looked solemn.

Meanwhile the man was trying to speed up the tractor. He jerked his head round angrily, several times, to look at something behind him. I saw then that his face was already brick-colour from sun and wind. The whites of his eyes and his teeth flashed savagely against this darker colour. He laughed and spat and said something to the other man.

At Ightham I came to the Chequers just as Mrs Munro was unbolting the doors. I went into the jug and bottle section and asked for gin and lime. She herself had some queer orange cloudy liquid when I asked her to join me.

She was very refined and smart and careful, keeping the conversation in the upper walks of life. I thought that it was nice of her to take so much trouble with her appearance, and to keep her pub so clean. Even the outside lavatory was well washed down with Jeyes' Fluid! On one wall someone had written, "God=Love=Truth=Power", on another, "Corabush", and below that was a rude anatomical drawing and the closely written case history of someone who wanted to meet someone else, sometime, somewhere.

It's all really poetry, I thought. If the writers had more stamina and restraint it would be poetry. You must search the walls of public lavatories for heart-cries.

Farther on, at Ivy Hatch, I came to soldiers practising manoeuvres. The first two I came on wore leaves and twigs stuck into the netting stretched over their tin hats. The effect was wild and pastoral and fancy-dress. The careful, camouflage greens looked specially chosen for their prettiness.

Round the corner I found lorries and little gun carriages draped in painted net. Some soldiers clustered round a fire which they'd built in a nuttery nearby. They seemed to be holding a large square tank over the flames. I wondered what they were cooking, but smelt no smells. On the hill above Fairlawn I came to two logs across the road. The soldier straddling them said in a very curious accent, which I could not place, something about the road being blocked and I'd have to go round. "Do you mean I'll have to turn back?" I asked, not knowing what road I should have to take. "No, no," he said with exasperation, "I only meant go round the logs." Wasn't it silly? What did he expect me to do? Ride over them?

28 March

Tomorrow is my birthday, and I shall be twenty-eight to match this date. I spoke all day to Noël Adeney. Lying in the Hurst Woods we ate our hard boiled eggs and talked about homosexuality. Her probe is so uncomfortable; she tells you just the things to ruffle you. And yet all the time you think she rather admires, or at least likes, you.

She ate my chocolate, which I resented although I broke off large pieces for her. Then Sir William Ceary and Phyl Ford[6] rode by on horses. I think they thought we were lying in the leaves making love. Wasn't that queer! Quite gruesome.

She asked me if I talked to middle-aged women, like her, better than to young ones. I found it difficult, because the moment one begins openly to talk about age with anyone, one always ends up by offending. Always one dates them just a little earlier than they expected, or places them unconsciously with the generation two years earlier.

Airmen flashed by on bicycles. They all wore that intent look of people who are grimly determined to enjoy themselves for their few free hours from slavery. It's an almost fanatical look. The anxious eyes seem to say, I *must* drink, copulate or what you will. I must, I must, I must, or I am nothing and my leave is wasted. O tomorrow and tomorrow and tomorrow; they'll all pile up until I die. And each pattern weaving, each quirk and twist are building something.

29 March

My birthday, so I went to Tunbridge Wells and nearly brought a Georgian teapot, but then I didn't, because the engraved shield had no crest on it, and I hate signet rings or engraved shields with no crest on them. They

---

6 A tenant of Peggy Mundy Castle's.

look naked. Before the silver shop I went to Mrs Heasman's and found two charming, stumpy cut glasses for 2s 6d each.

She stood in the doorway talking to me, telling me how when her husband came home on his last leave in the last war she didn't know him. "I heard a knock at the door," she said, "and I thought, oh, that's only someone come to borrow something. Then there was another knock, louder. We used to use the back room then as a dining room, so I came out of it and go to the door and open it and almost fall back with surprise. There he was with his equipment up to his eyes and a thin growth of beard all round his face. I hardly recognised him. Of course, after a bath and a shave and a good lay down he looked all right again." Her eyes glittered and smiled behind her winking glasses. "Then bless me if it wasn't the Armistice ten days after he'd arrived home. He had to go back again to France though, and he said the difference! Why, it was as quiet as quiet. No guns. Quite uncanny," he said. She mused for a little and smiled again. I had no idea she loved her husband. I had only heard him, once before, shouting angrily up the stairs for his dinner. Isn't it strange to think of the continuity of lives? In the same shop and home for the space between the wars. It seemed to me quite like the landed gentry.

8 April

The night before last, I sat in Hadlow churchyard, on the memorial to the thirty hop-pickers drowned at Hartlake Bridge in 1853.

Some of their Irish names had crumbled away, but others I could read — Donohue, Murphy, Clare. Their ages were inscribed too. Some were nineteen, twenty-three, fifty-two, four.

I thought of them all, swept along with the bridge, floating on the surface of the water.

Just ninety years ago those young ones turned up their eyes. And all their dirt, their thoughts, their joys were washed away.

The hops have been picked for ninety summers, and nobody thinks of the thirty bodies in the churchyard, that were fished up out of the water.

9 April

This evening I saw a white bicycle; and whenever I see a white bicycle it spells madness to me, for when I was small the doctor's wife in our village was mad, and she rode a white bicycle.[7]

Dressed in her mauve riding-habit and her thick veil she could be seen all

7 In Henfield (see 1942, note 49 above).

over the village, riding her white bicycle, pouring milk down the drains (to feed the German prisoners confined down there), carrying her badminton racket, going round to each house in an attempt to get people to join her badminton club.

Once, my aunt told me, she was discovered directing the traffic dressed in football boots and shorts.

The poor doctor also had his Sunday joint thoroughly washed under the tap, to get rid of the poison.

Often the doctor's wife slept in a barn in the hay, but at other times she would go home and sleep in her room as she used to do.

It was after the last war that she finally went mad. My aunt said that she had always been a little eccentric.

I remembered wondering, even as a child, how it was that she was left entirely to roam freely.

"But mightn't she do something dangerous? Mightn't she hurt herself?" I asked.

"The doctor says that it is much kinder to let her lead the kind of life she likes. She doesn't do anyone any harm," my aunt answered.

I think she and the doctor were right, although it is obvious to me now that the reason for leaving the mad woman unmolested was an economic one.

She really seemed to lead a vital life, however fantastic and ridiculous she made herself. Shut up in a home, or with a keeper, she could not direct the traffic, could not be of heroic service to poor imprisoned aliens, could not organize thrilling badminton clubs, sleep in the hay, wear mauve riding-habits, decontaminate the Sunday joint, ride on her romantic white bicycle over the common in the evening, talking and singing to herself mysterious and important words.

Oh how my heart bled for her! I thought of her alone in the hay — the whole wreck of her life — the fiendish laughter of the village children who were worse than devils.

It was shaming, utterly shaming to think that no one cared what she did; that no one would ever take anything she did seriously.

Entry undated

Today I have been to Ightham Moat. It was less spoilt than I remember it. I wanted so much to own it and undo all that was done in 1889. The drawing-room could be lovely, with its Chinese wallpaper, if the two blocked windows could be opened, if some of the garish paint could be taken off the Jacobean mantelpiece, if the "exposed" beams could be covered in again and if the appalling little 1889 fireplace could be swept away. How lovely to have elegant nostaligic tea out of a Georgian silver teapot and urn-shaped milk jug in such a room properly restored and furnished!

The great hall too needs stripping of its dreary panelling and the old medieval windows opened to air again. Then the courtyard, squalid with weeds and a huge dog kennel, large and elaborate as a Gothic chapel. What a waste!

I biked out on to the main road where I rode a little way with a dark, wide-shouldered, football-bottomed youth. I could see where his pants stopped, the flannel of his trousers was so thin and meagre. He took off his coat, rolled up his sleeves, bent only on getting to the top of the hill. Dark, sulky, good-looking. I guessed that he was probably a little simple minded. Sulky looking people nearly always are.

13 April

Yesterday evening, after tea with Mr Churchyard was over, I got on my bicycle and pedalled down to the river, over the bridge, past the Red Cow and up to Tudeley where the tiny Goldsmid cemetery hangs to the side of the railway embankment.

I went down the footpath to the church and wondered if it was always forbidden to ride in the churchyard. I got off halfway across, as a compromise.

The church door was open, so I went in. How cruelly it had been restored! I hunted along the choir stalls for a piece of waste paper, for I had some lines of a poem that I wanted to write down.

I found the order of service for Passion Sunday, and wrote my lines on the back. Now I am wondering whether Passion Sunday is past or is to come. Perhaps they will look high and low for the piece of paper I have taken.

When I could do no more to my poem I got up and walked into the chancel. There was an old brass in the middle of the floor and I knelt down to read the inscription.

"Hic jacet Thomas Stydolf" was all I could decipher. I knelt still lower to decipher the old writing. Some of the letters were made impossible with their Gothic flourishes.

Suddenly, as I knelt there, I had the desire to lie on the tomb and kiss the cold brass faces of the medieval man and his wife in her horned headdress. That is silly, I thought, resisting the idea. What would anyone say if they came in and saw you lying on the chancel floor, kissing the tombs? They'd think that you had fallen down in a fit.

But I knew that no one would come in. Swiftly I lay flat on the stone and kissed the man's face first. It was pleasant and comforting to feel my body pressed close to the hard stone. The cool brass on my lips was pleasant too. I moved an inch or two and kissed the woman's face, then I straightened my arms, raising my body into a physical-jerks position.

I left the church and sat down in the dry grass in the churchyard.

17 *April*

Yesterday I had a wire from Edith Sitwell, asking me to lunch at the Sesame Club on Monday at 12.45. I can't think what it will be like. I'm wondering all the time.

Maurice Cranston was in the room when the wire came, and he contracted in the way people do when an unwelcome piece of good news is brought to someone else.

[*At this point, Denton broke off his account of the arrival of Edith Sitwell's telegram to begin a first draft — later much revised — of what was to develop into his second book,* In Youth is Pleasure. *It bears little resemblance to any published section and is reproduced for that interest alone. The narrator, Orvil, is Denton; Ben is his second brother, Paul.*]

In the early 1930s a young boy of fifteen was staying with his father and two older brothers at a hotel near the Thames in Surrey. The hotel had once been a country house and before that a Royal Palace. Now the central court was glassed in to make a large tea lounge. There was a glistening range of downstairs lavatories, and a whole new wing with ball-room, and a little box bedroom above.

The young boy was unhappy and nervous. He was frightened of his eldest brother and his friends, and he lay awake at night, longing to go to sleep and not being able to. He hardly dared to eat the rich hotel food at dinner, for he thought that it was this which kept him awake. He would go down into the village to buy condensed milk and ovaltine, and these he would heat over his little solid fuel "Meta" stove which he had bought in Switzerland. The stove made him feel happy, for it made him think of Switzerland, and he always liked the things he cooked on it. Only once, he remembered, had he had a failure. He and his middle brother Ben had decided to cook sausages in butter. They saw the sausages hanging up as they passed through the village street one evening at Wengen. They looked such good sausages and the delicatessen shop man seemed so amused by their bastard German-French-English. Whatever Ben said in German, Orvil added to and obscured with stumbling French that melted into English.

They went home laughing with the sausages wrapped in greaseproof paper.

In their flimsy wooden bedroom, with its enormous puffed-out, belching eider downs, they started to cook the sausages over the tiny "Meta" stove.

"More butter," Ben said.

They both delighted to see the butter melt and bubble round the sausages. When they were done to a dead bracken brown, the two boys picked the sausages up in their fingers. They were burning hot and so they had to keep moving them about. At last Ben took a bite and made a face. Orvil looked angry.

"He's trying to spoil the fun," he thought. Then he took a bite and let the morsel lie on his tongue.

"Garlic," he shrieked at last. "Oh, they're awful, Ben, they're awful, they're stuffed with garlic."

[*Denton then resumed his account of the arrival of Edith Sitwell's telegram.*]

We were both drinking coffee out of my two mandarin cups in odd blue saucers, so pretty with bright paint and little figures — old, ancient, something to cherish. The handle was loose on the silver coffee pot with smug Victorian double B's and earl's coronet. (It's even got Breadalbane stamped on the bottom, so there could be no doubt about its owner.) I paid £5 for it in a shop in St James's and not all the "B's" on the bottom or the side will ever take it back to that Victorian Lord Breadalbane's again.

As I say, I was pouring out more coffee, holding the pot close to the lid with my handkerchief because of the loose handle, when Lydia came in with the well-known exciting, thrilling, anti-climax yellow-orange envelope.[8]

"It's pre-paid, twelve words," she said.

I took it expectantly, but telling myself it was sure to be nothing but disappointment. I read it not quite grasping, because of queer writing and bad spelling.

Will you lunch here 12.45 Monday Stiwell Sesame Club Grosvenor Street W1

In spite of "Stiwell" I knew it was from Edith Sitwell, but because of my preconception that she would ask me to Osbert's Chelsea house I had the idea that I did not know where to send the answer.

I started to write Renishaw Hall, then I dismissed the waiting girl without a tip (which I am told is quite rococo nowadays) and rushed upstairs to ask everyone where I should send my answer to.

It was really so carefully worded, her telegram, with the name in front of the address so that I should know she was staying there, but I did not see this until Maurice pointed it out.

When he left I sent the wire and then went to a telephone box and waited nervously to get through to the Sesame Club.

8 Evie Sinclair (see 1942, note 4 above).

The woman at the other end would insist on calling me Madam, while I gave her my message. I wanted to be quite sure that Edith was staying there.

"Yes, madam," the woman said.

"Don't call her," I shrieked. "I only want to leave a message."

"Is it Mr or Mrs Welch?" the woman asked right at the end, still definite in her own mind about my sex. I wanted to laugh.

"Mr," I said, "Mr Welch."

Was my voice fluty and high through nervousness? I am not usually taken for a woman on the telephone.

19 April

Now it's happened, now I'm going up. It's rained in gusts. I've been reading *Street Songs* and eating breakfast with tickling contracting feeling in the centre of me. I think I will wear my blue suit. What will it be like?

[*Later the same day.*]

Now I am home and I will not write about it till the morning, for I have too much to say and I must think.

The nightingale sings, it [*illegible*] through all the night. The moon shines. All is cold after the heat. I live, am growing older, ever-dying now.

20 April

Yesterday, up early in the morning — the washing, the dressing, the brushing; then to the station on my bicycle. Everything planned, everything done, the ticket bought, the clean gloves in the pocket.

How late the train was — waiting, waiting there. Then the bursting carriages and all the passage filled with soldiers — their tin hats, bottles, knapsacks hitting on the walls when they turned. I wondered how I could stand to Charing Cross. I looked into two lavatories, but they were too smelly to lock myself into. I tried to sit down in the loop of a strap, then on a fire extinguisher. Sore, painful, I felt desperate. How ill and tired I would be if I could not sit down.

I gazed at the fat suitcase for some time, then at last dared to sit down on it. Pleasure, bliss, gazing out of the window, sitting down at last. The fields, the feathery trees, wonderful poison green, fresh as new lettuce. The large lonely young man carrying a huge implement across unending fields. Then the long, long tunnel with its whistle and the belching white smoke, not escaping, flowing over the train in a thick cape. Sparks flew and faded. The red demon glow on the white smoke belchings and the growing of it till I was really ready for some catastrophe. Can something be on fire? Will the engine burst and the driver be burnt to death in the steam, as I have read? Will I be groping in wreckage in the dark tunnel? All this through my mind and more. No change from early childhood.

Then the sooted wall seen faintly, the lamps of some workers, like miners' lamps or the lamps of gaolers in a dungeon. It is like the haunted house in the Luna Park at Margate. The green, luminous skeleton should descend, champing its terrible jaws, grinning. The concrete grime, then at last the air, on, on, quite happy now, almost peaceful. The very young petty officer in the carriage, cutting his nails with his mother's scissors:

"You should not cut them, you should file them," said his red-haired sister.

"I've got better things to do than to waste my time filing my nails," he said, in an extra manly voice, still puffing at a large, new, extremely smoking pipe. He wore glasses.

In London, walking up to the Leicester Gallery, then back again because I did not know whether to pay to go in, or take it as my right to enter free, as an exhibitor.

Then to the National [Gallery] for the pictures and, more important still, for W.C.s and wash basin. Nice for Art and Nature to be thus allied.

Looking at the face, hoping it would do, no smuts, no dirt, no shiny sweaty bits at nose base or on forehead.

Off in the taxi to Grosvenor Street. Emptied out at the wrong door, so I walked and bought cigarettes and then went on feeling parched, so dry and yet about to be wet all over.

Into the rather drab hall of the Sesame Club, basket chairs, ugliness; in a fright that I might not recognize Edith Sitwell.

Sitting down, feeling embarrassed with the other old women there. So incurious on the surface; yet I felt watching.

"Miss Sitwell will be down in a moment, sir."

The waiting, almost too much.

Then the tall figure dressed all in black, black trilby, Spanish witch's hat, black cloak, black satin dress to the ankles and two huge aquamarine rings. Wonderful rings on powder-white hands, and face so powder-pearly, nacreous white, almost not to be believed in, with the pinkened mouth, the thin, delicate, swordlike nose and tender-curling nostrils. No hair, I can remember no hair at first. The rings, the glistening satin, and the kid-white skin.

Down the long passage, this figure sweeping in front. Everything arranged for me.

"You will have Gin and French, or Bronx?"

"Gin and French, please."

Nervousness gaining on me.

"Now about your book, when is it appearing?"

I told her that it was still held up, but that I had heard it was oversubscribed before publication.

"Isn't that wonderful," she said.

"It's due entirely to your Foreword," I pushed out of my mouth. More nervousness. Hot, red.

"No it isn't. I think it's due to your article on Sickert." Here a laugh.

We began to drink our cocktails. Ice in them. Ice is lovely, I thought. Ice is luxury.

The Sesame Club was queer. Elderly ladies, attempts at sprightliness in the decorations, basket chairs, unfinished, things, drabness, brooding, unenjoyment of what meets the eye.

"And Gladys, we will have beer for lunch." Edith Sitwell called the maid by name, although Gladys is only a substitute, for I have forgotten [her name]. We move into the dining-room.

"You will sit there, won't you, and then the window won't be too much for you," she said to me.

I sat, with the light full on my face; better to sit with the light behind you, I thought. I wanted to sit under the window, not opposite. But I did not move.

The menu was brought.

"The tongue is very good today, madam."

"Shall we have tongue, and would you like some soup first?" I am asked.

"Yes, tongue," much rather than steak.

"What is potage paysan?" Edith Sitwell asks the maid.

"Sort of vegetable soup, madam."

We both decide not to have soup. The tongue comes. It is good, soft, sweet-tasting. There is Russian salad, beetroot, lettuce, potato.

Edith Sitwell has no lettuce. We begin to eat quite hungrily. I am like Byron over women's mouths for a moment, not being able quite to reconcile beetroot, tongue, potato with the mouth of a person who I have only associated before with poems in books. I had never thought of things going in, only coming out; dividing body from soul.

The Russian salad is full of garlic or strong onion. I will smell, will smell, I think. My mother, when I was small, laughed and would eat no curry (which she loved) because she was going out to a dinner-party that night.

"Darling, they will smell me," she said. "It doesn't matter however much I clean my teeth. You don't want them to smell your mother, do you?"

Edith Sitwell says suddenly, "What does your family consist of?"

I tell her that my father died in November. This stops talking. Sensitive people do not say anything when people unknown to them are dead. I am sorry, I want to tell her so much, to let her ask so many questions, but it does not develop.

I ask her about Renishaw; again, I do not hear quite as much as I had hoped.

She begins to talk about my *Maiden Voyage*.

"You really did like the book?" I ask.

She flutters her hands in hopelessness.

"Well, didn't I write to you all about it? No one could say more."

Edith Sitwell does not often say so much.

"I know, I know," I said hurriedly, "but I can still hardly believe it."

She laughed at this. I was pleased; she had got my amazement at her interest.

"Now I think is the time for you to do something violent and vulgar," she said.

The words struck a bell in me.

"That's what I'm longing to do," I said.

"That bit in your book about the terrible Chinese hotel — quite remarkably terrifying."

Silence for a moment.

"I will tell you what your danger is; it is your ingrowing toe-nail. Everything in, in, in."

She bent her very dignified head and brought her two hands up to it in movements rhythmical, swirling, in-turning.

"It is perfect in that book," she said, "but you must not do it again."

Her remarks had bolstered me in what I wanted to do. She was very right. How I hoped I was not boring her.

"Amusing that bit about your being good-looking in your Sickert article," she said, smiling with amusement.[9]

I was very disconcerted, very anxious to explain that whatever sort of face one had, one always tried to compensate by insisting on good looks, if someone lumped one together with himself in ugliness.

"Especially if they're about eighty!" And she laughed.

I felt safer. How many times I have wished that I had not written that sentence which I really felt at the time.

"What will you have now?" Edith Sitwell asked me.

"I think rhubarb," I said.

"Won't you have cheese? Rhubarb is poison."

"I think just the opposite. I love its taste."

"Then I will have cheese, Mrs Blank."

Three times she called the elderly maid Mrs Blank.

Very polite, very gracious, a little too much.

A lot of talk about the Poetry Reading.[10] Some cold remarks, some cool, some praising.

9 Sickert had linked Denton with himself as being ugly, whereas Denton saw himself as the best-looking person present (see 1942, note 2 above).

10 On 14 April 1943 Osbert and Edith Sitwell had organized a poetry reading at the Aeolian Hall in aid of Lady Crewe's French in Great Britain Fund, attended by the Queen, Princess Elizabeth and Princess Margaret.

"Eliot reading *The Waste Land* is very wonderful. You wouldn't expect it to be read with feeling and exuberance, would you? It would be altogether too overpowering. W. J. Turner went on and on and on, until the chairman had to clap his hand, and then we all clapped him so much that he had to stop."

I asked if the princesses listened well.

"They sat very still in the front row, and stared straight at one," she answered. "The Queen has a real interest in books."

I asked her about other writers. She liked Graham Greene's book *England Made Me*. We had both just read it. She thought Rosamund Lehmann very bad. V. Sackville-West bad. I asked her about Dorothy Wellesley and W. B. Yeats — why he suddenly took so much interest in her. She paused a moment, then: "I think it was just love, don't you?"

"I liked reading their series of letters to each other, didn't you?"

"Yes, but the more I think of them, the more I think that they do no one any credit."

"I think you should read Kipling and Willie Maugham, as wonderful story models," she said.

We got up. I felt a little top-heavy, as I always do even after one glass of anything. Lydia says it is because I am drunk without wine all the time, and the wine on top is fatal.

I followed Edith Sitwell down the long passage. She seemed to be talking to herself as she swept along. I wondered if I should say, "What is that?" or pretend not to hear.

We went and sat in the forbidding, aquarium-dark drawing-room, together on a sofa.

Then I remembered that I had left the book, her *Notes on Poetry* which she had just given me. The book with "For Denton Welch from his friend Edith Sitwell" written in front, which I had placed on the far chair so that no grease could get on it.

I jumped up.

"I've left my book," I said.

"I knew you would," she laughed. "I told you you'd leave it in the train."

I went swiftly down the passage. Mrs Blank was clearing the table.

"I've come for my book," I said.

She smiled. The other diners looked at me interestedly, I thought. Nice, nice, to eat with famous poet, lovely, magic.

Back in the dark room again we went on talking. Edith Sitwell turned her head and watched the door. Is she bored with me? I thought. She is bored, she looks at the people passing.

I liked to be in the darkened room talking to her. A little old woman passes us, stops, retraces her steps.

"Miss Edith Sitwell, is it?" she asks so carefully, gently. As if one could mistake that black satin and those aquamarines!

"Yes," the grave reserved answer — a little bow.

"Would you be so good—?"

English Women is thrust forward, open, ready to be written in at once. Edith Sitwell takes it.

"But at your leisure, there is no hurry." She waves her hand, smiles, floats away, disappears.

Edith Sitwell makes a face.

"I suppose this happens all day long?" I say, feeling glad that I have not brought two books of poems.

"This is the book of all books that I hate signing," she answers. "You're told that it's a patriotic duty for you to do it. You're only given £50 in consequence. And then you have a terrible amount of work to produce something which is so small that it's no good to anyone."

"Yes, they are tiny," I said. "How to get all English women into a quarter of an inch! But aren't they popular. People love them, and if they've never heard of most of the English women, think how much instruction as well as pleasure they get."

"Oh, I daresay it's nice for them, but is it nice for us — it is a ramp."

Edith Sitwell did not use the word ramp, but it conveys the meaning. The real words I have forgotten.

We got on to malice, insults, rudeness, libel. It was interesting about Wyndham Lewis. I could not really tell if she liked or loathed him. She laughed and talked about Lewis's terrible, hurting remarks which were always the things one could least bear to have said about oneself. Then I heard about them, the Sitwell joint libel action against Reynolds Press.[11]

"To teach them manners," she said. "We decided many years ago that if certain things were said we would fight, and we did. But it is a terrible business. One always feels, is it not better to leave it entirely alone? With past friends, people like Lewis, it is. If they attack you personally, leave it alone. If they attack your work, defend yourself. When the judge appeared with his terrible black face, we thought, now we are for it. Now we are going to be scalded, are going to have to pay, as well as being horribly insulted. All three. It is too much. But the black face was not for us but for our enemies. His rage against them was terrific. What a relief."

I mentioned something about the censorship. She said, "The law, I think, is absolutely right. As Bernard Shaw said to me when we were all called to give evidence over the *Well of Loneliness* fuss, 'Here I am, asked to say something about this pathetic book, and I don't know what to do, because I know it's

---

11 In 1940, while reviewing an anthology by Edith Sitwell in *Reynolds News*, Hamilton Fyfe, instead of attacking the book, had taken the opportunity of saying that oblivion had claimed Edith and her two brothers. They joined together in suing for libel. Edith and Osbert got the better of G. D. Roberts, KC, defending, and Mr Justice Cassels, a man of culture as well as learning, awarded the Sitwells £350 each.

serious, unpornographic, but it's so bad as literature.' "[12]

Edith Sitwell went on, "Let those poor people think or behave like that, if they cannot help it, but don't let them write bad books about it. It is dangerous. In the hands of young people they might do great damage — not because of stimulation, but because of the terrible revulsion they might cause."

I was not certain what to answer, so I began to talk of a passage in one of D. H. Lawrence's letters which has to do with *Lady Chatterley's Lover*. He hopes there that the book will be successful, for if not, he will be quite without resources.

"That sort of book must often be written chiefly for money," she said. Then she began some criticism of Lawrence's book with the words, "Lady Chatterley is just—" but now I shall never know what Lady Chatterley was to Edith Sitwell at that moment, for something distracted her attention, and she never finished her sentence. It hovered in the air above her head.

At half-past two, I said I must be going.

"No, no, you can't go," she protested. "Osbert said, 'Wait for me till a quarter past three. I'll try to come if I possibly can.' I'm sure he'll come; he's the one who really introduced me to your essay. He came into my room, sat down on the bed, and rolled about with laughter. He says he'll dance the minute he sees you, as Sickert did at the tea-party."

I laughed and we talked on for a little. I heard something of their life together at Renishaw, during the war — how most of the rooms in the great house were shut up, and about the two old servants.

"When they ask for me," she added, "Osbert says, 'Yes, Miss Edith is in; she isn't busy — she's only working.' "

There was more laughter, and as it died away I looked over my shoulder and saw that someone was approaching us. Edith Sitwell saw him too, and said, "Hullo, darling."

I stood up to be introduced and there seemed a general shuffle and swirling. When I was back in my corner again, the atmosphere had quite changed. We were three now, and a sort of vivacity had replaced the seriousness. I was told anecdotes with great skill and grace, but I can't remember them, because of the new buzz in the air. Sickert, George Moore, Arthur Waley were mentioned. Only the names remain. The rest has disappeared.

Edith Sitwell began a remark, but her brother followed closely with something of his own. She leant back, silencing herself at once. It was as if she left him to talk and be amusing, now that he had come.

He turned to speak to her about the poetry reading. There had been trouble or disagreement of some sort, and a letter had to be answered.

12 A novel by Radclyffe Hall about lesbianism.

"But why write to me?" Edith Sitwell complained. "Why not write to the chairman? It's nothing to do with me. I won't be the villain of the piece."

"Oh darling, don't bother about that — we all know you're not." He seemed impatient to have the matter settled with as little argument as possible; but Edith Sitwell still brooded on her answer.

This was chiefly a listening time for me; but when the reply to the letter had been decided upon, Osbert Sitwell turned to me and said, "You ought to write some more things like your Sickert article."

I was anxious even at the mention of this article now, so I answered hurriedly, "But I don't think I know any other famous people at all."

"Well, it must be arranged," he said, smiling rather inwardly.

"Yes, it must be arranged," agreed his sister, smiling too.

A house, not very far from me in the country, was mentioned. "He could do a lovely one, if he went there!" Osbert Sitwell said.

This atmosphere of a suppressed mischief was delightful to me. I felt that, for the moment at least, I was with lively helpers and well-wishers.

A few people were named; but I had seen Osbert Sitwell glance down quickly, I supposed at his watch, so was prepared when he said, "Now I must go, else I shall be late."

I stood up too, and held out my hand to Edith.

"Good-bye, thank you so much."

"Good-bye," she said. The black folds rippled, the marvellous rings winked. She seemed taller than ever in the underwater gloom of the long room. The end, like the beginning, was over so quickly; long before it had been properly grasped by me.

"Come and see me too, won't you?" said her brother, in one of those quick businesslike voices.

I was out in the passage, collecting my gloves and stick, wrapping my book in my coat, because the rain had begun again.

I stood in the porch, waiting for it to stop.

Suddenly Osbert Sitwell appeared from the hall.

"What are you going to do now?" he asked.

"Slowly make my way back to the country, I expect."

"I'm determined to get a taxi. Perhaps we could share it," he suggested.

I offered to try to find one and walked quickly towards Grosvenor Square. The rain spat on my face. I waved my stick, but all the taxis were full, with their little flags down.

I walked back, feeling rather helpless; and as I reached the door, a taxi drew up.

"Fine! Is this your doing?" Osbert Sitwell exclaimed.

"No, it isn't," I said, wanting to be disbelieved.

We climbed in together.

"Are you quite out of the war?" he asked, turning to me.

"Yes, you see I fractured a bone in my spine."

"Well, it has left you free, so I suppose you think it almost worth it now."

"Perhaps in a sort of way, although it was rather gruesome — no picnic," I added, rather strangely, since it is not one of my usual expressions.

"What do you think of the war? Don't you wish the whole thing would stop? Or perhaps you don't."

"I do. I think it's appalling."

We both seemed pleased with each other.

"We'll none of us know what it was all about in twenty years; it's utterly mad."

I looked at his elegant cane with amber, or agate or tortoiseshell top, a little too chichi for the rather rich, severe brown suit. I am so glad he carries it, I thought, it is nice to like nice, showy things all through one's life. This reticence, dullness, safe taste — horrible, cowardly!

He asked me about my family. America somehow came up. I found myself telling him that my mother was American, but brought up in Florence at a convent.

"Do you know the name, because I used to be in Italy a lot?"

"I have forgotten, but I have it at home."

"What was her name?" he asked very gently.

"Rosalind Bassett." I thought it sounded so pretty.

"Oh." It was said in the triangle at Hyde Park Corner, then I forgot everything outside the window until I came to Carlyle Square.

"Now I'm going to give you something for the taxi, because I've dragged you so far out of your way," he said.

"Oh no, no," I said.

"Yes."

"No," I was about to add, "if you want to pay anything just pay for your fare here."

This is exactly what he did. He thrust half-a-crown into my hand, and the meter said two and threepence. I took it, feeling confused and a little inferior, schoolboyish. He was so firm, so much the master of the situation.

How glad I was that I had not mentioned the reasonable suggestion about paying. I had at that time thought that he was about to thrust five or six shillings into my hand to pay for my fare right over to Church Street, Kensington.

"Good-bye, Mr Welch," he said, shaking my hand, although he was by this time outside the taxi. "Now that you know where I live, come and see me."

He looked up at the house and called out the number.

As if I were ever likely to, unless properly asked. Still it was nice, the idle sentence.

As we drove away I thought of him. He'd told me that he was going to be massaged. I thought of him, for some reason, lying on a marble slab and being pummelled by a tough young butcher with grubby, sun-bleached hair which kept falling over his eyes as he slapped and kneaded with his iron hard arms. But perhaps it isn't a man, they'd all be in the army, perhaps it's a woman. But no picture came with this new arrangement; unless it was of a giantess in spangles. I thought of the amusing thing Edith had told me earlier in the day: "As Osbert always says to the servants, 'Yes, Miss Edith's in, she isn't busy, she's only working.'"

Yes, I thought, he was like that, rather ruthless and teasing, but nice, nicer than I'd imagined, and so bouncing, still so resilient.

I wondered if he realized that I would never have gone in a taxi if he hadn't suggested it. I would have walked and wandered about and gazed at things. At Church Street I got out of the taxi and got into a bus going to Olympia. Hilda and Irene Dallas were both at home in Edith Road.[13] They were sitting in the back room with everything on top of them, because the front room was being painted. They were very happy for me over my book and my visit.

We had tea, and then I went back to Charing Cross. I was early for the train, so I wandered down into the Adelphi. A sailor was standing on a corner. He asked me for a match. I wanted one too, so I waited till he'd got a light off another person, then lit mine from his.

His fingers were dirty, nicotined, something from another world, faintly shaking. Mine were shaking too.

We stood and talked about the East. He'd just come back from Ceylon.

"I've nearly done my seven years," he said.

"Are those clothes hot?" I asked.

He held his raincoat open, looking at his body in the hairy blue serge.

"Yes," he said, "bloody hot."

Remember the atmosphere in that drawing-room again: dark, aqueous, cold, with figures passing, repassing; the glistening door opening and shutting; Edith's head turning, her white hand lying on her breast so that the huge ring sparkled like ice on fire in the gloom.

11 May

(*Maiden Voyage* came out at this time, I think May 3rd).

I went to the dentist that day and felt dulled and unenlivened.

Surely rather a good post. A fine letter from E. M. Forster full of very *sensible* praise of the book. But how I wish I knew all the nasty things they want to say too! Or rather I don't wish I knew them, but I wish praise did not make me think of them always. One from Lord Berners, nice but not exciting.

13 Sisters, and Christian Scientist friends of Denton's mother.

17 May

Yesterday, Sunday, a respite from excitement because there was no post, I thought! But Phyl Ford bicycled up (being bitten by the Alsatian on the way)[14] and presented me with James Agate's review in the *Daily Express* headed "Ah, these three can write", and likening me to "blooming Proust if I'm not damned careful". Not quite as forced hearty as that, but almost.

Now today I have Edward Sackville-West's letter asking me to lunch Thursday twelve-fifteen at Brooks's Club.[15] Oh excitements. I must wear sober blue suit, but I'm afraid my face will be quite tomato colour from the sun. I lay in it all yesterday afternoon by the river; then I walked on to the lock and two airmen passed me with a sporty-looking dog. Their blue-grey jackets were unbuttoned and one of them had hair which glinted gold. The other one jerked out to me, "How do." I answered gruffly, "How do you do." This is what happens, people say civil things to each other roughly and then walk on.

It is wonderful in the fields. There is nothing else that is so good for me. Now I am sitting on Shipbourne Common in only my trousers. The sun is burning me. The wind is blowing. The flies are buzzing and the birds rising with the aeroplanes.

Last night the Germans were over. Guns banged. I half woke up and lay thinking how strange it was that I lived in millions of tiny almost unconnected moments which gradually would build up until I lay in my grave.

18 May

Today I am by the river below East Peckham. I'm writing letters, roasting in the sun, sweating, burning, turning red. The feathers of the grass tickle me and I am almost stupefied. Oh, how lovely it is. Bang in front is a concrete pill-box covered with nets, slowly being swallowed up by weeds. *They'll* win, every time.

21 May

Yesterday I went up to lunch with Edward Sackville-West at the Café Royal. I sat in the hall waiting, wondering if I should ever recognize or be recognized. Always as I steeled myself to meet him a fat lady or a fat man or a couple swept in.

14 Gina; she belonged to Mary Sloman, Denton's landlady at Pitt's Folly Cottage.
15 The novelist and critic, heir to Lord Sackville and a cousin of Vita Sackville-West. He was then working for the B.B.C. When warned of Denton's sometimes outré taste in clothes, he changed the venue to the Café Royal.

At last someone rather small and quiet came in. I knew it was him and wondered why he walked straight through without looking round him. I waited for him to come back and then went forward; he had the rather uncertain, careful, don't-want-to-make-any-mistake sort of look on his face. He spoke rather drawlingly, his face was pale, a little spotty, sad. He wore two rings on his fingers (rings that seemed innocent of devices or crests) and an identity bracelet, a thick gold chain, reminding me of those chains which were finished with a heart locket.

We went to the downstairs eating place, but the waiter rather insolently said, "Have you booked a table, sir?" "No," said Sackville-West, rather haughtily and ashamedly.

"Come, we'll have to race up the stairs," he said, turning to me. "I'm afraid we won't get such a good lunch, but that can't be helped."

We went up and found a table in the gallery.

I chose hors d'oeuvres, he had soup. The quantities were huge. Everything of mine, the beans, the beetroot, the tomato pickle, the potato, seemed stewed in salt and vinegar. We both left a lot.

We began to talk about my book and about the rudeness I might expect as a result of my frankness. He said laughingly, "Sometimes your unpleasantness seemed quite gratuitious. A long pin comes out and in you push it." He thrust his hand out, and we both began to laugh at the enormities of my book.

"You'll probably hate it in a few years," he said. "But that won't make it bad, you'll just be like most of us, when we grow older — less willing to give yourself away on a plate."

Suddenly he looked very staid and distant and rather primadonnaish. "When one is out of one's first youth," pause, "or perhaps out of any youth at all, one gradually gives less and less away. But that is what is so disarming about your book, the fact that you don't in the least mind making yourself out unpleasant or ridiculous."

We went on and on talking of writing, and he advised me never to go outside my own experience; he said he thought this absolutely fatal.

"How near us do you live exactly?" he asked grandly. And I suddenly saw that if one had a place like Knole it would seem natural to suppose that the whole of the rest of the neighbourhood revolved round this. I stifled my slight resentment at this royal "us", because I was terribly keen to hear about many historical things. I was also quite ready to be disappointed, for I always have been before. You invariably get the least information straight from the horse's mouth. He told me that he had taken all the silver and put it in banks, that the pictures were in Wales or some such place. But the furniture had been stacked on the ground floor, where it could be got out quickly in case of fire. I asked if there were cellars, and he said, "Only the crypt where the central heating is now. It never had tombs in it, they are all at Withyham near my cousin's place."

He went on to tell me of the vault there, with the studded plush coffins and the babies lapped in lead, looking like paperweights, with their names just inscribed on them.

I said stupidly, "You ought to have one out to decorate your desk at the B.B.C."

And he answered, making it up there and then, "Well, I had thought of it."

By this time my vol au vent had arrived; it was stuffed with bully beef, bright red in colour. Salt again to the point of horror. I had asked for lager when questioned on drinks, and then heard him say that he would have ginger-beer. It was annoying not to have the courage to ask for a soft drink and then to hear one's host do so. When the chocolate éclairs came he said, "Oh, it's got custard in it!" and straight away began to scrape it all out. When I asked him if he expected real cream he said, "I thought it might be that soya bean stuff, which sometimes isn't so bad."

The best time in the conversation was when we both got excited thinking of my absurdities in the book. When he got more languid again it was not so good.

Afterwards when we'd said good-bye and I was alone in London, in the heat again, I looked about me at the houses, the people — everything seemed closed against me. People with handsome faces and the ugly ones all seemed equally shut away. I saw my book in Hatchard's and another book-shop. I wondered if this was a good thing or whether they ought all to be sold by now. I grew drearier with everything rushing past me. It's always like this, I thought, when I come to London. Men lie with their faces on the grass in the park. I pass, looking at them furtively. I see the broad red stripe on the trouser of some unknown uniform. A sailor rolls by with two girls. Painted faces, American soldiers. Everyone's eyes seem glazed, unseeing. The pain in missing all this excitement in other people's lives is horrible. I feel the awful outpouring waste. I want to be back alone in the country as I cannot share at all.

When I knew that I was going to live with my eldest brother in Adam Street I was horrified. I had wanted to be on my own, and this arrangement would not be the same thing at all. It was the last thing I could have wished for.[16]

5 June. Twelve o' clock at night.

Often at this time of night or in the early morning, or at any idle moment of

16 This paragraph is a reference to Denton lodging, when he first went to art school, and before finding a room on his own at 34 Croom's Hill, with his brother Bill in Adam Street (since renamed Robert Adam Street), off Baker Street. He wrote about the inhabitants of the Adam Street house in "The Earth's Crust", first published posthumously in *Contact*, October 1950, and reprinted in *A Last Sheaf*.

of the day, my thoughts turn suddenly to a street scene in Shanghai, when I was a small child. The sun is shining, and there is nothing to be seen but the asphalt road, the pavement, a piece of suburban wall with inset iron grilles. Then from round the corner emerges a procession. As it winds towards me I see that it is a funeral, but there is something curious about it, a hint and threat of mockery. As the coffin is borne past me, I become aware, with a shock, that it is paper, flimsy black paper, stretched on wooden laths; some of the mourners' clothes are paper too, I now see. Their curious grins, gesticulations and posturing are frightening and disquieting. Slowly the procession disappears with clashing cymbals, wails, low singing and sudden piercing notes.

I continue on my way home, wondering what can be the meaning of this macabre and elaborate show.

"Daddy," I ask, when I see him sitting there in his chair on the deep violet library carpet, "what does it means when you see an imitation funeral? I met people with a paper coffin and paper clothes all grinning and screeching and wailing."

Then my father began a long political disquisition. He told me of the present troubles between the Chinese and the foreigners. He explained the funeral as a demonstration staged by some hot-headed students — they were always qualified by this or some worse adjective.

But in spite of all his words, all of which were utterly in favour of the white man and against the students, I carried away with me the feeling that I have still, that the students were mourning for one of their comrades who had been killed, and as they could not recover his body, for the foreigners had destroyed it, they did it in this way with paper coffin and paper clothes.

7 June, afternoon.

I am sitting in the cool in Capel Church, under the medieval fresco. Against a dim salmon pink ground two figures seem to be hanging long coats and gowns out of the windows of a castle turret. Other figures seem to be banqueting; they all wear very satisfied expressions. There is a large cartwheel and the effect of stonework painted on the plaster.

Outside, the birds are twitteringly quarrelling, and a yellow-orange rose tree is spilling its too-ripe petals all over the tarred path. The only other noise is the aeroplanes' buzzing.

I tried just now to climb up the staircase to the tower. It has a charming, if home-made, attempt at a Chinese Chippendale fretwork baluster, but the worm-eaten treads creaked so ominously at each tread that I only lifted the trap door, looked into the tower room with its water cistern wrapped in rags, and then came down hurriedly. I pictured the whole crazy staircase coming down with me on top of the wreckage.

Across the way from the frescoed wall are three of the most unforgiving restored windows in the fiercest carved stone, but I tell myself that I should long ago have given up bemoaning the fate of all our churches in the nineteenth century. The twentieth is really no better; it simply has less material left to spoil.

I have been eating my lunch in the fields nearby (Ryvita, cheese, apricot jam, chocolate, bar of squashed dried fruits, coffee), sitting on my coral air-cushion, given me by May, reading for the fourth or fifth time an outline of the Brontë sisters' lives.

Charlotte's success, as always, delights and excites me. I cannot help thinking of my own book. I keep wondering if mine can really be called a success. Edith Sitwell says it is the best reception of a first book she can remember. I have letters and wires and lovely reviews, but how and when does one know? When the fat cheque rolls in? Is that what one is waiting for?

Bicycling up the hill to this place I passed two strange young men and a child piling chopped branches into a wagon. One of the young men had a bright turquoise pullover and lighter shirt, the other a small, squashy, curiously other-century mushroom hat. His face was atavistic, with gold-red skin and two longish projecting teeth. The child was quite pale and wore a beige beret. They just looked at me and said nothing until I was out of ear-shot.

Further on I came to two people cutting the hedge, one old, one young. The young one, with coarse nose and big leathery lips, held a billhook on a long handle. As I passed close to him, I had the feeling that he looked unreliable, almost simple, and that he might easily attack me with his weapon. A cart with a barrel on it passed me at the same time. The barrel seemed full of some curious wash to put on trees or plants.

From a treetop nearby I heard whistling. I looked up and saw a faded blue shirt and a slouch cap pulled smartly over one eye. Some rakish youth was picking the cherries there. You could tell how cocksure and brutal he was by the whistle, the cap, and the way he looked down from his high perch.

Earlier, in a field of hay which had just been mown, I saw another youth of the same sort, but this one was in a white shirt and a heavy leather belt plastered with brass badges of all sorts; they looked exactly like horse brasses only smaller. I could not tell if they were regimental badges. I wanted to go up and examine it. He was using their favourite word "fucking" just as I passed. It rang out cheerfully. One sees and knows how hard they all are in these sudden sights and sounds.

Last Monday I went to supper with Noël Adeney. We had cold soup flavoured with claret, and fennel in long green shreds; then a sort of pilau of rice, onions fried, pimento excitingly scarlet like dogs' tools, and grated cheese. The tiniest new potatoes and salad. Afterwards plums, and creamy mild tomato cocktail to drink. A charming meal.

We sat and talked a long time and then went looking for a pair of fisherman's red trousers which she said she wanted to give me. We turned a whole trunk out, but could not find them. There was printed velvet, linen, a Jane Austen period dress of Indian chintz with a waist under the arm-pits. (The arm-pits were padded with white cotton, against sweat.)

In the cupboard was a tin of Earl Grey tea which she threw at me to take home.

You see, this is what goes on in nineteen-forty-three, the year of the greatest war to stop all wars, if I have the quotation right.

Now I shall leave this cool church and this medieval fresco and get on my bicycle again.

This may be read about in years to come and then people will know what I did on this June day.

(The alter rails have "Michael Davis 1682" carved on them beautifully clearly.)

12 June

Up to Noël Adeney's for tea, and the *New Statesman* review of my book; then afterwards to the Chequers at Ightham (though I said I was going to Carpmael's to supper).

I drank five gin and limes at Ightham and after each one grew a little more outward and demonstrative, but deep down was sorrow, pain, fear, death-longing, all crouching inside. Afterwards, in the lavatory, I noticed someone had written "God is Truth and Love."

I left about ten and rather swayingly jumped on my bicycle to go back to Crouch, for Frida Easdale had asked me to coffee. It was late when I got there. Noël, Bernard and Charlotte were talking and I was given a chocolate biscuit and started to talk too. Too loud and too vivaciously, but it really didn't matter. We ended up on ghostly footsteps and poltergeists. The light faded, the moon began to shine in; we still talked and went on till twelve.

Frida walked a little way back with me. As we stood talking a couple of bicyclists went by and shouted goodnight. I followed on soon after them and just as I was about to descend the hill I saw one of them drive into the bank and tumble off just in front of me. I quickly jumped off and bent down.

"Are you hurt?" I asked. He was holding his head.

"Just a bit," he said, after a moment. The other rushed up, saying, "Are you all right, Martin?"

He pulled the lamp off his bike and saw the blood on his friend's face. There was a cut above the eye, but for one moment I thought the eye was filled with blood.

"It's not deep," the friend said, as if to reassure himself. "You're all right, Martin, aren't you?"

"I'm all right," said Martin, now much less shaken, "but where's me bloody glasses?"

We switched our lamps in all directions. Nowhere to be seen until at last I came on them several yards away; thick pebble lenses, quite unbroken. We all rejoiced. Martin muttered something about "and it was last night they said I was drunk". The other laughed.

"I think we ought to walk the rest," he said prudently with a rather charming solicitude.

15 June, afternoon.

Raining, aeroplanes droning, trees soughing.

I am lying in bed now, so I imagine, as I have imagined how many times before, a stone cottage on some heath or moor. A cottage that is reached by a footpath winding through wet grass and heather, bracken, harebells, thistles.

The rain is beating down, blown in waves by the wind.

Inside the cottage is a room with uneven, rather smoke-grimy white-washed walls, the dust lying in grey shading on the curves of the stones.

There is a fire in the grate that is not burning really very well; it is rather smoky, filmy, blue-grey, with damp wood and spitting sparks. The room has not really any of the charming things that I would try to have in a room; no lustre drops, no sparkling wood or marble or ormolu, no painted furniture or porcelain. Everything is very home-spun. Rough tweed curtains, cottage china, scrubbed wood chairs with drab-coloured, very comfortable cushions. There is the feeling about the whole place of utter solitude, stealth, the ghostly, un-lived-in, fascinating feeling of week-end houses. One knows that the house has been unopened for days or weeks or months; that it has stood waiting empty on the heath.

Off the living-room opens a kitchen, and an enclosed box-staircase mounts up in one corner. In the kitchen the large brass tap gives widely separated drips. The white cups stare down lonely from their shelf. They have coarse patterns of red and blue — a sort of imitation peasant ware that has become almost decent again through mass production methods.

The Valor kitchen stove has a brown oily film over the fierce turquoise enamel.

24 June

Yesterday I walked up the side of a steep wheat field. The wheat in the wind rippled into patches, some silver white, some soot black, the shapes always changing. I lay down in the sun, on some thyme which immediately began to smell. Ants crawled on me.

25 June

I'm sitting now in Nettlestead Church, which has huge perpendicular windows and fine glass. But all the glass has been removed and most of the windows are blacked out. In 1763 a great hailstorm damaged the windows badly. The little church is all alone, close to the river. I had to go to the rectory to fetch the key, a great clanking thing. I clanked it as I walked along the footpath. A man was swaying at the top of a tall ladder, picking cherries. A very small boy stood at the bottom with some cherries in a bottle, whinning. On the main road were gypsies sitting by their caravan. All men, mostly young, evil, exciting-looking. How can they still retain this outward traditional look?

I picnicked at the top of a hill by Mereworth. An Air Force sergeant said, "What's happened, mate? Have you lost yourself?" and then told me to climb over the fence and sit on the bank. I read Boswell on Johnson just at my age, when he first went to London.

In the peculiar little vestry, behind the organ, I looked at the cassocks (bright blue, one violet), at the brass vases and the hymn numbers. I thought that this was an exciting place for silence or secret meetings.

Not even a fly is buzzing now; only the drone of the planes.

Outside in the churchyard is someone's grave who was called "Dulcibella, beloved wife of George Acott."

I took a handkerchief out of the bright blue cassocks in the vestry. In size the cassock was between that of a full-grown man's and a boy's. It was almost new. First I found a clean handkerchief folded, then a used one, crumpled and quite stiff.

In front of me now two tombs, 1598 and 1636, Ladies Elizabeth and Catharine Scott.

26 June, four-thirty p.m.

I'm sitting in the Oxon Hoath pew in Peckham Church, looking up at the lozenge shaped [*illegible*] fastened to the sloping roof. The coats of arms are all various for Millars, Bartholomews and Gearys, but all have rams heads in them somewhere.

The pew is huge, like a theatre box, high up above the rest of the church. One looks down on the two altars and the rows of ordinary pews.

In front of me is a lovely little Wren or early eighteenth-century doorway, newly painted with very ugly graining, but of a lovely shape, surmounted with oval scutcheon, pediment and flowing carved leaves and flowers.

The openings that look down on to the church are supported by tiny Corinthian wooden columns with Jacobean-looking bases. The window near me is filled with delightfully inartistic nineteenth-century glass — a lot

* hatchments?

of full-bodied mauve, crimson and yellow. The walls are covered with Miller, Bartholomew and Geary plaques in black marble, white marble and brass.

A Victorian cast-iron stove like a highly decorated pagoda stands close to one of the sides of the pew. The seats run round the side of the square and have coarse squabs on them. On the ledge above rest large prayer books, mostly with the date 1837 in them.

There is a private entrance to this theatre box pew up several steps. What appears to be a pew for the servants (with curtains) is on the left as one mounts the stairs.

This delightful relic makes one groan and gnash one's teeth for what has been lost in all other parish churches. Only a few years ago there was another pew something like this belonging to the Twisdens at East Malling. It is all torn down now by the Anglo-Catholic parson who told me that it was an outrage against God as it jutted out into the chancel.

1 *July*

Today after my lunch (leaning against a hay-wagon, looking across to the shallow valley where a small engine puffed, and reading Colette's *Chéri*) I biked on to a pale baked-mud lane which led into a rich green wood. I passed two cottages and soon was ploughing over thick wood shavings and chips strewn inches deep all over the road. The lane wound on and up, past chopped bundles of poles and past little huts where the woodmen took shelter. It was like a tiny lost valley in a foreign land, Switzerland or China. Somewhere hidden, concealed, exciting and warm. I sweated hard, and the thick cushiony track still led up. At the top, my face was pouring. The sun stung it and the wind cooled the seat, but only on one side. I took another track which I hoped would lead me back to the road, for although I was rather enchanted by the wood I felt too tired to explore any more. I dipped into a green mosquito-ey little dingle overgrown with grass and nettles round a thread-like stream. I became angry now because of my tiredness, the heat and my feeling of being lost.

At last I reached the edge of a field, from where I recognized the roofs of cottages and a hop-kiln above Tudeley. I decided to go down by the edge of the field, hoping to find an openable gate at the bottom. The field was so bumpy and treacherous that I had to walk. Just as I was getting to the bottom I looked through a hedge and saw a brown face staring at me.

"Do I come out on a road down here?" I asked.

"If you come this side there's a gate," he said friendly.

I went through an opening into the other field where rich graceful hops were growing, and saw that the man was digging the earth round them with a glistening spade. He seemed quite alone.

"I got lost up in the wood," I said, plopping down by the hedge to rest. He sat down too, on his spade, and smiled at me very charmingly. I then saw that several of his upper teeth on the right side were gone. But in spite of this he was still good-looking; small bullet head, brown tough skin, dark stubble turning into gypsyish tooth-brush moustache, dark eyes, thick arms with wiry black hairs lower down and smooth rounded creamy muscles above. The open khaki shirt showed a paler chest with fine pectoral muscles and hair growing delicately in the clearly defined pattern of a cross. He pushed his small worn cap on the back of his head and seemed utterly willing to be gay and natural.

"You just having a ride round?" he asked.

"I've been picnicking and I lost my way in the woods. I want to get back to Tonbridge," I answered.

"Oh, I come from Tonbridge too, this isn't my real job," he said. "I used to drive a lorry, but then I was in the Fire Service until I got invalided out. I've had lumbago for twenty-two weeks."

"You look all right," I said, touching his arm in recognition and respect. It was so pleasantly brown and strong.

"Oh, I'm fine now. I've got brown too working in the fields." He rolled his sleeve higher, childishly pleased to show me the change of colour. He pulled his shirt more open at the chest and I saw there too the creaminess merging into brown and the blotches where skin had peeled.

"I got quite sore one day," he said chattily, and then went on to tell me of his lorry driving, which it appears he had really enjoyed. He told me they had often to work more than eleven hours a day (although it was illegal) in order to get enough money. The whole thing, accidents and all, seemed to satisfy him, a really happy disposition.

He straddled his legs and felt in his pocket for pouch and cigarette papers. I saw then that one of the thin brass fly-buttons of his dungarees which he wore over brown city-looking tweed trousers was undone. He did it up in a matter-of-fact way and then held the delicate white paper between his teeth as he fumbled with the tobacco. He looked more than ever like a raffish, Dickensian, slouching, dare-devil character. One could look at the gaps in his teeth without any real repugnance. (Interesting how some people can almost manage to be unrevolting under nearly all circumstances.)

Next I heard about hospital, where he had had infra-red treatment from a lamp.

"The lamp burnt a little spot here," he said, showing me a brown mark on one of his arms. He told me how it nearly burnt him all around the lumbar region too. "But it's good for you," he said with conviction, "I'd tell anyone to go and have that treatment."

"Do you think you'll get back to lorries now you've been discharged from the Fire Service?" I asked.

"I dunno, I hope so," he said. "This may be healthy, but it's not fast enough, is it?"

I agreed, liking him so much for enjoying what I had always thought of as one of the most dreadful of lives.

The whole moment with him in the rich hop-garden seemed something rather unexpected and idyllic. After wandering so wearily in the alien wood to come out and find so pleasant a human being with that rare animal quality which only comes with contentment.

I got up to go on my way reluctantly.

"Good luck," I said heartily, thinking to myself, we'll never see each other again, we'll both grow older and older and uglier and uglier; the earth will bloom, the hops bristle and curl, when we'll both be too disgusting to think of. And then when we're dead other young men will meet casually and talk and part. It's all too never-ending for words. I felt hard and sore-hearted and battered about.

"Cheerio," he said, with real pleasure at my friendliness. (How is it we can quite artlessly invest even single words with much more meaning then can ever be written down in a hundred words?)

2 July. Ten to four. Afternoon. Hot sun.

I am up in the belfry of Shipbourne Church, circa 1870. Stout walls, every angle sharp, hard. Before me is the intricate oiled brass mechanism of the clock ticking and stirring and whirring alarmingly. There is an old oak chest, painted; inside was a postcard dated 1930 calling the bell ringers to a meeting. There was also an old copy of a paper called the *Virgin World*. Outside, the gardener is harshly sharpening his scythe.

The old hatchments decorate the walls, Cazelet or Fane arms I suppose. Black goats' heads and three fences on a blue ground.

I feel like a Pre-Raphaelite person on a Pre-Raphaelite tower, alone, cut off, comfortably ill, and mournful and desolate.

The bell ropes are gathered gracefully together into a tangle of woollen barbers' poles. Gaudy and decorative.

There is only one diamond in the faintly translucent lancets, through which one can see the outside world. It looks miles away, frightening, remote, backed in the sun, uninviting.

The clock has just gathered itself together to strike four o'clock; like steel fans beating the air and like brass serpents hissing.

A bedroom in a tower like this would be lovely. Serene, remote, beaten on all sides by wind.

3 July, 3.25 p.m.

Today I went towards the river at East Peckham. Near the farm called Kent

House I heard a machine chugging; then I saw a dark faced youth gazing into the hop garden and discovered that the trench, which is being cut from coast to coast to bear oil in a pipe for the invasion armies, came through this part. All the men working on this are Irishmen. Two passed as the youth and I talked in the road. One was large and loose-looking, fair-skinned with turned up nose and trilby hat; the other rather short and squat, muscly and tramplike, with yellowish hair. Neither of them spoke and neither of them looked particularly Irish. I went on to the river down the very bumpy lane through the fields just by East Peckham post office. Being Saturday the river banks were not deserted. Children were bathing and screaming and splashing in a shallow tributary, and oldish men were fishing solitarily, not speaking or even looking at each other. They gave an indescribable effect of wonderful resignation. I chose a place by one of the camouflaged pill boxes close to a may tree on the edge of the bank, and spread my mac and blew up May's tomato red air cushion. Then I started to eat my cheese & honey & biscuits & chocolate and red-currants in earnest. I drank all the coffee and lay back, shutting my eyes on J.C.Powys's *Philosophy of Solitude.* I heard voices and saw two boys on the opposite bank debating where to settle for their fishing. They came quite close to me and I heard them joking and swearing through the barricade of thick grass.

I tried to write a little but I could not, so I lay in the sun and then went on my way. As I came out of the bushes I saw that one of the youths had lain face downwards in the sun and forgotten about fishing. His back was naked and had turned a dull rather creamy purplish brown. A slight tremor passed through it every few moments, and then one saw the very minute drops of sweat glittering frostily between the shoulder blades. I watched carefully until I had remembered the sight and then crossed the bridge and moved towards the weir. Three small slightly ragged boys with braces, like a Wilkie painting, were fishing with a curious contrivance.

Beyond, by the powerful, massive new locks, where water gushes perpetually from many square mouths and there are little iron platforms and bridges, I saw a naked youth of about sixteen with very square shoulders and head, sitting on a piece of round black machinery. One could tell that he worked in the fields, for there was a sunburnt V on his chest where his shirt opened, and an arresting change of colour on his upper arms where his sleeves were rolled. The rest of his body was rather swarthy white, and when I came nearer I saw some reddish spots.

He shook all the dark wet hair off his face, and said the water was lovely. I sat down on the grass and watched him dive. He did it specially for me. "Do you ever go off there?" I asked him, pointing to one of the little platforms quite high in the air. "I did once, but I hit my head," he said shyly. We went on talking. He told me how last year some of the hop-pickers rushed down to the river, all lit up from the nearby pub, and how they began to rock the old high footbridge which used to be near here until at last the whole thing crashed into the water with two men of nineteen or twenty on it. He mentioned their age for some reason. They managed to scramble out all right but that was the end of the bridge.

He lay back in the sun and said, "My mate ought to be down soon. He'll dive off the high platform, you wait for him." I said I would.

We were joined at this point by a small gold-brown-haired girl who was wheeling in a pram a still smaller boy in a cotton sun hat whose left leg was completely encased in plaster of Paris. Under the instep was a shiny metal support.

"Has he broken his leg?" I asked obviously. "Yes," she murmured, too quietly to hear.

Suddenly there was a whoop from the boy on the bank. "Here's my mate," he yelled to me. I looked up and saw a very light-sandy-haired boy on a bike dashing towards the weir. He leapt off and darted across the bridge, a tremendous sense of urgency about him. "Quick, Ginger," his friend yelled unnecessarily to him, "get your clothes off and come and dive off the high platform."

Ginger disappeared into the long grass by a mound, and I caught glimpses of clothes being pulled into the air, and the sudden dead whiteness of his shoulders.

He rushed out of the grass, dead pearly white except for his freckled face, with little, lumpy, rather over-developed stomach and pectoral muscles. A rather broken up, not pretty, surface fussiness. Different from his friend's smooth lazy-looking body.

Pulling his mouth back and showing his teeth in a wild, mad, excited gesture he rushed at the water and dived, going so deep and straight down that his legs almost turned a somersault.

"He dives too deep," I said to the friend.

"Yes," he said indulgently. Then, when Ginger came up spitting and gurgling, "Get up on the board and do your dive!"

"I can't," Ginger said with assumed babyishness, quavering, making his limbs tremble.

"You're a bleedin' liar," the friend said.

"You got to come too," Ginger insisted.

"I'll go off the lower one; I hit my head last time," said the first boy.

Ginger got on to the top board, about eight or ten feet up, and dived again very deeply. The other boy shouted, "Coo, you've hit the bottom, look at the mud."

Ginger swore and said he hadn't. The other boy dived off the lower board quickly to get the ordeal over. Then they both swam about, talking and spitting and dragging their hair back. Ginger's hair now looked metallically shiny and yet dead at the same time.

At last they both came out of the water and sat down on the grass beside me. The first boy lay flat on his back and half shut his eyes. He looked charmingly coarse and young-animalish now, with thick brown neck, smooth arms and hairs round each brown-red nipple. Ginger turned his extremely white and nobbly back to me and almost bent over his friend, talking to him about his work, and how he had been late because he had been staying at home, pressing his trousers for the dance that night.

"Aren't you going?" he asked.

"No," the other said scornfully.

"I thought you was."

"Well, maybe I will, I don't know yet."

They went on talking about work. There was something about a saw breaking, and the work being all right, but—

At last Ginger turned to me and said with exquisite politeness: "Well, is it warm enough for you?" He evidently felt that I had been neglected.

"It's wonderful, isn't it," I said. Then I asked him if my clock was right. It said a quarter to six.

"It's more than that," he said. "It's more like six." I got up.

"Then I must get on. Good-bye."

"Cheerio," they called together.

I hated to leave the happiness there. It made me think of Dorian Gray. (I suppose the youth-age business.) I thought of the boys in years to come. They would not be nearly so nice, quite horrible in fact. They had both talked about going into the services; one plumped for the R.A.F., the other for the Navy. All the happiness would melt away. I began to think of Oscar Wilde and Lord Ronald Leveson-Gower and all the people who have longed to become young again. I don't know why 1890 should leap to my mind the whole time. Is it because they worshipped youth? Or is it because it always seems to me a rosy time for young men to be gay and wilful and wasteful?

5 July. *Three-fifteen p.m., at the top of Gover Hill, in the avenue that leads down to Oxon Hoath.*

A woman on a chestnut horse has just ridden by, looking romantic against the background of steel-blue shallow hills and bleached cornfields. The sky is thickly clouded, heavy with rain that won't fall. I've eaten chocolate and cherries and read two stupid short stories by Somerset Maugham.

I would like to build a tower here, on the top of this hill, with three storeys, a kitchen and living-room on the first, a bedroom and bathroom on the second, and a gazebo and workroom on the third. Perhaps on top of that, pillars holding up a lintel, but no roof. I would like to lie in the tower quietly for ever.

6 July. Twenty to two, on Shipbourne Common, leaning up against the wooden palings round a tree called "Cryptomeria elegans" (on a zinc label).

Boys of the land army or whatever it is called are chopping, burning, tearing down the bushes, clearing the whole thing for growing wheat. I am sorry, for it is one of my favourite places for eating and meditating, but one old local in the churchyard the other day said that it was a very good thing, and that he could remember the common without a tree or a bush on it, that it is only within the last thirty years that the bushes of may and the small trees have sprung up. I look across to the tower of Shipbourne Church and think of the early eighteenth-century church (1722) that was torn down to make room for this quite soulless thing. It seems an enormity, to have destroyed the whole meaning of the landscape and the history of the place. But once reconciled to this smug solidity, and one can enjoy something about it; certainly not its beauty, perhaps its feeling of security, and the freedom which comes from not caring in the least what happens to a thing.

The boys work in all stages of undress and raggedness; some wear coloured shirts and drab waistcoats, but others are stripped and have shiny café-au-lait backs, while one has trousers with so many holes in that one is immediately reminded of those Elizabethan slashed breeches and sleeves.

Just now there was a shower of rain and I huddled under some trees with them. They talked of one of their number who only appeared fitfully. "He must have some money behind him," was their verdict.

14 July

I have got a poetry bout on, but I keep on wondering if I'm producing semi-demi A. E. Housman. I should hate this, although he is a lovely poet.

This morning I had a letter from a Mr Julian Goodman, 10 Gower Street, hand-made paper, to say that he liked my book so much that he had gone to the Leceister Galleries and bought my very nice Piebald Cat.[17] I knew this picture would sell, so it is so nice to be proved right almost on the first day of opening. An absurb cat with a sleek, well-fed, conceited look is really irresistible. I wonder what Mr Julian Goodman is like. Is he a rich Jewish financial gentleman? There is nothing nicer in the world than having one's productions appreciated.

On Saturday Marcus came for the night.[18] We drank tea, then gin, then beer, then coffee, then port, then barley water. Wasn't it extraordinary?

He told me all about the gaiety of Poole Harbour where there are the

17 Currently in the collection of Mrs Anne Gallon.
18 Marcus Oliver (see 1943, note 1 above).

dearest little pubs in which soldiers and sailors and civilians dance madly and feel awfully friendly. "Just like the South of France," he kept on saying.

Yesterday I bicycled to Mildred Bosanquet's at Seal.[19] She was out so I looked at her old Georgian silver in the sideboard and at the few remnants of old china mixed up with all the modern muck in the pantry. Old families are just as squalid as others, except for these tiny remains of past days.

Marcus told me of an earl of about sixty who had fallen in love with a schizophrenic youth down in Dorset. The youth was put into a coma with insulin and has now come out of it very prim and sober.

The earl has got very friendly with the whole family now and often goes to stay. This puts the mother into a great flutter. Apparently they are all very peculiar; for the mother and the other air force boy son sleep together in each other's arms. Isn't this a nice picture! I imagine them as gypsy but perhaps they're very upper-middle-class.

Francis came this morning and started baby talk and babble to show what a distressed state he was in. He has no money, his mother has no money. At last I gave him two-and-sixpence to buy cigarettes with.

Now I am on the edge of a cornfield with rain clouds over me and [*sentence unfinished*].

15 July. Twenty to ten a.m.

Have just this minute got a letter from the *Tatler* to say that they are going to use my photograph in the 28th July issue, and that the review on 7th July was by Elizabeth Bowen. This gives me great pleasure. I have always been put off by the upper-middle-class snobbery in her books, but nevertheless I like to think that she it was who wrote that nice review. I knew it was a woman, but not what woman. I think I would like to write to her.

20 July

The glow-worms were so bright tonight that they looked like the stubs of the fattest most expensive cigars glowing in the grass.

21 July

Today I picnicked on the road in Shipbourne, close to a man who lay in

---

19 Mrs Bosanquet had asked Denton to take care of a large eighteenth-century dolls' house, which he spent many months restoring. After Denton's death, Eric Oliver presented it to the Bethnal Green Museum of Childhood. It is illustrated and recorded in *English Dolls' Houses of the Eighteenth and Nineteenth Centuries* by Vivien Greene (London: Bell and Hyman, 1955).

the stubble, sunning himself in a white singlet. After my meal I walked up to him and we talked. He was a Norwegian sailor, and he was spending his leave at what he described as an A.T.S. camp. This sounds irregular, but I may not have got the facts right, as he only spoke very fragmentary English. He said the girls were nice, that they came from Manchester and that they drank almost as much whisky as he did himself. He said that he and his mate got into a train with two bottles of whisky and a smaller one of rum and they had quite finished the whole lot by the end of their two-hour journey.

"Is there any place for coffee further on?" he asked. "Tea or coffee?"

"Would you like to have tea with me?" I suggested.

He nodded his head, jumped up, tucked the vest into the neat little trousers and donned his sailor jacket and his shoes. Everything was very new and coarse and clean and rather childlike. I admired the tight fit of the jacket, with its zip. He ripped it up and down once or twice to amuse me. When he put the little beribboned cap on, the effect with his broad flat fresh face was almost Japanese — something strange, jaunty and rather amusingly and curiously graceful.

We both jumped on our women's bicycles — for they had both been borrowed.

When we got here no one was in, so I made the tea while he sat and smoked. He said the Earl Grey tea smelt good. I said, "Very rare to find China tea in England now." It is almost impossible to avoid speaking pidgin English to a very halting foreigner.

We sat on the bed and drank our tea and he ate honey and biscuits. Talk lagged. I brought out *Verves* and we sat close together looking at pictures like the two children on the annual *Chatterbox*. We just pointed, nodded, sucked in our breath, laughed. One picture of naked medieval ladies cutting their husbands' throats in bed particularly appealed to him.

At last he stood up and said, "I better go and get my cigarettes."

He straightened and patted his tight neat little clothes all over again and cocked the absurd cap rakishly.

"I no civilian clothes," he said ruefully.

"Those are much nicer and more sensible," I said with conviction, trying to comfort him.

"My hair going," he said, patting the crown of his head. Indeed I had noticed that his light goldy-brown hair was rapidly thinning into a bald patch. Some of his teeth were missing too. But neither of these things detracted from his rather monkey, child-like quality. He might have been over thirty. He might have been under. One did not necessarily associate any particular age with him.

When he stood up to go I was sorry. I imagined him pedalling off to get the cigarettes (of which he said he smoked seventy a day on leave — on board, he only smoked a pipe), then whizzing back to those gay A.T.S. girls who drank so much whisky. It really sounded such a sensible unofficial arrangement for a sailor's holiday.

22 July, 4.25 p.m.

I have just heard Viola Garvin cracking my book up on the wireless — saying that Edith Sitwell laid hands on my head like a priestess blessing a young neophyte or something.[20]

Very nice, very funny to hear one's name across the air. Lots of praise. I keep on wondering who was listening. She said people ought to listen when Edith says that she would not be surprised if I turned out to be not only a born writer but a very considerable one.

24 July, 4.50 p.m.

I have just been down to the sluice gates where I saw a procession. A Chinese-eyed, Hitler-moustached, smooth oily-skinned airman was walking in triumph with two little boys bearing a huge pike hung from his closed fishing rod between them. There was blood from the fish's gills and fish-smell and scales on the airman's hands. His face was childishly bright-eyed and exhilarated. The little boys were screaming to me in admiration. "He caught it! He caught it!"

"I've never seen such a size!" I said.

We walked along the river bank, the airman talking considerately to me, natural politeness on top of every other feeling because of happiness.

Then the fish wriggled, bounced in the air and disappeared into some undergrowth. I didn't know that it was still alive.

"When will it die?" I asked, as the airman fiddled in the ditch to get hold again of the fish. He did not care to touch it as it wriggled.

"Oh, in about an hour, perhaps," he said.

He hooked it up on the rod again, the cruel wire through its mouth, the head seemingly almost pulled off by the weight of the body.

"I've been waiting for this feller for several days," the airman said to me. Then, "Cheerio, this is where we go across the fields to Five Oak Green."

The two little boys were organized again into carrying the fish.

"Don't let it touch my back," the larger one screamed, "a dreadful slimy thing like that touching my back."

"Aw, don't be sissy," said the airman. The children screamed with more excitement, fear and delight, and the party set off through the long grass.

20 Routledge had sent Frank Swinnerton, the novelist and critic, a review copy of *Maiden Voyage* in the hope that he would broadcast about it. Swinnerton wrote to Denton on 15 July 1943 praising the book but saying he had no more broadcasts lined up so he had passed it to Viola Garvin.

Once more the fish leapt off the line. This time the man approached it so menacingly that I thought that he was going to bash its head to pieces, but again he winced away when its tail lashed the air.

He hooked it up again, then looked across the field to me and smiled for the last time, a deprecating humble smile, a smile that wished to include me in the joy of having caught the pike.

I thought of the fish and blood-sticky hands. He would hold on to someone very tightly with those hands tonight, I thought.

Francis wrote to me this morning, saying that his mother had fallen down in Tunbridge Wells and had been taken up by the police as drunk and incapable.[21] She had been allowed out on bail, but had to be taken to the courts this morning by Francis. He suggested that I might like to go to watch the proceedings.

She of the large Edwardian Tudor house, the "Castle Careless", with its butler and footman and page-boy, its silver tea-kettles and Earl Grey Blend, its greenhouses and lawns; she was now falling about in the streets, causing disturbances. I wanted to cry, seeing so clearly in an instant that everything goes from bad to worse. I wanted to back her against all the officious policemen, because she was well over sixty and quite lost and strayed. I marvelled at the amount of herself that she had managed to preserve, in spite of her lunatic life.

27 July, 4.15 p.m. By the river at East Peckham.

I have just been walking along the tow-path, wearing nothing but sandals and raw silk socks and khaki shorts I had eleven years ago, when I was seventeen. I walked along with the hot sun burning my back, eating plums, cutting the bruised parts off with my green-handled knife. It seemed so sad to be wearing the same shorts and silk socks I had when I was seventeen. I felt that I had changed much more than they had.

As I walked along the edge of a field of red beetroots I thought of myself as a child of five in China, passing through the peanut fields, longing to be alone close to the sea at Weihai-Wei. How I loved to be in the fields where the peasants quietly cultivated things. Only very rarely do I get the same feeling in England, and I had it today.

In a tributary a young man, two girls and a small child were bathing and splashing. I was surprised and pleased with the comeliness of all of them. I sat down on the opposite bank and stared frankly at them.

The young man rushed into the red-gold over-ripe corn and shouted to

---

21 Mrs Streeten was an alcoholic. She appears as the mother of Danny Whittome, in reality Francis Streeten, in "A Picture in the Snow" (see 1942, note 36 above).

the girls, "Now you just turn your backs." He fumbled about, evidently pulling down his trunks and drying between his legs. The girls said, "All right," but as he bent down, busy in the corn, I saw them both turn round and stare too.

I picked up a piece of paper that lay near me in the grass. It was a page of Alden's Oxford Guide. I learnt that Carfax = Middle English Carfuks, Latin Quadrinfurcus = four-forked.

A plane keeps on circling round as if it were trying to do an emergency landing, so I've run down to a shelf under the river bank, in case it should crash on me in the field. The wind is blowing hard, but the air is hot.

Routledge's wrote this morning to say that they hoped Alfred Knopf were going to do my book in America.

I am going to write a short love story, I think under an assumed name, for a magazine. I will take two family names and put them together. I am going to do this because I want to see if I am able to write what the average person thinks *is* a story.[22]

28 July

My picture in the *Tatler* today reproduced rather too small for my liking!

Down to the river again, where I spent all my time talking to and drawing a half-naked bather and confectioner called Eddy Link (isn't this a pretty name?). He said he was thirty, and he was very communist, very pacifist and very anti-haute bourgeois! His was a funny little figure, small but rather strong, very brown and hairy up top, very white and dirty down below when he took his socks off! He told me all about his champion fight with another huge Welsh baker, when he was only nineteen. His idea of heaven was to retire to a country cottage with a charming mistress, not a wife. He said he was now getting £4 a week, but he was used to £6 or £7.

29 July, 2.45 p.m.

I am sitting by the lake in Oxon Hoath Park, looking across to the house and imagining that I am a rich author who has brought it for his own. I think of all the things I should do — how I should pull the dead tree out of the lake and have deer to graze on the slopes round the house so that the grass should be smooth and silky. How lovely it could all be if it belonged to me. Sometimes the fish leap right out of the water; there is no noise except a far away aeroplane droning.

---

22 "The Fire in the Wood" (see 1942, note 4 above).

2 August

I am sitting close to the shut-up cricket pavilion on the Oxon Hoath estate under a young tree; close to a broken wire fence. The wind is blowing fiercely and the sky is thick with grey clouds.

As I was reading Robert Louis Stevenson a soldier ran past in his braces, swinging a brown beer bottle. He also wore a smart peaked cap, not a forage cap. I wondered where his tunic was. He seemed to be in a great hurry. I jumped up to watch him. He disappeared hobbling over the humpy path.

After my meal I went to look at a half-ruined cottage. Four rooms, an outhouse and a privy. The brambles were growing in at the door. The rose wallpaper had nearly all peeled off and hung down in weeping sheets. The leaded windows were nothing but a tangle of broken pieces and jagged wire. I thought of it all repaired as a house for me.

I think Oxon Hoath must be one of the most untouched estates in the country. All the cottages collect rain-water from their roofs or have wells. They all give that nineteenth-century impression of unselfconscious romanticism. There are dogs on chains, clematis, wooden barred windows with peeling paint, no wires or poles of any sort, only rough mud paths leading to dilapidated garden gates, like decaying stumps of teeth. These tiny cottages stand dotted about in the deserted fields, and over the low stone wall stretches the park up to the lake, where the house, with its French château twist, broods. Inside are the pictures and the furniture of the Millers, the Bartholomews and the Gearys. I think the house must have been almost completely rebuilt in about the eighteen-thirties, but it now has such an atmosphere of remoteness as to seem ages old. It is because nothing can have been changed for about fifty years. This left-alone quality gives far more the atmosphere of age than a licked-up medieval church.

9 August. Oxon Hoath, on the bridge by the lake. 3.45 p.m.

I am here again. I hug the warm parapet and gaze across to the charming house. The wind is blowing hard, the sun is hot on my back. The brown and white cows, as in some majestic picture, roam across the rolling slopes before the house. White fish leap in the water noisily. At the gate I saw two huge trees just felled. Are they going to cut many? I hope not. I saw also a green tent and motor bike, and I wondered if Tom was cutting the trees, and if I should suddenly come upon him, his skin a deep dirty brown, looking magnificent as he flung down the axe on the bark.

18 August, 9.30 a.m.

Last Thursday I went to tea with Mrs Littleton and she showed me the book plates and the little round wafers of her husband's grandmother. "Duchess of Northumberland, Syon House" the book plates had on them, and coat of arms and coronet. The little wafers were all different colours, pastel salmon, strawberry, apple, lime, larkspur, lavender, citron, marguerite. I imagined the duchess in the 1830s putting these little wafers on her notes and then pressing her seal on them. I saw her sticking her bookplates in her own books. They struck me at that moment as most charming relics, pretty, fragile, of no money value. There were also many old French bookplates that their Uncle Henry had collected. They were on coarse paper — delightful rococo, beautifully engraved yet archaic.

On Friday I climbed up the hill to Mrs Bosanquet's, over Shipbourne Common, past Fairlawne. Just out of Ivy Hatch I overtook two walkers, each with a small knapsack on his back. One was short with whitish hair and bald head, the other was tall with large beak and leather elbow pads on his jacket. They were both such perfect examples of schoolmaster-walking-tour-early-twentieth-century gentlemen that I let them pass me again, then got off my bicycle and walked behind. I was rewarded by remarks absolutely in character. The squat, broad one, who was considerably the older, was saying to the other, "Of course, what I liked about Johnson was that he was in every sense of the word a true Liberal. With him everything had to be done by discussion."

The other agreed. He managed to be jaunty, manly, deferential to age and yet independent all at the same time. I saw that he was quite good-looking in a heavy way. Age perhaps thirty-five; eyes rather dark and bird-like, yet sparkling with clean fun. A face so characteristic that it was hard to believe in it. The rough tweed jacket, the leather pads, the rather dirty grey flannels and heavy brogue shoes.

All was exactly as it should be. He started a story about a man (Johnson again, I think) who went into the dining-hall and, seeing the jars of sugar on each table, thought that one jar had more in it than the others; so he took all the jars into his study and weighed the contents.

The older man gave a hearty laugh. I knew they were schoolmasters now. There was no doubt.

The next thing the younger man said was, "Have you ever heard about how he sent back his fried egg?"

The other said, "That's hardly like him." He was firm and politely incredulous.

"Oh, but he did," the other insisted. "He was given a fried egg and bacon—" The story meandered on. I let them get well ahead of me. I would like to have heard more, but I felt I could not go on walking at their heels. I think that there is nothing more fascinating than watching human beings who have retained traces of another age.

In the woods near Knole Park. Hot, sultry. 5.10 p.m.

This morning I went into Tonbridge to get a manuscript typed, and on the way home I saw Prince Belosselsky walking on the pavement. He was dressed all in a thin flowing suit of some smooth khaki material. He wore old, beautifully polished brown and white co-respondent shoes and a sort of drooping, rather pointed trilby hat that he always affects. There was such an extraordinary and studied air of elegance about him that I was quite taken aback, and almost began to wonder if he would care to know me without my coat on and riding a bicycle. I gave him a quick darting smile and then looked away; but he called out in a loud voice, "Hullo!" It was a mixture of so many things, but chiefly it was a rather boisterous welcome. I felt that perhaps he might almost want to stop and talk, but I jumped on to my bicycle after giving one more look at his receding back. The sweep and sway, the curious lilting and at the same time padding gait, sort of imperial waddle, the feet pointed outwards and the head held stiffly like a wired carnation; the flowing clothes, the jacket very long, the trousers narrow, the soap-stone, rather esquimau face with many wrinkles and hawk eyes, all together held a fascination for me. Here was somebody not at all clever, rather foolish perhaps, who yet could create this interesting effect. There was snobbery in every movement and line, but also care, thought, discrimination, idealism and beauty. Yes, the image left in the mind was beautiful. I kept thinking as I rode away that that old, poor and probably ill man had made of himself, by endless contriving, a thing of beauty. It seemed very noble and heroic to me, to be over seventy, exiled, completely alone, with hardly any money, and yet to take this endless care with one's appearance. I realized at once that it is his only means of expression, but who is to see and who is to care? That is what seemed sad, that there was nobody to give their attention to this extraordinary relic. I would like to go to him and ask him many questions and write a book about the Russia he remembers.

When I went to his flat in the High Street (over the cake and tea shop) and saw the portraits of his ancestors, the tiny enamel box with Madame le Baronne Strogonoff (*née* la Princesse Belosselsky) engraved on it, the order of St Catherine in a glass case, I was filled with that passion I have for old, dead, past things. And I felt very sad.

19 August, 11.30 a.m.[23]

I met the most extraordinary person at May's yesterday. She had asked

---

23 The following entry, together with the entries for 25 August and 2, 3 and 4 September, are the genesis for the short story "Brave and Cruel", in which May Walbrand-Evans appears as Julia Bellingly, Elizabeth Plummer as Katherine Wade and Monte as Micki Beaumont (see 1942, note 28 above).

me in to meet what she had described as a ravishing young man. She had got to know this man right at the beginning of the war. She had come home to find an unknown bicycle left in her garden. Later a young man had turned up and claimed the bicycle, saying that he had left it in the garden because he was fed up with riding it. She asked him in to tea and then never saw him again till the other day when he rushed up to her at the bus stop and shook her heartily by the hand shouting, "It's the artist, it's the artist."

He told her that since their last meeting he had been all through the Battle of Britain as a pilot and now was invalided out of the Air Force though still on "E" reserve.

He told her that he wanted to have his portrait painted, and so she asked him to come along yesterday to talk about it over coffee.

I was very curious to see this person, so I went along too. The first remark to greet me was, "Oh, he's got leather pads on his elbows. I like them, don't you?"

I was called Denton in the first few seconds and almost patted on the back. I looked at the ravishing young man. This was certainly not the right description. He was saturnine, black, harsh-featured with thick waving hair and rather small square white teeth. Thick black hairs covered his arms and sprouted at the base of his throat. He wore an Italian shirt of white towelling with cord lacing at the neck. His trousers were dirty blue corduroy, patched on one knee. He was rather tall and rather heavy looking, somehow not quite thin enough at the waist. He spoke with extreme exuberance, directness and simplicity in a slightly cockney accent. It was impossible not to respond to his friendliness.

He took up my book which was lying on a table and said, "Fancy being able to write a book. It's marvellous. So you were at Repton, were you?"

"Yes," I said.

"Of course you know Tonbridge?" he asked shyly.

I nodded and mentioned a few names of people he might have known there too. He only gave vague answers.

Suddenly he asked me, with many uses of my Christian name, and many "old boys", whether I would like to collaborate with him in writing a book all about driving lorries through the night.

"Of course I did it for the experience," he said hastily, "but I know all about it, all the swear words, all the slang, how these chaps pick up girls by the side of the road." Here the gayest wrinkle of the face and laugh. I wondered what May was thinking. I was thinking that I had never before met so uninhibited a grown-up person (May told me afterwards that he was twenty-five). He seemed like a very frank child. Whatever came into his head was blurted out straight away.

He began talking about Italy and mentioned "honourable capitulation" several times, each time being careful to pronounce the "h" in honourable. I became panic-stricken, afraid that I might copy him and to be thought mocking him by the others. (By this time Elizabeth Plummer had come in.) She spoke very little and the man did not know what to say to the young girl.

"I think Elizabeth's very shy of me, I wish she wouldn't be," he said, turning to me. Then to Elizabeth, "Elizabeth, don't be shy."

He went back to the war and said, "Of course in the air I was very cruel. I'm very cruel you know. I can't help it, I have to give the devils all I've got. I can't stop myself. I used to love to sow a train with bombs, just as your machine sews a piece of material with the needle." He made prodding gestures in a line with his finger and then laughed gleefully.

We asked him many more questions about his air experiences and he told us stories with plenty of arm and leg movement. He showed shrapnel wounds, white and thin, on his arms.

Again with great excitement he said that we must together write a book all about his fighting experiences.

"It would be good, Denton," he said. "It would make your name as an author." Then when I laughed, "Don't laugh. I'm serious."

He said he had to go on to Sevenoaks, so I said I would take my picnic lunch and go some of the way with him.

"Good, that's fine," he said.

We started off after walking back with Elizabeth and listening to the Warsaw Concerto on her gramophone. Monte (for this is what we were told to call him) shook his thick black hair all over his face, sprawled out his hands and said, "We had a sergeant who played this the whole time. God, he threw himself about just like this, and the sweat poured off him. The next moment he'd be off in his plane. Nothing but playing the piano and dropping bombs."

As we bicycled along the road Monte said, "Of course I'm a direct descendant of le Sieur de Montaigne. Do you know who I mean?"

I said, "Yes."

"My father went to New Orleans in America. My full name is Francis de Montaigne."

I began stupidly to confuse de Montaigne with la Fontaine and muttered something about Fables, but it didn't matter a bit, because I don't think Monte had any idea what his ancestor wrote.

At Hildenborough he was getting so hot that I suggested his putting his jacket in my bicycle basket.

"Will it get in, old boy?" he asked. He took it off and said, "It's only a bought thing, isn't it awful? Squadron Leader Presland's wife wants me to have leather put on the elbows, just like you've got. She likes it."

"I've only got leather on my elbows because they were wearing through," I replied.

Monte looked down at his bare arms which were indeed very swarthy. "You're sunburnt," I said.

"No, I'm not. It's the filthy Latin in me." He clicked his

tongue and shook his head.

He then asked me if I could keep a secret and told me that he wanted to marry Elizabeth.

"But you've only just met her," I said.

"I know, but I think she's my type. I want to settle down. I never used to, it's come over me lately. But now I want to marry and have a baby girl."

It really was amazing. It was quite impossible to tell what this extraordinary person would say next. He went on talking about Elizabeth a lot, saying how he thought that one could take her *anywhere*, how pretty she was; she was his type, he'd had lots of women but he'd always been careful and kept healthy. Suddenly he said, "I like you, Denton. You wouldn't mind going up in the air Denton, would you? You'd be all right. You'd make a grand pilot. There are plenty of people like you in the R.A.F."

"Me!" I said in exaggerated amazement. "I can't even begin to imagine myself in an aeroplane."

In spite of the absurdity I was flattered by his calm acceptance of me as a pilot. I tried to imagine it myself, but it was too difficult. It was a peculiar compliment. By this time we had climbed halfway up River Hill. Just as we reached the first bend an orange lorry shot past us. The driver shouted something out; I thought he was just being derisive but Monte dumped his bike on the side of the road and darted away shouting back to me, "Wait a sec, will you? I know this fellow."

The lorry pulled up further down the hill. I sat on the bank and watched Monte talking to the driver. In the distance he looked more willowy; he seemed to wave his arms and shake back his hair rather gracefully. I wondered why he seemed different as he was talking to the lorry driver. At last he ran back and said, "I used to know that chap well. He's very aristocratic. He used to wear a reddish beard. He's French and he's a C.O.[24] He's working on the land."

We began to push our bicycles again; but we had only gone a few paces when another lorry passed, this time going up the hill, stopped, swayed, rolled back a little. It was heavily laden with logs.

"Look out," Monte said to me. "You've always got to be careful of those things."

His warning seemed specially sinister in some way. I felt that he had seen a lorry back on to someone and crush him. The lorry had now stopped in the middle of the road. Steam was belching out of the radiator. Monte rushed up to the driver and said, "You'd better let her cool off."

The driver was laconic. He asked Monte to put bricks behind the wheels. Monte ran to the bank where there was a whole pile, and then stuffed two under each front wheel.

The driver got out and stood by the side of the road, still hardly talking.

24 A conscientious objector.

He looked very young, fresh, yet tired and disillusioned. Monte said a lot to him, but got hardly any answer. We continued up the hill.

"Let's find a nice place and sit down at the top," Monte said.

We sat down on a green bank and Monte said, "Denton, do you think I speak very badly? Mrs Presland's always telling me that I'm much too careless. That I say 'knaow' instead of 'know'. You'd tell me too if you thought I pronounced things carelessly, wouldn't you?"

I was touched. I did not know quite what to say. I laughed and said, "Is Mrs Presland a beautiful elocutionist herself?"

"Well, old boy, she thinks she is, but I'm sometimes not so sure. I'd like you to meet her though, she's very nice. I like her daughter, too, only fifteen but lovely shaped breasts and very quiet and sweet. The little boy's a sod though; he's fourteen and last week when I asked to borrow something from him he hid it and said he hadn't got it."

Monte looked down and said, "I just wash and wash yet my skin is just as filthy looking."

It was so childlike that it reminded me of the negro who tried to buy something to bleach him white.

We both got up, and Monte said, "I haven't got much to do in Sevenoaks. You sit here and have your picnic and wait till I come back, then we'll ride back to Tonbridge."

I prevaricated a little, feeling almost exhausted by Monte's exuberance.

"I may be," I said, "but don't wait for me, if I'm not here."

"Oh, you're not going to write, you devil," he said. Then apropos of nothing, "After Tonbridge, you know I went on to Christ's at Cambridge."

I wondered if there was a Christ's at Cambridge. Monte managed somehow to make everything sound improbable. He didn't fit into any of the holes he so industriously dug for himself. He wasn't the French aristocrat, the English public school boy, the undergraduate, the lorry driver or the R.A.F. pilot. And yet I suppose he was a little bit of all these things in the most unexpected manner to make an entirely new pudding.

As we parted we stood by the horse trough. Monte turned to it and said, "Let's have a wash, Denton."

He buried his face deep in the water, splashed it all over his arms, and then went to the drinking fountain part and pressed the button. A jet shot out and hit him in the eye. He laughed. Drops glistened in strings in his black hair. I pressed the button while he tried to direct the jet into his mouth. With more laughing and splashing and swearing we parted. He tried to dry himself with a large dirty handkerchief and I went up the little side road along the edge of Knole Park.

25 August, 12.25 p.m.

I have seen Monte again today, just a week after the first meeting. He is now properly engaged to Elizabeth. It seems unbelievable but is true. He is the most fiction-like person I know.

He came up the drive and called up to me from downstairs to go down to tea at May's. He came bounding up the stairs, and began admiring my Donegal tweed coat and my coloured check socks. He, himself, was dressed in a violently blue shirt of a curious sort of silky linen. He told me that he knew a pilot in the R.A.F. who was extremely like me. "He was very artistic," he said. "We used to call him Louise, but that's only a nickname. He was a little like you and wouldn't stand a spot of dirt on his machine. Christ, he was fussy, and he wore satin pyjamas. He wouldn't let any of us tease him, Denton, but he'd let you because you're so like him. I'll ring the aerodrome up and see if he's still there. He was very brave, you know, and very cruel. You're brave and cruel Denton, aren't you?"

After tea Monte sat, and May and I drew him. He was delighted with our drawings, which were both bad. He wanted us to put his R.A.F. wings in silver paint, and underneath the strip of a D.F.C. ribbon. His vanity was most refreshing. He took it quite for granted that he had all the manly virtues and beauties.

Afterwards he mimicked his friend Louise, with rolling eyes and swaying hips and lisping talk. He really was extraordinarily animated; a sort of pure spirit of fun flowed out of him. When the others went out of the room he put his arm round me and muttered in my ear, "Everything's going fine, old man. I like her and she likes me."

31 August. 4.15 p.m. Near the lock gates — Golden Green.

The most perfectly lovely dragonfly has just come to sit on my bare knee. It had a deep browny blood-red body, palpitating, and wings completely transparent except for veins as thin as the finest hair.

The corn is all cut. I have just explored a round corrugated iron hut with wire netting windows and an iron door, a sort of louvre or vent in the ceiling. The whole thing mysterious and sinister with dirty manury sheep lying round it; all alone, isolated in the fields behind the river. It was nearly falling down, and when I stood in the middle of it, looking down at the torn newspaper and the excrement, I thought that it might collapse on me. I ran out quickly and wondered if the crazy thing were some left-over from the last war, re-erected here.

2 September

It is frightful, Monte is either mad or the most foolish crook. He has now got a special licence to marry Elizabeth on Monday. He's been telling lie after lie. The Tonbridge School story has been disproved. The D.F.C. more or less so. The endless romances about jobs, air fights, murders, wills, glamorous ancestors, amazing R.A.F. friends are now completely shown up as fictions.

Yesterday he told May that he had been to Brighton and there had been an air battle and a murder. He told me that he had not gone to Brighton after all. He also tried to sell me his typewriter for £30 as he said that the allowance his father had left him in his Will was not coming through properly. He tried to hint to May that his watch was for sale too.

I have no idea what I ought to do. He seems to imagine that I'm going to be best man. I'm waiting now to confront him. I must try to ask him why he tells these preposterous lies.

I have never met this sort of lunatic rogue before, so am at sea.

He also told May that his mother lived in Chelsea, then he changed it to Inverness.

Last night when he came to see me about the typewriter I walked back.

Late at night.

I went down to May's to ask if she knew any more about Monte. The whole house was in blackness. She pulled the curtains apart at an upstairs window and looked down on me; then she came to let me in. As I stood there I heard Monte and Elizabeth, I think, talking in the road. I was terrified that they too were coming to the house, but they must have passed by for May and I slunk up to her bedroom with the torch and sat there. The light hidden in the pink curtains of her French marquise bed glowed down on us. It was quiet and warm and sinister with the walnut tallboy and the Italian gesso table. We talked of nothing but Monte and what would happen.

3 September

The thing has come to a head. Today I had lunch in the fields near Oxon Hoath and then went to see Mrs Bernard to find out if she had discovered anything about Monte from her niece, who has a husband in the R.A.F., but she was out and so I bicycled home and called on May at the foot of the drive. She had locked her door (a thing she never does in the daytime) in case Monte called. She was telling me in horror how he had got a special licence for the wedding which was to take place on Monday and how Oliver Atkin was to give Elizabeth away and I was to be best man. She was saying how she had met the vicar's daughter, Miss Monypenny, yesterday, and also Mrs Plummer, Elizabeth's mother, and how she had told them all the lies we had discovered that Monte had told and how she knew nothing of him before he threw his bicycle into her hedge, but that Mrs Plummer seemed quite determined to go through with the wedding, saying that Monte put his head in her lap and wept. "You want to do something for the boys who saved you in the Battle of Britain, don't you? Then let me marry Elizabeth."

Just as I was saying, "Do you think someone ought to go to the police?" and May was saying, "Oh, no," we saw someone pass the window going up the drive to Pitt's Folly. I rushed to the gap in the hedge to see if it was for me, but May called me back and I was confronted in her drive with someone holding some papers and fixing me with two rolling black eyes. He looked exactly what he was, a Detective Inspector, but I in my flurry mistook him for a renegade publisher I knew and then for a tradesman. He came up to me quickly and said, "I'm a Detective Inspector but there's no cause for alarm. Do you know of anyone who goes by the name of Montaigne?"

May and I looked at each other, and I said, "This is just what we've been talking about."

We heaved sighs and smiled and led the Inspector into the house, May unburdening herself to him volubly. I was pleased that she was there to do all the work.

We began to ask questions, and he said importantly, "I'm afraid I'm here to ask questions not to answer them."

He smiled complacently, and like a cat rolled those black eyes.

"But is he mad?" May asked irrepressibly.

The Inspector said rather carefully, "This man is not certified, but I think he is!" He then whipped something out of his pocket and showed it to me. "Do you recognize this man?" he asked. There, on one card, were three terrifying views of Monte. He looked much thinner, with a sort of "hanged" or "broken neck" look about the eyes, the mouth and the way the head was held. There was an indescribable air of degradation and vice about the horrible little card. One could not look at it without feeling ashamed that any human being should be seen like that. It seemed brutal and mean. One hated the police for taking a foul advantage of someone in their power.

The Inspector was coming to his plum. "You must understand my hands are tied. I can't do anything, because a crime has not yet been committed, but I'm here to prevent bigamy." The word was mouthed and savoured a little.

May and I were suitably impressed. The extreme squalor of bigamy has always been very apparent to me. I thought with disgust of the dirty, swarthy Monte getting in and out of bed with various wives.

The Inspector was going on smarmily. "Of course, you'll appreciate the fact that we don't have photographs of people for nothing." He turned to us both with a smile. "We haven't a portrait of Mrs Walbrand-Evans at the station or one of Mr Denton Welch." May and I both grinned and laughed.

We talked for some time telling all we could of Monte. The Inspector seemed particularly keen to know if we had been told of his R.A.F. career. This, I suppose now, must be a complete fabrication.

I went down later tonight to May's and we went on to the Plummers, but a car was standing outside the house. We went back later and the car was still there. We saw that it was the Hadlow policeman's car. We came back and waited a little, but no one came, so at last I came back to bed. I wonder now what will be the final phase. Has Monte done a bunk? What does poor Elizabeth think? Has she woken up at last? And I am sorry for Monte, too. Rogue or lunatic, it must be terrible when nobody believes a word you say.

4 September

May rushed in in the morning shaking her head and saying, "It's awful, awful." Then she began to tell me that the Plummers went to London on Friday to buy the wedding dress. They stopped in Tonbridge and paid the vicar for the special licence as Monte could not do so.

They bought the dress, came back in the evening and found Monte at the house. He had been in to Tunbridge Wells to buy the ring at Wagner's. He took it out of its little velvet box, showed it to Elizabeth, and said, "Won't it be lovely, darling, when we are married."

At this moment, just as everyone was feeling untroubled and affectionate, there was a knock at the door. Elizabeth said, "Oh, I'll go, Mummy, don't you bother, you're tired."

Monte looked from an upstair window and said, "Don't go, Elizabeth, don't go." But she answered, "Of course I must go, Monte, if somebody's knocking."

She opened the door and two plain clothes men advanced on Monte. He threw himself on Mrs Plummer and Elizabeth, imploring them to save him, and then, when the policemen took hold of him he began to hit out and fight and scream so violently that they could do nothing with him. One of them had to rush out to the Newfoundland soldiers nearby, to get them to help to control him. Mrs Plummer described the horrifying change in his face when he became hysterical. He screamed and wept and clung to them and then fell down on the floor and went completely rigid.

After they had taken him to the station the policemen came back and interviewed Mrs Plummer. They told her that Monte's real name was Bone and that he was the son of a farmer at Fordcombe near Penshurst. His mother had completely given up hope of doing anything with him. He had a very honest brother in the navy. He also said that he was already married and had two children, but this now seems to be not altogether proved. The police apparently know all about him, although they will not tell everything. He appears to have done this imposturing time and time again, always using the name of de Montaigne, which seems strange. The whole thing is still very mysterious. It seems obvious that Monte is in some way mentally deranged, yet they will probably treat him as an ordinary criminal. He has been remanded till 14 September. That means, I suppose, that he is locked up in solitary confinement. The Inspector told May that when Monte got to the station the grovelling and imploring and complete degradation were too horrible to watch. He seemed to disintegrate and dissolve.[25]

September [probably the 5th]. By the river near Hartlake Bridge.

This afternoon, just as I was going to Golden Green with my picnic, an elderly man with a brown tweed hat and moustache said, "How do you do." I answered, and he slowed down to bicycle beside me. He said, "You won't know who I am, but I and my wife have often seen you. You used to have a little car with a roll-back top, and whenever you went by we used to say, 'There goes our Ron.' You see, you're the same type as our son. The shape of the head's the same. He's your stamp."

He went on telling me about the son's mining engineering brilliance and how he couldn't get a job at first, but suddenly found one at the B.I.E.T.(?) which is a sort of correspondence college. "He goes over the students' papers and corrects them," the father told me. He told me a lot about myself, how I used to live in the Hadlow Road, and how they had often seen me and always had a soft spot for me.

At first when he accosted me and told me that he had seen me in a car in the past, I was suspicious, not knowing what he wanted with me. It is a pity that one grows more and more suspicious. Then when he went on, I felt melted. It is charming to think that I appealed to their imagination. I am glad.

When I turned down by the river he said, "I'll come that way too." I began to feel that I should have him with me a long time. He began a story about his wife's hernia after an operation for appendicitis; then went on to varicose veins.

I longed to escape in spite of his kind feeling towards me.

"Are you going fishing?" he asked.

"No, picnicking." I began to revolve the pedals of my bike and gradually to edge towards the tow-path.

"Good-bye," he said, "and remember some people have been interested in you all these years, without you ever knowing it."

16 September. In bed. Ten to four p.m.

I seem to have spent a great deal of my childhood in prison — other people's prisons. The Black Tulip prison, the French Revolution prisons, the Spanish Inquisition prisons. And the horror of those prisons was so real to me that I often look back and vaguely remember the straw, the filthy

25 Monte was charged with masquerading as a warrant officer and received three months' hard labour.

food, the oozing walls and the toads on the floor, as if I were really once in that situation. Whenever I hear about prisons I seem to imagine that I have experienced confinement myself.

29 September

Yesterday I got a letter saying that my book "almost certainly" had been chosen as an "additional" by the Readers' Union, and that this would mean six thousand copies or so being distributed. I still don't know whether they buy these copies from Routledge or whether they buy the right to republish themselves.

2 October

I have just been asked to the poetry reading in Tunbridge Wells, by Lady Gerald Wellesley;[26] and in the same post arrived Peggy Mundy Castle's letter asking me to go with her. It's going to be very difficult manoeuvring.

22 October

The other night, as I was coming home in the dark, I saw a strange ungainly thing in front of me; then when I drew closer I saw that it was a man giving a piggy-back to a woman. They lurched a little. The woman said something. I looked at them quickly and saw that the man appeared very young with dark hair and eyes, a round face and short, stocky body. They laughed quietly together and said something more. I overtook them and left them quietly piggy-backing in the country lane at night. I wondered if they were just lovers, or whether the woman's legs were paralysed. They stuck out awkwardly on each side of his tough little body, like thin stiff chickens' legs.

I have discovered that Julian Goodman, who has asked me to paint her pug, is Lady O. Morrell's daughter. I am going to take the picture up to her next Tuesday and have tea with her. I am wondering what she will be like.[27]

26 October, 9.5 p.m.

I have just come back from London where I first went to see Lesley

26 Dorothy Wellesley, the poet; later Duchess of Wellington.
27 Lady Ottoline Morrell was the half-sister of the 6th Duke of Portland, and a much maligned hostess to the Bloomsbury Group. She had, somewhat confusingly, named her daughter, later Mrs Vinogradoff, after Mother Julian of the Truro Sisterhood. The painting of the pug, Alex, remains in Mrs Vinogradoff's collection.

Blanch of *Vogue* who wants to come down and do an article on me and my surroundings, in about two weeks' time. She said she wanted to do me in a suitable article, not all mixed up with Frances Day! She was nice and said that she must reproduce the pug in a future number.

At three ten, about, I left to go to Julian Goodman's. Just outside the door of *Vogue* I saw what looked like a whore in brown suiting and snood arguing with a tough little man. She was saying in a strong foreign accent, "See here, what you think you mean?" She was menacing and alarming. The little tough melted away. I walked into Bond Street to find a taxi. One stopped and a Chinese woman got out of it. Fairly pretty, but a little loose faced. She dropped a pound note under the taxi and it had to move on. She picked up the note, scraping her fingers along the street. The taximan, I think, was tight. He was old and wandering. The taxi jerked up at every light or crossing.

10 Gower Street had a brilliant scarlet door. I rang. A rather sluttish, middle-aged woman smiled and looked round the corner of the door. She let me in and said, "Come in here, will you?" Then she called up, "The gentleman's come."

I waited in the back room. Eighteenth-century marble mantelpiece; John picture of girl craning her neck over it. Fascinating little glass-painting in tiny frame on mantelpiece. Also photographs of pug and Lady Ottoline. The furniture looked "Dutchy", Italianish cabinets. Tiny German compass on desk. Cabinet of famille verte. An interesting Walter Greaves. A nasty something Bergen.

Julian Goodman came down the stairs. She was young broad-faced and fairly full-bodied.[28] Pretty with very good nose. Vivacious face with longish browny red hair. And brown-red coat and skirt. Victorian gold ornaments and stones winking. She immediately took a Turkish cigarette and lit it without offering me one.

I began to unwrap pug, saying, "I don't know what you'll think of it." She crooned, "The darling, I must see the darling." I unveiled it and she clutched her hands together and raved nicely. We talked a lot about the picture and the real pug, who was ill in the country.

She said, "The only thing is, he doesn't wear a bow."

I told her that one of the photographs she sent me showed him in a bow. She said, "Perhaps sometimes for parties or birthdays he wears one. But it doesn't matter anyhow, as he's so virile that he can wear a pansy bow and get away with it!"

We laughed, and she said, "You're not a bit like your photograph in the *Tatler*. That made you look rather loopy and you're not."

Talk went on about the pug, the pictures and the china.

28 She was thirty-seven years of age at the time.

Julian called out for the woman to get tea early. We went to the dining room. John's portrait of Lady Ottoline Morrell hung over the mantelpiece. Julian said, "I had an awful time getting that back from the Tate. When Daddy died it was on loan there, and John Rothenstein told me that it had been given to the Tate.[29] I told him that people do not present valuable pictures to the nation without putting it in writing. There was quite a scene. In the end I sent a man in a taxi to fetch it. I felt awful. I felt as if I'd never get the picture into my possession again. It's all very well. I know that these things should go to the nation, but they're extremely valuable and I have three children. I don't think I have the right just to give them away like that."

She went on talking about her mother's portrait. "It's not a caricature, but it's cruel," she said.

I looked at the other things in the room; the eighteenth-century Venetian ground glass sconces (little figures on mirror backing). There were Italian altar candlesticks turned into lamps on the sideboard. The table was long, I don't know what, perhaps some sort of late foreign refectory.

I lit the gas fire and we sat down, both on one side of the long table. I cut gooey Bee-zee-bee bread and we spread marge and jam on our slices. Julian poured out of a lovely little many-sided late-Georgian tea-pot with ivory handle and pineapple finial. It stood on its own charming little stand. I remarked on it and she let me hold it. "I got it out specially for you," she said. "I told Mrs Thing we must have the nice tea-pot out, and she said, "Who is it coming, M'm? Mr de Polnay?" I said, "No, it is not."

Julian laughed and added, "Do you know Peter de Polnay? He drinks like anything. The tea-pot belonged to an ancestress, Mary Anne Chapman. You can see her initials on the side."

I passed the tea-pot back to her, and she said, "My God, it's hot. I nearly dropped it. How on earth did you hold it?"

Quickly she began to talk about her mother and herself. How her mother was not a good mother. She did not want to have a child, and the child never quite gets over knowing this. How all her childhood she was made to fit into a role which did not suit her. Her mother made her play the sweet-tempered rather brainless little girl part when all the time she was not good tempered and had a certain modicum of brains. She said life was so terribly difficult for her as a girl that she made up her mind to get married as soon as possible.

She talked well and interestingly about her mother and fairly, telling me the faults of her mother, how vain and dominating she was, how nobody

29 Augustus John's 1926 portrait of Lady Ottoline Morrell is currently in the collection of Mrs Igor Vinogradoff, formally Mrs Goodman (see 1943, note 27 above). Sir John Rothenstein, director of the Tate Gallery from 1938-64. Julian's father was Philip Morrell, a Liberal member of parliament.

was any good to her unless he gave his whole allegiance. How the quarrels always arose from the withdrawal of some part of the other person's mind from her control.

"It was impossible for a daughter," Julian said. "No child can give that sort of worship and gratitude to a mother. It isn't natural that they should. Daddy was always saying to me, 'You don't realize what a marvellous woman you've got for a mother.'[29] I realized perfectly what gifts my mother had, but I couldn't bow down and worship her, could I?"

She told me about Garsington and how D. H. Lawrence was very kind and sweet to children.[30] She told me of her mother's absolute passion for helping artists of all sorts. She said, "All her passion went into that. People said that she was violently sexy and in love with them all, but it wasn't that. After she'd had me, she had to have an operation. She was awfully ill and both her ovaries had to be removed. After that I think she had no sexual desire left in the ordinary sense of the word and all her energies were given to helping people with ideas. Everything was sublimated into that. It just consumed her. You can't imagine it, unless you'd seen it."

We were both eating the Bee-zee-bee bread and some peculiar, rather nice, doughy currant cake. The hot water was in an ugly arty beaten copper flagon. I think the china must have been ugly and insignificant or I would have remembered it. The whole house had this mixture of beautiful and very valuable things and rather commonplace things. In spite of this it did not give the effect of a rich man's house; it was more an artist's house, with just the faintest touch of artist's squalor: chipped paint, charming old rugs, just a little too worn to be put on the floor, an unexpected gas-ring for the gypsy to heat his cocoa on in the would-be grand dining room. John's portrait of Lady Ottoline sneering down, all the teeth showing. The Venetian sconces broad and flat and steel coloured.

We began to talk about living in the country and how the chief lack one felt was the complete blank of conversation in the evening.

Now for some reason Edward Sackville-West's name was mentioned, and Julian said, "Oh, Eddy would adore you." I said that I had once had lunch with him and how sad he seemed. She told me that he was the most hypochondriacal person she had ever known, but he was nice and kind and not really malicious, like so many of his temperament.

Julian said his weight of sadness was due to the fact that there would not be an heir for Knole after him.[31]

"It's easy to say that he's probably reconciled to all this by now, but still I'm sure that's what weighs him down."

---

30 Garsington Manor, from 1915-27 the Morrells' Tudor house near Oxford.
31 Sackville-West was forty-two and unmarried. There was in fact an heir, his cousin Lionel Sackville-West.

She asked me if I'd ever seen Knole, because then I'd know what she meant.

I said, "I think if I were Edward I'd just quietly enjoy it for myself." Julian looked into the distance.

After tea she put a large chintz covered box on the table and showed me early pictures of her mother, in swirling gown, huge hats, scarves, veils.

"She's lovely there," I said, pointing to one. Julian was immediately up in arms. "Oh, yes, she was a very lovely woman when young," she said with emphasis. It was as if she were telling me that I ought to have known — that her mother had been an acknowledged beauty. I felt small and slightly put in my place, and I thought again how superstitious people were when talking about beauty. If a person has a reputation for beauty, she or he is never allowed to be anything but beautiful. It is a blasphemy to say, "She looks rather good there" or, "not so interesting in that one."

I remarked on Lady Ottoline's out-jutting chin, a repellent-attractive thing I always dwell on.

"That's a Bentinck trait," said Julian, quickly and uncertainly. Her eyes glanced at me timidly and sharply. "They've all got it." She seemed to be wondering whether I knew what she was talking about, and if I did, whether I thought she was being pretentious.[32]

Further on in the book were pictures, signed, of Sarah Bernhardt, Violet Manners, Julian's two uncles in their fur coats before they went to Russia.[33] Her father, looking an Edwardian clean young man with crimpy hair. Quiet and sensitive. Later ones of her mother, more and more posed and swirling. Several of Julian as a child in smocks; pretty, brown, like a boy.

There were many nameless ones which Julian could not place. "What a pity they haven't written underneath, because I can't tell who they are now."

We left the old book and went into the hall.

"Let's begin right at the door," said Julian.

We stood by it and looked at the first little picture, which was a John drawing of a woman's hand, early, picturesque, signed A. E. John. Next came a little John painting of figures in a landscape. Charming, sentimental. Children with big, blousy mothers. After that, something I've forgotten because I did not like it.

Slowly we mounted the stairs. There were John Aldridges, Henry Lambs and Etchells. Nothing I really liked. At the top, little Persian miniatures in frames and a lovely little mirror in a painted glass frame. I'd never seen one like it before.

32 The Duke of Portland's family name was Cavendish-Bentinck.
33 The Duke of Portland and Lord Henry Bentinck, a photograph taken in 1866.

We heard a baby crying in one of the rooms.

"That's the maid's baby, nothing of mine," said Julian laughing.

She led me into the drawing-room. It was more or less dismantled with two iron beds in it, where the children slept when they came to London. Julian's father had fitted it up as a library with book shelves and pilasters all round the walls. All the books had been taken away, except for one wall. The Adam ceiling was painted green too. The whole colouring was too heavy and metallic for me. It looked sprayed, somehow, like those wicker dirty clothes baskets.

Over the lovely Adam fireplace was a Duncan Grant set into the panelling. It was raucous, coloured, amorphous, dull, a mess.

"I'm not very fond of it," said Julian. "Nor am I," I answered.

When I asked Julian if the beds were in there because of the bombs, she said, "No, not really; it's because I haven't any more room."

I couldn't quite understand this, as London houses, although they look small and narrow, always seem to have several bedrooms.

We went up to the third floor. There was one junk room with blue and white china, on top of a rather too-polished up "Gentleman's Wardrobe" and a lot of cardboard boxes in it.

Then we went into Julian's room. "It's lovely," I said.

"Yes, it's lovely. It used to be my mother's room, and now it's mine," said Julian with quiet satisfaction. I wondered, suddenly, if she felt pleased to have at last got it for her own. The bed was a four-poster, with no top, but white muslin curtains all round it. They looked crisp and transparent. I nearly said, "Don't they get awfully dirty in London!" but then thought it too banal.

Julian went to her dressing-table and did a few dabbing, poking things. I carefully did not look for some reason.

She turned to a side table, picked something up and said, "That's the brooch Mummy wore on her wedding dress. Do you remember seeing it in the photograph downstairs?"

I held the brooch in my hands. It was made of pearls as big as button mushrooms. But what made it difficult to know what to say was that the pearls were obviously imitation. They had a backing of yellow metal that could only be called gold out of politeness. It seemed clumsy and pointless.

Next Julian held out to me an Italian pendant of emeralds, curiously coloured and shaped pearls, rubies, enamel and chased work. It had a chain made of little enamel tubes.

"But nowadays when can you wear a thing like that?" asked Julian.

"Could you in the evening?" I suggested tentatively.

"Yes, but there isn't any evening in that sense of the word," said Julian. "People hardly even change their clothes."

I looked at a curious engraving of Byron which made him look like a Scotch comedian in a Tam-o-shanter.

"Do you know Peter Quennell?" Julian asked.

"No, but I like his books," I said. "I haven't read all his Byron. I'd like to."

"I'll lend it to you, I've got it," she said.

I looked across the rooms to the long built-in cupboards with mirror doors, designed like sash windows.

Julian opened one of the doors and said, "I've got all mother's dresses in here. Daddy wouldn't get rid of anything."

She held out a mouse-coloured velvet dress to me. It had little pearls all round the square Juliet neck. It reached right to the ground.

She took it right out of the cupboard and said, "She was very tall." The ghostly dress hung down to the ground. I stood beside it and thought how small I would feel if Lady Ottoline were inside her dress.

Julian pulled another dress out, very like the first. Their colourlessness made them pathetic.

"She never changed much," Julian said. "When my mother used to go out in the street the little boys used to hoot. She had tremendous courage. I was terrified of walking about with her as a child. I couldn't bear the staring people."

We left the bedroom and slowly walked downstairs and out of the house. Julian came with me to take me to the taxi stand. In the garden I saw three statues. I said how nice they were and Julian said, "Those came from Garsington. But when we wanted to bring them here and put them up in the garden, the Duke of Bedford wasn't a bit pleased or grateful."[34]

"But they make the place," I said.

Above us loomed the huge new London University building.

I stepped into the taxi. Julian told him where to go. I saw in the out-doors light the powder on her face, making it a little too matt.

We shook hands. She held mine for a moment longer than I expected. I wondered whether this was the height of gracious compliment — something done specially to show how friendly she was — or whether it was her usual habit. I felt very inadequate, ungallant, wanting to be. I felt warm, because she was so kind and friendly. And I felt sad because I imagined her going back to her lonely house and because she had said that, not being creative, she did not like to be alone too much.

When I got out of the train at Tonbridge, I walked along the platform beside a not very tall, well-built soldier carrying a bag and suitcase.

"It's awful weather," he said in a polite, matey, Northern Irish, "gentleman-like" voice.

He turned a very pleasing, rather sporting face towards me. There was a

---

34 Landlord of much of Bloomsbury.

stiff little fair moustache, healthy curves and hollows, the cheek bones an especially nice shape.

I liked him immediately. I suppose it was the feeling that one could almost certainly trust this man not to get up to any sort of funny business ever. He was absolutely uncrooked and well-meaning. Everything about him seemed sober and controlled, yet jaunty.

I was marvelling at my rather surprising feeling, and so could do nothing but make more banal weather remarks.

"Oh, the fog in London was terrible!" he agreed. His curious, melodious, plummy, almost affected, yet very male and plebian voice interested me. It was something one could listen to and build theories about.

"Have you far to go?" I asked.

"Oh no, just —," I could not hear what his destination was.

We gave up our tickets and walked out of the station.

"I've been letting off some steam," I think he said as we walked towards the bus. He laughed and I imagined he'd been on leave with his wife or girl. I laughed too. He may of course have been only talking about the engine of the train which was making a noise.

I said "Good-night" and he did too, jauntily. I felt sorry that I would never know anything more about him.

14 December

I had last night a wonder dream. My mother had lent me a large maroon car and her chauffeur. It was war-time but we were able to drive from the country towards a town along a wonderful boulevard on the edge of a wide river. It was like the Thames embankment, but more spacious, and grander, set in rural scenery with here and there a comfortable white villa set on the steeply rising hillside.

I sat right in the middle of the back seat of this powerful and dignified car and the smart slim chauffeur in greyish silver drove without moving a muscle of his head. The road was almost empty, knots of soldiers here and there dotted the wide expanse. When they saw our rather ostentatious turn-out they made derisive and mocking noises. I sat very still, the gentle air blew on my face. The smoothness of our movement was utterly satisfying.

As we approached a bus stop, we had to slow down and avoid a crowd of people. This agitated me for some reason and I got out of the car and seemed to lead it in and out of the people, by walking in front. Suddenly I collided with an elderly man, very smartly dressed in greenish tweed jacket, leather jerkin, riding breeches, etc. He stopped and said, "Hullo, Denton, you out in your mother's car for a spin?"

I nodded and bent my head down in embarrassment. He then said, "There's no need for you to lead it through the crowd yourself."

At that moment the bus (or tram) appeared, and the crowd, including the man, made a wild scramble to board it.

Our car went a few paces further, then we seemed to have reached our destination, for the lean, very good-looking chauffeur got out, slammed the door and walked along beside me in the most hearty manner. We started to climb the hillside together. Suddenly the chauffeur with a winning smile said, "Am I going to be kept out till after midnight again getting old Piss's luggage?"

Rather outraged at this impertinence, but not wanting to be stuffy, I said, with a wry smile, "I don't know what on earth you mean." But I knew he was referring to Eric Oliver whom I had invited to stay and who had arrived sadly drunk the night before.[35]

Suddenly I threw off reserve and said, "Tell me, was my friend very drunk?"

The chauffeur made extravagant, manly, dashing gestures, raised up his hands and said, "Absolutely pissed. Couldn't stand up."

I began to feel sad that Eric should inspire so little respect. I longed for him to be suaver, better dressed, more worldly-wise. Then I thought that all this snobbery about appearance was ignoble. I was annoyed that the chauffeur was so obviously only impressed with the opulent.

35 Denton's residuary beneficiary and literary executor (see 1942, note 36 above). He had met Denton in the first week of November 1943, and by the time of this *Journal* entry Denton had fallen in love with him. He appears as Trevor Pinkston in "The Hateful Word", published posthumously in *A Last Sheaf*, and as Tom Parkinson in "The Diamond Badge", written in the last year of Denton's life and also published posthumously in *A Last Sheaf*, although the first half of the story had appeared under the title "The Visit" in *Penguin New Writing* No 38, 1949.

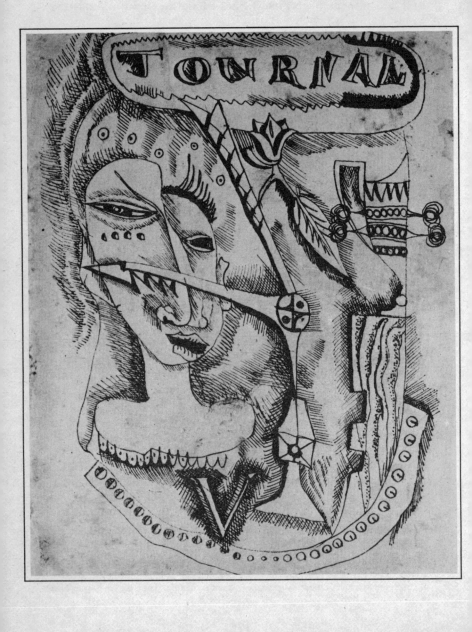

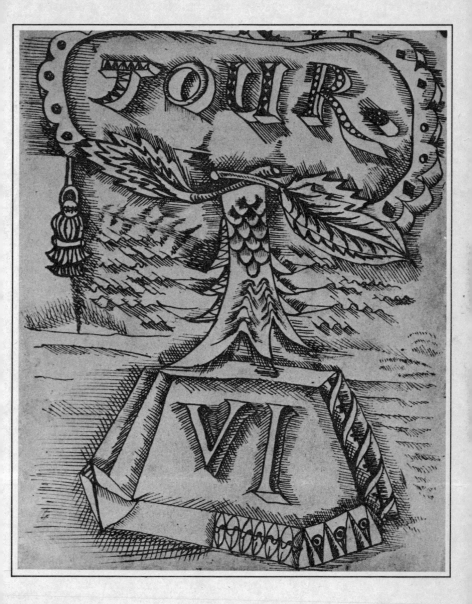

1944

YESTERDAY Eric (who had spent the night here because he'd missed the bus) and I took a picnic lunch and set off on bicycles to Crouch. It had been lovely in the early part of the day and Eric had wanted me to take him to the river so that he could swim. "Would you really swim, Eric?" I asked, and he had said, "Only dive in and swim across and get out, not stay in a long time." But I had not encouraged this scheme.

But by the time we were ready to leave, the sky was overcast with low scudding clouds which seemed at any moment about to melt and pour down in rain. A few drops touched us. Eric managed Evie's bike wonderfully. It did not seem nearly as small and uncomfortable as I had imagined. His shoulders looked very broad and heavy in his light grey suit, and his profile and dark hair seemed almost Egyptian. I have never known anyone whose looks seem to change so much.

We bicycled on towards Hadlow, past the Littletons' house, down Ashes Lane. Eric suddenly said, "Go slower, Denton; that's how you wear yourself out going at it hell for leather." The wind was behind us. We went easily. I felt happy and quite strong. We wondered where to have our lunch. It was now beginning to rain. I suggested stopping at the White Cottage and asking Trot and Prue if we might eat it in their parlour. I told Eric they were Sappho and he wanted to meet them. Then I thought of Harmiston's cottage, which he left empty all the week. He had told Noël and me to ask Mrs Williams for the key and make use of it whenever we wanted, but I did not dare do it now.

Eric helped me push my bike. He pushed it from behind. We managed the hill very well. I was tired but not dead. At the top I put on my macintosh. Then we swept down through the Hurst Woods to Crouch.

It was really beginning to pour and to gale now. We took the armfuls of our picnic and my manuscript which I had brought for Noël to read and went into the Chequers. We asked the landlord for gin, but he said, "No spirits at all, only beer, I'm afraid." So Eric had a big bitter and I a small one.

In the old primitive pub it was dark. There was a big log and coal fire in a curious grate which projected right into the room, with an iron hood above to catch the smoke. It was not imitation at all, very home-made, unperiod, just itself. All round the walls were narrow benches. There was a daddlums board and darts board, nothing else except a table and two chairs. As the winter wind and the bullet-noisy rain beat on the three small windows, Eric and I took the two chairs and put them near the fire. There was only one other old man in the room, and he stood at the hatch, talking to the landlord.

Eric and I had all this room and fire to ourselves. I realized that this was something I had wanted to do all my life — to eat a picnic meal by a fire in an olden room with Eric while the rain beat down outside.

I gave Eric his cheese, toast, Ryvita, tiny pat of butter, fruit cake, chocolate biscuit.

"I think not bring the thermos of coffee in," said Eric wisely; but he poohpoohed my anxiety over eating our own food in the pub. At last I asked the landlord if he minded and he said, "Not at all."

All was happy and warm. I poured my beer into Eric's glass to get rid of it. I couldn't put so much cold water into my stomach. I wanted to drink the coffee badly. We ate and ate. Eric was so hungry I gave him some of my cheese and all the fruit cake. The meal was just right. It was nice and right and only in the butter one felt the war. I thought as I ate: years after, I'll remember this, with Eric by the fire here in the dark room. Usually things are not romantic. This is romantic for some reason. It's like an old, old legend, and the weather's legendary.

Eric threw my peel and his own in the fire. We talked very little. We were separate people. I was a bit too much looking after his wants. He was his usual constrained self. But it was right. We wanted to eat, and we felt quiet inside. Sometimes we said, "What a pity there's no whisky or gin to make us warm and no port afterwards." We had a vision of hot fiery drinks which would make us feel rosy.

Eric wanted to pee so I guessed at a door and said, "I think out there." He ran out into the little yard, the rain and wind beating in after him. I heard him running on the stones.

And I sat quietly thinking. I wanted Eric to come with me to Noël's, and I was afraid that he would jib at the last moment. He has a horror of middle-aged women, thinking that he appears as nothing but a dull oaf to them. I cannot understand this, as they usually, I think, must like him. He seems only really comfortable and natural in the company of men. He can get on with any sort of men.

When Eric came back we drew nearer to the fire and I bought him another pint and we talked. He laughed at me. I was hurt a bit. He treats me with a mixture of thoughtfulness and solicitude for my precarious health and an almost cynical realism about my thoughts or feelings. All my actions are put down to very mundane motives. This may be all quite true, but it is a shock. I could do the same to him, but I don't.

At half-past two we had to get up and leave the fire. We burnt bits of paper, dusted crumbs from the table and made all neat. The landlord's wife said, "You two hiking?" and I said, "Yes." I suddenly wanted to be hiking and hearty and pre-war and pre-accident, everything young and careless. I wished that Eric and I had known each other when we were both eighteen and that we had walked miles together every day and slept every night in haystacks. I longed for it quite bitterly, and I felt the desperation that everything was dying and decaying and that Eric and I who were just made to be young and gay for ever together would go down getting sadder and older and more entangled every moment of the day.

We bicycled the few yards to Middle Orchard and knocked on the door. There was no answer to begin with. Eric hung under the porch, waiting out of sight, nervous. I said, "Come on, Eric." He steeled himself and came up to me. His nervousness was funny and tragic.

At last Noël came. She had been half asleep and was still illish from 'flu. There was much chattering and I opened the thermos of coffee and we drank it. Eric was tongue-tied, Egyptian-looking, smoking his pipe. I copied him and took mine out. He knocked it out and lit it for me.

Conversation was difficult. I wished and wished that Eric could communicate his thoughts more easily. I could see the tenseness and nervousness in him. I felt alarmed. He really looked so caged and frightened, and you can almost see the panic of thoughts in his head.

I went upstairs to the bathroom, and I hoped that Noël and he would talk together then. I stayed away for as long as I felt I could, but I now wish that I had stayed much longer, reading a book on one of the beds upstairs and letting them talk alone. It is much easier for two strangers to talk alone than to have a mutual friend making it easy for them helpfully.

When I came back and some time afterwards Noël left the room, Eric turned to me desperately and said, "Denton, how long have we got to stay?" He was imploring, like a child. I felt alarmed.

"I want to break the room down when I'm stuck in a bloody chair like that," he said. It was not so much boredom but the sense of some terrific restraint that seemed to be worrying him. I saw suddenly how terribly far apart some parts of our worlds were.

I followed Noël into the kitchen and helped get tea. While Eric was upstairs, Noël said, "I hope it's not too embarrassing. I wish Eric would talk." I told her how difficult it was to make him.

After tea when we left, Eric suddenly turned to Noël and said, "Good-bye, thank you so much for the tea and I'm sorry I've been so disappointing." There was a slight hitch. I laughed and said, "What did you think Noël was expecting, Eric?" And Noël said, "What do you mean? You haven't been disappointing at all."

As we rode off, Eric let out terrific sighs and puffs of air, as if he were recovering from some terrible exhaustion. He seemed really to have found the tea a terrible strain. I said, "It's good for you. You can't be so anti-social and boorish."

The wind was dead against us and the rain was soaking down. We banged into the wind and rain and loved the feel of them. Eric went down the hill much faster than I did, and I was left far behind. I felt sorry for myself, as I did when I was a child. A car passed and I was afraid that Eric, reckless and with no lights, might be run down. I waited for the noise, but none came. Eric was waiting for me further on, quietly and stolidly. He said nothing, I said nothing. I was beginning to be filled with bitterness, and I was determined to be cold and stoical and hard. Eric did not annoy me, but I made myself annoyed and grieved with him.

It was quite dark by the time we reached the main road. As we turned, Eric said, "Oh, there is the Rose and Crown." I said, "Yes," coldly. I would not take the hint, so we went on.

When we got in, utterly soaked, I said, "Take off your shoes and socks and trousers." He obeyed at once. I put on all the gas fires and soon the room was steamy from Eric's drying clothes. I threw him the old, old camel-hair dressing-gown, and I put the priest's cassock on myself.[1] We dried our hair. I left mine rough and wispy, but Eric combed his into the smoothest, sleekest of black Egyptian caps.

We sat by the fire and I covered my face with my hand. Eric looked deep into me and said, "You've done too much." I said nothing. I felt peculiar and unstrung. The wireless was playing lovely things, Gluck's Orfeo song and then other later things; everything famous, lovely, almost hackneyed. The music made me want to weep. Eric still looked at me with his funny guilty sad look, then he put his bare legs up on the arms of my chair and began to pull the hairs on them and rub his hands up and down. He bent his head down and put it on my knees resting it there. I touched his wet sleek hair. When he raised himself, I put my head down to the gas fire to dry it, and he, thinking that I had a headache and was unwell, took my head carefully between his hands and began to massage it as he had been taught, behind the ears, the nape, the temples. I let him do it. It was soothing, rhythmical, and I liked it. He did it very carefully. I felt grateful.

The wireless now had a reading from *Pride and Prejudice*. I liked to listen, but Eric didn't listen. Evie brought up the soup, and I lit the candles, and Eric wanted to burn the incense too, but as there was no charcoal he had to do it with a lot of matches. He put the hat on the little brazier and we saw the flames through the open grille-work. It looked exciting. He stood it on the tray between the candles and it smoked and smelt bad. The incense was being too much burnt. After the soup we had bean-pie and then apple-pie. It was nearly eight now. We had to scramble into clothes and leave the coffee to catch the bus. We walked furiously down the drive arm in arm like a pair of carriage horses. The rain had stopped and stars were shining. At the bus stop we waited leaning against the pole. We waited and we thought we had missed it, but then at last it came and we shined the torch and Eric ran and jumped on and I turned away before it started. As it overtook me Eric was standing on the step and he called out, "Good-night, Denton." He had done

1 A cassock in which Denton was eventually cremated.

it carefully to say good-bye to me properly. And I walked back and watched the dimly lighted bus disappearing along the road until at last it vanished in a soft blur round the corner.

Again I felt nothing but all the sadness and parting and dying and diseases in the world. All the accidents and hate and the long, long everlasting going-on-ness of it all. I thought that I and Eric and all people living were nothing but the reflection of all the thousand million people who had gone before, and I thought that in a little time, almost no time at all, we would all be gone again and swept away.

I remembered when I had first met Eric. It was some time in November, and I was ill in bed with high temperature and terrible headache. Noël and May had been sitting in my room half killing me with their talk. Just as they had left and I was trying to simmer down, I heard voices below and then Francis talking to Evie. I had told her not to let anyone else upstairs, but as the minutes dragged on and I still heard the talking, I shouted out, "Francis, I'm ill in bed. What is it?"

Evie answered, telling me that Francis had arrived with a friend and could they both just come up for a minute. I consented and saw, walking into the room after fat Francis, someone in green battle-dress trousers, Wellingtons, and a jersey and white shirt, open, also white tops of pants showing above the trousers, large leather belt, face red-brown, with very good throat.

This person looked at me in the bed and Francis said babyishly, "Oh, this is Eric, I've brought him to see you."[2]

I felt so ill that I couldn't entertain them properly. I tried to be very bright; but it was an awful strain. They had been drinking in a pub and had come on to me later. They were still mildly redolent of the pub and beer. They talked a little wildly.

When they left, Eric turned at the door and gave me a long sharp look. "Why don't you get up and come and have a drink with us?" he had asked the moment before. Now he knew I was ill and he was sorry and he liked me.

Then there was the time when Eric came and we walked in the moonlight above the pond in the wood.[3] We looked down from the revolving summer house on the dark treacle of the pond. We leant against the Chinese Chippendale balustrade and felt the moonlight on our faces. Eric's face was a snail-slime white, wonderful and like a ghost and I suppose mine was too. We leaned back against the summer house and it began disquietingly to turn round. We laughed and pushed it more; then we walked down and further into the wood, right beneath the bare wire of the delicate twigs.

"You like this, do you?" Eric said thoughtfully, as if he would like it too

2 Eric and Francis were living in the same hostel in Maidstone and were working for the Kent War Agricultural Executive Committee, Eric because he had high blood pressure, Francis because he was a conscientious objector.
3 5 December 1943.

for me. And I thought this so curious, so unimmediate when the moon was the wildest poetry all round us, but how nice it was of him to like it because I did.

After that, another week, when Evie was reading to me about half-past ten at night, I heard a shout outside the Gothic window. There was a high wind, so the shout in the wind was like a ghost. I listened again and heard distinctly, "Denton!" this time. Running down the steep stairs, I felt frightened. I wondered who it could be, what had happened. The voice sounded to me like Martin Miles's, someone I had not seen for years.

I went to the kitchen door and called out, "Hullo, who's there?" But there was no answer. I waited, then went through the garage and heard again, only this time quite frantic, "Denton!"

There was rage and despair and frustration in the voice. I fumbled with the big doors, then pushed them wide open. There was Eric in the rain in a macintosh looking hopeless and guilty, and I knew he was drunk. He leant back against the door and said, "Denton, will you lend me your bike to get home on?"

"But it's at the mender's," I said. "It's got a puncture."

He didn't seem to understand this. He made a haggard face and said, "Please!" with fierce despair. He seemed about to break down.

I took hold of his hand and pulled him in saying, "Quick, Eric, the door's wide open and the German bombers will have such a lovely target." I wanted to make everything lighter, happier.

"You can't get back," I said decidedly, "there is no bicycle."

"Then I've got to walk," he almost shouted. "I walked all the way here to see you, I can't walk back."

"Of course not," I agreed.

He looked at me.

"Then may I stay here the night?" he asked.

"Yes," I said.

His whole body seemed to get lighter and he was happier at once.

I led him upstairs and he told me how he'd set out at five o'clock to see me, suddenly taken by a whim because he had no peace to write a letter, and as he walked all the twelve miles from Maidstone he felt that he must have a drink at Hadlow. He went into the King's Arms and stayed there till closing time, dancing and singing and drinking with the Newfoundland soldiers who all tried to get him to stand them drinks. They sang "I came here to search for Joe". Eric sang it again for me, and it was poignant.

Upstairs he caught hold of me, because he was not steady, and his eyes were very bright and he looked wild. His hair stood out in long tufts. I tried to calm him and made him have tea, then we made the bed up on the floor. He suddenly caught sight of my gold cigarette-case and, picking it up fiercely, he said, "I could get a 'pony' on that!" Then he put it down again, curiously.

Then at Christmas I had made all the table pretty with china, glass, leaves and silver. The glass lustre shone, the red pepper looked pretty. Evie had made a nice meal with make-believe turkey, soup and plum pudding and hard sauce. It was all ready. I had Algerian wine and beer, Turkish cigarettes and Virginian, chocolate peppermint creams.

We waited and waited. One struck, then two. No Eric. Evie and I sat down at the table and began to eat the food, looking out of the low window and commenting on the lateness, and the taste of things.

Suddenly there was a telephone call for me and I had to go into Mrs Sloman's house.[4] It was Rosemary Mundy Castle, so I asked her to come round after lunch.[5] When I got back to the cottage, there was Eric talking to Evie in the kitchen. He had just arrived and I saw again that he was drunk, only this time more so. He was smiling and standing very still. He had asked Evie if there was anyone else with me before daring to come in.

I took him upstairs and sat him down at the table. I told him how late it was, and that we had begun to eat. He bowed his head on his knee and groaned. It was quite real. He held on to one of my hands and didn't speak.

"I thought someone else was going to be here, and I couldn't face them, so I got up a little Dutch courage on the way."

I smiled at him and said, "A good lot, I should think. Now begin to eat; you're about two and a half hours late."

"I'm not drunk," he said in an affronted, bewildered voice.

Again his hair was sticking out in a bush and he wore an old thick jersey, and grey flannels tucked into Wellingtons.

"Do you mind these?" he asked, touching the Wellingtons. "I lost one of my shoes yesterday in the mud outside a pub and I haven't been back for it yet. I've only got one pair of shoes in Maidstone."

He was about to pull the Wellingtons off, for fear they might offend me, but I told him to leave them on.

He hardly drank his soup, continually stopping to fix me with his eye and ask why my invitation was not more explicit. I had said no particular time for lunch and I had suggested that someone else might be there. I had hinted that I might go away the next day to my aunt's. The whole letter was cold and unsatisfactory. He was angry about it. I wasn't a true friend. I was cold and ungenerous.

"Oh, Eric, you're like a child," I said, worried and exasperated.

Again he looked deep, deep into me and seemed to be floating in a mist and a cloud; then he brought out in a voice which was a curious mixture of

---

4 Pitt's Folly (since Denton's death, destroyed by fire), of which Pitt's Folly Cottage was adjacent. Denton lived at Pitt's Folly Cottage from June 1942-March 1946. Mrs Sloman was the estranged wife of Harold Sloman, headmaster of Tonbridge School from 1922-39.
5 Peggy Mundy Castle's daughter. Her other daughter (page 290) was Jenny.

clearness and stutter, "Denton, you're just talking for the sake of talking."

I felt very snubbed, for some reason. I poured out the Algerian wine, which Eric had opened badly. I poured out the dark wine and we drank it. It was like iron water.

Suddenly Rosemary appeared, big, bouncing, spectacled, a little Christmas merry from drinks. She had brought me a handful of nuts and sweets and a baby cracker. She threw herself down in the armchair and we all had coffee together. Eric, I was glad to see, was not horribly ill at ease, as he swore he would be if anyone else appeared. He seemed to be able to manage Rosemary easily. He even looked interested, and Rosemary seemed to be so, too.

She began to ask him questions about his home and work. And soon we were all merrily talking and laughing. Rose and Eric were mildly drunk. We laughed for no reason, and Rose told us of all the drinks she had had for lunch.

By that time Eric was sitting on the floor by the gas fire, as I had the deck chair and Rose the arm chair. Gradually Eric began to sprawl lower and lower on the floor and his comfortable look suggested to me that I too would like to be warm, on a level with the fire. I left my chair and lay down beside him on cushions. I looked up and saw Rose sitting in her chair.

"Wouldn't you like to get near the fire, Rose?" I said on impulse, a little wickedly, to see her reaction. Then I patted the floor the other side of Eric and put a cushion for her. She looked at me sharply, and then said, "Yes, it might be nice. You both look so comfortable."

She left the chair and lay down on her back close to Eric. Soon she was holding his hand and mine and we were all tickling one another's ears and pulling hair like a lot of children. We talked hilariously and giggled, and through it all I could tell how attracted Rose was to Eric. Sometimes she grew very quiet.

Suddenly May blew in and found us all sprawling about. She was in a great hurry to get on to a tea party, but she managed to tell us that Mr Churchyard was dead and that Mary Brooks had gone out of her mind! She gloried in these grisly details. Eric stood up the whole time she was in the room, afraid of turning his back on her, as he told me when I asked why he didn't sit down. Such punctilio was quaint, after our lolling in a heap on the floor.

When May left we all had tea, then we talked and dozed till supper, after which we went down to the Rose and Crown. I didn't want to go much but Eric and Rose did.

The pub was full of Newfoundlers and their very prim, chic-looking girls. They had all drunk a certain amount, but were behaving perfectly until suddenly one of the soldiers sat down on one of the girl's laps. She didn't seem to mind, although he looked enormous. She just held him there like a child and he looked round at her with a moony smile. Then another began to talk baby language with a pathetic, lost expression on his face. It was a little painful to watch him.

I was terribly bored in the pub. I could find nothing to say to Rose, and Eric was alone at the hatch buying drinks.

Elizabeth Plummer and her mother came in to buy bottles of beer, and Elizabeth sat by me for a little. She looked very pretty and groomed, I thought.

There was nothing to do. I felt that the Newfoundlers were making a mock of us in only just inaudible voices. I wanted to go, but Eric would stop till closing time.

When at last we were outside again he said to me, "Denton, I ought to see Rosemary some of the way home. You must be tired so I can do it alone."

Of course I knew exactly what this meant. I made rather unfeeling ironical comments out loud to myself, so that they could not hear unless they were very sharp. We bicycled along the road in silence. When we got to Pitt's Folly gates, I turned in at the drive and left them on the main road. I said "Good-night" sharply and contemptuously. Rosemary's little lost, "Perhaps Eric will see me to just where the houses begin," I thought ludicrous and dishonest.

Of course I knew what was going to happen the moment they were alone together.

I went back to the cottage and sat down and had some tea, then I began to get things ready for the night. I knew that Eric would come back very late and that I would have to put him up.

It was after twelve when he did appear. Just before this, Rose's mother had rung up to ask if she was still with me as she hadn't arrived home yet and they were wondering what had happened to her.

Eric, when he came in, looked utterly forlorn and hang-dog. He sat down on a stool and again held his head in his hands. I wondered if he had the super-tension in his head which he sometimes had. I asked him if it ached and all he answered was, "She's a passionate girl, isn't she."

He began to pour out all that had happened and all his own troubles and shortcomings. He poured it all over me and I just sat back in the chair and listened and watched. Then suddenly I began to cry. Everything seemed so frightfully muddled and stupid and sad, and utterly hopeless.

Eric understood. We were terribly morbid and gloomy and felt that we were both going to die.

The next day Eric spent on my bed recovering from his drinking bout and reading my book. I sat in the chair finishing my little cat picture for Julian.[6]

In the evening I suggested that we should go out and get some air on our bicycles. We went down towards the river, crossed Hartlake Bridge and

6 A miniature, inscribed "Julian from Denton, Christmas 1943", currently in the collection of Mrs Igor Vinogradoff.

passed on in the direction of Tudeley. At the Red Cow I suggested we might have a drink, as I thought it would please Eric. We went in and he found a boy whom he had been cutting down trees with. We all had beers, as there was nothing else.

Eric said, "Now, Denton, you feel as much out of water as I feel when you want to take me to tea with old ladies."

It is true that I wanted to leave soon. The pub was almost empty and extremely dreary.

"I must go back to supper," I said, "even if you want to stop."

Then began the long conflict, Eric debating in himself what he should do. He said he knew he ought to come back with me, but he wanted to make a night of it.

I said, "You do exactly what you like. Don't have so many heart-searchings and worries."

He followed me out, saying that I was good and he was bad, I was strong-minded and he weak, I stood for his better nature, the pub for his worse.

I tried to make him light-hearted. I was tired. I felt sad and I wanted to be alone too.

I rode away with his promises that he would be back in about an hour ringing in my ears.

He never appeared till eleven-thirty. And then he came into the house covered with mud all down one side and with mud on his face and his eye.

He looked utterly forlorn and dishevelled. He glanced from side to side but never at me. There were terrible long silences. I didn't know what to do. Again there were long confessions and self-accusations. He had hurtled off the bike into the ditch coming home. He had stayed till closing time, not being able to tear himself away.

It was well after one now, and I said, "You can't go back tonight." But he insisted, saying that he wanted to sleep all the next day.

"You'll fall off again and perhaps kill yourself this time."

"No, I'm all right now. Talking's made me better."

I let him go at last, as he seemed so determined and I was so tired.

I walked down the drive with him and he said, "I won't come to see you again for a whole month, then I'll be good and sober again. I won't drink anything in 1944."

And he hasn't been for a whole month, and he arrived very sober. That was last Sunday.

I have just remembered what he told me about his land work.

In the summer he wears nothing but bathing trunks or trousers; that is why he is still so brown. And even when the sun shines in winter he takes off his shirt and the others think he's mad.

When it rains they all go into a little hut and play vingt-et-un and gamble. Eric wins and he says the others are bad losers.

When they want it to rain, they all cry out, "Send it down, Jacob! Send it down, Jacob!''

Eric is not quite sure whom they mean by "Jacob". It is a mystic name. Something between God, the prophet and some sort of Guy Fawkes.

For lunch they make a little fire and all squat round, and when Eric wants to be alone he walks away and lies down in the grass, or in the pew of an old church. He and another chap lay down in the pews of Mereworth Church and drank from their tea-bottles quietly, and rested.

It sounded an idyllic life, and curious too, with sometimes fights and quarrels.

2 February

Eric has told me how, when he was about nine, he ran away from school at Salisbury and walked to London, taking four or five days for the journey. At night he slept in ditches or in haystacks — once in a clover-stack — and he said that this was dangerous, because the clover sucks up all the air, and he might have been suffocated. (Is this superstition?)

He lived on the milk left on people's doorsteps. And this strikes me as extraordinarily poignant in some way. I can see nothing but a picture of a small boy early in the morning, snatching up nacre-white bottles of milk in the half-light and drinking them hungrily. It is tragic.

His feet were bleeding and cut, the shoes worn through, and when he reached home his father, who loved him, "made a fuss of him", as Eric put it. They were not angry, they solaced him.

He had run away chiefly, he said, because he wanted to be out in the world earning money.

Another time, when he was sent back to school, a master tried to make him eat, because he had gone on hunger strike. The master said, "I shall·beat you one stroke for every minute after now that you don't eat."

Then Eric took out a table knife that he had on him and pretended to try to stick it into the man, but two prefects rushed forward and held him. This is a sort of melodrama recounted like this.

I would like to hear it all in its real deep detail.

6 February. Eleven-fifteen p.m.

Eric is gone, and tomorrow he is moved to Appledore. The lorry calls for him at ten. I don't know when I shall see him again.

Today we took our lunch into the cold morning sun and went out on bicycles. We hurtled down the hill to the Volunteers, because Eric wanted a stirrup-cup.

We found the bar parlour full of old men; no other human beings. They were all using the word bloody.

We had gin and Eric drank his with half a pint of stock. We did this three times. I looked at Eric with the sun on him, and saw the tiny red veins on his cheeks and the acid spear-points of yellow and green-brown in his eyes.

One of the old men started to cry, and another said, "It's no good crying now, it's too late." Still the old man went on gently crying and wiping the corners of his eyes. He was a disgusting-shaped old man, and another of them had a dead swivelled eye. They were all disgusting.

The gin went a little to my head. I talked louder.

A very young sailor came in and was given a drink on the house. He wore an amazing expression of gentleness, almost shrinking nervousness and longing to fulfil his own and everyone else's obligations. I could not help staring at this extra-ordinary modest, blushing, conciliating expression. It was so naked that it was painful. One felt in some way that everyone gave him an awful time. He seemed quite unprotected.

I muttered something to Eric, and a little later, tactfully, he looked round. We said no more till afterwards.

An old bag of a woman came in. She had tight grey curls and Eric said, "She's a London woman. You can tell."

All the old men said to her, "Where's Bill, Annie?" She said with the straightest of faces, "He's out cherry picking," and all the others laughed tremendously. Just as she went out carrying her bottles of beer, she gave the most preposterous wink, a sort of screwing up of her whole face, difficult and an effort. It was quite ludicrous to watch, it was such a business and a labour. We all shouted with laughter. And the old men began to chafe her more and more.

When she was outside, she looked in through the window and gave another of her tremendous winks.

The old man was still crying gently. When I told Eric, he said, "No, his eyes are watering."

The other old men showed no sympathy. They said again, "It's no use crying now; it's too late."

There was a bowl of purple and yellow pansies and purple polyanthus and snowdrop leaves on the bar. Their careful beauty in an ugly dull black pottery bowl looked artificial, out of place, precious. And yet their little shapes kept drawing my eyes. They were like the sailor's nakedness.

All sorts of little gadgets were fastened on the wall behind the bar. Little horns, jugs, horse brasses and various instruments I did not know the use of. There were cooked-crab-coloured jugs and sage-coloured ones. The whole scene was very clean, very picturesque, genuine, commonplace all mixed up in one. And the sun played through the tight closed window on to the dust motes. There were plants in the window. The stove burnt without noise, yet very hotly.

At last we had to go. It was curious suddenly to see everyone out of doors in the daylight, harsh, and everything cold-looking because one was a little drunk.

I said, "Don't let's ride our bikes just yet," because I thought I would fall off. Eric agreed and we wheeled them down the road towards the little wood where I thought we would have lunch.

Eric talked about the expression on the sailor's face. He said exactly what I had thought. "He's always wanting to please everyone, and everyone gives him a bad time."

We saw him waiting for the bus. He still wore this same expression.

We walked on, talking loudly and a little drunkenly. Eric said, "When I take you into a pub, I feel like my father when he took me in for the first time." And I agreed that I felt like the son who was being shown his way round.

When we got to the opening which led into the wood, we pushed our bicycles up over the brambles and leaves; we came out at the charming clearing that I knew, and we laid my coat on the ground and spread out the lunch. Hard-boiled eggs, toast, coffee, beer for Eric, biscuits, apple tart, blackcurrant purée.

The world was slightly hazy and in a whirl. The weak sun shone. We were warm from the pub and the drink. We lay back against the tree trunk, close together because the wind was cold.

It seems unbearably sad now to think of that picnic, so unsuitable for the time of year, so lost in the wood and in time and with only two tiny points of humanity to remember it. In strikes at me and bites for some reason whenever I think of it.

We ate happily. I realized that I had been feeling quite drunk when it began to wear off.

Eric knelt up beside me and tried to put his coat right round me, for he saw that I was getting cold.

There we sat and knelt, smoking our pipes. I knew I would remember it afterwards and always. It was too sad to forget. And there was a lovely quality too, because of the drink and the wood and our hunger for the nice food.

Eric saw how sad I was and he kissed me and lay down on the ground and shut his eyes. We both felt then, I think, how doomed we were, how doomed everyone was. We saw very clearly the plain tragedy of our lives and of everybody's. A year after a year after a year passes, and then you look back and your sadness pierces you. We were very sad from the drink, and clear-sighted.

I told Eric that he couldn't go to sleep there on the ground, as the sun was disappearing behind clouds and it was getting colder and colder. We got up to go, leaving the egg-shells on the ground. I think of those terribly sad egg-shells lying in the wood now. I feel that I shall go back to visit them.

We bicycled on across Shipbourne Common where the church bells were ringing; then we climbed up the hill and came back home. We sat by the gas fire and had tea, then we lay down and rested, we were so tired; for the night before we had talked nearly all night.

The time came for Eric to go and he went, leaving his ring and his snuff box for me to take care of, as he thinks that they might get stolen in the hostel at Appledore.

It is Tuesday now [8 February] and he has reached there. I wonder what he will think of it.

On Wednesday I had his letter. A good one, which at the end hurt me so that I wrote a ten-page answer, probably very silly and bad-tempered and unwise.

11 February, 8.30 p.m.

This evening I bicycled to Penshurst. I climbed up the hill easily because I was with a man who worked at the railway and he talked all the time about the last war.

At the top he said good-bye and I went on, on, down the hill past a soldier and the old neurotic home, "Swaylands", which is now a military hospital. Two idle loosely hanging soldiers stood at the lodge waiting for something to be brought to them. They looked at me lazily and curiously as I sped past. The light was just fading and I thought how picturesque in the old sense of the word Penshurst was; unusued gateways, cottages clinging together, a little stone bridge, the charming little stone bow fronted house near it, and the Victorian attempts at romantic Elizabethan. I went on past Leicester Square and the Leicester Arms; and as I passed the pub, I thought of Eric who lived near here, on a farm, when he was twenty-one. He told me that once he won a race in the village sports and Lord De L'Isle gave him a money order for ten shillings which he spent on cigarettes.[7] I can imagine him running, running in Penshurst Park with the ancient trees round him and the people in white and colours. I can see it; the heat of the day and Eric younger, chubbier as he puts it, with his dark hair stuck on his forehead with sweat, and the Adam's apple swelling up and down in his throat. I can imagine him afterwards with the village youths and girls and I long so much to have been there too so that afterwards we could have had a lovely night talking and drinking and singing.

Nothing can make up for the fact that my very early youth was so clouded with illness and unhappiness. I feel cheated as if I had never had that fiercely thrilling time when the fears of childhood have left one and no other thing has swamped one. The cheek is plump and smooth, the eye and the teeth are bright and one feels that one would lie down and die if these first essentials were ever taken away.

7 The 5th Baron De L'Isle and Dudley, father of Viscount De L'Isle, V.C.

When I passed the great house it was nothing but a grey and faded silhouette, peaked roofs of chapel and great hall, battlements of the front restored part. Across the ha-ha the grass was smooth from the mouths of innumerable sheep or deer. I stared and stared at it, wondering what I would do if I lived in the middle of that huge pile, all alone. At the top of the hill I asked a soldier on sentry duty the way to Leigh. I remember now that I passed in the village street near the Leicester Arms a cook all in white with tall hat. It is curious to see their traditional clothing still, alone in the village street at dusk, like a ghost.

When I passed the Fleur de Lys at Leigh, again I thought of Eric, for he told me that he used often to get tight there.

Curious to think that all this time while Eric worked on the farm, hated it, was utterly lonely, got tight as often as possible just for something to do, I was only a few miles away in Tonbridge, walking the streets in my restlessness, trying to make myself iller and iller by any foolishness, wanting to die.

And we never met and all the years in between, seven, eight, we knew nothing of each other, they all melted away and were wasted.

2 April, morning.

So much has happened and I have written nothing. The work on my book decorations has somehow made writing seem difficult, outside my sphere, something to be kept for later.[8]

After three weeks of letter-writing and keeping away, Eric at last came from Appledore to see me. I went to Tonbridge to meet his train on the Saturday morning. I was late and so I looked in all the pubs round the station for him. At last I ran him to earth in the one near the public library. It was warm and dark and dismal in there; and there was Eric looking lost, distraught, restless, unhappy, his shirt all frayed, a large black pint in front of him.

"Hullo, Eric," I said as gaily as possible; then I went out again to take the pump off my bicycle. Eric quickly followed me and said, "Wait a minute, Denton, let's leave this pub, a chap in there is boring me."

I waited by my bike and the next moment Eric shot out of the door. We walked a little way, finding it difficult to talk. Then Eric clapped his hand in his pocket and said that he'd left the eggs he'd brought me behind in the pub.

He ran back and found them still wrapped in their sugar bag.

Just by Angels the jewellers I heard a patter of feet behind us and then

8 Decorations for *In Youth is Pleasure*, Denton's second novel, accepted by Routledge on 17 January 1944.

someone called "Eric", and he turned round and found a friend he hadn't seen since he was living at Penshurst. The friend had a red face and the ears stood out. He called Eric "Chicken" and Eric called him "Birdie".

They talked about racing, and Birdie said that someone they had both known had just had four fingers cut off in a circular saw. Eric and I both smiled and laughed. (This always seems to happen when catastophes are reported.)

"Have I changed much?" Eric asked Birdie anxiously, and yet not very anxiously, more with idle curiosity.

Birdie gave him a careful look and said, "Not a lot. I know you by your walk."

All this time I was looking in the jeweller's window and longing for the talk to stop as I hated to stand in the High Street with everybody streaming by while I did nothing.

At last Birdie melted away after I'd said something about lunch and Eric had mentioned the time.

We went straight into the King's Arms and Eric took me into the bar parlour. There we sat in a dark corner and Eric smoked the Dunhill pipe I gave him and we both drank gin. Eric had beer with his too.

"Oh, Denton, don't let's even think, just let's sit," said Eric desperately.

I agreed at once, seeing how anxious and worried he was. We just puffed our pipes, drank till we felt rather affected, and then at closing time poured out into the road.

We missed the bus for Eric, so he walked beside my bike. Then I got off and he rode a little.

He was not drunk, but he was stumbling and uneven in his walking and his riding. I think it was to do with his mental state. He wound my yellow scarf round his neck and looked dark, saturnine and rather gypsy with the bright colour.

At home Evie had kept the lunch hot, so we ate it after three o'clock. Then we rested and tried to sleep off the gin.

The rest of the day we spent talking very little, just happy to be together again.

I took the frayed shirt off Eric and gave him one of mine, which luckily fitted. I said I would get his mended.

When I went in with him on Sunday to go back, there was no train to Appledore till 7.12. So we went and had tea in crowded Aplin's and I pointed out Jack Easton's surgery over the way, and after tea we walked about the town, up towards the school round by the footpath through the fields. And Eric told me of his life in 1936 at Penshurst, when he used to come into Tonbridge. And I thought of us probably quite often passing in the street, never meeting or making contact, just when we were both so horribly lonely. And the wastefulness of this is one of the dirtiest things that life has done to me I think.

Those endless days and nights of 1936 alone and desperate, and Eric then wandering about too. To have missed all those young years together is very sad. I can think of no other word.

On the station we met another person who works on the land with Eric. His name is John and his face is quite cracked and he has a great tone of culture with a capital K.

I didn't want Eric to call out but he longed to, and at last he yelled at John as he walked about on the platform and introduced him to me.

John gave me a look and said, "Oh, I've heard a lot about you."

I didn't know what to answer so I said, "And I've heard a lot about you."

John said, "Go in!" incredulously.

Then he told us how a woman friend of his was walking home with an American doughboy, who, when she reached her door, suddenly gave her a great biff for no reason and then disappeared.

This story seemed horrible to me, but John didn't seem in the least perturbed. "My friend thinks he must have had a brainstorm" was all he said.

When the train came in, Eric and John jumped in a first-class carriage, slammed the door, and that was that.

I was left, rather mournfully, to push my way out through the crowd on the platform. It was all rather nightmarish. The night in wartime with the people coming and going, pushing and lusting and leering in the dark.

Eric came again two weeks after that, on 11 March. Later this time. And I was not very well and lying on the bed. He put his hand on my stomach and we lay contentedly talking and I began to feel better. He had a restful, good effect on me.

We did nothing that night because I was not well, but the next day we again bicycled madly to the Volunteers, only this time we sat in the public bar with soldiers, rough-riders, Home Guard.

I wanted suddenly to get drunk and we hadn't much time, so I ordered double gins, and Eric frowned. I think he thought it rather hysterical. Outside the window Italian prisoners were mooching lounging and the boys in the bar swore at them and called them lazy bastards and asked if our chaps would stand about lazily like that.

It was so warm in the bar we took off our coats and sat in our shirt sleeves and two little children looked in at us from the open window. At closing time we looked everywhere for a place to picnic and then decided to go back to the wood where we had eaten before. We pushed through the bushes and found those blessed eggshells lying there still. Eric marvelled, as I hoped he would.

I was much drunker this time after five gins and when we sat down at the foot of a tree in the delicate warm sun I suddenly burst into tears. Frightful, but true. And this flood set us talking, talking, talking about friendship, love, hate, fear of death, on, on, on.

Eric bent over me as I lay on the ground and said, "Oh, you're drunk, Denton," and I had to admit it.

Then we ate the lunch. The eggs, the raisins, tart, the beer, the coffee and chocolate.

My tears were dry but I felt emptied. We walked through the narrow paths of the wood, Eric supporting his drunken companion. Round and round we walked, talking softly, happy, feeling fated, doomed, waited on a moment of time, knowing death at the end of the path.

We were there till 6 o'clock. All those hours in the wood, in the open air!

We got back and missed both early and late buses. This made me happy. And Eric stayed the night. We slept the sleep of dead exhaustion. All night we slept with only minor wakings.

In the morning we took out our lunch again and climbed through Oxon Hoath to Gover Hill. We lay in the charming haystack beside the avenue. It began to sleet and we hid in the warm hay. The wind beat about us insanely. We laughed and ate pilchards and toast. We talked little. Yesterday had drained us.

Afterwards we went round the corner of the stack where the wind was tearing mad dogs, and we lay there in the sun, close together until the corner of the haystack collapsed on us burying us in the hay. I saw Eric's eyes glinting at me through the mass of hay. And I wished that I could always sit in haystacks with Eric, feeling the sun on us and eating pilchards.

But we had to push on to Crouch, where I was going to visit Noël. Eric was going on to Maidstone to see one of the Land Army officers. We wanted to smoke and had no matches, so I suggested that we should go into the White Cottage.

Trot and Prue were both there. Eric had never seen two lesbians before and so he was boyishly curious. I laughed. Trot liked him at once, and said he had buccaneering Kentish eyes. We played with the pregnant looking dachshund which had a sweet, pointed face. Its tits seemed as large and unending as castle puddings. It was happy in the White Cottage.

Eric came a fortnight after this again, last Saturday.

I was in bed with a temperature of 104 and Eric came up to me and he put a towel under my head and a flannel soaked in cold water over my temples and eyes. He did this many times, soothing me. He told me he had learnt it when he had all the terrible hangovers of his early youth.

He told me more stories. How he had tried to commit suicide at eighteen because he had taken £12 from his mother's suitcase with which to buy drink and did not know how to face her.

He was at an older friend's house, the chap with whom he had been drinking. He locked himself in the bathroom and began to take two hundred Aspirin tablets. He said that the taste was awful and the amount of water he had to drink was enormous. And as he took them he thought of all the other people in the world who did not have to die and he envied them with all his heart, and longed and longed not to have to kill himself. But at last he had swallowed them all, and then the friend, Jack, came battering on the door, shouting for him to open it.

At last Eric did and he told his friend what he had done, and said, "I don't want to die here on you. I am going off into Dulwich Woods. Good-bye."

But the friend, although tight, immediately regained some wits and telephoned the ambulance and hospital at once.

Eric was taken off in the white van, pretending to be more unconscious that he was. He had lost the use of his limbs, but he knew what was happening. At the hospital the young doctor used the stomach pump on him which was awful. And then Eric heard him say, "See if it's aspirin," and they put something with the contents of his stomach which turned it blue, and it was aspirin.

Then the doctor turned to Eric and asked kindly why he did it. And Eric was at such a loss to know what to do that he said, insolently, "Oh, I just had a fat head." The doctor turned away and said, "You'll hear more of this."[9]

And after that they tried to charge him, but somehow his father managed to dissuade them; but Eric was kept for weeks in a sort of workhouse, where they tried to make him appear certifiable. They gave him absurdly easy puzzles to do and such things. At last he was out, and now he cannot bear often to think about this time.

When Eric tells me things like this, life seems so terrifying that I want to die. And I long wildly to have known him all my life. I know it would have been different if I had. Perhaps not better, but different, less mad.

He told me too how with this same Jack he went drinking and they lost a pound note and they went back to London Bridge to look for it. And Jack, being boozed, darted out into the road and got run into.

Eric was walking about fifty yards in front of him when he heard Jack roaring and running to the parapet and screech of brakes. He stood dead still until a policeman approached, then he walked hurriedly on, never looking round.

He did this through fear and horror and because he was drunk, but also in the hope that Jack would get compensation if it did not appear that he was in drunken company.

The next day he found that Jack had broken four ribs, dislocated his neck and broken his leg.

The concentrated horror of this story I cannot get down on paper.

This was the same Jack who sold his grandmother's piano when she was away. And when Eric went to see him, he found him lying blind on the bed with a carpet of bank notes scattered all over and around him. That night he would let Eric buy nothing and they seemed soused and soused.

"But he was fascinating," said Eric simply, "he was fascinating. He had

9 Attempted suicide was at that time a criminal offence.

S.A. and women fell for him.''

He was ten years older than Eric, whose father so disapproved of him that he had forbidden Eric ever to be seen with him.

Another story Eric told me also happened when he was seventeen or eighteen. He was drinking in a pub and had been for days on end, waiting for them to open. And suddenly the publican saw him plucking at his shirt and knew that something would happen.

Then all went black and Eric rushed out into the yard, and the next thing he knew was that he was lying on the ground in a horse box in the stable, kicking and screaming, and people were trying to calm him and hold him down.

Then he was taken to hospital and stayed there three weeks. And he saw the sides of the building fall down and windows crash and doors dissolve, and animals unreal and terrifying.

Surely this is enough to make anyone cry, especially as it happened to one naturally sweet and kind, terribly young, foolish, generous, utterly without guidance and judgement.

Again I say how I long to have known him then, to have seen what was gnawing at him all the time.

As a result of my picture in *Vogue* I have had absurd fan letters. One Free-French Volunteer girl wants to come down in the bright spring sunshine. Another, a man, offers to come and nurse me when I'm ill and a third wants to paint a portrait of me! I keep them all at bay, being terrified of their disillusion if they should know me.

On my birthday on Thursday Noël brought me, as I lay in bed, a charming little eighteenth-century watch. Rich gold pinchbeck with a lovely disc of gorgeous blue glass at the back. The face wonderfully smooth and white with spidery Roman numerals. The hands two delicate gold antennae, beautifully, thoughtfully and strangely shaped.

The original old label is in the back of the outer case.

I played with it all afternoon, but it had then to go back to the maker to be made to go. I am waiting impatiently for it.

Noël has also made me a birthday cake with a pink "D" on it. It was nice suddenly to have a birthday recognized. And strangest of all, my brother Bill sent me a wire from the Conservative Club, where he had just arrived from Africa.

10 April

Yesterday, Easter Sunday, about six o'clock I heard a knock on the door, and then someone talking to Evie. It was the Free French girl who had written me a fan letter about *Maiden Voyage*. When Evie came up to tell me I cursed and swore and then had her up.

She was quite pretty and small and neat and spoke English quite ordinarily although she put on an accent for Evie.

We quickly talked quite naturally and easily, if rather conventionally, about her adventures in finding this place. She hitch-hiked from London and asked ten thousand people the way, she said. She told me that her father was naturalized English, her mother English, and they lived in Scotland.

She said she had been absolutely determined to find me out and present herself. Strangely enough I was not as alarmed by this determination as I thought I'd be. I told her my watch was broken and she promised to look out for one in London for me. She bemoaned the fact that she had not set out to see me much earlier in the day.

Over supper I noticed she wore a little signet ring, with two tiny crests and a coronet over them. I don't a bit know about foreign heraldry, so these signs and symbols didn't help me. Her name is Rose-Marie Aubepin.

I saw her down to the bus, and just as we were passing May's house, she leant out of the window and offered her a bed for the night. (Later she suggested that this would be a very nice girl for me to marry.)

When we reached the stop, Aubepin wanted me to write in her copy of the book, so I took my pen out and she presented me with her back to write on. The bus came up with us in this crouching position. I waved good-bye and said, "See you soon."

13 April

Last night as I sat in my chair, after lying all afternoon in Oxon Hoath Park, by the lake, in the sun, I heard a voice crying "Denton!" outside in the wind. And this has happened before, so I wasn't altogether surprised; but it was when I got down and found not only Eric there, but Eric plus another land-boy friend called Peter Clements. They had missed the last train to Appledore, by getting out at Tonbridge and having a drink, and so Eric had come to ask if I could put them up.

I felt rather dazed from the sunburn on my face and a slight temperature I was running, but I said, "Come in. Tell me what's happened," and I led them upstairs. After some laughing and smiling and slight confusion I made them both sit down and gave them beer. Eric got biscuits out of his bag and gave them solicitously to Peter.

He also brought out something wrapped in newspaper. It was a charming old, cut-glass tumbler from home, which he wanted to give me as a birthday present. I wondered if he had taken it with his mother's permission or not.

I kept wondering as I talked to them brightly how I could possibly manage to have them both in my room for the rest of the night. It would be impossible, I knew, for me to sleep with two people in my room.

I wanted to put Peter downstairs on a mattress, but the floor in the kitchen is stone, and I did not feel that even I could be so inhospitable and cruel.

Soon the floor was covered with the spare mattress, blankets, flea-bag, torn pillow cases; and after a lot more talking we began to get undressed.

Both Eric and Peter snored and so there was no sleep for me, and soon the nightingale began to pour out its never ending song. On and on through the night tremule, sucking, weeping, trilling; until the moon began to shine through the window on to my face.

It shone on to Eric's face too, and I saw his curved nose in outline, the hollow of his cheek, and his pushed back hair, like a dead face floating on the water.

In the morning we all had breakfast round my bed, eating porridge from bowls, and reconstituted scrambled egg, coffee and Noël's marmalade. Peter talked about the nice police sergeant he knew who was friendly with Somerset Maugham, E. M Forster etc. He also talked about his crook friend who likes licking girls all over in Hyde Park and who made £900 out of the Black Market. A curious mixture. Peter was rather alive and enquiring, but at bottom inescapably shallow and rather vain. I listened, amused, and Eric sat quietly smiling and smoking his pipe.

Afterwards we walked through the wood and then I went to lunch with May, carrying my own roast potatoes with me, and Eric and Peter went off to Maidstone (stopping on the way for four pints, as I learned afterwards).

17 April

Eric was coming for this week-end anyhow, so I saw him again on Saturday.

We looked at some old photographs he had brought, of himself and family. (This is always such a curious mixture of sadness and ribaldry.)

Then afterwards we went to the post with my story for English Story[10] and the thing I'm sending to the Cornhill.[11]

After supper we were talking of the picnic with Peter on Wednesday, and suddenly Eric and I began to quarrel, or rather I began banging against Eric and he became almost tongue-tied, except when he came out with rather hurting home-truths.

How we quarrelled, and how terribly unhappy I grew, and how hopeless.

In desperation, in the long silences when Eric drank bottle after bottle of strong beer and I smoked cigarette after cigarette until my fingers were brown, I took up Rothenstein's Men and Memories and opened it at the place

---

10 "At Sea" (see 1942, note 47 above).
11 "Narcissus Bay", first published by Peter Quennell in the Cornhill, July 1945, and reprinted in Brave and Cruel.

where Oscar Wilde wanted to sit near the band because he liked one of the musicians and how this angered the prim Rothenstein.

And then Eric made it up with me and sat on the stool and took my feet (which were already on the stool) on to his knees. So we sat in this curious position and made friends again, and I felt I would forgive him almost anything.

It was after two before we got to bed, but for a wonder we slept well. Only once or twice I woke up to see the moon on Eric's face, making it look like lean, lovely, hollowed sculpture, and with the sound of his breathing was mixed the wonderful nightingale which never stopped. And I felt so much better and less worried by my body that I rejoiced, and could not resist telling Eric how eased I was.

And it seemed a miraculously pleasant end to our trouble and unhappiness.

All morning we lay about undressed, and all afternoon too, Eric in my priest's cassock looking strange and interesting and historic, his hair all rough, bits of his body showing through the black as he pulled at his neck or tossed his legs about on the bed or in the chair.

I thought that it was easy always to be friends with Eric and difficult, terribly difficult, to keep up a dignity and grievance. I wondered how much like butter I would appear to other people.

I don't know what will happen in the future to our friendship, but now it is good to keep it alive all I can. And I will give all I can.

I have written nothing to him this week for several reasons, some good, some not so good. He shall write to me when he wants to. He knows he can always depend on me, but I think he wants to [sentence unfinished]

21 April

This morning I had a book, *Planet and Glow-worm*, from Edith Sitwell and a letter with her love. Then I went out in the sun and, feeling so much better, I lay on the top of the haystack and sunned myself and ate and actually fell asleep, and I forgot unhappiness and trouble and only felt in a daze with hot sun and cool wind on my face.

Edith just mentioned my *Horizon* story which appeared on Wednesday.[12] Cyril Connolly sent me fourteen guineas and said Hamish Hamilton wanted to know if I had a book of them in mind, because if so he'd like to publish it.

Lately I have had a poem in the *Spectator*[13] and two in *Life and Letters* and a story in *New Writing*[14] and one in *English Story*.

12 "When I Was Thirteen" (see 1942, note 40 above).
13 "A Mistake", first published in the *Spectator* on 28 January 1944 and reprinted in *A Last Sheaf*.
14 "The Barn", *New Writing and Daylight*, 1943-44; reprinted in *Brave and Cruel*.

Also I have sold two little pictures to a Mrs Serocold.

It is happiness to have things liked, but when I'm ill as I was on Wednesday and other days lately everything pales to nothing and I want to die more than anything on earth.

I think all I can do is to keep my work going as long as I can. And if I can no longer, then I will die.

4 May. By the river in the afternoon. Grey and windy.

Yesterday I went to London to see the specialist. And as I expected he had nothing new to suggest.

I remembered going to the same building in Brook Street (No. 26) to see the psychologist six years ago. The psychologist had a tiny room on the top floor; the neurologist a large one on the ground floor.[15]

After the specialist I took a taxi and went to Guy Allan's studio in Glebe Place.[16]

He opened the door and ushered me into the large, uneasy atmosphere of a lofty studio with holes in the skylight where shrapnel had come through.

Stacked in great masses were his own and his boyfriend's canvases. They were really a little better than I thought they would be.

While I was in the lavatory a sort of gypsy woman who had been Augustus John's model came, to fit Guy for a coat she was making him. She stayed to tea which we all drank out of thick earthenware bowls. I had a Jewish currant bun, but did not eat the rounds of bread spread with herring and radish slivers.

There was a strange half-Eastern cat, grey and fawn, which wore Guy's naval identity disc round its neck.

After tea we went into the hole under the stairs where Guy had his bed. Opposite the bed was a hideous sort of throne topped with Lyre-bird's feathers, which Guy said had come from the old Duke of Connaught's sale.

On the walls were pictures of Guy's friend Derek, Prince Youssoupoff in his grandfather's Russian clothes and some other people I did not know. At the bottom was one Guy had done of me from my *Vogue* photo. Two other people had arrived by this time, a Belgian artist, Roger Descomes, and someone else.

Guy showed me photographs while the others talked. He was not so extraordinarily dressed as he was when he came to see me for the first time

15 In 1936 Denton had consulted a psychiatrist (he always confused psychiatrists with psychologists). In March 1944 he had begun to pass blood, and had been referred to a neurologist by Dr Caterina Easton, the wife of Dr John Easton.

16 The fan who had written offering to nurse Denton; off King's Road, Chelsea.

last week. Then he wore harlequin socks and open-toed sandals. A Chinese crepe shirt and a jersey with a belt round it. Large Etruscan silver rings on his fingers and a Canadian lumber jack's jacket. His face looked slightly painted but that may have been my imagination.

When I left, he gave me a parcel which he said was a little Chinese earthenware teapot for my early morning tea! He wants to come and see me again this Wednesday.

It is strange meeting people who have written to you out of the blue. Guy must be forty-five. He is now a Christian Scientist. But when he came to see me last Wednesday he told me how about fifteen years ago a very charming Chinaman kept him drugged in a studio in Paris for some time. At last Guy couldn't work and the studio became indescribably filthy.

Some acquaintances finally came and dragged him away and got him back to England. Guy puts all this down to Christian Science. He also says he was cured of consumption. And now he thinks that God has sent him specially to succour me. I wish he'd begin his work. I should love to be succoured.

Guy also told me that the Duchess de Choiseul's daughter was once very fond of him, and her Belgian husband became so incensed that he nearly killed them both in a car crash by mistake on purpose.

8 May, 11.15 p.m.

When you long with all your heart for someone to love you, a madness grows there that shakes all sense from the trees and the water and the earth. And nothing lives for you, except the long deep bitter want. And this is what everyone feels from birth to death.

16 May

This afternoon as I went down to the river I saw three children with their heads in a ditch and they were chanting on and on like church-intoning, "Keep right on to the end of the war, keep right on to the end of the war!" They sang it with such delight. It seemed to be a sort of charm to them. When they heard me pass, they all looked up and began to giggle guiltily. Then the day before yesterday I found two small boys trying to push an enormous cart up an incline. And I helped them and at last we got it going. The boys had taken their football boots off and were paddling along the road in their socks. They thanked me between sweating groans and smiles and deep breaths.

Yesterday I went to Tunbridge Wells to be X-rayed.[17] Quite an ordeal of lying about with nothing on for over an hour. And the peculiar injection in

17 He had been referred by the London neurologist.

arm made my head spin and alarm grow in me. They took many plates of spine and lower down. All the room was blue, with baby-blue blankets and horrible little glass fishes and china rabbits and bronze dogs and clay horses and woolly birds on the mantelpiece. Also pictures of darling children and little wife. Why *do* doctors always go in for this sort of thing? It was as if they would obtrude their private life on you against your will. One could not miss so many toys and photographs, however blind.

I was so delighted that it was all over that I bought a little old print of "Pomona, Goddess of Fruit" and a little cut-glass dish. One shilling.

I stopped on the way back on Bidborough Ridge and drank my scalding coffee, gazing at the wonderful air. There was sleet in the low flying clouds, and I looked across and saw the white puff of a train, and Tonbridge in the valley, and I thought of Eric at Penshurst in 1936 and me in Tonbridge.

And it reminded me of our last week-end together when Eric brought pheasants' eggs which we ate on toast, and how afterwards we went out and spent all day by the river in the sun with only shorts on. We wandered across the fields like this and came to a stream and Eric saw a nest on a tiny islet so he took off his shorts and waded into the freezing water and brought back some moorhens' eggs.

Afterwards we discovered two bomb craters with irises growing at the bottom of them.

I have had Allen & Unwin as well as Hamish Hamilton wanting me to submit books to them because of my *Horizon* story.[18] And it has been mentioned by Vita Sackville-West in the *Observer*, and also in *Statesman* and *Time and Tide*, all very favourably. *English Story* paid me £15 this morning.

19 May, afternoon.

Today as I passed a cottage on my bike a little girl came out of the door, dressed in an old chiffon ball-dress that reached to the ground all round her. The V of the neck came to her navel almost. She looked at me and gave a self-conscious touch with her hand to the waist of her dress. Then she touched her hair at the back, and looked at the other two ordinarily dressed children that had come out with her, contemptuously.

Further on, by Hartlake Bridge, where my favourite haystack for picnicking is, I found soldiers and lorries. The soldiers were dressing and washing and changing behind the lorries. One could see pink chests and brown arms and necks showing from the rings of white singlets. They were laughing and swearing and shouting, the whole scene extravagantly noisy and male. And one understood so well what was meant by the tradition of the Army. It was something that exaggerated or completely changed the

18 "When I Was Thirteen" (see 1942, note 40 above).

ordinary behaviour of ordinary civilian men.

I walked after lunch along the tow-path and into a little wood with bluebells and little bits of excrement deposited nearly with newspaper. And when I came out, some soldiers passed through a gate and all began to shoot off their rifles. I hated the noise and hid behind the concrete of the bridge.

Now I am going into Hadlow to buy tobacco, cigarettes and beer for Eric tomorrow.

22 May, 11.15 p.m.

I have just written to Eric to say that I shall never see him again if I can prevent it. We walked through the fields by the river this afternoon and our legs got stung with nettles and I can feel them pricking still. We parted amicably, but I knew all the time I would write like this.[19]

23 May, 9.15 a.m.

The postman has just come to take the appalling letter that I have written to Eric. I hear the slam of the car door and the starting of the engine, and now I know that he will really get it. It is on its way already down the drive, to the road, to the office, to Ashford and at last to Appledore.

The face at the other end, as it reads it — what will it be like?

26 May. Five to eleven p.m.

Now I am utterly alone on my bed, on the too-hot velvet eiderdown in the close room. And outside, the moon is showing sharper and clearer every moment although there is light from the sun still. And I think all the time of Eric at Appledore. And I wonder what he thinks and whether I shall hear in the morning.

I have had two fan letters, from a Peter Cromwell of Mount Street, Berkeley Square, and from a Sheffield schoolboy.

28 May, 7.15 a.m.

Every night now comes over me the terrible restlessness just before bed, which I thought would never come again. And I feel that I must tear the

19 The basic problem in the early months of Denton's relationship with Eric Oliver was Eric's difficulty in accepting that Denton loved him despite his own inability to commit himself, coupled with Denton's fear that Eric was seeing him only to please him, not because he wanted to.

walls down. I must go anywhere out of the house to wander in the lanes on my bicycle. I cannot keep still. And the thought of Eric haunts me like a ghost.

Last night, just as I passed the tiny chapel "Fish Hall", I looked up and I saw the text displayed on the "Wayside Pulpit" board, "Let not the sun go down upon your wrath", and I felt madly that I must telephone to Eric.

Of course when I did, and after I said that I was sorry, I made everything much worse than it was before.

Now I am just waiting to telephone again, and I am going up to London if I can, to try to settle something.[20]

This whole week has been such drab monotonous pain. And nothing to hear or see. No letter.

My work has somehow died to nothing, and I think of nothing but dying or killing myself. I could kill myself so easily with tablets, no other way. The right time and place really only remain to be found now.

How nasty the talk of suicide, yet how inevitable it sometimes seems.

29 May. Whitsun.

I'm here now in this bed at Eric's flat in Streatham. The sun is beating on to the gauze curtains and I hear a wireless. Last night we went to the Greyhound in Dulwich Village and had eight gins and I talked and talked.

Now we have had breakfast in bed and Eric has gone to the refrigerator to get ice to put on my head.

To live this way is death and I know it, for me, and yet something extraordinary for me seems to come out of it.

How the trams whirr and buzz, how the birds chatter.

3 June. On Shipbourne Common in the afternoon sun with a few large raindrops falling.

And I have told Eric that we should not meet for some time but eventually we would be stupid if we turned against each other and quarrelled.

My weekend with him ended disastrously.

On Sunday night we went to the Greyhound at Dulwich. I thought everything would go fine, because that afternoon we had talked for a long time in St James's Park under a plain tree. When we looked down before we sat we saw a used contraceptive lying there, so we went round to the other side of the tree.

20 Where Eric was staying with his mother.

And talking there under the tree, I really thought that we had decided only to be friends and not quarrel.

But at the Greyhound I drank eight gin and limes and it was gloomy and tragic and we talked too much and walking home was swaying. Then just as we got off the bus (close to the old eighteenth-century tombs in a churchyard round which all the railings had been removed for the war) we ran into Eric's mother and I had to walk home so carefully. When we got in I must have seemed tight because Eric said, "Put your feet up on this stool." Then Mrs Oliver got hot cocoa and we all drank it. I thought it tasted extraordinary after the gin.

In the bedroom Eric came up to me and said, "Denton, we must go straight to sleep." But I lay in my bed restless and buzzing for most of the night.

Once or twice I got up and went to the window. I saw the little paved garden in front and what I thought was the cement statue of a cat. But it was a real cat, white and long-haired, standing as still as death. At last it moved. The trams scrapped and screamed all night. And army tanks thundered through devilishly. Eric woke up and said, "Denton, are you feeling sick?" and I said "Yes" and grunted.

In the morning, when at last I had got up, I went into the sitting room and found Bunty, Eric's sister-in-law, there with her two children Janet and Howard.

Howard aged two sat on Eric's knee, and Eric said lovingly, "I hope you don't leak." He really loved Howard and asked, "Don't you think you'll turn into a champ, Howard?" He felt him all over and we all said what a fat, strong child it was.

Then it sat on my knee and fell back against me and lay there quite still with its long-lashed eyes closed. I had never held a small child ever before.

Afterwards Eric and I made the beds and then walked on Streatham Common. The heat was overpowering. Eric had already had one pint. He lay dissatisfied in the grass, telling me how he had hated the rackety friends of his early youth, and how he had never had any real friends because he had always wanted to be alone sometimes and kick off from them. I saw how out of sympathy he was getting but I could do nothing.

As we waited for the bus to go home he suddenly said, "Christ, there's someone I don't want to meet." So I tried to screen him and we walked back to another stop. The woman was some barmaid who talked too much. Eric was really nervously upset now. He said, "I feel absolutely trapped and as if I couldn't go home now."

He saw another pub and dragged me into it. I would drink nothing. I looked at the raucous dripping scene, somehow so meaningless and undesigned.

Things were going from bad to worse. We traipsed home almost silently. Then after lunch we lay down on our beds and tried to rest. I read the

Book of Snobs until I could bear it no more. I jumped up and said, "I'm going." I packed my satchel. Eric said nothing. I asked him what bus to take. He said, "I'll come to the station." I said, "What for?" as freezingly as possible.

Then I went and said goodbye to Mrs Oliver and flapped out of the house with Eric following me.

I walked fast and he kept up behind. Just as we reached the stop a 59 bus approached. Without looking at Eric I heard him say, "This is the bus."

I didn't turn but marched on to the bus as if I had never known him in my life.

Suddenly as it was moving off I had the longing to see if he was looking after me. I dodged this way and that, and I thought I saw the grey Aertex of his shirt stretched across his broad back, but the conductress stood four-square, worrying for my fare, obliterating. I went right up to the front of the bus upstairs, and then I began crying in total disregard of all the passengers. I had dark glasses on but I suppose no one who looked could fail to see the tears trickling down. I really felt done for in some way.

In Whitehall I jumped into a rare taxi and told him to drive to Helen's in Ladbroke Square. I felt that someone somewhere must give comfort or distraction.

But, of course, no one was in, only some foreign girls gibbering in the gardens; so I wended my way to Charing Cross and sat in the sweltering heat of the bus with a little fair haired boy who had caught a tiny silver fish in the Round Pound and was taking it home in a jar. He said that the last one had died and he hoped this one wouldn't. I was so grateful to have someone uncomplicated to talk to that I quite loved the little boy for a moment or two. He was so amusing and precocious and somehow religious about the little fish.

I came home in the train with a vast woman in pucey red crepe floral dress. The journey was terrible. For two pins I would have poured out all my sadness to her.

6 June, 10.30 a.m.

Just heard that the invasion had begun on Northern France; and the weather is windy and sunny and I have nothing but an aching feeling in my heart, and I wonder if Eric has been made to leave Appledore or whether his idea about the coastal district being cleared for the invasion was incorrect.

Yesterday Peter Cromwell, alias Neville, came down. Smooth, quiet, timid, egocentric, uncreative. The sort of person I would quarrel with in no time. He seemed to like the things I write enormously. I wonder why? He had come all that way especially to see me. And we had prawns and lettuce hearts and partridge eggs, and macaroni, and plum flan and peppermint creams and coffee and apple juice.

He knows Connolly and Toynbee and all these people and he'll tell them all about me. Awful.

7 June

What a day of aching and giving up! The day nine years ago on which I was run over and my health ruined for ever. And Eric, I think of him all day and hear nothing. Last night I woke up hot and steamy and dulled and peaceful, until the thought bit into me. Then I heard the continuous stream of bombers through the night going to the battle, and the whole world seemed more wicked and mad than seemed bearable.

Today after quite a fruitful one and a half hours on my book I went down to the river to picnic with guava jam. Then I went on to the sale of Churchyard's things. I was too late to get any of the things I'd marked out yesterday — the Georgian tea-pot, cigarette case, snuff box, etc.

Yesterday, after May and I had seen the things, we went to tea with a Mrs Ford in the old Port Reeve's house (at Tonbridge). She was very right and tight and clean and so was the house with all modern conveniences. And the neat garden was full of roses, one called "The Doctor", to smell which one had to stand on a soap box. There was an old stone coffin lid with a cross on it, from the priory where the goods station is now, and the old outer dyke of the castle passes through the end of the garden, making a deep cliff.

I thought how strange to sit with elderly ladies in such a clean, such a Tudorized house with radiators and frigidaires, while the most unspeakable atrocities were happening in masses only a hundred miles away at least.

I have sworn that I will not write to Eric for a whole month; but now I hope that he will write to me before that.

8 June

Irene, when she came last Friday, told me how my grandmother Bassett was stiff and fierce and snobbish and seemingly stern and unlovable and how my mother was so pretty with her child's face looking up between the gold brown curls, and her nose and the eyes that almost turned into slits when she laughed. She said that she thought that it was to my grandmother's credit that she could produce a child so different, so lovable, so uninhibited and unworried by life.

And I thought of all those years ago, in late-Victorian Shanghai, with the sun-blinds drawn down for tea on some wide tiled veranda. I thought of Irene and my mother as children having tea together with honey sandwiches and molasses cake, and afterwards my stern grandmother coming to inspect them and saying to Rosalind, my mother, "I like you to be with Irene, because she has such good manners."

I would love to know all the facts of my mother's life from birth to the time she went to the Florentine convent.

15 June, 3.30 p.m. by Shipbourne Common close to a dead tree.

Yesterday Guy Allan came down and told me that the day before, Nina Hamnett had been lunching with him, and he asked her if she had read my book.[21] She threw up her hands and said, "Have I not! All the homosexuals in London have been shrieking at me, wanting to know how anyone could write a book like that. They're furious with him." I wonder why?

Guy also told me how he and Nina were once at lunch with Princess Violette Murat, and it was a very hot day and Nina wouldn't take her coat off, until at last Violette said, "Nina, I insist on your taking that coat off, you'll melt if you don't."

And Nina shrieked out across the room in French, "My dear, I can't, my bottom's through my dress!"

Violette threw up her hands, and yelled with laughter, and then she took Nina and gave her a beautiful dress.

He told me other stories about himself when young. How a friend called Sir Eric Williams, I think, was so fond of him that when Guy refused to go and stay with him, because he had a high temperature, Eric went out of the house at Southsea, down to the beach, where he hired a donkey and tried to make it swim out to sea with him on its back. The donkey rebelled, the owner cried out. A huge crowd collected, and at last Eric came back to the house wringing wet and shrieking with laughter. He was only twenty-one and Guy was three years younger.

This same Eric had been the third son and his older brothers were good at sport and he was not, so his mother used to have him publicly beaten before the butler and all the other servants.

It so happened that his two brothers suddenly died and he came into the title very unexpectedly.

Then there was hell to pay. He did everything his mother could not stand. He knew terrible friends, he drank, he drugged, he spent money madly. He draped a room all in black velvet and had nothing but a portrait of Beethoven with extraordinary things in his hair.

He became obsessed with Guy and wanted him to live with him. Whenever Guy went to stay, Eric would have none of the other friends near him, because he thought Guy was childlike and innocent and he wanted to keep him so. When Guy was at an Army crammer's, Eric was very sensible and did not try to disturb his work.

21 A painter and a famous habitué of Soho.

More than once Guy was summoned hurriedly by the housekeeper, because Eric had taken an overdose of ether. Eric did this, as he knew that it was the only way to get Guy, whenever he wanted him.

Eric took a troop of actors about the countryside and acted with them himself. One day Guy's mother said, "Let's surprise Eric and go down to so-and-so to see his play."

So they went and sat in the stalls.

When in the middle of the piece Eric suddenly saw them there, he said, "What, you here! Why didn't you tell me, I would have given you a box."

Then he realized that he was supposed to be a character in a play, and he roared with laughter, and all the audience roared too.

One night he tied Guy up to the four-post bed and started to beat him and to yell because Guy would not submit to him in everything. He was almost mad with possessiveness. Guy gritted his teeth and tried not to let even a murmur out. Secretly he was frightened of and overpowered by Eric.

One of the maids heard the violent beating and banged on the locked door, saying, "Oh Master Eric, stop, Master Eric, stop, don't kill him."

Guy just hung on until Eric's fury had abated.

At last things were getting to such a terrible pass, and Guy was getting so nerve-racked, that he said, "I will live with you, Eric, if you agree to live in Paris and not in England. You are too wild for this conventional England."

So Eric went to Paris and then sent for Guy to come; but then Guy saw his escape, and because several other people who were fond of him persuaded him, he meanly went back on what he had said and refused to go.

Then Eric, as he had always threatened, really did kill himself, and Guy has felt guilty about it ever since!

Guy also told me of a boy of about nineteen who came to see him at the beginning of the war. The boy was charming and good-looking, but he'd lost all interest in life and was horrified by the war. He had gone to his grandmother and said, "Grandmother, give me a few hundred pounds. Life is an utter swindle. I want to have a good time, then I will kill myself."

This extraordinary grandmother said, "Quite right, my boy. You could not do anything wiser than have a good time and then kill yourself. Life is too rotten to be believed."

So she gave him the money and a car, and when he had spent every penny and sold the car, he went down to the embankment, sat on a seat and shot himself.

Another story was of a Russian boy whom Guy found in Paris shut out of Lord Tredegar's house.[22] The Russian boy, who was rather drunk and distraught, told Guy that Tredegar seemed to have turned against him for

---

22 Presumably the 2nd Viscount Tredeger (1893-1949). His second wife was a Russian princess.

no reason. Guy, who was going in to see Tredegar, decided instead to walk home with the Russian boy and try to calm him. They walked along and the Russian boy poured out his heart, saying how terrible it was to have no money and to be dependent for your living on pleasing others and trying to make rich friends.

Just as they were crossing the Seine, the boy jumped on the parapet and was about to throw himself in, but Guy caught his arm and pulled him down. The gendarmes blew whistles and were about to run the boy in, but Guy said he was drunk and had had a row with a girl and he, Guy, was now in charge of him and would look after him. So the gendarmes left him unmolested. He spent the night with Guy, and Guy sent him off in a better frame of mind the next day.

Guy's mother towards the end of her life went blind; and because she had had such beautiful eyes and been a beauty, she would see none of her old friends, only talk to them over the telephone. When Guy became interested in Christian Science and gave up a lot of his so called worldly life she became terribly upset, because she seemed to live all the time through his contacts with the world.

16 June

All night long, and just now too at breakfast, have been coming strange things, rocket planes, mechanical toys with thousand-pound bombs in them. They make a rude noise and the soldiers shoot off a little gun that sounds like pepper exploding. The rocket planes are radio-controlled, with no one in them, and when they crash they explode.[23]

I wonder what will happen if the soldiers so near by will hit one.

20 June, afternoon.

On the stone bridge at Oxon Hoath with a tearing wind, and two boys fishing near me. They have caught twenty-seven roach, and they are all flopping and gasping and dying in the grass under the may tree; and the eldest boy tells me he is going to give them to the cat.

The day before yesterday I was by the river, near the bridge which used to have a diving-board fixed to it. I was dressed all in my green battle-dress, but I took it all off and walked about in only my khaki shorts.

I picked two yellow irises and something purple which I call in my mind melon flower, but I know it is not.

I also found two boys there, one fair, in a sailor's square-necked blue-

---

23 These were the V-1 flying bombs, nicknamed by the public "doodle-bugs". Denton lived on their direct flight path to London. The first had landed in Kent on 13 June.

taped top and one darker, more Mediterranean type, in collarless shirt and braces. They were camping, and had brought their tent down the night before from London. They had a fire, and so I asked if I could light my cigarette. I gave the fair-haired boy one. The other refused. I think they could only have been fourteen or fifteen. The fair one was making tea in a can. He put a piece of cloth over the cups and poured the tea in, saying, "I'm sorry we haven't a third cup, we didn't expect a visitor." This was somehow polite and charming, not a reminder of my sudden appearance.

They went on to tell me how disturbed a night they had had. They said about fifty pilotless planes came over and the tracer bullets were bursting all about them raining down shrapnel. First they dashed from the tent, where they had just made themselves cosy, and hid under the deep overhanging riverbank; then they left that position and fled to the trees.

At last they shut themselves for about half an hour in an old hop-picker's lavatory. They got hardly any sleep at all.

They told me of their memories of the blitz in London. They lived near a railway bridge. This bridge kept recurring in the stories. Two mad boys lived near them, and one of those boys, when a bomb dropped and everyone downstairs was playing cards, rushed up to the top floor and began playing the piano.

This same mad boy was not too mad to work in a munition factory; and every week, when he got his wages, he would take seven or eight little children up to the West End and give them sweets and seats at the pictures and any other treat he could devise. He loved kids; as the fair boy said, "He's crazy on them."

The boys of course knew far more than I did about the pilotless planes and everything else to do with war.

They said that near Bethnal Green, where they lived now, only the young women went into the shelters. The men wouldn't, and the older women wouldn't, and the children just stayed in the street, playing and singing. They said one little girl put her fingers in her ears, and if a sound penetrated she would begin screaming madly. She seemed to be the only screaming one.

Poor Dick Bosanquet, at twenty-five, has been killed in Italy.[24] It was in yesterday's paper, and I have written to his mother. He had reddish hair, a high voice and was attractive in some ways, though not easy to talk to, and wrapped in a certain amount of quiet complacency because of Eton scholarships and King's.

He was the first person to talk a lot to me of Housman's poetry. He said, "I'm rather a fan," and he lent me all the three books and Laurence Housman's *Life*.

24 The son of Mildred Bosanquet (see 1943, note 19 above).

I remember turning to the poem,

> I did not lose my heart in summer's even,
> When roses in the moonlight burst apart

and saying, "That's a wonderful poem," and his vital upsurge of agreement. And in those moments I liked him so much; but then everything would go dead and dull, and he would say to me, "Why don't you go to Cambridge, Denton, and get educated? You've got the time and the money."

I remember when I went to borrow a book from his room, looking in the drawer and seeing all his drab, rather wistful-looking socks and shirts. And I remember thinking then, "Poor Bosey (his mother), if Dick should never come back to wear any of these."

23 June

This afternoon, while I was walking through brambles under the trees in Oxon Hoath Park, I discovered a Gothic arch in brick looking as if it led into the ground.

I pushed through chest-high nettles which smelt, and came to it and found that the Gothic arch was the opening of a small brick tunnel. At the end was what looked like a gaping black well. I lit a match and held it up, but could see nothing; then I threw the match down and heard it patter on the ground not far below me. My eyes were making more out now, and I saw that there was a domed roof and round walls. I realized at once that it was an ice house, perhaps eighteenth century or early nineteenth.

And I thought of the great blocks of ice stored here all those burning summers ago. I saw red roses bursting their heads, and strawberries and custards and syllabubs and sherbets in cut glasses, and mandarin china punch-bowls.

I thought that this deep dark forgotten place would house a murdered body, or lovers on a rainy evening with the leaves dripping outside.

On the ground was an airgraph envelope, with "Mother asks you—" written on it.

I went out of the mouth and saw that on the huge overhanging beech tree to the left was cut "23/4/74" and then the word "Loose".[25] Just seventy years ago someone had cut that date.

Then as I was staring at this date and at the domed earth, tumulus-top of the old ice house, a most amazing burst of fire sounded from a nearby gun, and I realized that one of the doodle-bug pilotless planes was coming over.

25 A village outside Maidstone.

I had got some way from the opening now, but the gun-fire was getting so smashing and loud that I hurried back to the opening and took refuge in the Gothic tunnel.

There seemed to be guns from all round, and above them the doodle-bug's droning. Shrapnel came scattering down through the branches of the beech tree. I wondered if the plane would be hit and blown up. If so I wondered what it would be like in the tunnel, whether I should be buried and, if so, how long I would be left undiscovered.

After two doodle-bugs had flown over without being hit, the noise slackened and at last I ventured out.

Already the wood pigeons had begun to coo again and the land girls and men to go on building their haystack.

I had to stop writing because another came over and the sky was punctured with black puffs of shell bursts.

I ran to the stone bridge. I saw the landgirls running to the trees and two children throwing themselves down under a bush.

More shrapnel than ever fell this time. I heard its wicked whine and thud.

Just after, I went up to the children, and they showed me evil jagged pieces they'd found, enough to kill one.

26 June

On Thursday last I went towards the river and I saw truck after truck with a huge red cross on it winding slowly along the road — quite fifty of them. And I thought of the soldiers inside — their wounds and torn bodies.

I picnicked by the river in the boiling sun, in only my shorts; then I bicycled right along the banks until I felt the sun burning into the dip between my shoulder blades.

At Yalding I sat down in the long grass, close to the medieval bridge, where the water falls away in a thunderous roar; and an Italian prisoner in pinkish chocolate battledress came up to me and asked if one could bathe at that spot. We got talking and he told me that his brother was a postman in Sicily and he himself was captured at Tobruk in 1941. His own people lived near Naples. We smoked cigarettes. He was nice. His face was brown and coarse and good-looking and his body thick-set.

Another prisoner approached, a more Egyptian-looking type, and the first one said, "He is my cousin; caught the same day."

We all sat together in the grass until about four-thirty, when they went to get back into their lorry to go home.

Then I walked up on to the bridge and gazed down at a young man in a white singlet who was trying to catch fish in a bag of wire-netting on the end of a long stick. He had a large wad of bread and he threw bits of this into the water.

He must have seen my shadow far above him, for he suddenly looked up and smiled shyly and flashingly, wiping it off in a moment. It was a surprise to me — his face I mean — for it was strikingly handsome, not just ordinarily so, but regularly beautiful, the hair springing from it harshly and exuberantly. I wondered if he too was an Italian prisoner.

In old Yalding village I saw my face in a shop window and I became depressed. I wandered into the church and felt suicidal; the whole horror of churchgoing rising up, generation after generation, to confront me. I left and pedalled back furiously (stopping by some boys who were paddling in the water to find live bait) and going on with my letter to Ronald Benge in Italy who has just been awarded the M.C.

On Saturday I went down to the river near East Peckham, and just as I had crossed the wooden bridge where a man was fishing and his woman was watching him, I stood irresolute, wondering which way to go and where to spread my coloured handkerchief for my picnic.

When I turned the corner of the bush I expected to see a bathing party, but instead there was only one youth there lying on his stomach with no clothes on at all, reading the *Reader's Digest*.

He jerked his head up and we confronted each other and smiled spontaneously if rather nervously. With no more ado I plumped down on the ground quite near him and began to unpack my picnic, asking him how warm the water was.

Soon we were talking quite solidly. I learnt that he lived at East Peckham, or rather stayed there at week-ends with his grandmother. In the week he worked up in London at a music publisher's in the Charing Cross Road.

I began to take him in more carefully physically, as he looked rather interesting, quite naked except for a wisp of towel, against the vivid green grass in the violent sunlight. There were no clouds at all. For once a pure azure sky. His skin was very white, not yet sunburnt, his hair very full with blond streaks on top, rounded limbs, not very strongly built but what is known as "shapely". He sat up with cross-legs, rather like Buddha, and I offered him some of my picnic lunch to save him going back to his grandmother's. He gladly accepted so we had cheese and toast there together and treacle and coffee and raisins and cherries (provided by him) and chocolate.

After, we smoked his cigarettes and still went on talking. The sun was burning us now, and my head was beginning to throb, so we went under some trees further down and I took out my proofs and said I ought to try and do some corrections.[26] This lead to talking about books, and from books somehow we got to talking about hospitals, and it all came out that we both knew Dr Easton and liked him.

26 To the proofs of *In Youth is Pleasure*.

We talked about him a lot and our various troubles and times in hospital.

My new friend told me that he had only been to an elementary school, that his father could have sent him to a better school and didn't. I learnt that his mother had died at the beginning of the war and that his father had grown gloomier and gloomier and now lived with his grandmother. He liked his grandmother very much. She was attractive and must have been beautiful. She started on her marriage day with her husband and they only had sixpence between them. They never looked back. They grew things and took them round and sold them. She was wonderful at growing things. They just seemed to come up beautifully and abundantly. Her garden was full of pinks and honeysuckle and roses and fruit. She said that fifty years ago when she was a young woman, she and her husband, when they were cold, would go into the pub and get for twopence each a wonderful whisky toddy with sugar to be crushed up, and boiling water and a slice of lemon. One could have a fine glass of beer for a penny ha'penny.

John James Bloom, for this was the name of my friend, laughed and smiled at this wonderful bargain.

At last I suggested that we might go back to my place and have some tea.

We put on our clothes and pumped up our bicycles and set off. John James told me his grandmother's maiden name was Soult, and he said that it sounded as if it was French.

When we got in he seemed to like my place and stared at things appreciatively. I lay on the bed and watched him as he sat in the armchair. He told me how when he was having his tonsils out in the Cottage Hospital, his mother brought him a cold fried plaice to eat.

He also told me that he bled for a week and they had at last to get a specialist from London to deal with him, as he was about to die. This was the time when Jack Easton was good to him.

After tea we walked in the wood and then we came back and had some beer which was quite strong and rather made my head ache. I was getting ever so slightly tight until Evie brought me hot soup and supper which sobered me.

We went on talking until about ten-fifteen. Then John James said that they would be worrying at home and thinking that he would be struck down by a doodle-bug bomb, so he'd better be going.

I lent him *Maiden Voyage* and bicycled a little way back with him. We agreed to meet again next Saturday by the river in the same place, if nothing prevented either of us.

I wonder if he will be there?

27 June, 6.30 p.m.

Two doodle-bugs have just been shot down, one on each side of the house. They shook it violently, and I saw one of the dark patches of smoke hanging in the air. One is overhead just at this moment.

I was in Oxon Hoath Park this afternoon, eating my lunch in pouring rain and violent wind. Afterwards the sun came out and I dried out, lying at the bottom of an old bomb-hole just in the Alphabetical Avenue.

The lake today was all wildly ruffled and khaki colour. The lake is really called the Banyard which is a corruption of bagnio.

1 *July*

In the path through the barley field by East Peckham sluice gates I found a little flat red stone or piece of glass with the Masonic symbol on it; and I have put it in my pocket for my fortune. Up above, the doodle-bugs are whizzing up to London with the guns banging black puffs in the sky.

Just in the river was a vicious plop, which is a spiked finger of shrapnel diving.

Back now late at this twelve-thirty moment from the King's Arms, Tonbridge, where I have drunk and sung all night; "Trees", "I can't give you anything but love", and oh so many others. And afterwards I walked back with one of my close singers, a soldier called Alwyn, who sleeps in a lorry and has been three years in Gibraltar. We lay in some hay recuperating out of the pelting rain, and we talked, and then a doodle-bug buzzed and guns banged and we got up to go. He was nice and mild and sane, and I was so tight, feeling that it was comfort to have him there like that. He called me "Kid" and wants me to go and sing there again on Wednesday, "really organized", as he says.

I wonder if I shall go? And no sign, no tiniest sign from Eric at Appledore. I thought tonight that it should really have been he who was drinking and singing there.

To see the fat old tipsy woman, dancing the Lambeth Walk with the young gay soldier, who had a look of Eric, not facial somehow, but in the glisten of the eye[27]. So good, so bright, so bristling with life, swamping one into this drink and din, and after years of decay, no joy, no daring, and no glory, only the old [*illegible*].

And in the drink and the closeness of so many other people, my love for Eric seems to have died away. So real a love to die away into love for everyone, for the whole world.

The people in the pub, so many in their early teens. Boys and girls who should be in bed or school. Really children. The whole room seemed to be full of these children. More children than adults.

27 "Gay", one of Denton's favourite adjectives, did not in his time denote "homosexual".

7 July

Yesterday evening, near the Red Cow below Tudeley, I saw a half-naked man standing in the garden of his semi-detached cottage amongst the summer flowers. For some reason it was an arresting sight. He was leaning against the white gate and had a youngish, flat, ugly face. The whole effect was rather bizarre and beautiful and humorous, like a Noah's Ark or a cuckoo clock.

Then when I got home, May came in to read a story to me by old Sir William Geary of Oxon Hoath. It was good in its way — about his life on the Gold Coast. He said of himself in it, "Lecher that I was—".

11 July

Eric is here and with me now and has been since Saturday. All has gone swimmingly and he is staying for a week. The hostel at Appledore was bombed and ruined — one person killed, one badly injured. They were moved to a nearby mansion, and now his friend Peter has left and he feels that he doesn't want to go back to the strange place with no friend, so he wants to stay a week. I was surprised and delighted when he suggested it to me. On Sunday we went over to Chiddingstone Causeway and visited three pubs that Eric used to frequent when he was twenty-one. Many people recognized him at once and welcomed him. He said that he used to spend £5 or £6 a night, that he was hardly ever sober.

We ate our lunch in a Dutch barn because of the pouring rain.

13 September, at 18 Endsleigh Mansions, Leigham Avenue, Streatham, S.W.16[28]

Today I am in bed ill, but yesterday Eric took me to Dulwich Village to see the picture gallery hit by a flying bomb. And we walked down the road by green fields which was the way to his first school, now with all the windows blown out and derelict. He told me of the singing master who reeked of beer; and he told me of his rackety friend Jack who got drunk and strapped a screwdriver to his shin and said he was going to break into a club, and would Eric come too. It all came to nothing.

We sat on a seat looking on to the grounds of Dulwich College and we both smoked the same pipe and then walked back down the road where Eric's house of all his childhood used to be. Now utterly destroyed by 1941 land mine.

It was nearly dark. We walked over the ruins of the house, almost flat, and down the garden path with the vegetables of someone's allotment

28 The home of Eric's mother.

growing on what was once the lawn. And in a curious pine tree I saw a beam and two hooks and I said, "That was your swing?" and Eric nodded.

At the bottom of the garden was still the little tool hut which had been Eric's where he had played and peed out of the door to save going back to the house. And in the evening light the poignancy of this garden of his childhood transformed it.

How tired I was trudging back, thinking of myself and him and childhood and age and everything decaying.

The whole city falling to bits, gradually obtruding its skeleton. The war has made the city and everything grow older with a rush.

And now today Eric showed me a 1933 Sunday paper with his picture in it holding a black-and-white cat and underneath the headline: "Boy risks his life to save cat." He ran up the stairs to his father's burning factory and saw the cat lying there and brought it down.

In the picture a young Eric with diffident face, holding the cat lovingly. Something different, all strange over those years. I had a mourning feeling. To feel that I could never know any of that now.

A letter from Guy from Inveraray Castle where he has been staying with the Duke of Argyll for a month.[29] The lake, the ferry, and pipers round the hall.

On Sunday to Chelsea, where I saw the ruins of the church and Carpmael's studio behind. Nothing left but the ground plan to this favourite place of my childhood. The weeds waving round me and the tiles of the stove.

Eric and I have lived together now since July at Pitt's Folly, at Middle Orchard (Crouch)[30] and now at Streatham. And in some ways it is the strangest thing in my life — to share almost my whole existence like this. I have not even written in my journal, let alone at my book. But I have had to do a picture of an interior for *Vogue*'s Victory Number and have chosen the end of my own room with the baroque angels and the iron table. It will be reproduced in full colour with four other painters' work — Julian Trevelyan, John Armstrong, Francis Rose and Kenneth Rowntree.

They have also asked me to do a "feature" and decorate it myself with drawings. I must think. Blank.

Edith Sitwell sent me her new poems with love. And I took them out with me in the cold sunshine at Middle Orchard and walked down the hill reading them and rejoicing somehow as I have not done since childhood. The happiness and rightness of the morning struck into me. I came to the clear spring and then the factory hidden in the tiny valley. I skirted the

29 The 10th duke, who died in 1949, and to whom Denton was to send a copy of *In Youth is Pleasure*.

30 For the last two weeks of July, while the Adeneys were away, to avoid the worst of the doodle-bugs.

sewage works and climbed up again under the damsons until I came to brilliant stone-heavy plums of magenta colour brushed thickly with steel-blue bloom. I sat down opposite them and read the poems.

My happiness stayed with me for some time.

Now I stop writing because of the fading light. For two months not to have written.

A few days ago I suddenly got a cheque for £7 forwarded by *Horizon* from Hambro's Bank. Nothing else except that it is to the debit of a Swedish Special Account and comes from Stockholm. Could anything be more mysterious! I can't know ever who it is from or what it's for. It is an anonymous present, I suppose, for something I have written.

I have heard too from someone in Australia and from the editress of the *Laundry Record*!

17 September

What shall I write about? Shall I write about the bright morning with the sharp bird notes and the declicious spongy cooings of the pigeons on the roof of this house? Shall I write about the noises of the aeroplanes, the last flower on the wisteria that I can see mauve and pitiable out of my window? Shall I write about the war ending? Or my breakfast of porridge, toast and marmalade and coffee? Or just about autumn. Waking up cold in the morning; coming back cold through the low blanket of mist by the waterfall last night — from the pub on Shipbourne Common, where Eric bought me a thimbleful of cherry brandy for three shillings, and we heard the loudmouthed woman holding forth on cubbing before breakfast.

In this house now[31] — in the big part which Eric and I are sleeping in because Mrs Sloman is away, I have an eighteenth century wooden mantel in my room, taken from an old house. Then there is a china green basin and brass locks with drop handles to the doors. The furniture "limed oak", ugly, and a chinchilla Persian cat is sleeping and grunting and dribbling on my bed. Outside the window a tractor is humming. Eric is having a cold bath, so that the water pipes sing.

19 September, Pitt's Folly big house.

Yesterday Eric and I went to the dentist in Sevenoaks, and while I was sitting in the waiting-room with him, I idly turned the pages of *Vogue* and suddenly came on my own face there in the March issue. Then I went out and bought hair stuff and when I came back Eric was waiting with his tooth pulled out and looking a little strained. We sat in the public gardens — Eric

31 Pitt's Folly.

spitting blood a little into the flower beds. Then we walked up to Aplin's and Eric had only green salad while I had Welsh rarebit and tomatoes and cake, with imitation cream and coffee.

Afterwards we looked at the church, into which I walked all unawares with a lighted cigarette in my mouth. And on into Knole Park, between the two little lodges, towards four dappled fawn-coloured deer with delicate branching antlers. We climbed up towards the wonderful house and it began to rain, so we hid ourselves in a cavity under a fallen tree and lay there snugly with our feet out in the wet. The large beeches dripping round us, our cigarette smoke rising like tiny autumn bonfires.

Afterwards on towards the house where we saw that some windows had been blown in by a bomb and that a few tiles were off, but nothing serious. I wondered if Eddy Sackville-West might be lurking about somewhere, but we saw no one except an old man in pepper-and-salt with a fat spaniel. We walked right round the house, saw the little Gothic cottage and the sham ruins. I felt suddenly I knew it all so well that I longed to live there.

I thought again of our snug place in the leaves under the fallen tree, looking out on to the rising hill with the smoky curtain of rain falling into the stiff still green bracken, and the curious high squeaking of some solitary wood pigeons and then their gurgling coo. An eternal moment always dissolving which will yet re-occur a thousand, thousand times to a thousand, thousand other people when we are dead, who will look out in the same way through the windows in their heads and see the falling rain, the bracken, the pattern of the oak bark, and wonder, and go on wondering for years.

24 September, Pitt's Folly.

Yesterday I was sick and ill all day. So ill that I couldn't eat or think, only lie in pain, waiting for the next wave of sickness to come over me. And Eric looked after me wonderfully, staying with me all day, watching me, making the bed, and putting the cold towels on my face. I thought it would never pass; all life seemed an agony of sickness. But even then it was wonderful to have a friend near you, to help you all he could. The desolation of sickness was lessened somehow. In the night I woke up much better, and I turned the light on and read poetry, with my creeping, hardly recovered eyes; and I looked across at the stripped pine eighteenth-century mantel in front of me, and I thought of all the beautiful rooms I could make in a house of my own. Always with sickness come these reveries.

8 October, 11 a.m.

On Friday was Eric's birthday, and we quickly dressed and got on our bicycles and pedalled through the windy day to Penshurst. Leaves were falling, red apples on the trees, the ponds looking black. The wind made it easy, blowing us there. As we swept down the hill, the village, grouping itself on the rising ground, looked old, arranged, somehow at its best.

The lid flew off one of the picnic tins in Eric's basket, but we didn't stop. We swept on, over the bridge, where a lorry was just backing away from the pub. And then we found ourselves in the yard of the Leicester Arms where we left our bikes near a crate of champagne cider bottles. We went into the outside lavatory and there was written "Down with the Nazi Bastards".

Upstairs in the hotel we sat by the log fire and had gin and beer and Eric took out the silver cigarette case that I had given him, engine-turned, small, but nice. We sat there, smoking from it, banging the cigarettes on the lid, listening to the other conversations.

Francis Streeten's sister, of all people, was there, with what I thought was her other brother. Then her husband Lincoln came in, looking extraordinary in pork pie hat and plus fours. A sort of curate effect enhanced with the walking stick. We studiously avoided looking at each other the whole time.

The lunch gong went and we were left alone by the fire in the bar. I was wearing the corduroy riding breeches Eric had given me, and Wellingtons, with roll neck grey sweater.

After two when the bar closed we went down the private road near Leicester Square and found further on a haystack full in the sun and so warm that we forgot the winter wind. Eric sat there on the straw eating cheese and tomatoes and drinking coffee. Then we lay back, took off our sweaters, and enjoyed the heat.

A farmer came along and said, "You won't smoke there, will you," but he didn't molest us in any way, which struck me as just right and fitting on a good day.

Later we went back to Penshurst Place and walked round it in the wild windswept grass and Eric showed me where he had won the prize for running when he was twenty-one. The house looked utterly blank and dead, because so many of the windows had been smashed by a flying bomb, and boarded up. We couldn't get in at all and so we left it and went into the church, where the windows too were broken, and the wind whistled through the beams, soughing and whining. In the Sidney chapel, the important tombs somehow deserted and not considered any more. A feeling of pastness and dulled memory, no kindling.

We wrote in the visitors' book and then had tea at the Green Tea Rooms, run by two austere sisters, ugly, short, most ungiving! ("You can only have a scone and cake each.")

We drank a lot of tea and then started on the journey home. I left the village, as I always have, with a sort of wistfulness. I like it better than I did when I first saw it.

Up the hill, higher, past huge oaks and two badly bombed houses, on till Leigh, and then the Plough and the Flying Dutchman. Home just as the light had nearly faded. Pink sky, violent autumn orange leaves, wind terrifically against us and the night crawling up.

Then we had chicken here and dark green stuffing and tomato soup and nut-and-jam pastry, then chocolate peppermint creams and coffee dripped from the percolator into the old Nankin teapot.

When we were in bed that night Eric didn't say anything for a few tense minutes, then he brought out, "Thank you, Denton, for the day."

I thought it was a good day too.

Now I have to write a "feature" for *Vogue*, on "Ghosts and Dreams", and do decorations for it too. What am I to do? I wish it would all come in a flash but it won't, and I must begin to evolve something. Always the actual subject before one stimulates and then flummoxes.

In so many ways it is lovely to have Eric living with me here for the winter in this tiny garage cottage with only this one room, but I find myself getting swallowed up only in living with him. It changes all my feelings about work. I want to work so much now. But I haven't yet readapted myself.

11 *October*, 10.00 *a.m.*

Yesterday Eric and I went to the dentist. It was clear and fine, a most beautiful morning, and we bicycled to Tonbridge, left our bikes and went on by bus. Eric had bruised his foot by putting it in the way of an Alsatian which was going after another dog, and so he limped a little.

We sat right in front of the bus and stared at the sights.

We were just in time. I went in and I thought he was the best dentist I had been to. He told me how to brush my teeth and massage my gums, so that I should keep them in good condition.

We left him and had lunch at Aplin's, in the draughty, barnlike, hideously Tudorized room. Welsh rarebit with tomatoes for me, baked fish for Eric, then awful buns and imitation cream and coffee.

Afterwards we wandered round to look at the shops and I bought two Chelsea Derby plates, broken, but beautiful with grey urns, very delicate, and husks and medallions and little butterflies over the faults in the paste. At the back the little golden "Ds" and anchors. Also I bought two Flight and Barr Worcester plates, damaged too, but quite strange and charming, marbilised, with gold key pattern border and in the middle the large grisaille painted crest of a child's head with a snake coiled round its neck. Chelsea Derby, five shillings each, Worcester four shillings.

After looking in the shops we walked right through the town to Eric's uncle's and aunt's in Uplands.[32] A right, tight little house. The uncle

32 Mr and Mrs Harry Barnett.

antagonistic to me and rather rude to Eric, gradually thawing into a bore; the aunt nicer, more sensitive and delicate and gentle. She asked me all about the watercolours on her walls, when she knew that I painted and wrote. And she said about Edith Sitwell's helping me, "It's not surprising at all. Artist's aren't jealous, not if they're big."

I was surprised at this and even at the fact that she knew of Edith Sitwell. The uncle gave one the feeling that he had hidden his head under his arm all his life. After our quiet cheese sandwich, tomato, chocolate cake tea we fled and caught the bus home.

Alone together in the room at night, in stockinged feet, looking at the plates, reading in the china book, listening to the music.

Now Eric has gone over to Noël's to be painted and I am going later, after I have written some of my book.[33]

Letters yesterday from Robin Cornell, four air ones, all saying that he's rather "thrilled to have found you!" Australia has no intellectual life. What does this mean? Professorial people are cold. "They talk about classical philosophy and then want to whip you into bed." (This doesn't sound cold to me at all.)

Also letter from unknown gentleman at Chingford who has bought Gothic flower piece at Leicester Galleries and wants to know more about it. Very queer, meagre letter, paper, writing, etc. I must write very nice, delighted letter back. It made me extraordinarily happy to know I'd sold a picture when the news came at breakfast.

12 October

Raining violently today and Eric has gone to Crouch to do Noël's garden. Yesterday she began to paint him and I went up after having picnic lunch in Oxon Hoath. A horse came up behind me and tried to eat my toast and paper bag. The rain suddenly beat down, and I was reading Dorothy Wordsworth's diary until the page was soaked and almost falling to pieces.

Noël gave me a fine sweater from the Hebrides or some islands. Natural wool, black-grey and white in pattern, very hairy, oily, warm and suits me down to the ground.

After we had come back from Crouch we had to go in to the Slomans next door for coffee. I took my peppermint creams and wore the new sweater, to cause talk to flow.

I have written this morning and this afternoon. I must paint before Eric returns.

---

33 *A Voice Through a Cloud*. Although on 18 October Denton was referring to his third novel as his "new book", perhaps to differentiate from *In Youth is Pleasure*, not yet published, he had begun work on *A Voice Through a Cloud* in January.

18 October

Today I had a letter from Doubleday & Doran asking me to submit my new book to them for publication in America, the New York directors admiring my stories in *Horizon*. Eric and I were sitting up in bed, having breakfast, and we made jokes about earning the rent and ending up with silver-plated Rolls-Royces. The myth of American riches will last for ever in Europe.

Now it is fine clear sun after rain. Eric has gone to get glass for one of my pictures and to do household shopping. I have been writing all morning on my new book — the part where I sit up in the wheel-chair with the red blanket over my knees, in the sun, in the hospital common-room.

26 October, 3.35 p.m.

Day before yesterday Eric and I went to London to take pictures to the Leicester Gallery, to buy green and red-brown pyjamas at Swan and Edgar's and to show my portrait of Julian Goodman to her.[34]

It was a year since I had been to her last with the picture of her pug. When I got to Ottoline Morrell's red door in Gower Street I saw that the windows were smashed and boarded. I rang twice, then knocked, and at last Julian came to the door dressed in green, attractive, high-coloured, with new shoes on. We went quickly into the hall and I saw that the house was quickly becoming a slum. John drawing, Condor lithographs, old tortoiseshell cabinets, and the chipped paint, torn curtains, grime of war-time London.

Julian took me into what had been the dining room and told me that they were living in that room only, the others uninhabitable through smashed panes.

We talked brightly and nervously and Audrey Lucas who was staying came in. I undid the picture and we all made remarks. I had made brown eyes when Julian's were grey-blue. Audrey Lucas said *Maiden Voyage* was a lovely book, and although she had been prejudiced and would not read it, a friend won her round by shouting passages of it from the top of the house, until she had to get it for herself.

We had tea, white modern china, big cake, small cakes which I couldn't get my hands on. Too much sugar in my tea. Nervous smiling, talking about Julian's son's first term at Eton and the other little one's unhappiness at his school. The pug there on the floor, looking awfully like my picture of him. The great drooling, weeping eyes rolling.

Audrey Lucas left and went down to the basement to wash Murray

---

34 A three-quarter length painting from photographs, for which he was never paid. Its present whereabouts are not known.

Maclaren's socks — he also staying there — and so Julian and I were alone. She showed me the silver gilt very pretty eighteenth-century continental snuff box, big enough for cigarettes, that she had found in the bank; and I wished she would have the sense or the generosity to give me this in exchange for my picture of her, but I suppose she won't.

We went on talking about school and her children and I felt silly and a little bored — not as good as last year. I was not feeling so well, rather ill really, and she seemed shallower, more metallic, more only wishing-she-was-interested-in-the-arts.

She began to tell me about the boys, fifteen and sixteen, who broke into the house after the doodle-bug had broken all the windows, and lived there for two or three days. They left their filthy shirts and trails of burnt matches wherever they went. They had only just come out of an institution. They broke an ebony cabinet to pieces because they found a letter saying that it had a secret drawer. They also took some little trinkets and a suitcase full of silver, but when they found it was covered with crests they left it just by the Queen's Hall, and by great good luck a policeman picked it up. So after two months of waiting to be claimed, Julian's family silver was returned to her in this strange way.

Julian also told me how her mother's lapis-lazuli watch was stolen off her wrist in the train, by a man who helped her and her Belgian maid out with her luggage.

Somehow the whole meeting was a little wrong and dislocated. We wandered upstairs to look at the damage in the library and at the wonderful, faded yellow Chinese silk of the curtains. Julian wanted to bring them down as nearly all the others were in rags.

In Murray Maclaren's bedroom the leg of the old French harewood commode off, supported by a pile of books, the paintwork dingy and cracked as transparent as dragonflies' wings, the bedspread Julian's grandmother embroidered in 1890. Everywhere a mixture of squalor and interesting or beautiful objects.

I started to leave and Julian asked me to a party on Thursday with two bottles of gin and three of wine. Only eight people because of the small room, but I could not go.

When the doodle-bugs began, Julian had gone down to the country with an Augustus John under each arm, which she hopes are worth £1,000 apiece. A little bit of dust sheet stuck to the portrait of her mother and pulled a piece of paint off. Small and insignificant, Julian thinks.

I still thought about the old silver gilt snuff box and decided that I should like it really very much.

Yesterday I had to go to the dentist in Sevenoaks, and after quite a nice time with him, Eric and I went into the churchyard and jumped over the cemetery wall and sat in the grass by the side of the public footpath to have our picnic lunch.

There were cows in the field opposite, in the misty atmosphere, and beyond on the opposite hill Tudorized houses lost in the soft mist. We ate cheese, fruit cake, biscuits, toast, drank coffee and I ate the only orange in pigs.

Then we smoked the Dunhill cigarettes that I had bought, and an old lady came behind us and said over the fence, "Excuse me, but would you like any boiling water? Can I get you any boiling water?" I told her we had just drunk our thermos of coffee and she went away immediately to her house saying, "I see, quite, quite."

After lunch we got on the bus to Westerham and there we wandered about in the church and then sat down in the pew near the offertory box and were quite still for a little because we were tired.

The stillness, the extraordinary gloom of an empty church, sank into me. I thought that I would remember sitting there for years to come. I leant on Eric's shoulder because of my back and then we went out, him still supporting me and humming gently.

We walked through the grave-stones down to Wolfe's house, but it was shut, so we climbed back, passed Army and Air Force in their billets, waiting for tea with mug and plate.

We walked right through the town, looked at the antique shop and then at a watercress stream. Then we had tea at Pitt's Cottage, on a William Morris mortifying sofa round a corner, so that we looked at nothing but packing cases of cooking fat.

A big tea was brought of scones and home-made bread and cakes and jam. Eric ate scones, I ate a cake, then we smoked and Eric went a little to sleep and I read bits of Kilvert's Diary that I had brought in my satchel. It was nice there, hidden. I heard a couple come in, a drawling, thin, delicate man's voice, a more practical woman's. I amused myself by guessing the appearance of the two human beings. I had an academic middle-thirties body for the man and a rather doggy country lady for the woman's, but when I got up to pay the bill, I found the man to be a boy of about nineteen, the woman to be perhaps a schoolmistress — all wrong, although strangely enough the face of the boy was much better and *not* much worse than the one I had reconstructed for the voice.

We came back gently on the bus and all went well; but the night was bad and today I am ill with headache in bed and Eric has gone to be painted.

I had this morning the most extraordinary letter from someone in Sheffield who has written to me before about my book and story in *Horizon*. It can only be described as a very uncomfortable love letter, and I am wondering what on earth to reply. Very difficult. Perhaps not reply, though this seems mean. Also, on Tuesday, I had a letter from King's, Cambridge — would I go and talk to them on "Contemporary Literature"!! Delightful if I could be persuaded. What would I feel like, talking to and looking at the undergraduates? Imagination falters. They say nothing about lodging me or anything of that sort. Do they ever get any writers to go, I wonder?

I am painting a new picture, which I have done first of all in pencil outline, carefully then with turpentine to darken and strengthen the line. Now I put on, rub on, colour very gingerly, very little. The board is whitened and rubbed down so that the mahogany shows a little in places. Now I think that in some ways I have found the technique for my painting, direct, simple, permanent and utterly unlike what is usually understood as oil painting.

9 November, 8.30 a.m.

In the morning now, with Eric in the bed by the window and the red sky over him. Yellow leaves, wind, me in a nasty state of mind, bad-tempered, snapping. The clock ticking. I must go to the dentist this afternoon. [*Illegible sentence.*] The cat on the kitchen window-sill trying to get in, encouraged by Evie against all injunctions.

Eric being silent, not accusing me, except by silence, of being unbearable to live with.

With what a knocking and banging I got the early morning tea, trying to make everyone feel guilty.

Then away to the dentist's after working quite well at the first part of the Broadstairs bit in my book, when I was taken to the nursing home.

The dentist pulled my left upper wisdom tooth out, the first tooth I have ever had pulled out. He said wisdom teeth that are not sound are better away, and that it was pushing my teeth together. I felt the crunch, the sort of dragging, and the sight of the tongs was grim. The way he pushed on one's forehead too. He talked about Switzerland and the Count and Countess Vogue at Schiedegg.

Afterwards we went to the antique shop and paid for my two Flight & Barr Worcester plates and the antique man seemed to take a fancy to Eric and sold us a slightly cracked Nankin cup for two shillings, which is just what we wanted, as Eric broke his the night before last.

We went on by bus to Westerham again and saw Wolfe's house; the white-panelled living-room with Tudor mantel and eighteenth-century basket gate with blue Dutch tiles surround — pretty. The old maid in blue with white apron was rather nostalgic and pleasant too — gentle, soft-spoken. We saw the relics, but could not look over more than the hall, the two front rooms and the staircase. Disappointing.

We walked on up the hill and down to Pitt's Cottage again where we had tea in a crowded room, this time with a large party of officers, some in Tartan trews, at one table. They were furtive and repressed, terrified of shaming themselves in each other's eyes. It was painful to watch. It reminded me so much of school. No ease, or grace or enjoyment, only anxiety.

We looked out of the window and saw three swans flying high in the sunset sky, their white bodies not silvered as I hoped they might be. They looked flying to the other side of the earth; they were so remote, so ageless and so ancient.

Later when we left the cottage after chocolate cake and scones, we saw them, mild, tame, ornamental on a pond with rushes — quite different birds.

And I thought of the young waitress with two spots near her mouth, and the extraordinary walk, a sort of roll of the hips and a hobble, and her impudent answers to the owner of the tea-shop.

On the bus coming back in the dark, in the front, close to the pane of glass, I felt that I was in a great eye which was rushing forward, eating up the landscape as it went.

Now this morning, 10th November, I hear that my book *Maiden Voyage* has been taken by Fischer in America and will with luck be printed early in 1945. Ragg at Routledge points out what a small and select list they have.[35] It is interesting to learn the language of publishers. I never realized that there was as much exclusiveness as there is with dressmakers.

Marcus also writes that John Hesketh in India has been staying at Vice-Regal Lodge, Delhi and that it has caused a slight flutter there.[36] I wonder in which part.

30 November, 6.10 p.m.

It is night now; Eric is sleeping on the bed. I have been tearing up letters and making a mount for one of my pictures.

The gas fire gently burns. Outside the moon is rising.

I was ill in bed for a week till today; then I went out and walked under the trees in the wood, past the black pools, the rushes, the banks, violent with moss. I have grown a beard in bed, which I have kept. I think it looks nice and it is so natural and easy. It quite changes me, makes me look from another age.

Collins sent me *English Story*, with my own story in it, mixed up with Elizabeth Bowen, Rex Warner, Henry Treece.[37] I suddenly began to read it with great interest, liking some bits — other bits not. Usually I am overcome with shame when I see something of mine in print, and never dare look at it. Even someone else reading something of mine in my presence fills me with horror.

---

35 Murray Ragg, joint managing director.
36 At St Michael's, Uckfield with Denton. He appears as Alec Gale in "Evergreen Seaton-Leverett", published posthumously in *Orpheus 2* in 1949, and reprinted in *A Last Sheaf*.
37 "At Sea" (see 1942, note 47 above).

I had an air letter from an Aircraftman Parker in India, who apparently read *Maiden Voyage* and then started to track all my other work, writing and painting, just as Symons tracked Corvo in his book *The Quest for Corvo*.

This Parker has been amazingly persevering and has almost found out everything there is to know about my published things, even down to little poems in queer magazines!

He has been undertaking the search with another friend. And everything they found about me, they put into a book labelled "Denton Welch — His Book".

Now he wants to buy a picture to round off his search! He wrote to the Leger, the Leicester, the Redfern. And the Redfern forwarded his letter to me.

Isn't it crazy! I wonder if he will have the determination to do anything like it again! He might do some quite interesting research on a dead and gone obscure author.

It made me feel, when I heard of it, as if I had been preserving myself on a top shelf for years, waiting to be discovered. As if I were dead and done with, and watching some future person ferreting me out.

The moon shone through the Gothic window on my face. It had nothing to tell but stillness, dead wonder, magic that changes everything from heat and fear to the silver of a snail's forgotten trail.

When Eric was away and I lay in bed so still with books, my thoughts, the pretty things I have collected, I thought that all I really wanted was to be alone, to think and to dream in a daze about work I shall do. But now that he is asleep on the bed, I find I can still think and dream, and I even feel better physically because someone is there if I should not feel well.

There is always this question with me, to be alone or not. Really, to be alone is my nature. If it were not so, I would not have been alone as much as I have.

Is reverie really what people live for, and do they just do things to feed their reverie?

4 December

It seems that I have nothing this morning to give or say. There is a white frost. We are going to Trottiscliffe. I don't feel as well as I did when I woke up. It is sunny.

11 December, 12.10 p.m. Middle Orchard, Crouch, nr. Boro' Green.

I never got to Trottiscliffe last Tuesday. Eric and I climbed up the hill and came to rest here before going on, and I flopped down on the couch in the drawing-room and rapidly developed a high temperature. Eric made the fire, wrapped me in an eiderdown and I lay there hour after hour, until it was dark. Then we finally decided that we should have to stay the night. It was frosty, moon-lit. The window was thrown open, the fire blazed up the chimney. Eric lay down on the mattress on the studio floor, and we tried to sleep. But my fever made me talk and wake up with strange imaginings. I thought someone was getting through the window. I imagined that bombs or rockets would land on the house, for two exploded fairly near. A light was in the window of Mrs Archdale's till well after midnight, which made me wonder. The moon flooded in and I thought it was the dawn, and then, when it wasn't, grew terribly dissappointed. Everything ached. Eric came in to tuck the clothes round me and make up the fire.

At last the awful night was over, and we waited for Noël and Bernard to return from London. They didn't come till late Wednesday evening. I was still on the couch in a fever, unable to bike back. So I was put to bed in Charlotte's room, facing east, with a balcony and two windows and a bookshelf running by the wall, and I've been there ever since; the electric fire playing on me, reading Henry James's In the Cage and bits of several other things, doing nothing, half enjoying it, broken in on all the time by people from outside.

My beard grows neater and smoother.

My meals have come up served in little pieces of old china, mandarin cups, and a little gold and green Derby cup with puce mark that I gave Noël. One fluted blue and gold late eighteenth-century tea dish suddenly snapped into two almost perfect halves just as Eric poured the coffee into it. It was an extraordinary, rather supernatural sight.

And my thoughts here, locked away, disconnected, floating — they have been pleasant-unpleasant, peaceful-anxious, bright-gloomy, unfruitful.

Last night, when I got up for the first time, we were sitting by the fire after I had been trying to play a Mozart Romance, when we heard a buzzing overhead. We went out into the freezing orchard and saw a fiery ball in the sky, slowly descending like a basket or a balloon. It moved down through the sky jerkily, the light sometimes nearly going out, the engine uncertain. Then it cut out, the light was downed and we knew it was going to land for certain. We waited, standing about, turning our eyes away from the glass. There was a slight flare up when it touched the ground, then blackness and a loud explosion which sucked away the air and made one feel buffeted.

We all thought it was something new, and imagined that more were coming, but none did.

We made it an excuse for waiting up, though, till after one-thirty.

Eric does so much of the work here, making the fires, making the breakfast, washing up, sawing wood. I've never known anyone so willing to take on the work like this. It makes me think of Cinderella.

Evie suddenly appeared yesterday for tea. She had biked over from Pitt's Folly Cottage, full of life. She brought a cheque from C.E.M.A. for the hire of one of my pictures, and she recited the queer poem she had written about me.

Noël told me that I sometimes say just what is in my mind after I have said some politeness that completely clashes with it. Several times she has caught me doing this and I am unconscious of what I have done.

When she asked me if I'd stay here a day or two more and try to do a little work, I was very polite, and then I added: "I'll see if I can stand it"!!

Eric says I asked John Bloom interestedly all about his life in London, then turned away and said, "Oh, I wish you'd go." Does this sort of double conversation grow on one? If so, I shall soon be a very strange companion indeed.

The light this morning was so thick, dark and heavy that it seemed as if a great pall of snow was hanging over the world, but it wasn't even rain. It might have been a fog from the Midlands, it was so yellow.

The laziness that creeps over me in a strange environment is like an animal that ought to be fought, but is just looked at and then turned away from. I have been wondering too all about my health, how much of the rest of my life is going to be lived lolling about, waiting to feel well enough to do something. And I think I cannot have a great deal of time to do anything and that even if I do not write in my diary, I shall regret it.

Is it in Montaigne that I have just read that the way to know what to write about is to think of all the things you wish writers in the past had mentioned? I wish that people should mention the tiny things of their lives that give them pleasure or fear or wonder. I would like to hear the details of their houses, their meals and their possessions. I would like to hear the bits of family or intimate history they know.

18 December, 12.10 p.m.

On Saturday came John Butler from Cambridge, tall, skinny, bearded, smelling of scent, too stupid to be interested in life — everything I dislike mentally and physically. We sat through lunch — me in my cassock offering him rice, sardines and raisins with hard-boiled egg, he with his legs cocked up, his hands drooping and twisting. Tiresome is the only word for it all.

Then, the night before, an Eton boy, Robin Hamilton, came in with his poems all based on Hiawatha. He was rather nice in spite of them, and talked about mountains, Scotland, castles with curses, and sleeping in tents on moors.

27 December

On Christmas Day Eric and I were alone here. I got up for the first time and we walked in the sunshine in the frosty wood. All the ground was white. Then we came back and it was late and we sat down at the conservatory table and had the chicken and soup and plum-pudding. We lit the pudding with brandy Eric had brought from London; and then May came in and sat down on us. It was getting dark by the time we had finished our lunch, we had it so late.

I remembered last year when I waited and waited by the window, and no Eric appeared till about three o'clock and then he was drunk.

Now I am all alone here in the afternoon, with freezing mist outside, and nothing in me.

29 December

A cake in tiers, made as for a wedding, but iced in black, with crying cupids at the corners by the fluted black columns, and gold ivy leaves on it. Skulls in black sugar wreathed with gold laurels.

31 December

Sir William Geary is dead, so I wonder what will happen to Oxon Hoath. Eric said in the moonlight it was wonderful the other night — with a horse moving soundlessly over the grass and the lake reflected. In the Cedar Avenue he smelt a strange smell, and he looked up at the gate pillars and thought of Sir William all his life walking between them from a little child to old age.

All still in the moonlight, stifled, spun into a glass picture.

Now we are by the gas fire here on New Year's Eve — Eric sleeping on the bed, me writing my book, trying to pick my own brains.

All the years are too short — over before they have lost their newness. Nineteen-forty-four still has a novel flavour, but it is going into the grave.

This year has taken a stranger turn than any I expected. If someone had told me at the beginning that I would share everything before it was out, I would never have believed it.

It had seemed something so impossible for my temperament that I would have laughed.

In my wall is the mouse that scratches and dances. It seems as immortal as we are, and it is all a painted lie. No mouse or man after a hundred years — no cottage in the trees — only the earth, the water, the dripping woods and the low sky for ever.

I will hardly look at the back pages of this diary for fear of boredom, pain, dislike.

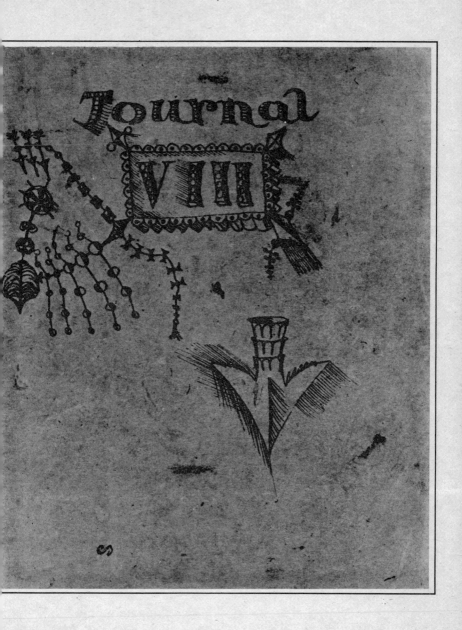

1945

4 January

BEFORE midnight on New Year's Eve we drank punch made of tea, lemon, ginger, marmalade, syrup, boiling water, and we ate almonds and chocolate. Evie sat there too.

Then on New Year's Day, after writing in the morning, Eric and I went to Tunbridge Wells on the bus. The sun half went in and mist came and it was cold. I hid my beard in my two scarves, blue and yellow. There were hilarious soldiers in the bus and very young girls, making a joke each time they opened their mouths.

Eric and I sat right in front, looking out of the windows. It was the first time I had been out for a month.

In Tunbridge Wells we got off at the Opera House and walked back down the mean streets to Mrs Heasman's junk shop, but when we opened the door and went in we found women all pulling out old clothes and pieces of flannel, and there was such a smell from the kitchen and the clothes and the women, and I remembered that Mrs Heasman had been in hospital to have her breast cut off, that we hastily backed out, saying that we would come back later. It was a pity because I saw a little blue Nankin tea-caddy with its own little stopper, and a Nankin bowl and cover, rather delicate and gilded, but I think broken.

We walked on down the town to Rosemary's old shop, but it was shut, so we could buy no nice biscuits.

Further down still we left my manuscript at Webb's to be typed. Then we ran into Peggy Mundy Castle and Rosemary. Our noses were all red and we did not like to look at each other. We were rather hearty and Eric touched Rose's shoulder and said, "We are just about to go into a shop and buy a fur-lined French letter."

She pretended not to like the remark at all.

Then we left them and I saw a Georgian teapot I wanted but I would not go in to ask the price.

We went down behind King Charles the Martyr's Church and looked at the books. Then we went on to the Pantiles and climbed down the steps to where the spring water comes out into a brown bowl. Eric swivelled out the iron cup on its heavy chain, and then drank cup after cup. I had some too but kept thinking that it tasted of iron, because of the rusted cup.

A small child came and watched us. He seemed intrigued with Eric, staring at his thrown back head and at his coloured belt. Eric hit his chest and said: "Ah!" as if the water were too delicious. The child gaped, and then

179

Eric pouted out his lips, making an amusing face for the child.

I shrieked with laughter; the child smiled uncertainly. His older sister called him urgently, but he would not turn away. Then she began to smile too, and we were all smiling like madmen.

We walked to the end of the Pantiles, over the flags which were covered with a layer of ice, and had tea at Binn's.

I imagined that my beard made the waitresses laugh. The gas fire was hot. Eric had tea-cake, dripping, and I had chocolate cake. We filled ourselves up with hot tea; and the light was beginning to fail outside.

I thought that in a lonely life with no jaunts in pairs, everything looked different. Tea shops were different places, shops were changed, the whole street was alien.

Sometimes one loved the alone life in a town, but only for moments. There were always other moments, which could never properly be enjoyed alone.

And I thought how many times I had sat in tea-shops and restaurants alone, listening to others talking, watching them fitting into their lives, then watching them walk out of the door and away for ever.

Yesterday we had Ted Nichols, friend of an unknown fan who wrote to me from Australia, to lunch.

We tidied and polished, because the place was completely tousled. Evie made lunch early and hot punch again and he came soon after eleven.

We watched him from the window — tallish, fair crinkled hair, brown freckled face that looked almost powered, funny dull blue eyes and smiling mouth.

Likeable but pointless, I felt. Too easy to get on with, with fat Passing Cloud cigarettes in his chromium case.

He showed us pictures of Robin Cornell (the fan) and others in strong Australian light. All without any complications, flat and straightforward.

He drank the punch, smiled, laughed, raised his eyebrows.

We had tomato soup for lunch, egg and celery pie, melba toast and mince pie. I poured out light ale for him and watched the bubbles rising.

He talked about Robert Helpmann and his sister. I was finding it all rather an effort.

Those good-natured people whose eyes take nothing in and rove continually. They are almost insulting.

Mrs Sloman came in afterwards and talked on the bed about Australia. Then we all went down the drive and put him on his bus.

I left them at the gates and went into May's garden to search in her hut for any bits of china I had left there.

I came away with a riveted Wedgwood Queen's Roare dish, painted with bearded barley, a broken Sèvres cup, rose Dubarry, and a riveted milk jug with pretty sprigs.

They seemed to have so much weight and sense about them after Ted Nichols.

8 January, 5.20 pm. Grey half-light.

My life is a great unfoldment with many marvellous things about it. I would not have thought that I would be damaged and ill so soon (twenty) or that so comparatively late (twenty-eight and a half) I should find someone with whom I could live in almost complete peace. All of life before that had seemed quite necessarily a solitary affair — and so it still is, but with an utterly different quality of solitude.

In my heart are hung two extraordinary pictures: one is called "Accident and Illness" and the other, exactly opposite, tilted forward as if to meet it, is called "Love and Friendship".

Now they play Bach concerto (for harpischord, but on a piano wonderfully) on the wireless, and the gas fire, with steel blue and orange flame, roars. Down the windows dribble long tears of condensation. The birds are snapping and creaking out their calls before bed.

13 January

Eric, when he was on Gover Hill the other night in the snow, thought, "What if I felt a warm drop on my hand and looking up saw, hanging in the bare trees, ragged corpses waving and dripping blood."

And he thought before Christmas as he walked through London at three o'clock in the morning of all the ghosts there must be — the people who have been burnt to death — crowding out of the bombed houses to walk beside him until he was in the middle of an army of ten thousand people.

21 January, 7.10 p.m.

I think of it — there in the dining room at Croom's Hill eleven years ago — sitting with Charles Lamb's essays on the table, drinking the tomato soup, crumbling the brown toast, gazing out of the window at the children in the park, wondering what will happen next, thinking, scheming.

And the old eighteenth-century room with everything just thicker, wider, more generous than absolutely necessary, seemed to hold me within its walls as if I were valuable, worth taking care of.

Over the wide floorboards my light rubber shoes would move, leaving faintly dulled marks. I would sit on alone with the perfect book, feeling the warmth of my smooth stomach separate itself from my shirt and my navy sweater as I draw in deep breaths.

And in the winter the fire would snap and I would long for the perfect friend who I knew could never exist. (For in those days even the possibility of a day-to-day friendship seemed utterly remote.) I lived young, alone, secret in my room or at the Art School, walking over the dark heath at night, staring down at London and the puce glow it made in the sky.

The river sirens hooted, the trams far away sparked and rocked down to Woolwich. I was lost in my own world, with no one to speak to. Then when I came home and fell down on the bed, covered with the brilliant wreck of my grandmother's Kashmir shawl, I would almost groan to think that nothing had come out of me that day, only the ghost of an effort to be great.

24 January, 8.35 p.m.

This evening as I walked along the Hadlow Road towards Maidstone a little way, with the snow all about me on fields and twigs and branches and hard on the road, and with a mist creeping over everything, I heard a soft whirring and then the blur of two lights. And as I stood at the side in the deep snow to see what passed, a pedimented bonnet like the Parthenon loomed out of the mist and I knew a Rolls Royce was come. Then it passed me, a fine old hearse, high slung, with bevelled windows, empty, the two men sitting in the front.

The hearse without a coffin sailed by almost silently. The hush of the snow and the make of its engine were in league with silence. I looked after it, then walked on, saying to myself, "The Muffled Hearse."

26 March, 7 o'clock p.m.

For the last few weeks I have been mending the mid-eighteenth century dolls' house (which Mrs Bosanquet of Seal handed over to me in 1941). It has been in her mother's family (Littledale of Yorkshire) since it was made. Mrs B said glibly, "I suppose it was made by the estate carpenter."

I first saw it in B's cellar on a winter afternoon. She said, "Here's something that might interest you, Denton," and shined a torch into a grey oblong box, amazingly dilapidated, on a stand. There were windows out in it, but I hardly would have believed that it was old, until she opened the doors and showed me the charming mantelpiece in each room, every one subtly different, with perfect mouldings. Then I saw that the tiny doors were two-panelled and that each room was wainscoted halfway up, just as eighteenth-century rooms should be.

But it was all daubed and coated with so much thick paint and there were so many sordid remains of Edwardian dolls' furniture, together with moth-eaten curtains and pieces of felt, that it had clearly become something to be avoided and forgotten.

Soon after this B said that the cellar was to be turned into an air-raid shelter for the village, and she didn't know what she would do with the dolls' house — she had no room. I volunteered boldly to look after it for her, and she was obviously pleased.

Then I waited for what seemed like a fortnight for it to be delivered at the Hop Garden (where I then was) by the carrier.

At last it arrived one morning when I was still in bed, having written *Maiden Voyage* for several hours. My head and eyes were tired, and I was almost trembling with excitement as the men climbed up the outside staircase with it and plumped it down in the middle of the studio. In my pyjamas I began to poke and peer and examine it.

First I tore away all the repulsive curtains and carpets which had been nailed on. The moths' eggs were as thick as a fish roe and the dust was like bat's fur. Gradually I emptied every room (dining, drawing, bed and kitchen). There were only two bits of Georgian furniture left. A charming dark mahogany Pembroke table with one flap, and two tapering legs missing, and a little chest, also very dark mahogany, but quite plain, with little brass knobs. I forgot the little oak stool for the kitchen. There was a tiny, perfect old brass saucepan, two good little pewter platters and some little Victorian dish covers.

The rest was muck, except perhaps for the curious little chair and chiffonier, perhaps 1880-90.

When I had stripped the rooms I saw how coated with ugly pink and green paint each delicate moulding was. Even the floors were painted pink and green. (Perhaps by some child with two pots of bright enamel.)

In the bedroom were two delightful cupboards, one on each side of the mantel, and they had been fixed with brutal brass hinges (the old leather ones having perished).

Nothing was left, scarcely, of the banisters. The classical pediment that went over the arched central window of the house was luckily in one of the drawers of the stand.

I saw now that this stand was also old and part of the original piece. It had straight little Chippendale legs and one old brass drop handle; the other missing one was replaced by a brown china knob.

As I looked closer at the body of the dolls' house, I saw that under the grim unfeeling coat of battleship-grey was a lighter fawn paint, and on this paint were the signs of bricks painted in black.

This excited me and I began to scrape. I soon found that under the fawn bricks were two other coats of yellower, bigger bricks with white outlines, and that right at the bottom the original coat was tiny red bricks. I longed to get down to this first coat, but it was impossible without ruining it in the process, so I contented myself with the first beige bricks, which by the texture and withered quality of the paint seemed to date from at least the early nineteenth century.

With a lot of work I gradually scraped nearly all the front and also the inside. It took months and covered everything with dust.

Inside I found that every room had originally been wall-papered with different pattened papers. There were fragments left in the hall (where I actually uncovered some delightful sprig, a sort of stiff tulip); also in the drawing-room, but these I did not uncover, as there was too little left.

Under the top thick green and pink daub, each room was well painted with a different colour (drawing, pink; dining, white; bed, blue; and kitchen, white and ochre).

I painfully scraped down to these, strippped the floor to its original plain wood, and found that the doors were meant to be bare mahogany and white surrounds.

When I had done all this laborious work, we had the fire at the Hop Garden and had to leave. The dolls' house in its fragmentary condition went with me to Pond Farm.[1] There I did more scraping and longed all the time to get a good carpenter to mend, and make missing bits. I saw one man who might have done it, but it fell through.

Earlier I had discovered that the draws of the stand, under thick chocolate paint, were decorated with a Chinese Chippendale fret design in ochre and white, very pretty but quite ruined by age and stripping. I carefully ruled out the shape of it, then painted nearly all of it in to preserve it.

I then got from May odd pieces of old brass handles, and made one composite one that more or less matched the original. This seemed an enormous advance.

Then came the awful stupid scenes and troubles before I left Pond Farm; and again the dolls' house had to go, this time to May's outhouse-studio where it was stored from 1942 till last month, when I suddenly had a passion for it again, unaccountable, unless it was just looking at it in its ruined condition and seeing again how lovely it could be.

And with May's tools I started on it, never having done any carpentry since the age of eleven.

I mended the stand fairly well, then one of the big doors, which was in three pieces. Gradually I turned to more intricate things, making the missing tapered legs of the Pembroke table, supplying two missing window-sills, the front door steps and the pediment and tops of the columns. The fanlight I made all of matches and putty, and it was good.

Then I did more stripping. The top landing to dark blue (the first and original coat) with white mouldings, and the wainscoting in all the rooms. I made little leather hinges, just like the originals, for the doors, and I began on the staircase, doing the chief newel posts in cedar, attempting to match the three originals left. The rest is still to do.

I have now nearly made one of the two chimneys and am about to begin

1 At East Peckham, where Denton was loaned two rooms for the first five months of 1942 after the Hop Garden had been destroyed by fire.

on the balustrade, which runs along the top of the house, linking up the pediment above the deep cornice.

Today Eric and I have been in to Tonbridge, where we found two awful Turkish brackets, with *exactly* the right balustrading on them, and two over the right number that I need. Measurement and shape could not have been more exact, if they had been made.

The woman said that the brackets were £3 the pair, but luckily it was a mistake and I got them both for £1. Tomorrow I am going to dismember them and put the balustrade on the dolls' house.

Nothing will look grander than the dolls' house, with its perfect classical door, window proportions, heavy Palladian coigning, cornice, and then the pediment and the reconstructed balustrade, all standing on the stand with its fret pattern revived.

All these weeks I have been doing it every afternoon (after writing) in May's garden. One has the feeling that slowly the house is coming to life again.

30 March

Well, yesterday was my birthday, and it seemed almost a festival. Eric gave me a charming, solid seal-top spoon (which I am going to drink my soup with), a little apostle spoon, and a tiny bottle of Benedictine, with all its labels on. Evie had made a cake for me, all Simnel, and also gave me a broken old cup, with scarlet and black flowers on it.

We started the day, loafing and laughing and bathing, slowly; then we went down to May's garden and had a picnic in the sun. Hard-boiled eggs, nut meat, cheese, pineapple jam, Ryvita, chocolate biscuits and coffee. Then cigarettes and an old cigar broken up and smoked in Eric's pipe.

Afterwards Eric gardened a little, and I fixed a moulding on to the dolls' house chimney and repainted the lost fret pattern on one of the drawers. When we had finished we got on our bikes and I went some of the way with Eric, who was going to Crouch for milk.

We parted at Stallion's Green. I came back, skirting Oxon Hoath, then through Hadlow.

When I got in I started to do one of the sashes to the dolls' house windows. Then Eve brought me a first pot of tea and some cinnamon buns. I ate and drank and she read me letters of Gaudier-Brzeska.

When Eric returned, we made more tea and brought up the birthday cake. He had also brought a cake from Noël, orange inside, white and pink dots and "D" outside.

And another parcel, which I began to unpack. There was a fret-saw, lots of wood mouldings, glue, a vice (all for my dolls' house), a block of De Brie orange chocolate, and then a little silky white-wood box, in which were the tiniest Bristol glasses you have ever seen. They must be late Georgian or early Victorian. There are four clear tall champagne glasses, two bulging wine glasses on stems, three beakers, one dark blue, two dark purple, four little white cups and saucers, a perfect jug and cover, a damaged one, and a fruit dish and plate. Even the champagne glasses are less than an inch high.

We all sat down to tea. I arranged the tiny glasses on the miniature Pembroke table, which I'd mended, and we were all busily admiring them, when May suddenly appeared, bringing rhubarb. She didn't know it was my birthday, but she had to be told, with all the cakes about. Then in the middle of all this, Mrs Sloman sent me two bars of chocolate, decorated with a coral Pyrus japonica flower. My aunt had sent me £1. I felt flooded.

Later, after supper, Eric made black coffee. We lit the candles in the glass lustres, had Turkish cigarettes and opened the Dom. We had thimblefuls each and dipped the mouth ends of our cigs into the honey liquid, because Eric had seen fat Americans do that on the films. The sweetness trickled down me and I felt satisfied.

9 April

I have said nothing about *In Youth is Pleasure*, and it has been out since 22 February (I think). So far everything is so much better than I thought it might be. Good reviews, except for Kate O'Brien in the *Spectator*, and quite long ones and lots. It was all sold out before publication, so now they are bringing it out again.

Even Charles Terrot[2], who is made use of in it, has written a smooth letter; and Lord Berners wrote to say that it had caused a sensation in his house. I have had other butter letters too from unknowns and one anonymous one congratulating me on resurrecting the scum and sewage novel of the twenties.

19 April

Yesterday Eric and I decided to go and see Chiddinghurst, the house where he first did farming in 1936, when he was twenty-one.

We took a picnic and started, after I had written letters. It was hot with a delicate breeze.

By Hilden Manor we met Phyl Ford who gave us two delicious lemon scones which we tasted later at lunch. Then we turned off by the Flying Dutchman and along the road by the Old Barn. I remembered, as always, the first time I went there with Bill in his Bugatti, when I was twelve and he was an undergraduate[3]. We tore through the roads and lanes silently, had a

2 At St Michael's, Uckfield, with Denton. He appears as Guy Winkle.
3 Denton's eldest brother, William, who was an undergraduate at Hertford College, Oxford.

neurotic tea there and then I was torn back to school again and left, while Bill sped away discontentedly in the snorting blue car.

Just by the Old Barn Eric and I quarrelled, because he wanted to take his yellow shirt off and I said that people would stare if he went along half naked on the road. Eric said, "What does it matter if they do?" and took his shirt off, so I bicycled on and we continued separated in this way for some time. We passed through Leigh. The village dominated so completely by the big house, that one can never get away from the parti-coloured brickwork of the wall, the gate, and the fanciful little estate cottages. By the church, with the avenue of poplars, the gate house and the gate, I suddenly saw the conception of the Victorian architect — his vision of grandeur, fantasy and completeness. Brooding benevolence of the great estate.

Eric was still riding on, and when I caught him up we began to be rude and quarrelsome. We came to the aerodrome by Chiddingstone causeway. I took another turning, then went back and followed him. At last we came to the house, Chiddinghurst, alone, at the end of a long, green lane. I still would hardly look at the pig sties Eric had helped to make, but we got off at some tiled cottages and Eric took me across some fields, and then across a dyke into an old orchard where the apple trees had fallen, so that the trunks ran along the ground, and then rose up like flowering cobras.

There was a great yew there with its roots coiling out of the ground, and behind it a quince tree in flower (delicate purple pink). Close by was a pond, an old barn with fine framework and a pump; so I think, once, a farmhouse was there.

We sat down in the shade and stopped quarrelling and began to drink lemonade. Then we had half a hard boiled egg each and nut meat and cheese and biscuits and toast and chocolate and jam.

Afterwards I looked at a museum booklet on dolls' houses and Eric told me how he had once fallen straight into the dyke when he was drunk and someone had told him that his chickens were being stolen.

We walked in the orchard, saw a mushroom eaten by an animal, but found no others. Higher up we came to a wood and a pond, but a farmer seemed inquisitive so we went under a tree lower down and sat in the shade. Eric fell in a pond looking for birds' eggs.

Then we went on to Chiddingstone to see it again and have tea. But when we got there the Castle Inn woman would do no tea. She sat in the back gossiping with a friend.

We went into the church and wandered about, admiring the candelabra and wishing I had a small one like it for the dolls' house. Then into the churchyard. I was getting tired and it was hot.

Suddenly, under a large yew we came upon iron railings round the opening of a vault. The top grating had been removed, and the gate at the top of the stairs was open. Ferns grew in the wall and stretched out their fronds over the opening. Eric began to walk down the steps, and as I watched him, he looked like the perfect figure of an explorer going down into the secret tunnel.

At the bottom of the steps was another iron gate with thick wire netting all over it, but this had been pulled away at one corner, and through it Eric looked; then he called me to come down quickly. I ran down, pushed myself in front of him, and looked in. There, quite plain before me, was a bare white-washed little room, and on a framework three coffins, a graceful, other-century shape. In the darkness they seemed to be of perished leather, studded with nails, but this may have been an illusion. For a moment I was only conscious of extreme stillness (although children were shrieking and playing in the rectory garden above us) and of three human beings in the coffins. I saw them through the lids of the coffins, and it seemed as if they were sleeping there till some later date when they would rise up again. The horror of the nailed down lids over those faces was very real, and the feeling too that here for more than a century was something untouched, undisturbed, protected and now perhaps on the eve of being molested, spoilt, obliterated.

We both realized that it was something that we might never see again. Three old coffins, extraordinarily refined, civilized and ordered, lying in their vault, in the coolness, the darkness. The world up above rushing by year after year and none of its heat and pain and misery meaning anything in that subterranean room.

I climbed up the steps again and went to look at the altar tomb memorial that was also enclosed in the iron railing. There I saw the name Arundel and a date in the early eighteen-thirties. There were other names too I have forgotten already, and a later date. One at least was a woman; perhaps all were women. I will go back one day and look properly.

As we turned to leave, I looked down behind a tombstone under the yew and there was a dead rabbit, lying on its side, with its fur looking washed and moth-eaten. I said "Look" to Eric and he made the neutral, held-in-check face that people do when they are shocked, even slightly.

We bicycled on past the castle and up a lane behind, whence we came upon a group of chattering Brownies, all in various shades of their tawny colour. They really did look like small goblins, because they were running with their behinds stuck out and they were looking round the whole time as if something large and powerful and ogreish were after them. They ran in front of us for some time; then they branched off into a field and we carried on through a wood until we came to another road which had two little round battlemented lodges on each side of it. We got off at once to look and found that they had recently been lived in by soldiers, for all the walls were scrawled over with slogans, obscenities and regimental crests. Over the mantelpiece of one, someone had inscribed a curse all to do with the pox and other gruesome things.

There were no windows left, not even frames. Each lodge had three rooms, one half the size of it, and the other two each a quarter of the circle. They were too cramped to do anything with, and they were sinister with their brooding, too-high ceilings and little lancet windows, but one could not help wanting to make them into charming habitable little pavilions. They had plain, late eighteenth century mantels and cupboards and must have been built when things were done to the castle.

We were now uncertain of our way but we still carried on through the wood on the rough mud road, and soon it took us through a farmyard, where the reddest, sun-bleached haired carter told us that we could go through right on to Penshurst. As we left the farmyard we both felt gaiety there, for there were two landgirls with the man and child and dog, and all of them were going in, bubbling to their tea in the cool evening.

Soon we were on a ridge that skirted the edge of the curling river, and the place seemed so forgotten and perfect that we said we must often come back to it.

We dipped down, crossed the river, and suddenly came up exactly opposite the great mass of Penshurst Place; because I was not expecting it, I saw it with new eyes, and forgetting all its restorations, was impressed.

The rest of our journey home on the road was an ordeal, for I was very tired and wanted only to be lying on my bed.

1 *May*

There have been upsets and troubles with Sloman, our landlady. She was insolently trying to make use of Evie and Eric. Evie was violent and told her not to dare to interfere with my morning's work, and I got so disturbed by it all that I wrote a note to say that we could not look after her dog and her house while she was away, I did not think that I ought to pay any more rent and that Eric could not help her in her garden for "pocket money", and that it had, of course, not been meant seriously and therefore I must not be annoyed.[4]

After this terseness, I thought that there might be an explosion, for I had never been so frank and plain like that before, always wrapping things up in butter as she has done. But instead, she and her friend Brenda[5] came into coffee with me, and were quite tamed, pouring flattery and charm all over me, saying that they tell everyone that for as long as I like it is "Denton's Cottage" and that I am not to worry.

In my excitement I had written to everyone about finding a place for me, and Julian writes this morning that she has been trying to telegraph me all the weekend as she thinks she has just the thing for me at Garsington. Home

---

4 Denton was paying £78 a year for Pitt's Folly Cottage. He now agreed to pay £93.
5 Brenda Cobb, with whom Mary Sloman lived. Denton referred to them as the Ladies.

Close — three guineas a week and she will dislodge the Colonel who has it now! One part lived in by Ottoline Morrell's ex-parlourmaid who's had it since 1916, and who goes to work for the Colonel!

Needless to say it is not just the thing at all. But it is so nice to know that people are looking, and I am wondering too if it is the cottage that Ottoline offered [D.H.] Lawrence. I think it must be and that interests me, as I always remember reading his letters when I was eighteen and thinking how foolish he was not to accept her offer.

Julian has also told me of a thatched cottage that may be empty in the summer, near her place at Newbury, but rich and semi-rich people never realize that a rent that is half or less than half their own is still "expensive" to someone else with less money.

9 May

So yesterday was Victory Day. A feeling of uneasiness all the time and wondering what to do, because I had been silly enough not to shut myself up in the morning. There we were sitting in May's garden. I was doing the dolls' house. (Did I say that in the kitchen, while I was scraping a block of wood on the right of the fireplace, I came across the initials M.J.D. and the date 1783 under a coat of paint? It was charmingly done in two shades of grey paint and black.)

Well, I was puttying up holes and cracks in the walls and sticking things, and thinking of the excitingness of finding the date a few days before; and May brought her lunch out and we undid our picnic.

It was all right and dreary in turns, and people bicycled by in red-white-and-blue clothes and everything and everybody seemed dislocated.

Then, just when I was coming back to the house, to try to settle to write, Noël turned up, and wanted to stay and have supper with us, and May, when she heard it, wanted to come too, so I had to come back and put new life into Evie. She really did very well. She made us clear vegetable soup, into which we poured our cider, and then we had macaroni cheese, cold carrots and fried potatoes. Afterwards the chocolate mousse was stretched with white of egg, red jelly, orange peels and cachou nuts. It made a delicious strange sweet. Unexpectedly good.

I was very tired by now, but May, as usual, had to be rude to Noël, saying "Perfect!" in a sneering voice, because Noël was making up her face to cover up her boredom with the King's speech. There was a black electric look of hate between them, and a little time afterwards May left to go to the bonfire at the Codringtons (unasked) and Noël was to follow on, but she stayed talking until her husband Bernard appeared and called up at the window. And they too began to squabble in the drive, when I left them. Horrible for a moment.

When the whole lot had gone, Eric and I went to walk in the wood — all wet leaves and grasses poking through our sandals, and the nightingale singing its head off with clockwork persistence.

Just as we came back into the drive we saw a bicycle light approaching. It was Noël returning for her coat and telling us that Sloman and the other women round the bonfire were like cascading blancmanges tied together with apricot ribbon.

Far into the night there was the noise of singing and shouting at the pub and fireworks going off, and in the sky the glimmer of some huge bonfire, or was it the illumination of London?

Neither of us could sleep, and there were awful thoughts and anxieties in the air — the breaking of something — the splitting apart of an atmosphere that had surrounded us for six years.

13 May

When all seems rubbish that you wrote, in this and all your other books — when you have nothing good to show yourself, to give yourself a feeling of delight. What can you do but plough on through thick mud?

16 May

So we are going to Middle Orchard, Crouch, today, for ten days, while the Adeneys are away. Last year when we were there it was all flying bombs and mental upsets, but this year it will be exploring on bicycles, painting, and eating meals in the sun, and reading other people's books and playing on their piano. Evie is staying here at least to begin with, so Eric and I must get our own meals and make our own beds.

17 May. Five to six p.m.

So we are here in Middle Orchard, and the sun is pouring down, and the white curtain is blowing and scraping on the matting floor. All day I have been restless in the new place, doing no work, wandering from room to room wondering how I would furnish it with my things. The big tapestry cartoon in the studio, tea made with the water from the rain-water butt, and in the garden a statue, a classic plaster cast from some art school painted with many coats of weather-resisting paint (this because any better form of statue would be such a tremendous price). I could be happy here, if there were no noises from nearby.

If you do no work you bemoan the fact by finding fault with other people or things all day.

This morning I went to Ightham Church and, as always, since I saw the reproduction of the picture of it as it was in 1827 I was dismayed and frustrated to think what had been done all over the country to the lovely things that have been left to us. But for once I did not go out disgusted but looked more carefully and saw that the restorers had really not entirely gutted the place. There were the three old tombs in the chancel, the charming candelabra, some old woodwork.

20 May. 8.15 p.m.

Today I feel as if my talent was nothing, coming from nothing, turning into nothing with infinite pain and labour. Everything buzzes in me, my tongue, my eyes, my face and my thoughts. They are the greatest buzzers of all. I wrote a page and a half of my Chinese story this morning,[6] and a letter to N. Adeney, and then this afternoon I tried to paint Eric with humiliating results. It is clear that I have no idea how to begin a straightforward portrait. I can only contrive and tickle fantastically and that only sometimes. But that would be good, and what I want to do, if I could rely on myself body and mind, but I can't.

I have just come in from a ride, much too long for me but interesting, and I could not get out of the feeling that I was really a child going for the ride after a very long illness. Things were fresh and biting like that, and it was an adventure.

At Birling, with the old church tower rising up and dominating so aggressively the curve of the road and the whole village, then behind to come to the Victorian gates all smothered in red bulls' heads, rosettes, portcullises, and "Ne Vile Velis" in Gothic lettering. An ordinary farm gate, only stouter and larger, and tricked out with all the history, snobbery, and exhibitionism of a secure time. In its dilapidation and with the dark green bushes swallowing it, it was pathetic and cruel and delightful all at once.

As I biked round this Nevill place looking up over the stone walled bank to the tops of the Scotch firs I seemed to remember being told that the house was burnt and done for, that in the heart of the trees there was a black stone shell; but I could see nothing. I went up to another gate, this time entirely made in the form of two portcullises. All the wooden points had decayed away and looked like broken teeth, but it was fastened with a huge new chain and padlock, giving one the feeling that some very real ogre or monster lived inside and kept his property in order.

Then I got lost in the lanes and came out at last in the midst of all the buildings of Laybourne Lunatic Asylum.

---

6 "The Coffin on the Hill", first published in *Life and Letters*, June 1946, and reprinted in *Brave and Cruel*.

22 May, 10 to 12 p.m.

The moon is on the white table now in the garden of Middle Orchard, shining through a ruff of rainbow mist; and an aeroplane drones — alone in the sky, flying on for ever. The house is in utter stillness and I think, think how I would have it if it were mine. And I think too of Huxley's *Time Must Have a Stop*, which I began tonight. Its novelettish extravagance makes you both hate and love "real life" the more; but everything seems garbage tonight.

25 May

I was sick all the next day, Wednesday, and it seemed as awful as if I were dying, just as it always does (even when you are a child crossing the channel in perfect health). I thought it would never stop, but it did towards evening, and Eric looked after me and did everything. So yesterday seemed easy and calm after the horrible threat and the melting of every rock.

Routledge have sent a cheque and told me that *In Youth is Pleasure* is now in a Swedish edition. There was no letter, only the bald mention of £20 for advance royalty. You see, you understand, how totally unimportant are your concerns to all but yourself. You have always known this but now it is flung at you, making you feel petty, and indeed you even lose interest and have the feeling that everything is nothing.

And it seems that a little literary success is not connected with more than a little money, for I now have a book in Sweden, a book in America, and two editions here, and what I have to show for it is £238.

6.45 p.m.

Now I have come back from the wood at Platt, laid out I think some ninety years ago by those same Nevills to whom the burnt-out house at Birling belongs. And I have heard that this wood was to be the wild garden round a house that was never built — I don't know why not. It is now a tangle of huge rhododendrons — all at this moment at the perfection of their flower — and the last survivors of Scotch firs, most of which were cut down by Tom the Woodman in 1940. Wandering there brought it all back to me, how I lived at the Hop Garden then, and how I went out one day and found that the trees were being felled. Behind a huge smoking bonfire I saw a half-naked man with a wide brass-buckled belt round his riding-breeches. His shoulders were thick and broad, and his skin had turned to a tawny brown. His hair was all in his eyes and dusty with wood ash. He looked extraordinarily glowering and wild. We grunted at each other and then we talked, and afterwards he came to the Hop Garden and I tried to paint him several times. He was gentle and strange and came from Yorkshire. I still see his hands black with turpentine from the wood and his hair full of minute twigs, needles, skeletons of leaves and buds.

The wood as I went through it today was full of memories of Tom and other people and things.

There was the pine where I sat looking out to a village of chicken houses, which I tried to draw at the end of the exercise book that was really given up to the book I began before *Maiden Voyage*. It was to be an autobiography from my birth. Through the months of 1940 I plugged at it. Then it suddenly died on me and there was a lapse, until in the autumn or the winter several tiny things suddenly crystallized into the determination, by hook or by crook, to finish a book that began with my running away from Repton and ended in China.

I remember the complete conviction that this was what I should do. It came over me after I had read *Hindoo Holiday*, which I liked, and after I had seen somewhere that true books of travel are always interesting. I knew instinctively that my book would be nothing like Ackerley's, and nothing like a travel book either, but there were commonplace pegs that I badly needed; they somehow made all simple, only leaving hard work and perseverance to be cultivated.

Every morning after that I stayed in bed and wrote from breakfast to lunch time, sometimes two, sometimes three, sometimes four hours.

It gave me a serenity which I had not had since childhood, although I dared not read what I had written, for fear of disgusting myself. All that mattered seemed to be that I should finish it, doing each piece as well as I could.

The wood brought back to me that beginning, and it brought back also the steaming day in June 1941, when Freddie and Rosemary came over, and the first draft of *Maiden Voyage* was done. Freddie was going to type it for me. He was not yet in the Air Force, and nobody could tell that he only had another year and four months to live. He chased us in the bushes, tried to trip me up, teased and sweated. I thought that to revise my first writing would only take a few weeks. I never dreamt that it was far the longest and most arduous part of the proceeding. I even suggested, half-heartedly, dictating it to Freddie while he typed!

26 May, 9.50 p.m.

Yesterday, as I was climbing up the hill at the beginning of Seven Mile Lane, I saw a dumpy woman in pale smoky peacock blue in front of me. I noticed her because she was walking with a great effort and she had a suitcase in her hand.

When I was about to pass her, she turned round with a weary, wary, dog-like expression on her oatmeal-coloured face and said, "Is this the way to

Mereworth Woods, please?"

Her hopeless quality, her exhaustion, her bludgeoned air seemed almost assumed, they were so obvious, and I said at once, "Put the suitcase on the bicycle-seat and we can wheel it up."

She thanked me numbly, and as we walked together it came out that she had gone up to London from Guildford to spend her husband's leave with him at the Union Jack Hostel. But when she got there, no husband appeared. That was on Wednesday. She waited till yesterday for him, tried to ring the camp up, but was told that no one could know the number of a military station. Then at last she cried, not knowing what to do.

She finally decided to take the train down, and here she was dragging her suitcase along.

At the finish of her story, told so lifelessly, without any effort at effect, she began to murmur almost inaudibly and still quite colourlessly, "I don't know where I shall sleep tonight. It'll be men only at the camp. I expect I shall have to sleep in the fields or in the wood. It doesn't matter, anywhere will do."

And she really seemed to mean that anywhere would do. She was in no way appealing for pity, fishing for a bed. She was accepting the inevitable, grimly, colourlessly.

I thought at once of the spare room at Middle Orchard and I saw her in it, and I had a repulsion, and I wondered what the words would be that I would utter. For a moment, they might have been anything. Then they settled down into:

"I live up that way" — I pointed — "it's another mile, but if you can't find anything nearer, you can spend the night there."

She said, with no enthusiasm, "That's very kind of you."

"Have you a pencil?" I asked. "Then I can write the address."

"No," she said.

"Well, the name is Middle Orchard, Crouch." I enunciated like a schoolmistress.

She repeated it after me and said casually, "I'll remember that."

But I didn't think she would and I said good-bye and bicycled off, leaving her plodding up the road.

Later, after we had finished supper and Eric had gone to bed, I suddenly heard a movement, and there she was looking up at the back door, peering, frowning.

"Come in," I said boisterously. And she plunked on to a hard chair in the sittingroom, not the arm one I had tried to steer her towards. She sat there breathing hard, talking in a whisper of exhaustion.

"It's not right," she kept saying.

I quickly made some tea and gave her that with cake, while I heated up the remains of the macaroni cheese. I expected her to be quite uninterested in food, but she wasn't when I mentioned it; she seemed touched, made vital for the first time. But when she came to eat it, she was moderate, not greedy.

She said, "God's good, he sent you to me!" but there was no real conviction. Life was on a level of amazing flatness. She showed me the front and back door keys and said that they told her at the camp that her husband had gone to Guildford, so they had crossed.

"He won't be able to get in unless he breaks a window," she said drearily.

Then I showed her where the bathroom was and she went to have a bath, while I made up the bed.

Long after she had gone to bed, Eric and I talked in his room. At midnight I left, but I was feeling very restive and I lay in a half-awake state for a long time.

All at once I heard a movement on the landing, and I felt ridiculously scared, imagining that the woman had come up to steal my money. I lay there hating everything, not awake enough to be sensible.

(Eric afterwards told me that he woke up and felt exactly the same.)

Of course the poor woman had only gone to the W.C., as I was to discover in the morning, for she was too considerate to pull the plug.

In the morning Eric got her breakfast and rang up the station, and I did not see her until I went into the bathroom, and looking out of the window saw her walking through the apple trees carrying her *wooden* suitcase, looking neat and worn and large-hipped in her smoky peacock suit.

"Good-bye," I said again boisterously, waving my hand to her, smiling, feeling guilty.

She turned as if I had startled her, then she waved back and said, "Good-bye, thank you ever so much."

And as I saw her go down the drive, I thought of her in London, on the train, with her husband, without him, eating, sleeping, washing, thinking of money. I didn't know her name, she didn't know mine. We would never meet again. There would be nothing but the memory of the chance encounter, the bed, the meal.

27 May

Some of the American reviews of *Maiden Voyage* have come. Auden's in the *New York Times* is the most sensible. Some of the others are buttery, others calling me a snip and a snob, effeminate and obnoxious, saying that I sit better with Miss Sitwell than I do with them.

There is something very different in them from the English ones. Something artificially sensible, standing no nonsense, something resentful and afraid of presumption, and something just dead and mechanical. But there are good things too. Even the least sympathetic ones point out what they consider good too.

30 May

When I read about William Blake, I know what I am for. I must never be afraid of my foolishness, only of pretension. And whatever I have I must use, painting, poetry, prose — not proudly think it is not good enough and so lock it inside for fear of laughing, sneering.

The post has just come and John Lehmann has taken my 'Judas Tree' story.[7] (Only in the bathroom, cleaning my teeth ten minutes ago, I thought: "What has happened about the 'Judas Tree' story?" I had completely forgotten it till then. Could the fact that Lehmann's letter was near me in the postman's bag have put the thought into my head?)

Richard Armorel Howden, the psychologist who wrote to me about *Maiden Voyage*, now wants to come and see me. I dread meeting him particularly, for some reason. He is so seemingly prying, unfortunate in his remarks. Or is it just that prejudice against mind doctors?

Routledge says that Bonnier's in Sweden will do *In Youth is Pleasure* this summer or autumn and will think of *Maiden Voyage* afterwards. And that Fischer's in America are going to "push my books for all they are worth" and that the second edition is bound to be sold soon. I suppose all this "pushing" is mentioned as a dainty to keep the author satisfied.

9 June. Pitt's Folly.[8] 12.30 p.m.

Well, we are back again, and I have been in bed again, with a black hard pain in my head, and being able to eat nothing, but today I am better and so I preserve myself, hardly daring to do anything for fear of bad results.

Everything looked so clean, so fresh, so rich as I came into this room, saw the angels[9], the Gothic window and the excess of red — red carpet, counterpane and lacquer screen. It was lovely to see everything pretty that one has, after living in the bare house, the wood house, furnished by someone else. This is so small for us three, and the Ladies next door are in some way so constricting, but there is something that suits me — the snugness, the being unable to expand one's everyday life, thus leaving all energy for work.

The picture of this room came out in *Vogue* this week, and the "fan", Peggy Kirkaldy, has written to say that it looks a "perfect fairy house"[10]. It

---

7 Editor of *New Writing*. "The Judas Tree" was published in *Penguin New Writing* No 26, 1945, and reprinted in *Brave and Cruel*.
8 In reality, Pitt's Folly Cottage.
9 Two carved wooden baroque statues, four feet high.
10 She appears as Susan Innes in "The Diamond Badge" (see 1943, note 35 above).

does not look that, but I could make it so nice if it were my own, and if I could turn the garage underneath into another room. One needs no more than a four-roomed cottage with bathroom and kitchen. And outside it should be sash windows, long downstairs, short upstairs, and a portico the height of both storeys. Ionic pillars and a pediment, or would a balustrade top be better so that one could get out through the roof and walk on an open balcony? It may sound boringly eighteenth-century revival, but it is just what would suit me; tiny and perfect, with old mantels and two panelled doors with brass drop handles, and one room with the walls panelled in pine.

14 June

Hector Bolitho wrote this morning from the Athenaeum, to say that *Town and Country* in America had asked him to write an article on me, and could he come down to see me, as he wanted to make it good. He said he wasn't very good at that sort of thing, so I must help him, if the idea didn't depress me too much.

I have asked him to lunch on Saturday and Eric is going to get strawberries and asparagus and light ale and cigarettes, so that we can give him a little something after his journey. We are wondering what he'll be like, and whether it will be a pleasant day or agony. I hope he won't ask embarrassing questions. Nothing could be worse than that.

I have often heard his name, but I don't really know what he writes. Is it history, at all? Or am I mixing him with Philip Guedalla? The name so harsh, Byzantine, has always stuck in my mind, because I have never been quite certain how to pronounce it, and I have wondered what nationality it was.[11]

Or is it the man who has written on flying and airman in the war? If he is it will be a great change to come here and find me "lolling on a lewd day-bed"! The "lewd", of course, does not apply, and so there is no point in the quotation, but I am always saying the words over to myself. I've loved them ever since my brother Paul chanted them to me when we were schoolboys.

It is so difficult to explain to strangers the state of one's health. One either says too little or too much. If he wants to know why I have to be so careful, I shall just have to tell him, I suppose, that I was once riding on a bicycle, when someone ran into the back of me and fractured my spine. But I hate to. I shall feel as I did the other day when Noël Adeney started a hateful conversation about me. She just wallowed in "death beds", "stricken deer", "tragedy", "the hurry to get work done". I am not a spectacle for

11 Hector Bolitho, novelist and biographer, was a New Zealander. His name is made fun of as Hector Bolithiero in "Brave and Cruel". Philip Guedalla had died the previous year.

198

curiosity, hers or anyone else's. I will not be dramatised. No one has been so blatent as she has been. She is truly sentimental, because she plays with her feelings, so that they shall excite her.

When we came back, I forgot to say that a Mrs. Seaton-Corfield (the mother of Robin Cornell, a "fan" I have not met) had sent us a most wonderful plum cake from Australia. It is made from the recipe of her great-grandmother, and when the tin is opened a heavy scent of brandy swells out, like an organ stop. The dark heart of the cake is damp, reminding me of the warm, watered earth in Grandpa's grape house at Whaphams.

17 June, 11.15 a.m.

Hector Bolitho came yesterday, rather early for lunch, while Evie and I were still getting things ready. I had lain the little marble-topped chess table with my mother's very flat, delicate Italian lace mats, the small squat cut-glass tumblers, the old straight-sided white-and-gold sugar-basin in the middle with a poppy, a marigold, briar roses, cat mint and some magenta star flowers in it.

The 1740 silver christening spoon, the big salt cellar, and the urn-shaped pepper pot were making the table look pretty. I was just putting the crispbread in the Gothic toast rack on the table when I heard the taxi draw up. He was a long time telling the man when to call for him again, so I wandered backwards and forwards uncomfortably and Evie went round the corner and then retreated. We both hated the moment before the encounter with the stranger.

At last he was walking up the dark stairs. I switched on the light and saw a small tubby man with large heavy rimmed glasses and a rather square "German" head with bushy white-grey hair.

At once it was really very easy, ordinary. I curled up on the bed and he sat in the armchair. I offered him a cigarette and he began to tell me that he was just out of the Air Force and he felt like a newborn child. He told me more about his life in the Air Force, saying that it stripped him of all his pretences. I listened, then said that I could not know what any of the services were like, because I had been entirely out of the war, because of my health.

"Isn't that strange!" he said, "for I had the idea that any young writer, who has not been involved in the war, would be very old-fashioned — but you had not struck me as in the least cut-off, and so I thought that you must have seen quite a lot of service somewhere."

I did not know what to make of this. Is it that I look as if I had been made to put up with a lot — accident, illness, pain, discomfort? Anyhow, there it was, and we went on talking easily, or rather he mostly talked, telling me that he once went through an ostentatious period, driving in a Rolls Royce, building a now unwanted wing on to his Essex Tudor house; but that was all gone and he wanted things much simpler. He told me that in London he had to move about from hotel to hotel, because each one could only have him for three or four days, and he couldn't find anywhere of his own.

Then he said, "But I am talking all about myself, and I came to interview you!" He asked me if I knew what sort of a magazine *Town and Country* was, and explained how much better the letterpress was than one might suppose! He explained that two other books of his had been serialised in it and added that the editor now wanted him to write an article on someone, and had told him that America was talking about me and wanted to know something about me. (Here I imagined an extraordinary sort of monster with a very large mouth asking — no, demanding — straight answers to the most embarrassing questions. Or perhaps was it a figure with a million, million mouths and one tail who was doing the demanding? Anyhow, my imaginings were as fantastic as his statement.)

He was smoking all this time, and I had at last persuaded him to have some cider. At first he would not, as he had already been into the Angel where the barmaid had said to him, "We have whisky, gin, Drambuie — and Benediction."

About this time Evie came up with the asparagus and we sat down to the chess table and he admired the plates and asked me simple-mindedly how I got them. He seemed surprised that anyone should love things enough to seek them out and prize them. I said, "This one is pretty, it is Chelsea-Derby. Although it's broken it is riveted, so it won't fall to pieces when you eat off it." I wanted him to turn it upside down and see the little gold "D" and anchor twined together, but he didn't; and I knew that he didn't really care what it was. But he liked his food and that was a good sign. I passed him the melted butter, and gave him more cider, more crispbread. He began to tell me that he had gone to stay with Beverley Nichols at Hampstead after he had left the Air Force, and B.N. had been so kind, bringing him morning tea and putting flowers in his room. He had a bathroom, a bedroom and a sittingroom all to himself. It was just the comfort and attention he had been wanting.

He said that Beverley Nichols had a rich woman "fan" who sent him present after present ranging from gold cigarette cases to monthly parcels of towels, soaps and toilet paper (delicately and discreetly wrapped up). I said that the last in this war must have been the greatest present of all, greater than the gold and the jewellery.

We went on to a dish of new peas, hard boiled egg, split lengthways, sardines, new potatoes with mint and butter, salad hearts and sweet dressing. He was quite greedy and couldn't resist things that were pressed on him, saying that things tasted far better in the country.

He said that Noël Coward was so witty and then told me a story which is perhaps very old. Lady Diana Cooper, at the time when she was acting in *The Miracle*, said to Noël Coward nastily, "I went to your new play last night and I didn't laugh once." "How strange," he answered, "for I went to see you the night before and I couldn't stop laughing."

Then he went on to ask me if I knew Edith Sitwell well, and when I said that we had only lunched once together, he told me that he too had only met her once, but they had corresponded a lot over her book on Queen Victoria. She had used facts which he had first discovered in the original letters at Windsor, and there were notes at the bottom of many pages stating the source of her information. So when soon after the publication of her book Noël Coward met Bolitho, he said, quick as lightening, "Hullo, has Edith Sitwell written any more books by you, since the last?" He said I must never tell Edith of this, because she had been so nice and generous in her tributes.

Do you think he really wants me to tell her?

We finished with strawberry shortcake — the pastry really beautifully made by Evie. H.B., after his second helping, said, "I feel like an overfed schoolboy."

I said, "You've had nothing!"

Then we lapsed into chairs and drank coffee and ate the whispy Swiss chocolate squares that Noël A. had given me.

It was soon after this that he said, "After I had written to you I regretted it, and I will tell you why now, although it may embarrass me."

He told me that the night before, he had been reading *In Youth is Pleasure*, and although he had felt that by now he had defences against life so that things could never hurt as they had at first, the reading of the book seemed to break all his shell, so that when later that night he had a quarrel with his host and the man was venomous and cruel, he retreated to his room and sobbed. "And sobbing is different to crying," he added. Later, the wife of the man came in and all was made up because she was so charming.

He said impulsively, "I think I am devoted to the man too." Then he dashed it away by, "But I don't know whether I am, because he is so cruel." There seemed bitterness and a wound there, and I wondered what else he would say, but he suddenly switched back to my book, saying, "But the quality that I was afraid of in you was the absolute honesty that strips away one's barricades, so that one can be hurt, just as one was as a child. I would not have sobbed last night, if I had not read *In Youth is Pleasure* before."

"How awful," I said, "that my book should do that." I was at a loss, not knowing how to take his tribute. Was it all a fancy thing, not genuine?

"It isn't awful!" he answered, "but that is why I regretted writing."

Now my mind has gone blank and I don't seem to be able to write any more about his visit, except that he told me how as a child at school he was not liked, and the master too caned him on the hand unjustly once. After this, as he was walking away from school another boy followed him and suddenly fished from his pocket a little silver pug — its head on a hinge — and pressed it into Bolitho's hand. It was extraordinarily hot in his palm, he said, and he could never forget the love and joy of that moment.

He kept the pug always — until the beginning of this war, when he gave it to his great friend, who was a pilot. He gave it to him because he thought it would help him and save him. And the man lost it, not on operations, but just through carelessness. Then resentment and misunderstanding and hate broke up their friendship, so that nothing remains. He put it all down to his friend's losing the dog.

"But don't you think that resentments, misunderstandings, come and go, but something else persists?" I asked.

"No," he said, as if the whole thing was dismissed.

Again I had the feeling that I was taking something seriously that might just be an exercise, a story not yet written.

The next story was of the horribly drunk American lieutenant who stopped Bolitho and a friend while they were carrying a suitcase home slung on a walking stick between them. The American said, "Say, how much do you want for that stick?" in a filthy, menacing tone. He seemed ready to do anything — evil and abandoned through and through. It was very late with no one about. The American seized Bolitho's friend by the tie and began to shake him — because, B said, he had bristled with aggressiveness. But B went passive, yielding, "feminine" as he put it, flowing with the man, so that there was nothing to fight. He said to the man that he knew all his country so well, that he loved it, and would hate to have it spoilt by the man's behaviour.

The man said, sneering, "What exactly do you mean?" But he wavered, and then the other American with him said, "Come on, leave them alone." So passivity had won the day.

I had a curious feeling while he was telling me this — one of embarrassment, of being put in a false position, of listening to something unpleasant on all sides. A mess of evil, passive and active and utterly unmeaning.

There were other stories about the extraordinariness of Ottoline Morrell, the uncomfortableness of T.E. Lawrence (he always would be God who knew). Then something about D.H. Lawrence, how he sat curled up on a sofa in Hampstead, drinking many cups of tea into which spoonfuls of whisky had been poured and how he told the young Bolitho that he ought to be able to live on £3 a week and so be free to do nothing but the work he wanted to do. "But by that time," B said, "I had already tasted claret."

He spent a lot of words on his desire to have money, his willingness to be a "hack" as he called it, to earn enough for comfort and luxury. He seemed to treat me as someone who would never behave in the same way. It is difficult to know whether people are really complimenting you, when they take up this attitude, or whether they are just thinking you a poor incompetent. They are doing both, I suppose — praising and blaming your supposed unworldliness.

The taxi was late in picking him up, so about three I took him into the wood and round in a circle. Talking out of doors was stiffer, more pointless. I was pleased when we came back and had early tea with Mrs Seaton-Corfield's magical cake.

He tucked into it and gloated on it, and said, "When I get presents of food from unknowns, I'm always terrified it's poisoned."

Eric was there when we came back from the wood, and when I went out of the room to talk to Evie, Bolitho said to him, "How nice it is to meet someone who is unspoilt by his success." And he said to me, too, "Your vocabulary is so unpretentious." What did he expect!

When the car came at last, we took him out to it, and he pressed both our hands with a meaning look. Something most understanding — put on, of course, but likeable, for in spite of all the little insincerities, that even a great person can't entirely weed out, he seemed to wish one well, "to want to live and let live", as Eric put it.

Eric said, the moment he was gone, "Well, that went off like a house on fire. What do you think he'll write? Something pretty good."

And we talked about it all, and I suddenly felt quite exhausted.

21 *June*

Eric has gone off today to London for a week, taking Julian's portrait, and two little things to the Leicester Galleries.

The "fan" Peggy Kirkaldy has written from Bradford-on-Avon, telling me how tasteless the Granby Hotel is.

And the little late-eighteenth-century watch which Noël gave me two birthdays ago has now been mended and is ticking beside me as I write. It is really perfect in its way — a modest, genteel, unrich way. Thickest pink gold plated on bronze, and a piece of deep, deep sapphire glass as a back. A pure white enamel face with little dots all round the edge, and delicate Roman numerals, and then the original jeweller's label in the back of the outer case. "Gregory's of Basingstoke. Watches, Trinkets, Music and Pianos let out to Hire." All in fine lettering on a yellow ground.

Inside, the gold works ticking away so busily (sometimes giving a little rush, or seeming to), the filigree watch-back, the name Bramwell, London and the number 617. I should like to know the exact date of it.

8 *July. In the morning sun, on the white balcony at Middle Orchard.*

We climbed up here on Thursday night, through the park at Oxon Hoath, up the Cedar Walk, under the huge uplifted boughs spearing their green pancakes of foliage, past the exquisite eighteen-thirtyish wrought iron gates, enclosing the uncut hayfield which used to be the smooth lawns of the approach. Past all this and then past the lime avenue where a new electrified fence has been erected with an ugly red jigging, zigzagging notice saying, "Beware, this fence is electrified." Like a concentration camp.

We went on climbing until we came to the middle of the avenue that leads up to Gover Hill. Then we sat down under one of the trees and spread our supper picnic while we gazed out over miles of country to the part of the Ashdown Forest which I think is called Jill's Lap.

To eat we had American shrimp paté (from the U.S. guys at Eric's mother's flat) spread on crispbread, then crumbly pastry and Pocetta's wonderful chocolates from Seattle.[12] Afterwards cherries and cigs, and barley water that was tepid.

Some Italian prisoners were down below us singing near the Coffin House and the Artichoke.[13]

When we had finished eating we got up and walked under huge beeches and smaller Scotch pines till we came to a smooth glistening sweep of grass where cows were grazing. Beyond it was yet another avenue, and then the view towards Goudhurst and Marden.

The sun was very low now making our shadows into little black men on cathedral-spire-stilts.

When we turned to walk back I pulled out my handkerchief, and my dull-orange Parker Duofold pen fell out with it, and I thought, "How awful if I had not noticed it!" For I write everything with it.

We did not get here till about half-past ten. Then we only made beds and fell into them after drinking hot Ovaltine.

13 July, 8.30.

On Wednesday night I went into the wood behind Beeching Wood at Platt and saw the old grey-silver horse in the field and the magenta heather, and covering of thyme, and rolling tide of bracken all as it used to be, only lovelier because I knew I couldn't see it always. I wandered down the tight closed-in little paths for a long time, past many orange-dotted butterflies, past pine trees, until I came to the grove where I first sat down to write a story, some time in 1940. It was hot then, as it was the other night, and I remembered sweating, and worrying, and the insects, and the feeling that I could get nothing on the paper, only words spelt out, but no body. I remember going back that evening, rather unsatisfied but pleased that I had written at all. Writing in the wood that day had been a sort of test of endurance.

Before I got out of the wood on Wednesday I nearly got lost, and pushing

12 Pocetta Saunders (Vesta Fielding in *Maiden Voyage*, see 1942, note 48 above).
13 The Coffin House was a building Denton painted, selling the picture in 1946 to Rose Macaulay. It is illustrated in *A Last Sheaf*. The Artichoke was a public house.

through the shoulder-high heather I longed so violently to be strong again that I thought something must happen. Something in me, or outside but in me too, could withstand. But I think really that I get worse all the time, so that I have the picture of myself draining away. The only thing that can withstand is the will, in its own weak, shabby, obstinate, joyless way.

Yesterday I went snopping round the outskirts of Bonhill to see what it was like, if it happened so to fall vacant. I slipped through the holly hedge by Winfield House, below the spreading flat cedars, and skirted the huge creamy swelling strawberry field on the other hill. I came to the little garden of Bonhill and saw how well placed it was, how nice really the lofty little early-Victorian stone house, in spite of the unfortunate small rough-cast additions.

Today I got into the very garden as I'd discovered that the tenants were away. I looked into all the windows, and was pleasantly surprised. It needs things done to it, but not so very much, and the garden in its too quaint landscape garden way is well done, though not good for the house. Even the rough cast addition to writing room and kitchen is good of its sort. Everything with a little work and money could be good and the view is wonderful. I pictured it all scoured, painted, polished and with my things in it. The garden all ship shape after Eric had dealt with it.

15 July

Last night was the most tremendous storm I have ever been in. Lightning continuously from perhaps nine-thirty to four o'clock this morning, and lightning that appeared like violent cracks in the curved sky bowl. Flashes of pink light that showed the orchard trees up in a sort of ghostly powder blue grey. Thunder crawling all over the sky. Two moths fluttering madly against the window pane to get out to their deaths, while we watched from the top windows for hours, drinking tea and exclaiming. Once I went to shut the metal fitting of a window, and I felt what seemed like a vibration through my fingers as a lightning flash split the clouds.

There were lights over towards Wrotham and the red flashing of the aeroplane signal tower, hailstones smacking on the balcony, the injured telephone ringing helplessly in little bursts.

At last we had to go to bed, we were so tired, and my ankles were aching and burning as if from the storm.

17 July, 7 o'clock p.m. Pitt's Folly Cottage.

22 July, 4.45 p.m.

Something must have happened to stop me here. Well, the next day Ted

Nichols and Robin Cornell arrived for lunch, late, and Robin, in his pathetic, arrested-development way, had to explain that they were late because they had drunk too much the night before, and that had made them sleep late and miss the train. It was sordid. And all through the afternoon we had to listen to his disgustingly commonplace titbits about his own fascination and charm. (He had one of those fish faces and underwater eyes which *always* are trimmed with thick horn-rimmed glasses.) This sort of person should be smacked and put to sleep for ever, but I suppose they live longer than most people and burden others for years with their extraordinary pretension and mental squalor.

I will write no more about them — except to say that we had thistle artichokes and melted butter, cold fried fish, peas, carrots, lettuce and Evie's sweet salad-dressing made with condensed milk, then cherry flan — coral-coloured cherries, stoned and bottled by Noël Adeney. Afterwards we smoked Dunhill cigarettes and chatted and shouted, till anyone who was listening must have thought that we doted on one another's company.

Before that, last Sunday, at Middle Orchard, I had just come down from an evening bath when who should appear but the Adeneys themselves.

"So sorry," Noël said, "but we couldn't telephone, it is out of order." The night before, as I wrote, there had been a terrible storm. So we had to make them welcome and appear as if we were not dislocated. I kept thinking that things in the house were out of order, but it seemed fairly normal.

After supper Evie's sister (who lives in the sinister Crouch House, which is an Anglican home for lost and derelict ageing people) suddenly came walking through the orchard. I could not face her with the Adeneys — there would be so much falsity and patronizing — so I slipped out through the French window and walked down the hill to the path which winds past hoppickers' huts — one lived in now with a table outside, a brass jug, a bowl, a bunch of lacy flowers, tightly packed pink, white froth, something greyish too like dirty lace. Further on one suddenly discovers oneself on the verge of a sewage farm, at one time laid out with trees and bushes, the whole rather resembling a private swimming pool in the little tucked-away valley with the overhanging trees on the hill, the stillness of the evening, the sky that had been scoured and cleaned by the storm.

And there I sat down on the tar drive close to the central clump of bushes and I watched the rich orange-edged ochre slug drawn out luxuriously on the wet stones. I watched it, for it seemed to have four horns and a hole, a cyclops eye in its side which it opened and closed. It was for me changing its form there, stretching and retracting, a wonder of nature. This feeling, so bandied about, seldom visits me in a form that is not mingled with history. But now I just watch the slug for its own intricate, perfect, peculiar self. So self-sufficing, seemingly so attuned to its home on the edge of the sewage farm. Delicate drifts of it came up to me — like a sigh — a mournful crying to the past, so poignant in the evening — the call of the sewage.

After a long time I got up from the ground where I had been crouching and walked back. But halfway I was caught and held by the sight of a striped fly, which had suddenly flown into a spider's web, and there the graceful, thin, pear-shaped yellow spider was flying over the threads, and then he had thrown himself on the fly and they were grappling belly to belly like lovers. The spider had arms like lobster claws and the fly's were tipped with minute shoes or suckers. The feet waved madly and the spider seemed to be digging its teeth into the neck of the fly.

I watched quite fascinated, never having seen such a thing before. Very slowly the fly seemed to sink into a stupor, its poor sucker feet went slower, and the spider's darting, horny claws seemed filled with tense excitement.

I thought at last the fly should be let loose as it seemed fitfully alive still — this was a guilty feeling that I had watched it, seized upon and done nothing — so I broke the web, then felt guilty towards the spider. Then at last I saw that the fly was done for so I put my foot on it to stop its arms waving.

I wonder if the alarmed spider came back after I had left to devour the squashed fly, or would it despise such a morsel?

The slug, the spider and fly, the sewage farm in the clear evening after the storm; I took all these back with me to the house.

23 July, 7.30 p.m.

We have just come back with May from Tunbridge Wells. She drove us there in the car. It was strange to be sailing in the car, to watch the people, the traffic, the hills from Bidborough Ridge, right across to Somerhill and much farther, all these sights suddenly laid out before me after being shut up in this room, or at Middle Orchard.

It seemed like going back to other years before the war. I felt that other me again — it was there, hiding under the surface — the circumstances recreated, and the old person leaps out as if from hiding, and one feels very sad thinking of all the past selves that are waiting to leap out and are shut away probably for ever.

We saw behind King Charles the Martyr's Church, down the little bricked path, past the Regency Gothic houses with their pretty windows and porches, and one with all the front studded with round stones, packed tightly together. Past all these, we came to a flight of steps under heavy bushes, romantic bottle-green light, overgrown excitement of the steps.

And there we were before an empty Victorian house with generous bays and wide windows. Inside, the rooms rather low and long. Something extraordinarily attractive about it, and also about the garden with its monkey-puzzle tree, its little terraced lawn, paths and greenhouse.

We could not understand why such a house in the heart of Tunbridge Wells could be empty at such a time. We suppose it had been requisitioned by the army and was still held by them.

May wanted us to divide it in half and share it. She was going to the agents but then forgot. I would not have wanted it in the town or with her, but it was good for what it was — delightful that there was only the bricked footpath in front.

After house-gazing we went to the furniture market in the old Corn Exchange, and looking up into the blue sky I saw for the first time how really lovely the statue of Ceres looked with her sheaf and the cornucopias and, I think, underneath the twining of vines.

It is all in some early nineteenth-century composition of terracotta, and in the sunlight the delicacy of this rather commercial statuary was remarkable. Pearly and charming and fine-detailed. One longed to be able to put her in a garden, at the end of a green valley against the view.

I went into the junk shop and bought a strange early mid-eighteenth century cup for one and sixpence — creamy paste like Chelsea, and with the ground smooth bottom. Must be that, or Bow, or perhaps some French or German factory. It had a woman in terracotta playing with a bounding dog.

I bought too a large Chinese dish, early nineteenth century — garden scene, figures all in brown — a tiny little boy chasing an enormous bee in the foreground.

I thought looking round that old cornmarket, what interesting things could still be found for a little. There was a French table, charming marquetry and ormolu, it does not matter whether eighteenth century or not, a round table with inlaid marble top, harp, wreaths, and a little cabinet for two guineas — rather amateurish chinoiserie, yellow-gold figures and palm trees stuck out black with nice brass mounts and keyhole.

There were lots of other things too, all rather derelict, but easily reclaimed.

To see all these old things, and Tunbridge Wells, which, in spite of spoiling, still has something left, and to be free sailing in the car, the first time for years, and the sunlight, all gave one a feeling of happiness. There was restlessness too, suddenly to see so many people walking and moving. One wanted to know what was unfolding in each head. Their eyes were looking forward, intent. I wanted to follow in the sky above to the end of the thousand journeys — nothing, nothing there I suppose for each one of them, but they are looking all the time.

May had just come back from Pevensey Bay where soldiers kept telling her that they'd found yet another mine on the beach, and where youths got hold of an abandoned gun at night and began to shoot live cartridges with it through people's windows. They nearly killed one woman as she was doing her hair. The police hid for them in a derelict house, but could not get them.

There were other extraordinary happenings, too. A falcon nested in the house and had babies and May had to feed them with raw meat, and one kept biting her hand and arm till she gave it to the butcher. She said that to feed them, she had to swoop down with the meat as if she had been the mother bird.

Then all the rooms were splintered with splinters of glass, so that footsteps scrunched everywhere, and there was nowhere to keep food so that enormous bluebottles settled over everything.

Her son and daughter-in-law were having matrimonial difficulties, and the daughter-in-law went about weeping and the son kept drinking and having asthma. Then the daughter-in-law had a violent attack of measles and thought she was going to die. Once she fell fainting out of bed so violently that May thought she really must be dead.

31 July, 7.5 p.m.

Last Wednesday Peggy Kirkaldy drove over from Colchester bringing cucumber, tomatoes, large cake, book on china, and two pretty George III teaspoons, the engraved sort, datemarks 1801, 1802.

All went very easily and I liked her more than I thought I would. She was tall, she had nice rings and diamond watch and was dressed in grey with white spots.

And today she has sent an 1809 edition of *A Sentimental Journey* with two coloured Rowlandson prints in it and nice marbled paper covers, lots of magazines, and a big box of her own lavender which I have been skinning off the stalks all this afternoon. She wants to bring her doctor friend Bob over on 12 August for a picnic in his car. Would we come out in it too?

On Thursday we went over to Trottiscliffe to look at Ivy Cottage which Mrs Carpmael offered me for 14s 6d a week — amazing rent for nowadays.

I remembered it on that half-term when I was eleven and at St Michael's. She and Irene had driven over to fetch me, and then we all sat in Ivy Cottage in the pouring rain and listened to the chicken roasting in the oven in the kitchen. The walls of the front room were (and are) panelled in a sort of lincrusta cardboard, and I remember so well the terrible consuming depression and excitement mixed, of the day, the darkness, the good food, the constraint with the elders and the dark threat of returning to school in the evening.

Then, in spite of its gloom, Ivy Cottage was a refuge, a haven of civilization and comfort, but when I saw it last Thursday, squalid after the last derelict old father and daughter had left it, I felt that I would be foolish to move there. Chief objections are that it is right in the village and that it is semi-detached, the gardener's widow having the other half.

And there was the feeling too that even if we could get the builders to put in electrical fittings and repaint it all, it would still be only a makeshift, a temporary place, a mistake.

I would go with pleasure if I had nowhere else, but that feeling is not strong enough. C will be offended, I'm afraid, and think that I am foolish to turn down her lovely offer. She would find it difficult to see that what was her was not found suitable by someone else. She is a very strange mixture of kindness and complete egoism.

Now that I am writing this, the sky has gone so green-yellow-grey and the room is so dark that I cannot see what I am writing. It is like the end of the world, yet the rain will not fall, only a few strangled, painful drops.

Did I say that a story had just come out in the *Cornhill* about me in China as a little boy?[14]

2 August

We had, too, last week, on Saturday, someone called Stewart Scott, an editor of something called *Eurasia*, which is to bind East and West together. His hair was coming out and Eric said his teeth were too, but he is only twenty-five. There was something nice about him. He had gone to Sandhurst at the age of seventeen because his father was a brigadier in the Indian Army and expected it of him — his eldest brother having been killed on the North-West frontier.

In due course he went to India and was soon court martialled for putting blank cartridges in his rifle when he was told to shoot at some rioters.

He was dismissed from the army and became a civilian living in the bazaars, Indian fashion.

He was then arrested (he does not know what for, he thinks because the authorities thought that he was stirring up trouble) and put in the most horrible jail for a month. He said that the conditions were unbelievable. Then he was freed, and immediately forced into the army again, this time as a private. He was in the army most of the war and at last got out because he was considered mad or unfit. He decided to behave as naturally as he could, taking no account of army conventions or codes. And so they thought he was mad. It was mad, he said, for him to talk to the Indians instead of the white men; and several other things were mad to the army mind which appear commonplace in ordinary life.

Now he is living in London and trying to edit this new magazine.

The facial spasms, the difficulty in utterance sometimes, the rapid fading of his physical youth, made him seem very childlike and helpless. He seemed to be a born victim. Eric thought that he would go mad soon or die.

He evidently found me easy, for he said, without considering the words at all, "Write to me, won't you, because I like getting letters and I like writing back."

He told us too that at his wedding party after the ceremony a girl came up to him and said, "Don't you wish that you'd met me before the wedding?"

14 "Narcissus Bay" (see 1944, note 10 above).

and he answered through a haze of drink, "But Mary, I've seen you about for a long time."

"All the same," he added, "she was damned attractive." It is a long time since I've heard anyone talk like that.

3 August, 3.40 p.m.

Yesterday afternoon we went again to Tunbridge Wells in May's car. First we went to Mrs Harmiston's shop in the slums, but the enormously fat daughter was blocking the gangway with her sandy-eyelashed postman, and there was such an atmosphere of smouldering sex that I could only glance at the china and oddments and then leave hurriedly, saying that I would return later, when the mother was back. The mother tells May that she thinks I am very nice. She has had to go to hospital to have one of her breasts cut off, and she tells you all about it if you are not very careful. She has a delicate beaky nose and wears glasses and swears quite a lot.

Next we went down to the Pantiles, where Eric and I managed to shake May off, asking her to go into Boot's to buy us a toilet roll, because we did not dare go ourselves. We then went to the fat woman who guards one of the springs, and we asked for a glass of water and paid our penny. The bottom of the glasses had gone an amber colour and I said, "Is that the iron in the water?" She answered, "Yes", with no expression, except perhaps a sulking one.

Eric then had another glass, giving her another penny eagerly, but again she did not respond, and I who felt that she was bound to be a little pleased with a young man eager for her water, was disappointed. It was as if she thought all the world very contemptible and ridiculous, and at that moment I had a sort of glimpse of the mad world, drinking these clear upswelling waters since the seventeenth-century; in this very place, century after century, the smiling people coming, taking the water into them, walking up and down chattering, going away and dissolving into the earth at last themselves.

Later when we climbed to the top of the common and saw below us all the roof tops, the faked copper-green domes of the Opera House cinema, and, nearer, the huge frog-shaped rocks squatting in the hay-like grass, and the little human bodies sprawled out in the sun, or sitting guardedly on the benches, I had a love for Tunbridge Wells and I wished that the Pantiles and the charming things remaining could be cared for and not ignored, degraded and destroyed.

But it is a truth that goes much deeper than we know, that men feel it indecent in some way to lavish care on things that never can be replaced. If a precious thing should get broken, there will be many people who in secret will sigh with relief.

It is as if care and love were too exhausting, too constricting.

Now I have bought May's car, so this afternoon we are going up to Crouch to get the milk.

There really seems some chance now that I may be able to build a tiny house, and I keep seeing in my mind exactly what I want. A long room downstairs with three french windows from floor to ceiling along one wall, a fireplace and an old mantel at one end, and at the other a blank wall for my tapestry cartoon. Upstairs three small bedrooms and the bathroom.

4 August

Last night we went up to the top of Gover Hill in May's car, for the first time. And there I drove it into the woods, where the aircraft red searchlight was during the war; and we got out and walked down the path through the bushes to the point where one can see straight down the Oxon Hoath avenue and on and on till the Ashdown Forest hills rise up.

The sun was a crimson hot-plate sinking down into the dusty, mousy clouds; but when we sat down it was hidden, and so I could not watch it disappear. We had brought the tomatoes Eric has grown, cheese, hard-boiled eggs, Darvita, chocolate and plums. It was like some time several years ago — a time before the war.

Suddenly out of the bushes an elderly, cheeky, business-looking man bounced and called out sharply, "Hullo, Dulwich!" and then went on down the path followed by two women. They talked about the view and the National Trust, and we were left to recover from surprise. The reason for his remark was that Eric was wearing his brother's blazer. I quite expected the man to return and ask absurd questions about Houses, masters, boys, games. And I wondered how Eric would take it, for he was not at the school.

It was quickly getting dark, so we hurried on to Middle Orchard to fetch the milk. We found them in, Noël wearing dark glasses, because she had broken her others. She insisted that we should stop for coffee, and we were quickly looking at charming 1870 guide books and at Chantilly sprig cups and saucers.

The coffee was very strong and I did not realize until too late that there was a whole jug of hot milk on the table.

In the dark, in the orchard, with a woman outside turning over the hay, and with the lights of the sitting-room flooding out, there was an atmosphere of newness, of expectancy, of waiting for a happening. Some promise somewhere in the air.

We drove back down Seven Mile Lane, past Italian prisoners walking home with sinister glacier-like faces turned to our headlights. Emptiness inside them and sadness and lust, to fill up the hours.

5.36 p.m.

Now Eric and I have driven to the ridge above Fairlawne and near Ivy Hatch. We are on the edge of a cornfield, the gold-brown sheaves stacked.

I left Eric sleeping and went for a walk into a wood that is being cleared. Tractors neat in tarpaulin jackets tucked in bushes, and deep zig-zag patterned ruts with sludgy mud and puddles under trees where mad flies darted and buzzed.

The view melting and consuming, changing and yet for ever.

I came out on the private road that goes down to Ightham Mote. I walked slowly up into the village and there I waited in the village shop. At last the woman sold me apple juice and coffee; but while I was waiting I was able to notice the old woman before me. She looked poor and she had cloudy eyes, apron flowered on a black ground and a thick swollen ankle under a black woollen stocking. But in her hand was an old Malacca cane with a gold knob — old greenish, pinkish, shallow worn gold. I wondered if she knew that it was gold. It was dented, so one could tell that it was thin, but still gold is gold. It had lost its ferrule and was worn down. It looked like the stick of the city dandy, come at last after eighty or ninety years to a labourer's cottage.

And as I walked out of the shop into the almost silent street a soft wireless voice said from an open window, where a net curtain was blowing, "In the year 1702(?) Louis the Fourteenth, known as the Sun King...from his palace of Versailles, which had started as a small château..."

What was it all about? The words were glamorous, thrown at me in the heat of the late afternoon, with the uneventful, unembellished village hemming me in.

In the wood, huge flies had collected on the freshly cut ends of the piles of wood, and as I passed they buzzed up into the air, leaving the white rounds of wood marked with red chalk marks.

And squirrels in the nut orchard bounced off the branches, ran about in the grass like grey kittens.

9 August

Yesterday I had a letter from Syracuse University, asking me about my story "When I Was Thirteen", saying that I had a following there amongst several of the younger members of the staff. The Librarian, it seems, gave his copy to a friend who was on a boat crossing the Atlantic. The boat went to the bottom of the sea and my story with it.

Now I am trying to find the manuscript of the story. I have found every other manuscript but that one. Could I have destroyed it? I wanted to send it to Syracuse University; then they could bind it in gilt morocco and keep it on their shelves for ever.

When I saw Syracuse on the envelope I felt quite confused. I thought it had come to me from the past, from classical times.

In the evening we went up to Crouch to fetch the milk in the car; and after we had escaped, we parked the car on the ridge just above the early fourteenth-century manor, "Old Soar", then walked down through the fields, past the potato plants in flower — a sweet smell past powdery-blue plums lying on the ground, until we came to the farm buildings, then to the tiny little medieval place itself — a stone box with two smaller stone boxes fastened at the corners.

Round at the front we saw the red Georgian farmhouse which has been built on to it. The fanlight over the door has little Gothic arches — suggested clearly by the real Gothic building. The woman let us in a little grudgingly, and we went alone up the spiral staircase into what I suppose was the solar; from it led the little chapel, and what the farmer later told us was the garde-robe (but I always understood that garde-robe was a polite medievalism for W.C., so I feel perhaps that he might be wrong).

We climbed up to the top floor, the floor that has been inserted in the hall or solar, cutting the charming pointed windows in two, and saw there the amusing early nineteenth-century drawings that have been done in red chalk on the ceiling. Childish little sash-windowed houses with belfries, trees with large leaves, horses, a man in a swamp shooting duck perhaps — and then two fat little pugilists with their fists up in the old-fashioned way. (Someone had been rude here and had pencilled in a long thin phallus that jutted out from one and poked the other in the ribs.)

The doodle-bomb of last year that burst near the gypsies in the orchard above has made the ruinous condition of some parts worse than it was, as well as breaking all the windows.

I longed to be able to buy the place and very, very carefully restore the manor part and live in both it and the red farmhouse.

I am going to write to the Society for the Protection of Ancient Buildings to see if they will do anything about it.

26 *August*, 11.35 *a.m.*

I have been ill now and in bed for over two weeks. That is why I have written nothing. And the new doctor gave me M. & B. tablets which, I suppose, made me feel even worse — black, dead, inhuman as a boulder — telescoped into myself till nothing could come forward. Now I am better, and so the other state seems unbelievable, but it is waiting for me again.

Very little has happened. Quite a good notice of *In Youth is Pleasure* came out in the July *Horizon* and there was also something from an Australian paper.

My brother Paul arrived with Aunt Dolly on Thursday from Ditchling.[15]

15 Dorothy Welch (see 1942, note 49 above) had moved to Ditchling, Sussex, in 1943, and Denton had very briefly considered living with her again.

He has just come back from Italy and all the fighting of the last three years. He looks extraordinarily untouched by it, for which I was very thankful. But I would not live with him for very long, I think, because he seemed so very prowling and roving-eyed. He could not sit still in the room, but had to pick everything up and look at it, or read anything that lay near him. My aunt's own Aunt Bertie has died, and left her and the other sixteen nephews and nieces about £2,000 each.

31 August

Today nothing grows out of my heart, nothing comes. I could do my pen-drawing with contentment and pleasure except that my eyes are tired from doing it all yesterday, and I do not want to make myself feel ill; so I am thwarted, for nothing comes to write. There seems a lot there, but it is plugged and stuck. Flowing from me is no essence; it is all walled up.

The day before yesterday I went out in the car, the first time for two or three weeks. We went first to get my new medicine from the doctor; then we drove on down Hayesden Lane, climbed the hill and went along the ridge to Penshurst, with the wide views on each side of us. Just past the mental hospital, Swaylands, we parked the car at the top of the hill and gazed out across a field to the village down below. We drank tepid tea, because the thermos is broken, and ate chocolate biscuits and Evie's home-made ones. It seemed strange to be in the comfort of a car after so much bicycling all through the war. It felt dead a little, and I wished I could bicycle anywhere, do anything with no ill effects. For a moment I felt horribly envious of ordinary strength, ordinary health.

After tea we went on through the village, past the desolate looking great house on the hill with the wonderful old trees in the park on our right, and so to Leigh, where we went over the green to look at a house that was advertised for sale. It had sounded quite good, but when we saw it, we found a horrible little stucco house, with a few meagre black boards at the gables, and its position was very bad, right in the middle of many other villas. We laughed and came away as soon as possible.

1 September, 7.15 p.m.

Yesterday we took lunch, ducks' eggs, nut meat, tomatoes, crispbread, cherry jam, honey and coffee in the car and drove to Peckham Old Church on the hill, where we stopped and ate, gazing down over the churchyard to the far view.

As we were eating, the rural district sewage tanks drove up and emptied their loads straight into the woods. We heard the sewage swishing and gurgling and then the smell struck us in the face in sudden gusts. We shut the car window on that side and soon it dispersed; but surely this is a very extraordinary thing to do, to empty sewage straight into a wood.

Afterwards a fair-haired youth, with a darker, very faint beard just sprouting, told us that they sometimes just emptied the sewage into a field, although people had complained, so he supposed they now came and dumped it into this lovely wood. He was gentle and docile, and so rather likeable and sad. One felt he was soon going to be ground down. We left him and walked down to the War Memorial lychgate, where we sat on the stones in the sun and looked down on to Hadlow Tower, seemingly so far away.

Eric's shirt had split right down the back, so he took it off and sunned himself.

We tried to get into the church, but it was locked, and the fair-haired boy told us that the money boxes had been rifled and other things damaged. He smiled at us and said, like an old, old person, "It's these gangs of boys, you know."

After some time in the sun we left the church and drove slowly down the tiny rough lane towards the ruined arch with Corinthian pilasters on the edge of the Mereworth estate. Just as we were climbing up to it, we passed an oldish man with a gun under his arm and a taller, younger, dark-haired man with a black patch over one eye. Their surface sinister quality was deepened when the short white-haired man seemed to direct the other one to get out of our way, as one would a very young child. He at last gently pulled him down the bank and the other stood there apathetically, with his back to us, just as a patient, obedient cart-horse would. We both felt at once that he was mad. There was something very piercing about his stance, his slightly bowed head with the one screened eye and the dark hair jutting up stiffly.

When we got to the ruined arch, we found that gypsies or soldiers had demolished most of the wooden fence and we could walk right into the grounds. This we did, I rather nervously, expecting to be turned out or seized by guards. The army had put a hideous little field telephone right through the arch and down the ancient, dangerously ruinous beech avenue, but even this could not spoil the absolute romance of the lovely villa seen far away, with rough ground and banks of bracken sweeping down on each side of it.

The picture was fine because the warm dust-coloured porticoes, dome and pavilions were set against a deep background of sage-green trees and hill. We sat at the end of the avenue and gazed for some time at this house, perfect of its kind and time. The old-fashioned architecture books point out disparagingly that it is a slavish copy of one of Palladio's villas, but yesterday it looked quite perfectly eighteenth-century English. It seemed as if the countryside cried out for it, and after we had left it I felt that everything else seemed unrealized and insipid.

At last, after I had said how much I wished I could have it to look after it and live in, we went back to the car. Eric had found some mushrooms and I had eaten a few autumn blackberries and tasted their mysterious juice, delicious and bitter and sad.

We went on down the hill and came to some cottages, and across the road were stretched many flags and the legend "Welcome Home Frank." I thought that it would be nice to be a soldier and find this waiting when one at last came home; but only the people who live in cottages treat their sons in this way.

9 *September*

Last Sunday Paul came and told me that if we get nothing else, we will eventually each get eighty shared in Wattie & Co.[16] and if the firm gets going again and is moderately successful, we should each get about £300 a year. But there is the mystery of what has happened to all the rest of our father's money. Did he spend it all? Will our step-mother be able to throw any light? It is all peculiar and just what one should expect, I suppose. He had about £4,000 a year in director's fees alone.

Then there has been the great scandal of my great-uncle Percy Bois, who has been sole trustee to his sister, Aunt Bertie, for several years.[17] She has died and it has just come to light he has taken between £10,000 and £13,000 of the £48,000 odd on the interest from which she lived. The money is now to be divided between sixteen nephews and nieces, and so they are each to receive £1,000 less than they would otherwise have done. It appears that Uncle Percy, who everyone thought was quite rich, had only £200 of his own for the last few years, and so he took Aunt Bertie's money to keep up his large house near Petersfield, his mentally deranged wife, his unmarried daughter and his widowed and penniless married daughter and her children. Now they have to leave the house. There is a sale on 7 September. Uncle Percy is ninety, frail and a little senile, his wife is quite unbalanced and peculiar, so the two daughters will have to manage on their legacies of about £2,000 each and Uncle Percy £200 a year. They are trying to find a small house.

I remember once staying with them when I was nine. They had a long, low house on the side of a hill somewhere in Surrey or Sussex. It was autumn-winter, I know, and Marjorie, the unmarried daughter, invited me into the old schoolroom one day, where she had a little saucepan simmering on a spirit stove. She said, "Let's make coffee and fudge, shall we?" I was excited, but a little bewildered.

She was a governessy, blue-stocking girl, quite ten years older than I was.

16 The firm in Shanghai of which Denton's father had been a director; rubber estate managers.
17 Another sister, Edith Bois, had married Denton's paternal grandfather. Uncle Percy appears in *I Left My Grandfather's House*.

I wondered if she was doing the sweet-making to amuse me on a dull afternoon.

She poured condensed milk in, added sugar and butter. I remember stirring the mixture, then watching it harden and glisten on the flat tin tray. I often think of that room and that moment. The low lattice and the glum sky outside, the smell of methylated spirit, and the enticing smell of the fudge (although I was afraid that the condensed milk which she had put in and which I hated would spoil everything), Marjorie's intent, peering, rather fierce face.

The whole house seemed rather too heated for me, and there was a load and jumble of objects. A chain-mail veiled helmet with a cross nose piece hung over the stairs, and I was told, I think untruly, that it was a crusader's. It was probably Persian. Then in the drawingroom were cabinets of satinwood in the Adam style as seen through late Victorian eyes — eplodgy roses and bows with perhaps a cupid on a cloud. I remember the cabinets because my great-uncle explained at length to my mother that one was french polished and one wasn't. He asked her which she liked best. I remember preferring the french polished one — it made the wood look silkier. I did not like the coarser, open grain of the other — but both cabinets seemed quite ugly to me. I could never quite make out whether my uncle wanted eventually to have both french polished or both only waxed. He seemed to make a great business of them as specimens of different treatment.

It is curious that the harsh glass of french polish should have appealed to me as a child, when I could not bear the lacquer put on brass bed knobs and fittings and other fierce hard processes.

It was just at the time of our visit to these Bois relations that I had been given an easel and oil paints. I went into the drive and picked spiky holly with red berries. Then I picked a sprig of tawny beech leaves and went upstairs to paint them on a little canvas block.

I secretly disliked the canvas board because I knew the canvas was only paper and the board only cardboard. Now I know that these seemingly impermanent boards are one of the best things to paint on — far better than real canvas or plywood.

I had the picture of the leaves for a long time. I can see it now — the red berries with the whipped-cream whorl of thick flake white for the highlight.

I did not see these relations again until 1933 when I was on a walking tour. They had changed their house, but I know the address, somewhere near Petersfield, I think. I was very tired and the sun was hot on my back and I wanted a nice bed for the night. I sat down in the grass at the edge of the long straight road and rested for a few moments. Children were playing near me, shouting. Then I took my courage in my hands and walked up to their house, down the drive, till I found a building so like their last house that I knew the same mind had chosen it — the sober tiles and bricks, the oak door, the leaded panes, Lutyens country covention watered down, made unspectacular.

I knocked on the door rather desperately and rang. I was taken to my uncle, who had just come in. I explained myself and brazenly asked to stay the night. He looked at me like an old turkey or vulture with a loose scrawny neck; then he said rather uncertainly, gently, repressively, "Of course, there are buses."

"I know, but I am tired," I said, determined to stay the night, determined to be made welcome, to reap the benefits of their comfortable home, to have a new experience, not always to miss new happenings and surroundings because of timidity and other people's dried, dead hearts.

It is only the sort of thing one does when one is very young, but there I sat having tea with my uncle until my aunt and cousin came in, gazing at their stag's head crest all over the tray, the pot, the cream jug.

When the others came back from a garden-party-of-work my uncle said quietly, "This is Denton Welch, he is going to stay the night." My aunt's eyes fixed on me (she was not then mad) and my cousin said, "Oh, then we saw you in the long grass on the side of the road. I recognised your blue shirt. We drove by."

I was made conscious of my lack of clothes, only khaki shorts and the skimpy Aertex shirt that wouldn't keep buttoned. I began to regret my ruthless gate-crashing, but I felt that it was weak to repine, that I must push forward, enjoy, not feel embarrassed. Were they not my relations? Was I not entitled to stay with them?

After the good, cold supper that night my aunt said to my uncle, "Now take Denton out on the terrace while Marjorie and I deal with things." I saw that she meant to clear the table and take the things into the pantry, so I said at once, "Oh, let me help," and went to pick up the tray. But my aunt seemed quite flustered and appalled that a man should even think of helping in the house. "Oh, no," she said agitatedly, "you must go out with Percy, he will show you the garden. We are suffering from the universal servant difficulty. The cook won't do anything, it is one maid's day out and the other has left."

I was surprised at all this explanation, at the refusal to let me help, at the almost shame my aunt seemed to feel because she was left to clear away her own table. She did not even have to clear up, only to clear. I saw that it all came down from another day, when servants were considered absolutely essential, as a part of life so important that they could not be done without under any circumstances.

At night I walked down the wide passage filled with curiosities to my bedroom, so Edwardian-bachelor that I half expected to see a hip bath in the corner.

In the morning there were horrors over the tip to the one remaining maid. How I rejoiced that the other one had left and that I should never see the cook!

But what should I leave? I had so little money for my journey that to leave two shillings would leave a painful hole, and yet to leave less seemed trivial and mean. I was so inexperienced that I felt everything had to be all or nothing. So I left nothing because I could not afford two shillings. I think now that the maid would even have preferred sixpence to this blunt nothing, but I was too proud to be little so I decided to be nothing at all.

I went into the downstairs cloakroom and then said my good-byes — so funny, so cold, so woolly. It was exhilarating to get out of the house and walk on the common road; yet I was glad in some way to have been and to experience their life.

18 September, 10.30 a.m.

Last night in the moon — head on my shoulder, and the screeching owl flickering across the lawn, through the trees and back again; while the cow mooed sadly for its bull. All stillness in the room, only the arch of grey light from the Gothic window living across the polished floor and the end of the bed. Moment that can never be *made* again, only *known* in years afterwards.

19 September, 11.10 a.m.

Yesterday, after a lunch of chopped egg (ham mixed in it I noticed), grilled tomatoes, mushrooms, scarlet beans and potatoes, then peaches from her flowering peach and cream off the milk, we went off with May in the car to fetch a parcel. She had begun in a very bad mood because she had been expecting Guy Allan to lunch, and of course he hadn't come. Half way through our meal, when we had eaten nearly everything, the telephone bell rang and I thought, that's him, he's waiting at the station — he'll be up in a minute and there won't be a thing to eat. But I was wrong; he hadn't even left London and he wanted to come today or tomorrow instead. May firmly put him off, saying that she couldn't cook another meal for several more months.

When we had collected the parcel, I drove through Tonbridge and out by the Pembury Road. We went right on to Pembury Walk where all the bracken was turning and signing to rust colour and where there were still notices to say that soldiers were practising shooting over the ground and it was dangerous to go beyond a certain point. I went right through though, down into the little valley where the water works and the sewage works are and up the other side, until after some time we came to a small empty house on the right and, just past it, a larger and much more interesting one. I stopped the car at once, and Eric and I went over the weedy drive to the window on the left. The front of the house was rather uninteresting late eighteenth-century, sash windows and a not altogether attractive roughish stucco — original though, I think. The porch was very bad, perhaps 1860-70. Pitched roof, dreary chamfered wooden pillars, timidly Gothic, but so timid that you couldn't even distinguish that style unless you analysed the sources from which such a dull construction had sprung.

But when we looked into the kitchen we saw a cavernous room obviously earlier than the facade of the house, although it had a not very good eighteenth-century dresser (all the drawers stolen) and a corner cupboard.

We looked into two other windows but they did not seem to promise much, except that I noticed the nice, thick panelled shutters; then at the right hand end we looked into a room that was entirely panelled in perhaps mid-seventeenth-century pouching — the sort that is called Tusloi. It had obviously been treated with linseed oil or something dark and sticky, but there it was, rather exciting. The wide fireplace seemed to be original too. We hurried round to look at the back of the house. Then I saw the huge stone chimneys and realized that a much earlier house had been faced with the disappointing Georgian front.

As we were going through the farmyard, a nice labourer asked us if we would like the key, and then told us his little boy (who was in long trousers — dungarees — and seemed about to go hoeing with him) would get it from the cottage; but the small child said with great assurance that he couldn't reach it and refused even to stand on a stool to do so. So the man, after smiling indulgently, went to get it himself.

When he brought it back, I took the large key and went expectantly to the front door. Excitement is the only word describing the feeling as one waits and fumbles at the door of an old, unexplored, empty house.

The hall was dull, narrow and unimposing in any way (I suspect that the little morning room on the right has been sliced off it) but at the end in a sort of large niche was a really fine staircase with amazingly thick carved posts and ample bulging balustrade — something that would have graced a much more important house. It again was seventeenth-century — early, mid or late. I'm not accurate enough to say. I think early to mid, because it was so very massive, but it might be later. It was the richness of its thick carving and simple heaviness made a strong appeal to me, who am not always fond of clumsy strength. It seemed a staircase made for centuries. It went up in short flights and wide platforms round a square. The width of it made you feel you could dance down it.

I half went up to it, then came down, determined to explore the bottom floor first. There was no new interest in either the kitchen or the pantry or the morning breakfast room — they were really quite dull — but the panelled room was good. One could see that the panelling had been white before the Tudorphiles had stripped it and smeared it with the horrible oil or varnish, for there was still a small white eighteenth-century cornice round the older panelling. The door was eighteenth-century too, so were the windows. I could not quite decide whether the white stone Tudor mantel had been put in when the room had been "restored". If so, it must have been done some time ago. If one could get the oil and varnish off the wood, I think it would be a lovely colour.

We went into the back room, which must have been the drawing room, I think. The fireplace was boarded up, but it had one charming Gothicized sash window and a little brass drop handle to the otherwise dull door. I later noticed that several doors had these pretty original handles and locks.

Upstairs was not very good, except for the wide old floor boards which one knew would look wonderful waxed.

There was one little closet room with very old lattice panes and moulded wooden mullions. The attics would make one fine long "chamber". There were those good arched "flat" beams framing the plaster.

We went down the back stairs and they too were wonderfully solid and satisfying. It was a house of fine staircases. All the pride of the house seemed to be in these flights. The back stairs were not of course so grand or so wide as the front ones, but they excelled in one particular, they had never been painted or stained, and so the oak was wonderfully hard, shiny, dusty, purplish, silver, greyish colour — quite indescribable, as can be seen from that string of adjectives.

These back stairs led us right down into the cellar, where we found a sinister skeleton of the central heating boiler and new posts shoving up the old beams. We did not like the look of this. It made me feel that the house would crumble into the cellar, until Eric said it may have been done to create an air-raid shelter. (The house had been used for most of the war for soldiers; one could see signs of them everywhere. One thought of them in a long pink, naked line waiting to get into the one old-fashioned bath, and in the drawingroom someone had written "Fuck you" in long chalk letters. The electric light switch covers had all been stolen too.)

Out in the garden we found an old walnut tree — very grand and august, though not very large. The back of the house was delightful in a rustic jumbled way, with tiling, and the staircase and closet projections, and there were some steps to a higher level of the lawn. All nice espaliers too, pears I think, and a strong stone wall.

There was the farmyard just next door and an ugly new gas storage apple barn.

One wanted so much to have the house and lots of money and clever workmen to make it perfect. But in my present state it would be nothing but a great anxiety — and when it was in good condition, it would be much too large.

Still, one hankers after that staircase and those little brass drop handles.

9 October

I have been ill for a week, and before that I had a letter from an Alexander Randolph, an American Criminal Investigation Department agent stationed in Salzburg. He wrote to ask me where he could get my books, as he liked my short ʼstories so much. Then he told me that he had asked for them in Bumpus and the "little woman" behind the counter suddenly brightened up and told him how much she admired my work. She knew quite a lot about me, although she has never set eyes on me, and she ended by sending him to the Leicester Galleries to look at my two little pictures of animals there. He says that she has some strange Polish name and that I ought to visit her if I am ever passing, as her "devotion is quite touching".

Then I had another letter from a Stephen Bagnall of Fog Lane, Manchester. His was very restrained and sensible — exceptionally so, and in a tiny carefully formed hand, on heavy white paper. I mention all this because my mind floats out, wondering what all these people are like, who say they like my thoughts on paper.

We had too a youth called David Carritt,[18] sent to us by Guy Allan. He came to lunch and there was a chicken and baked pears. He was nice really, very young, eighteenish, and rather clever. He played the harpsichord well and I gathered he was a very bright boy at Rugby — a precocious conversationalist, with a few spots on his face, excitable movments. He loved mentioning the names of minor old masters — obviously cut out for a museum worker. He only looked at things in the room that he could date and docket. Other things were quite missed. His eyes are not really sharp. I think he would be called a very brilliant boy. He says he once had an aunt who went to church with bright red toadstools worked into the thick plait of grey hair hanging down her back. When I mentioned my dolls' house, he said that at home they had the dolls' house that was once in Devonshire House. I questioned him about it, but he could not tell much except that he thought it dated from about 1850 and that it was in a bad condition with no furniture left. He is rather childlike in some ways, a simple snob and perhaps rather feminine.

On the day he was with us I began I suppose to feel ill, but I only put it down to the exhaustion due to his froth and nonsense. (He is humorous.) But in the night I began to shiver rather pleasantly in the midst of feeling warm. Then in the morning I was feverish, and the next day I was sick very often. It was like earthquakes inside splitting me, throwing up yellow sulphur bile from the depths. I was empty inside even before I began being sick. Black, yellow, splitting days like that make you wonder how you manage to exist through them. I have the feeling that my flesh is stretching. I'm glad it's so elastic — that the veins are not brittle like glass rods.

18 Later an international art expert. Through his friendship at Oxford with Ben Nicolson he was responsible for Denton's visit to Sissinghurst in 1948.

Then on Thursday Dr Ramsden appeared. I told him that Jack Easton was back and practising and I would rather return to him as my doctor again, since he had known my case since Broadstairs days. Not wanting to be boorish made me say to Ramsden that he should go on with his visits; but now Jack writes to say that he would like to come, if I'd like to have him. We are waiting to see him, after his five years with the army in Egypt.

Routledge tells me that *Maiden Voyage* is being published by *Le Sagittaire* in Paris next year or the year after.

18 October

Last week Eric and I went out in the car to Mereworth, then up Seven Mile Lane until we came to the little road between the brushwood just before the Beech Inn with its clumsy little Gothic windows and its wisteria. We stopped at the corner before the road dives down to Black Swanton Pool, and there we began to eat our toast and cheese and tomatoes and chocolate and walnuts. The sun was hot on our faces through the windscreen and we had to take our jackets off. A strolling soldier in braces passed us and got through the fence into an orchard. My bowels were rumbling and crumbling inside, so I had to leave Eric and run into the delightful bushes. All alone there, with the leaves cracking in the sun and the last insects being slow and dying as they walked along. The smell of all the things that had had their summer, lived their love and pleasure out. Only the greedy horse-flies lively for what they could find when I left. I walked further along the path, then sat down by a tree stump, so that I had all round me green light through the leaves.

We went on till we came to Trottiscliffe, then down the lane to the church. On the corner sat a fat-breasted gypsy woman with the inherited bold stare. Her hair was gold and her dress was so tight that it looked like rubber. We passed the church and came to Tin Town where the peculiar little huts and bungalows have been built. Then we turned into the lane leading to Coldrum Lodge. I wanted to see it again, to find out if it was still empty. The wide farmyard with the line of twisted walnut trees was full of activity. A woman fed something in the barn, a man stared, a black and white dog barked and landgirls were helping with a haystack. We saw that the house was lived in, so we left the car and walked to the little circle of Druid stones half on half off the steep ledge of ground that looked out to the ridge of downs and the far-off white pillars of the Medway factories.

We climbed up the little path. The National Trust have made of the Coldrum a little garden with a hedge all round and the grass scythed. There were the fallen stones sunk into the ground like giant bullets in an ogre. And the huge tree that jutted out, a little house on the edge of the small precipice, seemed to be launching into the air, the landscape; seemed to be sailing there for ever as a testimony, I can't think of what, unless it be endurance and cruelty.

We lay with our backs to the upright stones and watched below us, next to the broad field of sparse mustard a mock battle between soldiers who were training to be officers. A red flag was flapping helplessly and smoke was rising. There were bullet noises and whines and then the screeches and shouts of the soldiers running in lines, falling on their stomachs, disappearing over the hill-top.

Then we turned away from the Druid stones and the bullied soldiers and walked back to the farmhouse. We took courage and walked right in front of it. There were the two pines still in front. Some of the ivy had been cleared away and one could read quite clearly in the oval stone above the door, "Coldrum Lodge, 1796", in that charming lettering that can never fail to give me satisfaction. I remembered inside the two panelled rooms, with all the moulding very thin and delicate, because they were so late. I never remember before seeing completely panelled rooms so late.

We could not go in now, because it was inhabited, so we stared and then turned back to the car and went to have tea with Mrs Carpmael and her mad sister, Connie.

Connie met us in the garden, and because I had grown a beard while in bed, she knelt down on the grass in front of me and murmured something about Christ. Then she got up, looking very old and knowing and monkified, and passed close to Eric, saying nonchalantly, as she brushed his fly buttons with her hand, "Would you like these undone?" Her voice was so light, so almost social, sneering, that I could not feel that there was any real sexuality in her, only the ghost of frivolous excitation. Then she began to talk to me about dukes, the Dukes of Cumberland and Cambridge, I think. She always gets on to dukes with me. I wonder why? She told Eric, too, when he called me Denton, that I wasn't Denton. I suppose again the beard non-plussed her.

At tea we were made to smell the yellow quinces on the dresser. It was a curiously artificial smell that I have never smelt before. Mrs Carpmael poured with difficulty out of the Georgian teapot, and I wished so much that she would give it to me. We melted away at last after being given some fast decaying pears.

On Sunday, Bill and Anne came.[19] My brother had grown grey hair at the sides and he told me all about our father's latest Will. It appears now he has left everything to my stepmother unconditionally. She is sole executrix too. This, which seemed so very bad on the surface for us, is apparently not quite so bad, as Bill thinks that the whole thing can be settled, if he offered her an annuity on condition that she gives over the shares to our keeping. At

19 Née Stafford, Bill Welch's first wife; later divorced.

present she is staying in Shanghai and swearing that she is going to run the firm herself. It is just like the wicked stepmother in children's stories. Bill says that in a good year, when all is in running order again, the shares should bring in a lot and that in a year or two we should all have quite a comfortable amount. But I suppose Ada knows this too, and so I can't help feeling that she may be very difficult.

There is also the question of money of our own mother's that may now go into her pocket. For our father sold the house (bought with our mother's money) for about £15,000.[20] This should really have been divided between us instead of going into our father's estate. Bill says that he will rake this up if Ada will not agree.

I suppose money is so fascinating, so repelling and so tiring because it has the power to draw all forms of ingenuity out of people.

26 October

What has happened to my heart tonight? It could eat up all the world. I went out at five o'clock and the darkness came so quickly, the hard wind was blowing me back and the rain spat down. I had no light on my bike and near the town I got down to walk [21]. And on the other side of the road I saw another shadow walk and after a little it seemed to stop in a gateway and watch me, but it seemed that it might be all imagination, it was so dark and lost to me. I moved on, then looked over my shoulder once or twice wondering if anything sinister could be lurking there. Suddenly I saw the figure cross the road and I knew that it was following me. I walked very calmly, slowly, so that it should pass me under a lamp-post. And then I saw that it was quite a young sort of gypsy country boy. And it said, very politely, touching its slouch cap, "Excuse me, sir, but can you give me a light?" It then fingered the cigarette stump behind its ear, and I began ridiculously and confusedly looking in all my pockets for matches I knew weren't there. Somehow I couldn't just say no and leave it at that. He had such a curiously open, I suppose what you would call "English" face, that the sly words, the old, old opening gambit of getting into conversation with a stranger, seemed out of character and peculiar. I half expected him to beg and yet I didn't. His light hair stuck out jaggedly under his jammed down cap and he wore one of those very long old overcoats that somehow look dashing and rakish to the very last.

He fell into step with me and started to tell me how he'd taken the horse out, then it had thrown a shoe and he couldn't get it to the smithy. "If a horse gets anything into its head you can't do nothing with it," he said, "so I had to put it in the stable, and now I'm going home."

20 585 Avenue Foch, Shanghai, where Denton's mother died when he was eleven.
21 In Tonbridge.

We talked a little about horses — how soon we had learnt to ride; then he told me that he didn't ride for two years, after he was nine, because he was sent to Scotland.

"Where were you in Scotland?" I asked, and he quite non-plussed me by saying, "Well, near Derby for some of the time."

"Oh," I said, feeling at a loss. Then unaccountably I left him, turning down Postern [Lane] for no reason. I don't know why, for he seemed so nice, so simple, almost charming, the mixture of boy, man, child. Was it that I felt him sinister in his approach? Or just that my own inadequacy overcame me? Then I felt the lack of real contact between us, the complete hollowness of casual bonhomie — built on a lie — the lie of pretending that one feels no deeper. One pretends to be a dear little machine, when one is a devouring flame.

I went on into the town and got my M. & B. pills at the surgery, went past the Castle public lavatory and along that little side street, to revel in the controlled squalor of the backs of houses in a provincial town.

Near Ferox Hall, where the little pub sticks out into the road, I looked round and thought I saw the boy in his slouch cap again and my heart was all jarred and jumping, and I seemed for a moment almost to suffer from hallucination — a piece of crushed wood and bark before me on the pavement seemed to take on the semblance of a dead and bulging little rat or mouse. I can't tell you why I was swinging about like this. Sweeps of piercing sadness came over me. I was lost in the dark world, in the lighted streets alone, waiting to die...

Then I looked up and saw through the lighted pub window, with a sort of amazement, an extremely pretty Adam mantelpiece with, I think, a little chariot drawn by lions on the central medallion. It was all painted rather a hot pink, and a grey-haired woman sat before it primly cocking her crossed feet up to warm them at the modern stove. She was reading a book and wore glasses, and over this delightful mantel were two early Victorian prints of pugilists. It was just before opening time, and this quiet scene and the relics of the past spoke to me with an obstinate, insistent voice. It was the platitude that the river said: "Lorries tear past all night and people die, but we are still here wrapped in our ancientness in the quiet bar parlour." All false, this feeling of everlastingness that relics give us. That pub may be swept away any time this year to widen the road.

I walked down to the cinema, and just as I passed it I saw old Prince Belosselsky swaying with his fantastic other century walk up the step. He too wore a slouch cap and a long coat, with such a dignity and pomposity that they almost might have been crown and robe in Madame Tussaud's. I have never known anyone with this walk before. And his stranded figure bit into me too — to think of its sitting wearily through the film alone with its past stretching out behind it like a sheet of never-ending woolly tripe. To be stifled in one's tripes.

For a moment I sat by the muddy swirling river. I think lock gates had been opened, for it was very low, almost with the mud showing, and it should have been high and raging and flooding after these many days' rain.

On the iron seat I seemed to have reached the bottom of my sadness and hunger, and it was suddenly quite easy for me to see that I should go home at once to supper, not go on over-tiring myself and making myself ill, as I used to do so often in the past because of the thing that was eating me. It was all clear that I should never wander and grope about and gaze, that I should always make for something and do it, that I was lost if I did not make a pattern for myself. When I go back into formless days, feel stiffled with my lack of ability, feel that everything is smeared and smudged, I have the vision of true madness. Not melodrama madness but just dirty madness.

16 November, 10.20 a.m.

I have brought nothing to this book of all the days that have melted away — days when we have taken the car to woods or to hill tops and have eaten our food there in the shut-in snugness with the dashboard in front of us, perhaps rain on the roof and the view through the windscreen.

One day we went to Hurst Woods and I drew tree stumps, toadstools, dead leaves, and Eric found a skeleton snake all curled, and a dead squirrel with dense, bushed-out tail. I saw the place where Maurice and I and Freddie had the picnic in 1938 and Freddie had charged about, behaving like an ape in the trees. No one knew then that he would be killed in an aeroplane. He was much too like a troublesome, jumping flea to be imagined unmoving.

Afterwoods, he went on to Middle Orchard to find out what was really happening. It has been nothing but changing.

Now it is settled for the moment that they are not moving to London. Their house in Hampstead has fallen through, so we won't be able to have Middle Orchard.

I am very thwarted, impotent-feeling, as if we shall never have a house and garden.

19 November, 8.30 a.m.

Evie in bed with a temperature and Eric has been doing all the cooking, making spaghetti dishes, perfect fish pudding and clear soup with noodles in it.

Now it is eight-thirty and he is knocking about downstairs getting early morning tea. Heskett, the gardener, is just walking past with heavy, lumbering, sluggish steps. The milk girls have arrived on their motor bikes and are clinking their bottles, turning them into strange musical

instruments. Far away on the road lorries can be heard, their ty
seemingly sticking to the road and singing as they eat along.

Eric is talking to himself in his "Northern" voice, saying "bluddy" for
"bloody". The air is cold and damp, flowing in at all the windows with the
very pale whitey sunlight.

20 November, 7.29 a.m.

Great drops of water from the mist heavily plopping, everything milky
outside. I have my story to do for *Harper's*, another to do for *Kingdom Come*,
my *Vogue* drawing to do in four days, my book to finish, [22] pictures to finish
for the Leicester, and two for the Arts Council. How much of this will get
done soon? I am a snail worker turning out about four paragraphs a day and
messing with my pictures till they are an obsession.

25 November, 7 a.m.

So nothing — blank in me tonight after sickness and 'flu. All day
touching at the drawing with my black pen, turning away from the writing
always, because drawing soothes and lulls, and should do so, else there will
be no good picture. It must all be built up of little cat pats, love pats;
although many people will not believe this and think painters should be
half-drunk louts who paint with their large loo-loos. But writing ought to be
love pats, that tickle the patter with warmth as he pats; but it only is
sometimes for perhaps five seconds.

It is lazier to be a painter than a writer, but only if you are both. If you are
only a writer, then you are lazier, because you waste your hands. Only if you
copied out your books most exquisitely you would be better.

Black man on the wireless sings, "Don't want to be a Judas in my heart,
Lord". Gas fire roars so dryly. Maurice Cranston has been to tea. He can't
think one thought out of the middle of his own head, but only out of
someone's else's, and the heads he chooses are always secondhand too. It is
a puppy biting its tail of hollowness.[23] He reviews books for the *Church
Times* and he saw my last one on a Charing Cross bookstall labelled boldly
and baldly "Of Interest to Students of Abnormal Psychology". He thinks I
should tell Routledge to object, but I don't think it matters at all.

Writing is everything but the reality. Heavy as mud, powdery as

---

22 *A Voice Through a Cloud.* It took Denton four years to write.
23 This passage is typical of Denton's abrasive attitude towards friends, possibly occasioned by
his own ill-heath. Cranston was still only twenty-five, and Denton did not live long enough
to be able to test the mature intellectual abilities of his contemporaries, nor to have to eat his
words.

meringue, silvered all over with clouding slime, everything true escaping underneath the words, like insects scuttling away — like the cars and bicycles in Trafalgar Square beetling, skidding away when the huge hand in the sky, God's hand, is only just put down to pluck them.

When your life has nothing left in it but your writing, then it grows so dear that even the badness is loved and groomed and cared for. But if real love comes into your life, it cuts away from your work, so that if you laugh at it, almost despite it for what it is worth, yet long for it too, brood on the time when you had nothing else, when all you had to live on was what you made, when your thoughts were hotted up and sharp, for you dared not let them cool.

27 November, 7.40 p.m.

We went to the preview of Miss Awcock's sale at the Stewardess's cottage in the Cedar Walk of Oxon Hoath. Under the great saga pancake trees squat the little brick house, behind wrought iron grilles. Opposite is the walk with the round pudding bay-trees to the huge kitchen gardens with their grand gates.

Miss Awcock is over seventy. She and her father before her must have been agents for Oxon Hoath for nearly a hundred years.

Now she is being turned out because the new owner, Cannon, says she is completely hopeless and inefficient and Sir William Geary left nothing in his Will about the cottage being hers for life. She is going to live in one room in Tonbridge and a subscription has been got up for her. It reached £3751 I think.

The things in her cottage are charming, because quite untouched, unvarnished and unmessed about. Some are almost black with the rich grain showing through the polished dirt. A charming little Sheraton sideboard with Tambour cupboard was like this. Then there is a little castor dented-in, 1716, which Eric is going to bid for, for me. And a good country Chippendale chair that has lost its top splat and pieces off its legs. The seat also has been incorrectly rushed over, but it is nice and worthy, with crisp carving.

The rooms were pretty with old mantels, eighteenth-century, put into the older building, and fragments of panelling in the passages. Everything cared for over many years with no change. Very un-spectacular, but with that untampered air that is very rare.

There is no bathroom, electric light or water laid on. Not even a tap, I think, in the kitchen.

The step at the bottom of the boxed-in stairs was semi-circular. The room one entered into had a brown, thickly painted Adam mantel, and under it the only pretentious, ungenuine thing in the house, a strong bricky open grate, painfully with the pretty mantel.

We left in a hurry because we saw Phil and Peggy Mundane Arswhole appearing at the door;[24] luckily they went straight upstairs, so we wriggled out at once.

We went up into the Hurst Woods and picnicked with the watery red sun dropping down into the whippy bushes. Afterwards we walked and found a wonderful gnarled, knotted, bulging, swollen, gashed beech hedge — amazing in its growth, breathing out age, hardness, sleeping, watching, enduring in the weather. I saw 18 — carved on it, but could not read the rest of the date, it was so swollen out. I am going back to draw some of it.

Further down we found a holly tree almost sickened with berries, then a cottage and a litter of baby pigs; the dolphin one, as Eric called it, with a large knob underneath it, very nightmarish. There was a shaggy gruesome horse too. The cottage's position was almost perfect on the hill — if one could have converted it.

We drove on to Malling to see the red-nosed man who does repairs and has an outside stall. He only had three old finger bowls and he wouldn't mend my black ebony cabinet, but we went on and bought some kippers instead.

Then we visited the church, and the vicar was just going in at the side door, looking very lugubrious and ungiving.

We came back by Middle Orchard, and because no one was at home we let ourselves in and made tea and I played Handel's Chaconne with variations while Eric shivered over the electric fire and read *Picture Post*.

We hope like anything that Noël is going to buy 34 Croom's Hill and move there. It will be funny if she does.

It is where I first lived in Evie's house when I was an art student of eighteen. Lovely house looking on to Greenwich Park, all that a small house should be.

When we got back, May came out of her house screeching at Eric like a fishwife-parrot, and when I followed him I found her draped on the Récamier sofa with sticking-plaster over her eye and burnt-brown-red blood dripping down her face and dabbed all over the towel that was covering her full front.

It appears that she trod on a brush in her kitchen and threw herself down on the brick floor. She had felt gruesome and so she had posed herself and waited till we brought the car back.

At first I thought she had really hurt herself badly and suggested foolish things like doctors, but she only looked at me sneeringly, and soon she was jumping up and showing us how many of her unwanted objects she had sold to Mrs Johnston.

---

24 Peggy Mundy Castle (!).

She was like a sinister waxwork. She had that added touch of falseness which is much worse than the blood and the towels.

30 November

Yesterday we went to the dentist in Sevenoaks by Fairlawne and Ivy Hatch and Seal.

I saw the tall narrow dripping avenue of "Wilderness" and the sordid smug houses all along the edge of what should have been the park.

I saw the angle of the road by Knole where the German bomber, all in flames, nearly landed on me in 1940. I remember sheltering in great fear in the little hut of cloth and branches on the edge of the field, then running up the lane towards the golf house. It landed perhaps thirty or forty yards from me and immediately set all the field and pine copse ablaze, and all the bullets spat and the petrol tanks exploded.

I remember the violent heat that struck the back of my neck, and, after my terror, the relief that seemed to break me up and melt me away.

The German had jumped out before the plane crashed, and he had come down on the other side of the wood, his parachute licked up in flames.

When I reached the golf house an old caddie saw me and said, "Oh, you've had a fright, you sit down in here." He took me into a corrugated iron cabin and left me on a box. Afterwards I wandered out, and I saw two maids in the main clubroom. They were whooping and exclaiming with enjoyment of the excitement, and remembrance of their fright.

After a little while they looked at each other with a curious look; animal, furtive, naked, ashamed, greedy. Then one said uncertainly, "Shall we?" The other nodded sharply, like a jerky bird. Then they were all across the green in the direction of the wood where the airman had come down. They were going to gloat and be horrified and I wondered what would be left in their heads after the sight.

When I got to the dentist he was a long time grinding away the tooth and the old stopping, then building up elaborately his new creation. The jet of water spitting into the bowl; the chestnut-pink shiny walls; out of the window the bleak winter garden with the wooden bird-house and piece of ancient nut on a string; the little phallus drills with bristly mushroom heads standing up erect on the round swing stand.

And afterwards, with it all over, the freedom of roaming in the town, looking at the china and furniture, trying to find something worthy of being bought. I saw a Georgian milk-jug for £6. I saw a red-headed boy-man dressed in red Harris tweed, very conscious of his hair and face and hands, grimly intent on walking quickly down the town, sort of bouncing in his new shoes, laughable in his fierce seriousness, like a toy.

Then all the High Street near the church was rooted up with pneumatic drills and men with pickaxes. The men with pickaxes were bending and lifting like slaves, their pale grey faces clammy looking, and the muscles in their arms, that slapped about a little too slackly, were like slaves' faces and muscles. They tried and trembled and strained. One very big one had arms like a contralto. And all the time the mad jagging, splitting of the drill.

1 December

Yesterday, late in the afternoon, Eric and I went out in the car and came near the empty house, Little Hawkwell, in the dark. We got out and walked in the meadow to the right of it, close to the ancient stone wall. There was a footpath there, and I was reminded of the Priory wall at Repton.

The damp cold dark and the lights twinkling on the further hill — Pembury perhaps — and in front of us a shape that looked like a huge man. But when we came up to it, the huge dark man turned out to be quite a small old one leaning on a stick and going back very slowly to his cottage. We could see it dark and grim in front of us. At the end of the path we turned back, not wanting to go down the hill into the forbidding little wood. We talked of how things sometimes in the dark looked gigantesque. Then I thought of the empty house with its fine staircase, in the dark, the rain dripping through all the floors, the obvious gruesomeness of it, that was so much more effective than any subtle hints. Fright of a night alone in such a place. How is it that all over little congested coasened England, pockets of fright and mysteriousness are left?

There are ponds dark as molasses treacle where the antlered branches are covered with hair-fungus-moss.

4 December, 5 to 10 a.m.

Yesterday I did no work because my story had gone all to bits. I only rubbed and scraped at my painting with my leatherwork tool.

Then at about half-past twelve we set out in the car for Rolvenden to see what we could discover about Eric's Goble ancestors who had lived there as far as we knew in the eighteenth and the early nineteenth centuries. We had with us the photograph of the charming map of George Goble's "estate", as it's called. It is a map of several fields and below is the picture of a pretty eighteenth-century farmhouse and some oasts. Everything about the map so delicate and ornamental.

It was a clear, biting, pale blue, weak sun day, not autumn and not winter, and we found the way very easily. We picnicked in front of Pembury Old Church, eating our cheese and tomato-chutney sandwiches of crispbread and munching chocolate, Pat-a-Cake biscuits, chocolate and peppermint humbugs. Then Eric got out of the car and went into the churchyard. I was reading about German philosophers in the *Times Literary Supplement*. Soon he came quickly back to the car and asked me to come and look. Then he took me to a tomb, Ann Westlake, aged thirty-four, 1803, went to a half broken grille at one side and shined the torch down.

We could see the coffin all crumbled away like the skeleton of an ancient ship that has been sunk in a river bed — and cradled in it the human skull lying on its side demonishly lustful, as if it were consumed with excitement and greed. The ribs mounted up like birds' fingers.

I had never in England seen before a skeleton in a graveyard. Only these elegant coffins in the vault at Chiddingstone.

We left the skeleton of Ann Westlake quickly, thinking of the daylight. I started the car, the dog in the cottage barked, and we cruised down the hill.

We went down the Hastings Road, then branched off towards Cranbrook. We first saw a windmill on our left, then another older one on our right. We expected the village before we came to it, but when we really did reach it, it exceeded our expectations.

It had a stationary, overlaid charm. The street was wide and one kept wanting to stop and look at the houses in turn. At the head of the village stood the high church tower, a little raised, and directly in front of it was a house with a fine eighteenth-century bow-fronted shop window. I guessed that this was the house to which Ellen Easdale had moved from Crouch Farm House.[25]

We parked the car by the church. We were very excited, and as soon as we got out we spoke to a woman in trousers with gypsy dog-brown eyes and then walked down the most likely road with the picture map in our hands.

We had gone in quite the right direction, but we did not yet know that no trace of the house was left. Past the vicarage we called at a house that looked faintly like Brickwall but we learned that it was called Bull Farm.

Then we turned back and made for the church. Almost as soon as we were in the churchyard we found a tomb with Goble on it, fairly late, 1877 I think. I left Eric to copy it out, and went on to the ancient yew where there were some good seventeenth-century flat tombs with fine lettering. Then I found another tomb, eighteen-thirtyish, with the names Goble and Dunk on it.

I felt sure that we were going to find almost too many tombs. I went into the church alone. One of the windows had lost all its tracery from a flying bomb. The wind was blowing through the sacking and a workman was up a scaffolding. My mind did not count him as a human being, for some reason. I felt alone.

25 Gladys Easdale, the sister of Noël Adeney, by whom she had been nicknamed Ellen. Crouch Farm House stood adjacent to the Adeneys' home, Middle Orchard.

To the left of the chancel I immediately noticed the enclosed family pew. The wooden door and the monument in the archway by Lutyens were new, but inside I saw all the memorials to the Monypennys, and the long old oak settle.

I learnt later that this, for an unknown reason, was called the Scott Chapel and that its upkeep had been the responsibility of the Monypennys since 1722. It went with the great Maythem property, which had later been in the hands of the Tennents, who had put up the Lutyens memorial.

After I had finished exploring this corner, it was more than I expected to walk across the chancel and discover in the other chapel (Saints Catherine and Ann) all the Gybbon and Gybbon-Monypenny memorials, and a winding early nineteenth-century staircase leading to a gallery furnished with a wonderful set of Chippendale chairs, and an eighteenth-century easy chair and two side tables.

This was the Hole Park pew, belonging first to the Guilfords, then Gybbons, then Monypennys, then Barhams. The chairs, although with stupid modern seat covering, were in almost perfect condition, the wood bare and untouched, dry hard, the carving hard and thin — better than the condition of any other eighteenth-century chair I have seen.

I thought of them standing in the church since they were made, miraculous to escape so much.

My mind was dwelling on furniture after seeing them and I walked down the nave and found all the pamphlets and money boxes laid out on a little table with a drawer — country Chippendale oak, with very pretty Chinesey brass handles with original lacquer, and the wood again in marvellous untouched condition. It was as if the quite humble little piece had been wrapped up and put away all its life. No french-polisher, varnisher, dauber had been near it.

Eric had come into the church by now and had found a tomb of Thomas Goble, late of Rye, 1811, in the chancel. (Later we discovered that he was allowed to be buried there because he farmed the tithes.)

We went out of the church again, feeling lost and thwarted because we couldn't find Brickwall.

We wandered down a drive, saw a house very like it, but learned from the fur-coated Mongolian-looking woman, who was just moving in, that it was called the Old Parsonage. I think she giggled with the removal man as we walked away.

We were getting warm as the Parsonage was marked on our old map.

Then, just as we reached the church gate again, I saw the parson arriving on his bicycle. He was long-nosed, tall, nose skin coarse and granity, and I saw in a moment that he had a deaf-machine to his ear.

I went up to him and tried to explain, and he said rather impatiently, "One moment," and then fumbled in his bosom, to switch on his machine, I suppose.

I felt a little foolish, explaining about our family history hunt. He had that bad English manner that is too clumsy either to be properly rude or polite. I felt I had to provide all the delicacies and so seemed to myself exaggerated, affected, almost dripping with sensibility. Horrible to feel fancy. One is like a monkey or a decoration on a Christmas tree.

He was willing to be more helpful than he could or would show.

He took us with long, preoccupied, gawky steps into his vestry, where I saw another armchair of the set in the Hole Park pew.

He got down on his knees and opened the safe. I saw the Communion plate glistening, and wanted to take it out and examine it.

Then he pulled out a lovely long slender book, *The Survey of the Parish of Rolvenden, 1820*, and began to turn the pages much too quickly; every one should have been pondered on.

He was turning so quickly that he was almost past it when I called out, "There is Brickwall!"

We discovered then just where it should have been — next door to the vicarage.

"There is no house there now," said the vicar.

So it has quite gone, pulled down, burnt, no one knew how it had disappeared or when. The vicar said he would ask some of the older parishioners. He told us that the last Goble to live in Rolvenden died about eight years ago, and that he was a good cricket umpire!

Then we left the vicar. We wondered whether to go and see Ellen Easdale or not in the bow window house. We had asked him if she did live there and she did.

At last we went up the wooden steps and knocked. There was a little fumbling and a voice, then she was standing there, exclaiming with surprise and turning to the person already with her, explaining that I was an old friend whom she had not seen for a long time. Her grey hair very feminine and sheeplike and corkscrewed.

The person with her was Colonel Barham. Coming straight from the wonderful chairs in the theatre gallery pew with its sweeping staircase, there was a flare of interest in me as I heard the name.

He was like a dummy man; all dressed too sharply and newly and trimly. Everything too stiff and hard; and because he hardly talked but only nodded his head jerkily, Eric and I both thought that he was a little mentally defective.

I told Ellen what we had been looking up in the church and she poured out with her excessiveness, "Oh, Colonel Barham is the one for family history, he knows all about everything."

There was a sticky pause and then Colonel B said very offensively, as a truculent child would, "I don't know all about *anything*."

I smiled and laughed a little, and then there were other little lapses and beginnings, until I began to have the theory that Colonel B had come, all dressed up, to pounce on Ellen and that we had quite spoiled his frolic. (Eric told me afterwards that he had had just the same idea, too.)

Suddenly Colonel Barham jerked up stiffly and said, as if he'd been disgusted by an obscene remark of someone else in the room, "I shall be going now, Mrs Easdale."

"Oh, stay and have some tea, won't you?" said Ellen, titting-totting to the door after him, like a pretty little girl doll grown into upper middle age.

After he had gone and we had all been funny at his expense, snipping-snapping little bits off him, enlarging on the preposterousnous of his existence — all so age-old the badinage of ours, the laughing at shyness, gawkiness, pomposity — Ellen began to show us over her house.

It had a curius staircase from cellar to attic, narrow, almost spiral, unlike any other late eighteenth-century one I had seen, with not quite pleasant but very personal flourishes of thin wrought-iron. The boards, grey-purple-brown, silky.

The atmosphere reclaimed, not really comfortable with impoverishment under the new cleanness, but with its spicing and sprout of charm too. And upstairs her pink mantel and twisted rope basket grate, such pinched sharp smart design. The window looking into the churchyard with the lugubriousness of the tombs, they can be called nothing else; and one knew that there were huge bells in the tower. All the time they would be there waiting to ring, to clang, to mask everything with doom.

Opposite the other window, almost the first houses I have seen being built since the war soil and scratch all the fields opposite where Ellen before could see a long, long way to a pond.

We went down again and into the abandoned basement, where I wanted to sit down, but there was nothing, and I thought how so-called ill people like Ellen stand and stand while I am wilting.

We went back to the first green-panelled fireplace room and Ellen got out her seaweed cups — one extra large — and began to boil her kettle on the logs.

When we were drinking, Eric gave me the large cup and then gibed at once. "What a little fellow with a big cup," and Ellen opened her eyes rather wider.

She told us that she had had her brother to stay and when he arrived all his trousers were falling apart in front from moth holes, so she had to go up into the attic and get her musician son's corduroys.

Everything was like this — flitting about.

And we ate the scones and her jam and she said, "I never eat at tea." But how annoyed she would have been if we had not eaten.

So in the end we tore ourselves away, because my inside was turning over and over and I wanted to be alone with it.

A good day, even going back in the dark. We will remember it all; so much more fortunate and interesting than we had expected.

12 December, 7 p.m.

Eric is in London, so today after work I went out by myself in the car. I first posted my drawing to *Vogue* in West Malling, got three shillings for the gas meter, then walked about in the streets looking at everything.

The three old lipped finger-bowls in the open-air junk booth; the soggy outlines melting down in the about-to-fade light; then near the church in the white house on the corner, the glimpse of a richer than usual room — a grandfather clock, walnut, ugly rich red pleated silk lamp, smooth paint polish, old things looked after and valued above their money's worth.

I was held by the glimpse into the garnished house and the trimmed and dug and swept garden with its almost bald, so well rolled lawns, and stone cobbled stable-yard. Everything attended to and so much more placid than the world, the town, the dangerous bend in the road seemed to warrant. It was like looking into a ghost, dream, dolls' house, where nothing happened, only the things waiting for the never-happening happening.

Then round the bend, when I did not like to stare any longer into the softly lighted rich room, I saw the black, looming, extravagantly large half ovals of the Italian prisoners-of-war camp. And one of the doors into the long sections of giant toy tunnel was open, and I looked in and saw plate after plate after plate, tin or enamel, I suppose. They were like dogs' plates, and they seemed to be laid on the ends of beds which were covered with black-sheep-colour army blankets. While I looked into the amazing barrack kennel and thought of the cherished white cosseted house just round the corner — the almost too punching, violent contrast which yet at the same time was no contrast at all, and accepted by me as calmly as by anyone else — a young, thin, rather too flexible Italian with the dark glistening rodent hair came round the corner carrying a board piled with long gold-brown loaves. They were like the enormous ears of a nightmarish head of corn. They were a potent symbol of something. Were they just the echo of many, many Harvest Homes? They were very ancient, not to eat, to go on being held like that on the board, to be carried for centuries by the man round the corner, everlasting, each century after it would be the same. The picture caught and held. Loaves of bread being carried for ever.

I must have been staring, fixed on this picture, allowing myself to be swallowed into it too much, embroidering it, aching for it, because the man looked back and it seemed that his attention was held in some way by me. He looked quite frankly and went on looking. It is disrupting to be stared at — that is why people hate it so, it makes us feel frightened, excited, children again, disreputable.

I went away unsettled, made naked by his eyes, to wander in the unfeeling, torpid little town, at the mercy of it. And I immediately began to note the bedraggled and lost people. A sort of semi-tramp workman just behind me seemed to acquire the face of someone I had once known, and I felt that he might almost be followed me or begging for money. It was invention. And the children seemed to be about to shout insults. I got a twisted version of what they were saying and it sounded like, "Look at that old man — he's nine." Nonsense, and of course not to do with me. Complete contradiction in the children's mouths, paradox they love to scream.

16 December

There have been troubles all the time about 34 Croom's Hill. Evie's brother wrote to say that he could not let the Adeneys have it after all, because the woman who made the first offer would be placed in a distressing position if she were passed over in their favour. The lawyers told him that he was not bound and that the Adeneys should have it because they have done all the work to get it derequisitioned, but he still persisted. We sent wires, notes, letters. I told him that we should be homeless if he decided against the Adeneys.[26] They offered more money. He still was stubborn.

We were about to wire to say that Evie would refuse to sign the title deeds — luckily they are still in her name, although the house was given over to him — when we had a telegram from him saying, "Unexpectedly able to comply with your wishes over house." We have not yet heard any more and we are wondering what has changed him.

We think now that unless the L.C.C. or the borough council obstruct, the Adeneys are almost bound to go to Croom's Hill and we to Middle Orchard.

20 December, 6.25 p.m.

The Adeneys went up to London to sign for Croom's Hill on Wednesday; and we, after doing Christmas letters, cards and parcels all morning, got the car out and went into Tonbridge at about three o'clock.

Just as we came up to the bus stop, we saw John Bloom alighting, and of course he was coming to see us, so we had to stop, and I asked him to come with us to Tonbridge. Then it began to rain very heavily.

First Eric posted the parcels and went with John to try and get some aluminium saucepans from Timothy White's, while I went into Easte's in search of grand striped material for the living-room french window at Middle Orchard. They had nothing but flannelette and sateen and ugly chintz which needed "dockets" — everything gruesome and institutional

---

26 This was not strictly true. Denton could have remained at Pitt's Folly Cottage but he had set his heart on living at Middle Orchard.

and unreviving. Buying cloth, which should be so warming and pleasing, was made to be like buying toilet rolls, pumice stone, ashes.

I went out of the shop in slight confusion and met Eric coming in to find me. We all got back into the car and went towards the junk shop housed in the old skating rink. John and Eric had been thwarted over the saucepans too. They were all bespoken.

In the overarching great shack that was once the roller-skating rink, the rain had been pouring through the crude joinings of the flimsy roof. Old hip baths that brought to my mind pictures of naked men wallowing in Edwardian country houses on fine hunting mornings were placed in the alleys between the furniture, and there were slop-basins and bowls and jugs too, some brimming with the pure rainwater.

To one not interested in searching out objects there must have been the frightening, frustrated gloom that hangs over derelicts living and not living; there must have been it extremely in that cardboard St Pancras Station.

I thought of this as I nosed about — and the thought of the effect of the place on John and Eric made me hurry, turn away from things rather too unfeelingly. I was hurrying and there seemed nothing there to redeem the squalor, to clutch at one for rescuing.

Then I walked down the last aisle and saw in the middle what looked at first like a not very remarkable early-to-mid-Victorian little couch — Récamier thickened and toughened and having developed turned stumpy legs instead of delicate out-sweeping Greek ones. But what really held my glance when I looked nearer was the covering of the couch, the flat loose cushion and the round tailored sausage one. They were all of tomato soup *red horsehair*, dirtied of course, but, remembering its life of eighty, ninety, perhaps nearly a hundred years, really in wonderful condition. And what a wonderful stuff too, this never before seen red horsehair, glistening like glass threads, rich and hard and heartless, built to wear people out, not be worn out by them. The cushions made so stiffly and truly, everything about the couch showing solid worthiness, as much as any Victorian piece I had seen; and its ugly, Gothic, sharp parrot smartness simply calling out to be used, sat upon and loved.

Its appeal to me was so strong that excitement leaped up in me in a gulp. I turned it upside down with Eric and John, looked at the solidity of its stretchers and webbing — everything in clear-cut nearly fresh condition, although there was slight worm-holing in the soft wood. Then I lay down on its firm, smooth hardness and knew that it was mine. We called the older moustached man and, because it was newly in and he could find no chalk mark on it, he went away to consult his book; then he came back with a young one with rather fragile hairy wrist and one of those metal watch-straps like a chest expander.

"Five pounds," the older man said. I dithered, feeling it almost weak not to bargain, but knowing that I should have it after all, so realizing before I had begun the waste of words.

I wrote the cheque and the young one asked me gently for my address and even for my identity number, saying all the time, politely and persuasively, "It doesn't really matter. It doesn't really matter."

I had a sudden surge of liking for his nervousness, rather as I had for the hard glitter of the scarlet horsehair, then we took up the two loose cushions and went out, John muttering to me, "How cheap, isn't it good! What did you think he would ask?"

Eric said, "Anything from about three to ten." Which was just what I had thought too.

When we got to May's and were putting the car away, I told her about the couch and asked if the man could leave it with her the next day and if she could keep it for us till we went to Middle Orchard. She made a fuss about her lack of space and I grew impatient, for I knew she would agree perfectly, only wanted to make a to-do first.

All through tea I was thinking of the little couch, how I would take off the few remains of red braid and put on gold, or green, or gold *and* green, or yellow braid, polish the wood with beeswax, treat the underneath with worm-killer, brush and clean and beat all the red horsehair and the stuffing.

I began to brush the two cushions with Eric's nail brush dipped in warm water, then I rubbed them with a hot wet towel. They glowed, and seemed to bristle like a living animal. They were like coral gums.

Then, just before Evie came up to read, and as I was sitting on the arm of the chair looking down at a picture or book, something seemed to shift delicately in my eye and there was a slight swimming of which I took little notice.

I settled myself on the bed with Eric, about to listen to the reading, but before it began I said something about my eye, which he pooh-poohed rather, telling me that I was a little neurotic.

As Evie's voice, reading Sassoon, lulled on, I shut my eyes, thinking that the cloudiness might lift when I opened them; but it didn't. It seemed to grow, and I saw two teapots, two Evies and two warm lamps. I still did not worry too much.

There was an amusing piece about Ronald Firbank, fruit from Belheim and rich chocolate cake — and after that I jumped up, not being able to stay still any longer, and went into the bathroom.

I saw there that my lid had dropped down and that the pupil underneath was huge, velvet black, almost swamping the tiny coloured rim. The other pupil was normally small. The whole effect of my face was wickedly languorus and lop-sidedly un-me. I went down to the others to tell them and to show them, but they still pooh-poohed comfortably.

And so I settled down to a night of deep pain in the heart of my head like a tight little walnut. I took a Veganin tablet, and after that I seemed to be still in pain but too lethargic to be as restless as I wanted to be. My eye was weeping all on its own, apart from me, the water coursing down my check, and my heart was frightened. I felt abandoned. The watering of my eye seemed as gruesome as the dripping walls of the lavatory in an Industrial Revolution slum.

In the morning, the lid and the eye on my left side all seemed to be sinking down to the left — everything left, hooded, wilting.

Eric went out after breakfast to ring up Dr Ramsden, but as he couldn't reach him, he rang up Jack Easton instead; and very quickly after the message I heard a car draw up and knew that it was Jack. He came up the stairs without Evie saying anything to me, and I was not perfectly certain that I had not deluded myself until he opened the door and stood there. He was more or less the person that I had first seen ten years ago in the garden of the nursing home at Broadstairs; there was less hair on the top of his head. He was tireder, and I thought of all the disgustingness that he had had to deal with in Egyptian hospitals for the last four to five years.

The meeting would have been much more graceful if Jack had not suddenly said in a too social voice, "How are you!" What was I to do? Respond in the same tone, or at once plunge into my anxieties over the eye? I compromised and said with rather a giggle, "I'm quite all right if it weren't for this peculiar eye surprise." There was a tremor of dislocation and surface silliness, then I told him just what had happened and waited.

Jack walked up and down in the way that might be so annoying in someone else. I knew that if there were anything terrible that had to be said, he would say it more delicately, more protectingly than anyone else I knew; but still I did not care to wait for his verdict. It was a trying moment. I darted my head from side to side and smiled restlessly as if everything in the world were as trivial as could be.

Then he told me that he thought it was a temporary paralysis of the third nerve, and that it would get better but would take some time. First he said a few days, then six weeks or perhaps two months! The leap was not really a shock — the "days" had been said as if a longer period were implied. He explained to me that sometimes people wake up to find the whole of one side of their face paralysed, that after some time the condition rights itself. No one quite knows the cause. Perhaps it is tiredness, strain, a chill.

He said that I should wear a black patch over the left eye to stop me from seeing double. He said that it was impossible for the other eye to be affected at the same time.

There seemed hardly time to talk of anything but the eye. I had not time to ask about war life in the army, and all he said about my writing was, "Let me see, are you now on your third book?" Again social tone and the feeling that the words were like little bits of tin, twinking in the chair. What was it that was cutting him off from real talk, real contact? Even his good human manner seemed on the point of ringing false. Everything seemed nearly tumbling into acting, as if he, very tired, could not give solidity, only hollowness. Perhaps it was embarrassment that made the varnished serenity. I wanted it to crack and yet all the time I realized how marvellous his manner was compared with the boorish-aggressive-defensive fearfulness of most people. It was so good that he himself had at last realised its quality and so it had begun to set and lose the finer shades and delicacy.

And yet perhaps all that need be said is that a professional manner was turned on to me as on to any other patient — that the doctor's mask [*sentence unfinished*]

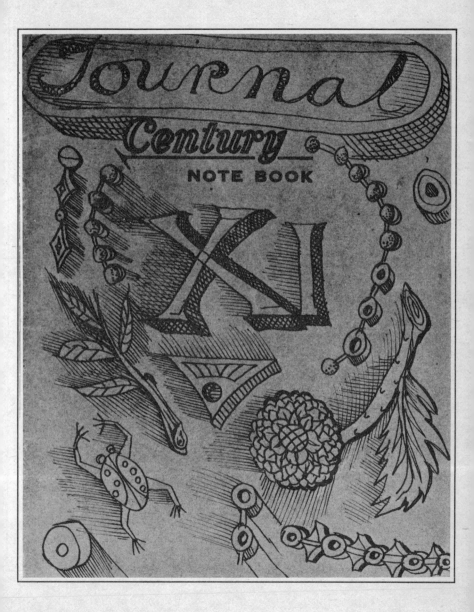

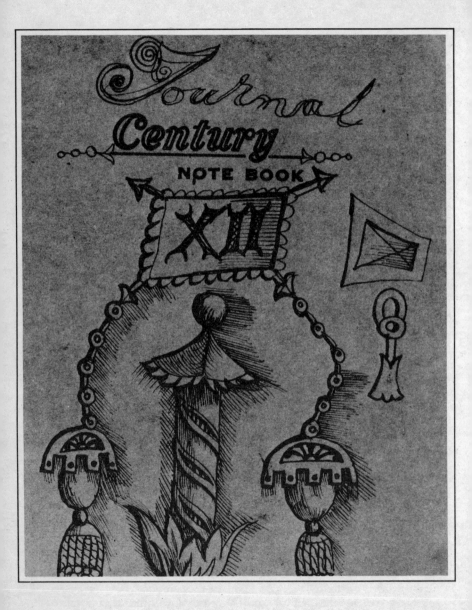

1946

MAY WAS burgled last night in the high wind. Or perhaps it was this morning just before dawn.

All the drawers, even the tiny ones in the bureau, were opened, and the dummy books were thrown out on the floor; but all that was taken were two Chelsea figures, a little comfit-box with a tiny silver spoon, a double rose Dubarry scent-bottle and the chocolate in the urn-shaped china sugar-jar.

The burglar also rested on her sofa, washed, brushed his hair, used the closet and polished his shoes. In the kitchen he ate spoonfuls of marmalade, but did not steel the Georgian spoon; then he spread the marmalade about and found biscuits.

When she came down in the early morning she found the front door open and the drawingroom curtain flapping out of the windows.

The man had opened the window with a knife and had tried to remove the putty round another pane.

Two other houses, Bourne Mill and Faulkners, were also broken into, and the police think a Borstal boy or a deserter had perhaps been at work.

Coming out of the pub at midday, Eric saw an unkempt youth with service respirator case, beret with land badge, an anxious retreating manner. He feels that this youth might have slept in the outhouse at Bourne Mill and then begun his chain of housebreaking, when everyone was asleep.

I side with the burglar unquestiongly and only wish that he'd helped himself to more. This, I suppose, is surely a malicious feeling, an amusement at an acquisitive person's discomfiture.

12 *January*

This afternoon we picnicked in Pembury Walk, by the pine trees, and then Eric drove the car on past the gates of Bayham Abbey and on until we came at last (after passing huge pines all chopped down and showing their white base) to Frant.

We saw in front of us the little untutored Gothic revival church — how much better, sometimes, only a little knowledge is! The person who built this church was unclogged with "book-learning" and so his church is unrepulsive and almost pretty and good. But I am well aware how dangerous this gospel of ignorance can be. It is, I suppose, the excuse for every inanity. Things only are good because they are good. Book ignorance or book-learning can help or hinder according to other circumstances which shall combine with them.

But all that paragraph is muck that I did not mean to write.

I wanted to write about the inside of the church with the lights on and a boy playing the organ behind the marble pulpit. There was something very warm and cosy there. It was holiday Saturday afternoon. He was enjoying himself alone, but he glowed to have an audience, and played for us eagerly, but without turning his head or speaking once. But one knew that they were his best pieces that he dashed into, and we sat in a pew to listen.

The organist hadn't got enough chin. There were some old angels set in the leaded windows. Many of the panes were blown in from bomb blast. One memorial plaque explained with neurotic care that Godfrey, Baron Wolf(?), was a Knight and Baron of the late Holy Roman Empire and that King George III had granted him a patent in this country too! Nothing else about him was mentioned.

Is it a sign of improved sense when a person of this generation thinks the anxious meagre snobbism funny? Or would he find my sober-sidedness equally pathetic?

13 January, 8.10 p.m.

Allington Castle and the river all cold and grey and swelling; something evil about its ancientness and turning inward, the windows like eyes that have turned into slots for money, nothing moving along the battlements, only the flag blowing glumly. It should not have been a Union Jack. It should have been something much less nationalistic and more narrow and family. It should have been as greedy and glowering as the rough walls and the business-man's-belly round towers.

Over everything brooded the greed and the joylessness. But it had its own beauty, which was a beauty of mournfulness and lack of understanding. One was not tempted to scrutinize it, to separate the restorations from the ruin, one took it as it was and dumped it down into one's mind as Gloom Castle, Castle Wet, Misery along the river.

We climbed up the steep bank above the river and looked down on its mass, and then we walked back to the huge lock gates where the water bulged through like wet bullocks tumbling with their buttocks in the air, all glistening.

We looked back, standing above the bellowing roaring water, and saw far away a bonfire on the river bank. Something tindery had just been put on to it and it was climbing wildly up like a vibrating pinnacle.

We went out in the car to [name of place omitted; Eric Oliver thinks it was Oxon Hoath Park] after Paul had come to say good-bye. He is flying to China on Tuesday.

He brought me four soft American khaki blankets, a tartan rug with D. L. S. Nairn on it in red embroidery, a quilted sleeping bag, sheets and a mosquito net. They are all his sleeping things that he had for the campaign in Italy. He also gave me some grey flannel and some greenish cord; so we shall be able to have some new trousers and jackets made. And how useful the blankets and quilt will be. I have been mending two round holes in the tartan rug that look like bullet holes — or are they moth?

18 January, 6.5 p.m.

Today we went towards Tunbridge Wells to shop, and first we stopped half-way up the narrow country road to Southborough Common to eat our picnic. As we were biting into the egg sandwiches, a thick-set dark youth passed us carrying a broad-bladed hay-cutter. His face was shy and a little glowering, but he had eyes that were remarkable for their up-pointing slant and length — rather unreal eyes, like long almonds. It was a strange face for England, and afterwards, when we'd got out of the car, I saw him cutting silage for cows. We talked, and he had told me that he didn't smoke because he didn't think it too good for people; then he jumped up and down, thrusting the blade deep into the tobacco-smelling, flattened stack. Some of it had a whitish bloom and dust. "This at the top's bad," he said. "It gets better down below. But we just put the bad stuff back on the land, so it's not really wasted."

There was a broad avenue cut through the copses on the hills for a long way, to clear the bases of the electricity pylons. They reminded me of skeleton guardian giants on the ceremonial way to a great tomb. The air was so freezing that I had to look up at the pressing low sky and say, "Do you think it's going to snow?"

"I shouldn't wonder," he said, staring up. When he grinned and looked straight at me, I saw that his face was even rarer than it had seemed at first. It was a picture gypsy's face with glowing cheeks, and the slanting eyes and quirky eyebrows made it innocent instead of wicked. I saw that he wore strange little leggings round his trouser ends.

"Good-bye," I said, walking away, and wishing that his face and body need never be spoilt.

This thought stayed with me all the time in Tunbridge Wells — the bodies spoiling all the time, the goodness and the rarity draining out of everyone that passed me.

A rush of sulphur-smelling smoke belched out of the station archway as I passed, and a soldier was walking in the middle of it in the maroon beret of a parachutist. His face was like an amiable costive pug's, and I watched his hesitation on the pavement and then his plunge into the telephone box. I wanted to know who he was ringing up. It is so tantalizing when one sees a face thinking, pondering, debating with itself before one's eyes. I wanted to follow twenty, thirty, a hundred people home. Everything is quickened when one has these moods of being nothing but a pair of eyes, but how much sadness and thwarting wells up! One has lost the cosy self-love and preoccupation, and only the concerns of others are interesting, but nobody realizes, of course, one's interest. It is almost as if one had achieved invisibility which at all other times (where one so wishes for it) is impossible.

Everybody is perfection (blemished outwardly) walking, gazing, swinging from side to side, waiting for the thing to click, and for their hearts and minds and bodies to be filled. They see nothing but their own images, and their thoughts encase them in an iron lung. Many million mummies swathed, spiced and embalmed alive.

As we came back in the dusk we saw the silage-cutting man climbing up the hill, his shoulders hunched over his bicycle, his remarkable face down. It was impossible not to think of him as everything quiet and good and sober, as industry at night-time going home to well-earned supper.

At home when I drank lemon tea and ate three good chocolates, I read more of Haydon's life, and I thought of his writing in 1823, my writing in 1946 — private thoughts, like toy mice dancing in each century, then lying silent, squashed flat between the pages of a book, piled over and topped for ever with later layers of dancing mice.

21 January, 3.45 p.m.

I went out into the wood with a temperature, to get some air and change for a moment, and there was ice all over the black pools and a little snow powdered on top. I stepped on to it, holding on to a tree trunk; then I went on to the stout square hut of thick branches that has been built mysteriously by someone. It was as squalid as ever. There were two metal spoons on a chair, and the chair was on the narrow iron bed. The only light came from the window of dim celluloid, perhaps from some ancient car hood. Frying-pans and four or five white composition mugs.

But what seemed new and so held my attention was the tattered book at the end of the bed. It had no cover, and when I picked it up, asking myself, "What will its title be?", I found that most of the leaves were frozen together in a crunchy squeaking lump. And its title was *Demon of Desire*.

I could not take all its richness in at first — it was so *much* more than I had expected. I turned some of the first leaves, the only ones that would move, and I found a sentence which asked what harm prostitutes did. They did their duty and were paid and forgotten; but the harlots, the predatory harlots, "many of them of aristocratic blood", were the real danger. They stalked the world and swallowed up men. It seemed that the author upheld professionals and could not bear dilettanti.

Then there was a passage where a poor man had to dismiss his pretty typist because she would lean over him when he was at his desk and she had such prettiness and smelt so warm and nice that he couldn't bear it — because he was keeping himself for his invalid wife.

The whole book, frozen part and all, was speared through several times by some sharp instrument, which had torn and made illegible parts of the pages; and it came to me in a flash that some boy had attacked it with his knife, for its wickedness, and for his wickedness in reading it, for its vile seduction and for his weakness in being seduced. Just as I threw *De Profundis* out of the bathroom window so that it landed in the roof gutter and could never be got at again. I did not think *De Profundis* vile, but I thought it very tawdry and mawkish and was frightened of the prison reek all about it. I had only just heard the gruesome Wilde story, and was filled by its disgusting quality.[1]

31 *January, 9.50 a.m.*

It is quite true that a general unwillingness to appreciate robs most people of their eyes, nose, mouth, ears, limbs. They are trunks of wood always repudiating; although they have *already* been deprived of all sense and movement.

19 *February, 10 p.m.*

Yesterday at lunchtime we drove in through the peeling archway of Hadlow Castle, threaded the leaning decaying trees and the black bushes and ended up in the wide stable yard where all the other cars were parked. It was the sale day, and just for this once, never again, we could wonder about.

We went out on to the front well -cared-for lawn, looking all the time at the amazing building, all the Gothic pinnacles looking wretched and unkept, the harsh white paint, misapplied to the mullions and tracery, making them jump out from the lion-coloured plaster, as if they were some gigantic swollen lace.

I loved all the Gothic-revival, mournful beauty. The gimcrack and the decay had their own peculiar fascination, and the monkey puzzle on the brink of the indented landscape gardener's lake seemed to be holding out its terrifying monkey arms to grasp one to mourn with it. One was weighed down with so much fantasy about one.

Then we went into the hall and saw the long passage the length of the house with the two white busts in their niches and the extraordinary lantern of coloured glass with pictures of saints carrying their symbols, Bibles, bells, churches, instruments of torture.

And up above the three windows of the stairs, damaged in parts, so that

1 Presumably it was the bathroom window at 34 Croom's Hill, Greenwich, from which Denton threw *De Profundis*, for he mentions reading it in "A Novel Fragment" (see 1942, note 4 above), set at the time he was an art student.

the billowing angel wings and draparies were cut away and left blank in panels.

Up on the top landing the auctioneer was droning and the crowd standing in smelling silence, chewing their pencils, fingering their dirty envelopes.

We walked the length of the downstairs passage, looking at the filigrane tracery and flamboyant work above the doors. The floor was stone flags, the woodwork ochre wood-grained. At each end was a window where the acid coats of arms bit at one, leapt at one, insisting on the amazing depth of their oranges and purples.

We tried all the doors, but they were locked because of the sale upstairs. Eric went to the furthest door, saying, "I'm sure this one is open." It was, but it only lead into a cupboard where a sad gas mask was hanging. We both smiled, and a rather conscious youth who was with us smiled shyly too at our fooling. He was dressed in an old khaki greatcoat, turned down Wellingtons and dirty peacock pullover that was lovely with the khaki. He was smoking very consciously and this made him seem a gypsy child, but the next moment he seemed the married young farmhand with grave responsibilities.

When he turned away still smiling, I noticed the tiny mark on his neck, as if once he had been pinched with tweezers and as if the wound had healed bunchily, making a little cushion with two dints on each side. There was dirt on the dints, but all the rest of his face looked very clean and fresh except for surface smudges.

Eric and I walked out again to gaze in all the windows of the locked rooms. We saw Corinthian pillars and a classic cornice in the biggest room, clearly the only relics of an earlier house, before the Gothic frenzy seized the owner.

And as we were looking and admiring and getting a pleasant gruesome thrill out of imagining the horror of having such a place tied round our necks, we saw the khaki coat and peacock pullover approaching us again, walking nonchalantly, looking this way and that, smoking and sweeping the hand away like a Victorian swell. Very stiff, very masculine, very aware of self and anxious.

Eric said, "He's going to say something to us," and I knew he was too.

A smile and a jerk of the head at the fantastic Boston Stump, Fonthill Tower (so fine for all the country round, but extraordinarily oppressive and threatening now that we were under its vast stiffness).

I found a little door and a winding staircase, but it was so dark I didn't fancy going on any further.

We at once walked in a trio and it seemed fixed without any arrangement that we should go together up the spiral staircase.

"I've found the door to the cellar too." We were all quite genuinely excited and pleased with one another — a true case of mutual aid and comradeship.

The sad peeling castle — too literary to be interpreted in plaster, brick and iron bars — suddenly was animated for us. We walked forward too quickly really for me; then began our exploration — through the grim pantry parts into the octagonal servants' hall. There, when I came to my Shell poster in 1937, I saw all the servants about to congregate and eat their supper.[2] The wireless was going and I thought, how funny for the mice to make such a noise, when the cats were only just round the corner in the parlour.

Now all was empty and bare, except for one cupboard of old china bits and remnants.

The peacock khaki boy was leading and I was behind him. We started up some back stairs where the plaster had fallen down in dusty pancakes that put the teeth on edge. After winding round till we were a little dizzy we came to one deserted tower room, then another, and a long narrow gallery. All bars. We trod about exclaiming, talking like children, as people exploring always do. Then we un-wound ourselves down the stairs again. I was getting worn and aching already, but I wanted to go on, and "Peacock" led us next to the cellar door.

It was all dark and the stairs were uneven. We looked down into a little room that Eric's match showed us had marble shelves, like a dairy. It was a strange shape, and another door lead from it in to the cellar proper.

Vast blackness and weight on heaps of ashes or coal, a boiler and the heavy, slickly cut beams holding up the ground floor.

We got into the passage running the length of the house with many of the black dungeons off it. "Peacock" said, "I wouldn't like to be shut up in those. Just like real dungeons." I said, "Yes, you could keep plenty of mad wives down there." Eric offered "Peacock" a cigarette and I saw their faces near together — peach glow, industrious lips, eyes slanted.

Right at the end was a dungeon that had been made into an air raid shelter. The beams, tea-shop blackened, the walls sage-green — where the wine bins had been like baby horse boxes. On the sill of the underground window that looked into a well was a lost gas-mask in its smug tin case, and an address book with only numbers in it. The boy rushed at this and looked through it, as if he expected something good.

I was really exhausted by now; but we climbed up one more staircase and looked at one more isolated groom's or housekeeper's room, with exuberant birdflower paper (puce, dark green), cupboards on each side of the mantelpiece and a gash window on to the stable yard. It was a very mournful room, where one would be lonely and in despair in perfect peace with no hope of interruption.

2 Denton had sold a painting of Hadlow Castle to Shell-Mex for a series of posters on Architectural Freaks, for which he was paid £20.

The three of us in that room, looking in all the corners — for what?

When we came down, the Peacock-khaki was making for the great tower again, gritting his teeth for the attempt on Everest after the lesser peaks. I made faces at Eric, for although I would have liked to have stayed, I had a feeling that I must stop moving or I would make myself much worse.

The boy was ahead of us reconnoitering, so Eric called out, "We're going now."

He looked round and his face was disappointed. It gave one a slight pang. We had broken what had been quite chance and gay. He would have to go on exploring alone. We had taken away his salt. I wished I was not a crock.

As we drove off, Eric saw him in an open doorway still looking this way and that. He waved to him and "Peacock" waved back. I wondered if he would find anyone to hire him, for he had told us that he had come on the chance of someone wanting furniture taken away. I wondered too if he had a horse or a car. Of course I imagined him with a horse.

So we left the groggy castle to the dealers and the other vultures. I would like to have enough money to make it fantastic and beautiful as it was meant to be. It should not be sobered up in bits and rotting in others as it is now. It should all be "Walter Scott" beautiful, with rich bright colours and stripes, much gilding and silvering, coloured mirrors, glass lustres — everything in what the painful people would be sure to call the worst possible taste. Why is timidity considered a virtue? Why is Whistler wispy wistfulness clung to even today by the great British public? Why are riches and freedom thought of only as vulgarity? It is all that gruesome snobbism that would tie the hands behind the back, then cut off everything a man has ever valued.

1 *March, 5.40 p.m.*

I am in bed today, but on Wednesday we started quite early for my aunt's at Ditchling;[3] and all night it had been snowing, so it was quite a white world of the specially wet sorbet sort, for the snow was not determined enough.

The roads were all wet and almost cleared till we got through Tunbridge Wells and drew near the Forest. I was so tempted when I saw the signpost the other side of Hartfield that I had to go on to it, so that we could eat our picnic lunch there as I used to do, so many times before the war.

As we climbed up the road, one soon realized that the snow was thicker, more undisturbed and menacing than before. We really began to quarrel about it, arguing about unwisdom and foolishness.

At last we came out to the ridge where the wide sucked-away grand sweep is dotted with little meagre hard-bitten firs. And now they were all heavy with snow and the hills were soft and downy with it. The gruesome luxury

---

3 Aunt Dorothy's house (see 1945, note 15 above).

of all that freezing breast of eider duck amazing in the sun, having the dull-polished glint of white grapefruit hide.

Almost at the top of the hill I pulled into the side of the road, then felt that we might never start again, but we remained there and had our hard-boiled eggs, bantam ones from Elizabeth, and golden treacle on golden toast. An air-force guy and woman passed us in a car all battered and rusty up one side. They took one look at the snow at the top of the hill, then turned round and fled.

A break-down lorry came slowly over the top of the hill, dragging a large car, a fat dead beetle or tortoise, behind it. Still I didn't think the snow was really serious. But when we moved on a little, we suddenly came on a spot where the wheels just churned and milled round helplessly.

Just at this moment another little car came over the crest and a large bony man, like a vet, jumped out and began at once to try and push us out of the thick patch.

It seemed impossible to begin with, and I was hating the sound and smell of the engine, and the heaving and grunting of Eric and the man; but then I felt it swinging, and soon I had it turned and we were thanking the man and winging away back down to the main road as quickly as possible.

On the way down we passed the air-force piece and his woman, a break-down lorry and another car with a horsey, whippy man standing by it, wearing breeches and a black pullover with a spidery white pattern through it. He had a villain's moustache and looked wicked and amused as he heard Eric swearing at me obscenely because I didn't want to pass cars, thinking there was a ditch filled up and masked with snow.

When at last we got to my aunt's we found her just about to "tidy herself" up for our visit. I had never seen her house before and found that it was a new bungalow that had been a nursing home. It is right in the middle of the old town, up on a high bank, closed in on all sides.

Something nice about it, in spite of its ugliness — the outside is rough-east and it is so unrealised that it seems to have no front at all. The front door cannot at first be recognized; the bedrooms are in the front, the living room tucked into the side. At the back my aunt has cut off two rooms, a tiny kitchen and a bathroom for someone else, so that she shall not be entirely alone. But even here there is peculiarity and inconvenience, for the two main rooms are separated from each other by a little court, and to get from one to the other one has to pass down a little covered way.

I suppose the strangeness of the plan is due, a little, to the fact that it was a nursing home, though I feel that even then it must have been eccentric and confused.

My aunt was very pleased to see us and made us coffee at once. She put too little milk in for me, just as she used to when I was a child.

There were all Grandpa's books, china, garden seats, early Victorian paintings (a bird's nest so soft and pretty by an old milk jug with cloudy mandarins on it, farmyard scenes by someone called Lara) that were in the drawingroom[4] — the Chinese table and stool ornately coarse, specially for Europeans, with little dancing white ivory men and warriors inlaid into the golden-brown wood. They had been in store for seven years and I had not seen them for perhaps ten.

Everything was shown to us, and it was a shock somehow to find everything in such good order, so fresh, so clean, and yet unremarkable, that one's eyes began to search greedily for any speck of beauty anywhere. It was a shock to realize that most household goods are quite unworthy of all the care they receive. It was as if a solemn shrine was found to contain only a celluloid cupid-doll.

Now I remember how, as a child, at the mercy of other people's environments, I was utterly delighted whenever I came into a house that contained more than a cupid-doll; how I glowed and felt that the inhabitants were really wonderful.

10 March

I think that the murderous part of writing, the trying to force thought into a form that can be shared by others, is something that one shirks and turns away from with sick distaste in the morning, when it calls, and at night when one tries to have done with it. But it will never stop gnawing. There is always the longing to put the thoughts into the crude mincing machine. It is as if a madman were determined to make all the delicacies of a perfect music come through a brass trombone.

The other horror is that we are not rich enough, cannot take in all the thousand million things that we would have in every story. If we try, we only overload and are cumbersome.

All we can do is to make a cheap little framework, that we hope is strong and resilient.

We are going to leave here in a few weeks and go to Middle Orchard. I have lived here nearly four years.[5] It makes me think of all the other places I have lived in — the flat in Hadlow Road, February 1936 to January 1940; the Hop Garden, Platt, January 1940 to December 1941 (bombed one year, burnt out the next by the kitchen boiler); Pond Farm with the Gardeners for about five months; then this Pitt's Folly Cottage from the spring of 1942.

17 March, 6.45 p.m.

Yesterday we drove Noël Adeney up to 34, Croom's Hill, Greenwich — her new house. I had not seen it since September or October 1935, when I

4 At Whaphams, Henfield (see 1942, note 49 above).
5 Pitt's Folly Cottage.

stopped there in the ambulance on my way to the nursing home at Broadstairs.[6]

To go in at the heavy, early eighteenth-century door and see the broad stairs and the sweep of the high wainscot was to have brought back to me all the feelings of my two years of life there.

It had been all fresh and newly painted when at eighteen I had come upon it in my agitated, inexperienced and determined search for a room of my own. Evie had opened the door to me and been as moony and as unattached as she still is. Strange to think that from that day to this she has been somewhere about the place. First I lived in her house, now she lives in mine. And she is as inhuman as ever.

But I must go back to our visit yesterday and not remember too much to muddle and confuse.

The house, instead of being fresh and painted, was now all war-worn and rather dirty. The Adeneys' things had been dumped in lumps and piles in every room, so that one could only walk in passages as at a junk shop. The first floor was let off to the L.C.C. for offices, and they stay there till three years are up. There was too much for me to think of as I went into each room.

The jut-out room with the thick-barred sash window on to the park, the indented cornice, the heavy moulded mantel and the window seat was the most inhabitable one, and Bernard had lit a fire in the watered down Art Nouveau grate that spoils the old scratched grey marble surround. It is a room that could be made beautiful, and although some of the wall-paper was weeping down, it was satisfying just to sit in it and take in all the details again, and to watch the bicycles in the park and the squabbling boys going up to the park.

The cellar where the fine stone-flagged kitchen had been was now divided up into small compartments, but the old fitted dresser was with its legs like plain, unfluted columns and the shelves in the curved bow were still there. If the dividing wall were taken down, it would be a fine room again.

18 *March, evening.*

Geoffrey Lumsden wrote to me this morning, sending me the beginning of a book which he had dedicated to me, because *Maiden Voyage* prompted him to write it.

I had to stop my description of our visit to Croom's Hill because I've been ill all day, but now it's melting away and I can think a little again.

I think I will copy out a bit of the dedicatory letter because I will want perhaps to remember it.

6 The incident is recalled in *A Voice Through a Cloud.*

THE TAJ MAHAL HOTEL, BOMBAY.

Sunday.
10th September, 1944.
My dear Denton,

I have just read *Maiden Voyage*. A fellow Reptonian, called Payne, who is in the same Battalion as me, said to me a month or so ago, "An O.R. has just written a book." I was amused by the way he said it, as though it was quite a feat that an O.R. should be able to write at all, let alone write a book. "A fellow called Denton Welch," he continued, "do you know him?" "Denton Welch," said I, "do I not!" And my thoughts sped back to Repton, to New Cross and Tonbridge.[7] He told me he was expecting a copy to be sent out from home and I impatiently waited and thought, "Good for Welch," "Damn good show" and so on.

Yesterday I met him on leave and asked if the book had arrived and he said "No" but that he had managed to buy a copy in Bombay.

He kindly lent it to me and I sat up reading it until three-thirty in the morning. This is the result.

I think the reason why I am so excited and pleased about it is because I know you and because the book is the product of a brain that I know and knew when, like mine, it was young and developing and which at that time contained the seeds of *Maiden Voyage* and no doubt so much more, and here is the first blossom, and more and greater will follow. Many congratulations.

I shall go back to our day at Croom's Hill. When I got to the top floor, to the room under the roof of the jutting out piece, I thought of the two years I had spent sleeping there, thinking, talking to friends, living alone with the things I was collecting.[8]

How dark it was with only its window looking on to the park! I remembered all this and it did not surprise me. Looking down at the sash bars, under the soot and newer white paint, I saw the lines of rose madder and ultramarine that I had made to follow the mouldings. I was pleased with this (transported to that other time, twelve years ago, when I ran home with

---

7 Denton noted in the MS, "Greenwich really"; his lodgings were in Greenwich, the art school in New Cross.

8 Denton occupied two different rooms during his stay at Croom's Hill. The first, described in "A Novel Fragment", was off a half-landing on the first floor. At some stage during the two years he lodged in the house he moved into the room referred to here (and in *A Voice Through a Cloud*), an attic bedroom on the second floor.

the tubes of paint to do the decoration), when I looked across at the door and saw that it had not been painted over at all and still was bright with lines of colour. It also had a curious black, dusted look. I went across to it and saw that the gold paint I'd dabbed all over it had all gone gangrene black. The old uneven boards were still ochred.

I thought how I would run down from this room in the morning, rather late, and burst into the jut-out dining-room, where I would sit at the table in perfect peace, all alone, with the moving picture of the park through the window, and the snapping fire behind me. I would sit there eating toast and rich, overcooked plum jam, the most delicious I have had, drinking coffee and reading — always reading and then gazing about me.

It was there, while I ate, that I first really read the *Essays of Elia*; the book was with a Greek lexicon and other things unreadable to me in a low dark bookshelf. I took it up, and almost at once realized that it was for me.

23 March, 2.15 p.m.

All alone at Pitt's Folly Cottage on the day before the last.[9]

Eric and Evie have gone up to Middle Orchard to deal with painters and cleaners, but I have a temperature through trying to clean a window and the mantelpiece, so have to stay here and leave everything to other people.

I have tried to tie up all my manuscripts neatly and even the effort of that has made me gruesome; but I was better after my boiled egg and Dr Johnson lunch,[10] and now I am thinking of all that has happened to me in this room built over a garage, how I fled here from Pond Farm after the absurd quarrel about nothing, how all my "fame", if that is quite the suitable word, sprang on me with *Maiden Voyage*, the notice of Edith Sitwell, Herbert Read and the others; the letters from unknowns.

All that held a spice that comes vividly back. Then my next book and stories seemed to be building up, and I was waiting all the time for something else to happen to me. Francis brought Eric quite unexpectedly, and because I was so ill and exhausted that evening I nearly did not see them. What would have happened if I hadn't suddenly changed my mind? Another door was opened on to a landscape that I thought would always be quite foreign to me. All those crags and pools and frowning storm-clouds; a degree of sharing quite outrageous if it had been prophesied to me; unhappiness and feeling of waste that I thought I had done with for ever; cosy snugness of friendship that I only remember very early with my brother.[11]

9 He was to move into Middle Orchard on Quarter Day.
10 A mixture of coffee and cocoa, according to Eric Oliver.
11 Paul.

Now I'm lying here in this corner for almost the last time; sun outside glistening on the tartan rug, shining the reflected light on to the angels' wood cheeks; trees gently, flutteringly blowing.

I seem almost at the other end, my heart has had to desert this place so much.

I had a poem in my head last night, flashing as only those unformed midnight poems can. It was all made up of unexpected burning words. I knew even in my half-sleep that it was nonsense, meaningless, but that forcing and hammering would clear its shape and form. Now not a word of it remains, not even a hint of its direction. What a pity one cannot sleepwrite on the ceiling with one's finger or lifted toe.

24 March, 4.25 p.m.

Last day, alone again, and I have been into the wood saying good-bye. I thought, under a tree root, I had found an amazing stump, gentian blue through and through, of a toadstool. For a moment it was a treasure to me, and I thought I saw too a segment of the violent blue cap as well, but when I went up to it and bent down it was the spout and end part of the lid of an old blue enamel tea-pot thrusting through clogged layers of dead leaves. There were the indented gums of gaping old shoes too, and primroses and iris shoots coming out of black slime ponds. Gnats were already dancing round and round in a mad swirl.

I went to the lately deserted mid-Victorian cottage — very taking in its way; but one of the walls is about to fall out, so it is deserted.

This afternoon the back door, which has always been locked, was open. There was a white dog snuffling about, but it seemed unattended by its human being, so I slipped through the door into the wash-house scullery with its narrow larder. Boys have broken some of the pretty, fanciful white-latticed panes, but the walls seem good.

The front kitchen-living-room had a minute bow, latticed again and with its own tiny tiled roof outside. If one could have made the front door of glass there would be all the light needed. The stairs were in a box, and I came to the narrowest landing I had ever seen, and off it were three bedrooms, one the size of a large closet, the back one the biggest, and the front one with a doll's Victorian grate, beautifully designed, slight, yet baroque and rich. I imagined it with a handful of juicy apple twigs in it, and jewel-like jet-like fragments of coal.

A weight of depression clapped down on me as I imagined living there, working to make it beautiful. Powerful breaths of sadness puffed at me. I thought of the black miasma swamps at the bottom of the clay pits so near. I thought of the swarm of mosquitoes that buzzed upwards in the summer air.

I left the house, thinking of all my life near here and of how I should never live here again.

25 March

The very last morning and the sun is shining through a sort of frosty mist. Coo-dove wood-pigeons coo and cocks are crowing further away. Last night they played Hayden's London Symphony on the wireless; and all the walls were stripped in here. I kept thinking of coming here in 1942, and as I packed my trunk, I found a piece of paper. It was a letter from my father's firm, dated 26 May 1942, telling me what my income was for the year up to April 1943. It ended, "We note that you are moving on June 10th. Will you please let us know your new address?" So that exactly dates the moving of the furniture here. I myself came earlier and had it furnished for a fortnight.

This journal, I think, was begun in July 1942, so its thirteen books almost entirely cover my life here. There are many things that I have not put in. Strangers have written to me and I have forgotten their letters, though I should like to have remembered them all. There was that long span in 1944 in the doodle-bug period when Eric and I spent every day by the river bank, when Guy brought Vernon down for a week of heat and bathing, raspberries, painting (only by Vernon) and, one night, roast duck.[12]

I was too bewildered then to write anything, but I wish now that I had made myself.

Twenty to eleven p.m. Middle Orchard.

It's happened, we are here. I'm in the quiet room all to myself and Eric is in his, sleeping already. The stiff new red, grey and fawn striped curtains are round me and I smell paint from downstairs. I ache all round the middle of me in a broad belt. There was an owl just now calling and calling.

30 March, 7.40 a.m.

Yesterday was my birthday, but all letters I might have had, or presents, must have been delayed by the post re-direction, for there was nothing here. Eric had given me a little child's mahogany stool with tapering legs, stretchers and hard delicately curved top, that we found in the skating-rink junk shop in Tonbridge on the 26th, the day after we moved here. We went out that day in the brilliant sun to go to the bank and do tiresome shopping. Then we had lunch in the Home-Made Cake Shop — very good in solid way; tomato-ish soup in earthenware, stewed steak, which I cannot have tasted for about ten years, mashed potatoes in lumps looking like soft tennis

---

12 Guy Allan (see 1944, note 15 above). Vernon was his German boyfriend. They camped out in May Walbrand-Evans's garden.

balls and cabbage stuff, then jam tart, and Eric had cheese and biscuits. Even the coffee was hot and milky.

Just before we left, the place began to fill up, and two maturing girls came to sit at our table. They were in very high spirits and pleased with each other in a cynical way, just as children are immediately after being let out of school. Their conversation snapped backwards and forwards between them like elastic in good condition. The smaller, least likeable-looking one seemed to have the whip hand, and she sometimes almost appeared to be rapping the larger one over the knuckles. When the larger one said, "I shan't leave unless I have to," the other asked:

"Oh, and why should you have to?"

"Well, they might find someone else who was better."

"Do you think that likely?" This in a very strong bludgeoning tone.

A little silence, then the other felt that perhaps a little fight must be shown.

"Not very likely."

An unfortunate effect, not enough conviction, too much assumed brassiness, and so there was an awkward little pause.

We left them talking with great animation about their churches.

"I gather," the tall one said, "she doesn't approve at all of St Bede's." (Or so the saint's name sounded.) "Apparently she went there one day and came away saying that she didn't know what anything was about."

"Oh," said little stony one. So much in her "oh", contempt of ignorance, of disapproving fools in outer darkness, who didn't understand the glory of the service at St Bede's.

To go back to the house here; we have now put the eighteenth-century cartoon for a tapestry that I have had rolled up for four years. It came about twenty-five years ago from a château in the south of France. It is all faded blues, greys, pinks, creams and greens, and in it Venus is leaning down from her chariot and her doves and blessing a young girl whom Cupid is fixing with a dart. An older woman looks on with an expression of amazement on her face. It is framed in a lovely rococo border of shells, wreaths and spiky fins or wings.

It is ten feet square so we had to fold two feet up and put one side a little round a corner. It has been backed with some finer material which is stiff with glue, so it crackles and is difficult to handle. When we folded up the two feet at the bottom, we had already hung the cartoon, therefore I had to pin it first, creeping all behind in the dark, then I had to thread a needle, sit on the inside, with Eric on the outside, and we had to pass the needle back and forth, through the stiff canvas, till we came to the end.

The walls of the living-room are light blue-grey-green, woodwork white, floors natural wood waxed; then the two terracotta rugs are in there, the little Regency rosewood side cupboard with mirror doors and ormolu gallery and pillars between the windows, curtains the old deep green velvet ones I had in my first flat, the Hadlow Road one, when I was twenty-one.

7 April, 10 p.m.

I bleed inside; and when it comes out of me, almost fascinating in its disgustingness, I feel full of snarling that I am spoilt. To have always to do every fragment of work with the gloves of sickness sheathing each finger, to have that added! The glove of flesh is thick and deadening enough, without the bewildering adventure of illness never-ending. And if a silly woman in a car ten years ago had driven straight instead of crooked, I should not be whining till I'm stiff all through.

Outside there is a young moon very bright in the coldness, there is what I imagine to be a young owl to-whooing, a stubborn dog barks. Evie has just been reading me Haydon's Journal, the Petworth visit and the debtor's prison, and Eric went to bed at half-past six. We quarrelled because I did not quite like the shape he was cutting round the honeysuckle hedge. He was changing a gentle curve into an angle. The verge cut in this way seemed to have much less reason and meaning; just as a bow window that is three flat sides and not a segment of a circle is usually much less pleasing. He did not like me to say this and told me that people must all be allowed to do things in their own way. I then said that I had spoken because otherwise I should have resented the shape of the lawn every time I looked out of my window.

How tedious the little details seem, written down, yet it is always this littleness that seems to have, banked up behind it, great walls of fight and resistance. I think it is true to say that criticisms on matters of "taste" bring out of children and ancients, simple and complex, the interested and the uninterested, great waves of animosity. It is as if each person feels insulted when his judgement on artistic things is questioned.

When there is resentment in a house, however passing, the walls seem thick with it and the floors muffled. The weight of it is like stone beads.

9 April, 10 p.m.

Yesterday, after working all morning and afternoon drawing my *Vogue* drawing and writing my "woodman" short story,[13] because I felt rather ill and restless and in need of different surroundings, I got into the car and drove up Wrotham Hill towards Gravesend. Half-way up the hill I saw a little fork road to the left and I tried to remember where it led. I was put against turning up it as it had a notice to say that it was the way to a pre-

13 "The Fire in the Wood" (see 1942, note 4 above).

O.C.T.U. camp, and I saw myself ending in an Army enclosure.

Further up the main road one of the youths from the camp "thumbed" me and said, "Are you going to Gravesend, please, sir?" He quickly dropped the "sir" when he was sitting beside me and I was trying to make conversation. This I knew was a compliment in some way. I suppose I interpreted it as a tribute to an umpompous or young appearance. But it may, of course, have only meant that he felt me too mild to demand such an old-fashioned form.

I dropped him at Meopham. He was unlighted with humour or any vividness. He was rather sincere; and he had rather specially big spots on his chin, brooding and smouldering like volcanoes between the downy fluff of his beard. One could see how difficult and painful his shaving would be.

I went on until I found a road to bring me back to Wrotham.

I went some way, until I came on the part where I had walked when I was eighteen, on my pilgrimage from Winchester to Canterbury.[14] Remembering it, I had a spear in me for my spoilt ease and strength of body. I whined for what appeared to me that suddenly taken away beauty of ease and agility. How I loved my lightness, springiness, endurance, tautness! I thought, "I shall always be this springing, dancing-wire taut person," then in two years I was flat on my back with the fear of no walking any more and the certainty of illness till the grave. Yet how amazingly my body has put up with it. I must look more worn with it than I should look; but it is not dramatic. It is horrible when the ill look is dramatic. It throws every friend into confusion.

Well, I left the road where I had walked before, and I wound down a long valley, the flat side of the hills gently shutting me in. There were no people, no cars, only me.

It was getting rather late now, just before the light failed. I came to a white cottage on my left and a little further up, on the other side of the road, I saw a ground plan of a house, heaps of rubble and the other signs of a bomb landing. Standing out of the tangled mess I saw at once a beheaded statue and a large decorative urn, so on impulse I stopped the car and got out. I walked towards the statue and saw the head, with a wreath of vine leaves round it, lying on the ground. I picked it up and fitted it on the statue. There was another head missing and an arm. It was an early Victorian group in

14 It is possible that this refers to part of a walk that constitutes the last section of *I Left My Grandfather's House*. The expedition, as recorded, tails off at Cocking in Sussex, but Denton may have continued to Canterbury without recording this part of the walk. It is unlikely that he would have commenced a walk from Wrotham at this time, as he did not live anywhere near the place until he was twenty-one.

terracotta. The ideal beauty so slimy as to be wicked, and so holding its own repulsive attraction.

Just as I was wondering whether to ask for information at the white cottage, I turned and saw across the tiled floors of the ruined house a tall man in city grey approaching. I walked towards him and asked if he could tell me about the statue, as I was looking for one for this orchard, "to seal a vista".

He said, "It's mine and I don't mind parting with it, but the council must decide. They've taken over."

He then went on to tell me that a flying bomb had completely demolished the house and that his mother was killed. He was waiting for the council to build him something in its place. He lived temporarily in the white cottage, though it did not belong to him.

All this time I was observing him in snatches. He was tall, rather floppy, loose in the middle in the city grey clothes, and he had thin hair and a large pale face crowned and cowed by a large and rabbit-nostriled nose. The whole effect was rather like that of a large, soft, grey-white rabbit or Easter hare.

When I moved back towards the car he said suddenly, "Er, perhaps you might like to see inside the cottage." He seemed uncertain and rather eager that I should go inside. I said that I would like to, but that I had to be back to a very early supper so mustn't stay more than a minute.

I wondered who would be in the cottage. I expected wives, even children, or at least elderly relations. The man himself I guessed to be in his middle thirties, but he may have been younger. He had the looks that seemed unstamped.

As we were going through the little gate I thought I saw a person in the room on the right, where a fire glowed, get up and pass across the window. I steeled myself for introductions, smiles and explainings.

But when we entered and he had shown me the tidy kitchen scullery with its oil stove and old copper, he took me into the front room and there was no one there. The "Ideal" boiler boiled alone, and he said, "I live quite alone here. A woman comes in every morning. A friend's been staying with me, but he went this morning."

He then asked me if I was interested in furniture, and began to point out the oak Bible-box, the modern little dresser, the curious black-and-gold round, dumpy, vaguely Windsor chairs. I had not seen old ones like them and I wondered if they were old, but he waved a hand and said, "About 1820, I think."

All this time he was pumping up his lamp. He had taken a bottle of methylated spirit and filled it. I had at first mistaken it for whisky or gin in the dusk and had expected to be offered a little drink; for there were two oranges on the table near the bottle, strengthening the suggestion of cocktails and stimulation (I seemed in this house continually to be following false clues to wrong conclusions).

I sat down rather uneasily because I felt unwell and tired. I tried to show as much interest as I could in furniture of the type least attractive to me. There was a dreariness about the oak so unrelieved, so spoilt and made to appear doubtful by its association with Tudor tea-houses.

The man seemed most eager for me to stay and talk, and I realised some of the isolation of his long evenings there, after his day's work. He told me that his work took him a lot into the Canterbury area. Then he told me that he used to live with his aunt at Ash, so I asked him if he knew Tom Hennell, whose father had been rector there.

He said, "Yes, isn't it awful about Tom."

I said, "Has he gone mad again?" He had once been put away for nine months. He said, "No, but you know he went out East as a war artist? Well, they say he was captured in Java by the Indonesians and hasn't been heard of since."

It was a shock. When the war was supposed to be over, to feel that people one had known could still be seized and done away with very painfully was doubly horrible. I imagined all the beatings and tortures and starvings of the vindictive. And I thought of Tom, very big and shapeless with his black lamb's wool hair, his mad, self-preoccupied eyes, the three or four waistcoats that he wore on top of each other, and the huge portfolio of old drawings he would take everywhere on the back of his bicycle.

He had hidden violence in his character that was always alarming to me, and I imagined him striking back frantically at his captors, yelling, his dementia clapping down on him again, until they thought him some true devil.

I was thinking hard of ways of escape from the little white cottage, because of my discomfort and tiredness, but the man seemed keen to show me the upstairs next. He took me up narrow stairs into his bedroom where there were two beds, a little oak chest, a Chippendale dressing mirror, rather pretty, and an old punch bowl, Chinese, but with European lovers and a ship painted on it. My interest was growing, so that I wished I felt better to enjoy the adventure.

When he opened the small chest and I saw packets of stamps, I said, "Do you collect stamps, too?"

"Yes, it's my business." He seemed rather repressive and guarded about it.

"I've not known a person before who was interested both in stamps and antiques," I said, unthinkingly. "They go together," he replied, waving his hand.

The other bedroom, where the friend had been sleeping, was full of china in one corner. Really pretty bits, blue Worcester, printed Leeds, Derby tea sets, a Chelsea red anchor cup. He turned over the pieces for me and held them very tightly in case I should drop them.

"If only you could spend another half hour," he said, "I'd get some good things out for you."

"I wish I could, but I must get back, you know."

"Just come into my junk room for a minute then, just for a glance." He took me down the stairs again and we entered the room on the other side of the staircase.

The floor was covered with boxes and packages. There was a large built-in cupboard filled with more china. I was delighted and would like to have looked at everything. I kept wanting to know if he also sold china. There were several things that I wanted to buy. Prettiest black transfer ware, Liverpool or Leeds, with little rococo ladies and bouncing pug dogs, against a grotto dripping with ferns. Every bit was nice; but I had to get away, feeling tired and uncomfortable.

"If you had half an hour, I'd unpack some really nice things," he said.

"But I must get back, I'm afraid."

Even when I went out of the gate he followed me to the car, still talking. Perhaps the night alone at that cottage, rather isolated, never quite appealed to him.

He wanted me to go again and he took my telephone number. I said, "Oh, but you must come and see us next. We've only just moved in."

There was a sort of checkmate, I think — each person wanting the other to make the pilgrimage to him. I saw too what a heavy person he would become, "squatting on one's face" perhaps for many hours, complacently telling one of china marks.

Just before I left he said, "I've got a telephone too. I'm under Clarkson, that's my real name, but most people here call me James, because that was my stepfather's name. It's not my real name but I'm called it."

"Which do you prefer?" I asked, feeling confused.

"Well, James really, but it's not my real name."

This insistence on reality, and the confusion of names, made me think, as it must have many others, that there was something a little furtive and criminal about him.

13 *April*

An amazing thing has happened; they have written from my father's office to say that Bill has asked for his Air Force gratuity, about £99, to be handed over to me on my birthday! How heartless and dead of them not to have told me of this on my birthday, instead of several weeks afterwards. It would have overjoyed me, for I got no letters that day — although some arrived the next. I have never had a present like this before. It delights one all over.

16 April

Gerald has been, fustulating, fabricating his flash trash — all tinsel from India, Cairo, Pretoria.[15] His endless stories pouring out, and he sitting on you from one o'clock till ten at night. Bullying insistence of such a talker and squatter, and underneath his sly snake eyeing you. Extraordinary innocence of his conceit, every story centring on himself — and what a transformed self, quite unrecognizable.

Between pats of butter he tried to be nasty too — a nasty pudding he mixed up into really, and he wants to come with someone else on Saturday.

Why has his type of person ever thought it wise to fix on to my type?

I suppose the terrible flaw in him is his lack of any brooding, sulky depth. He is a music-hall man recording his funny self for ever on a wearing-out gramophone.

He says he has loved the army because it has made him feel freer. He says he does love to meet all sorts of people, including well-known ones. Here he reeled off his list of names. Wavell, Mountbatten (Lady), Auchinleck, Turkey princes, Greek princesses. Again it seemed endless. Everything was endless. That is the other awful thing about Gerald.

I suppose underneath everything, though, he is the anxious little boy, longing to be popular, not to be overlooked. He longs to take part, to shine, to glory. But how lovely if the tiniest bit more judgement had been given him in that thick-behind-the-ears round head of his.

17 April

The American edition of *In Youth is Pleasure* has come. Very ugly, all debased cover. (Gerald said snarlingly, "There are several editions of *In Youth is Pleasure* in Viceregal Lodge, you'll be interested to hear.") Snarlingly is not the word, more sneering-snarling-joking-teasing-dismissing. I hate to see my own book tossed on the American world like an ugly bag of nonsense. The cover of a book that is coarse poisons the first few pages inside.

Peggy Kirkaldy was here on Friday, and she brought me a nest of ten eggs, and a fine old Norwich shawl — a lot of golden oranges mixed in tiny Persian pattern with all the other colours and a border of scarlet, cerulean, white, black and green squares. The last square in each corner had the woven initials, F.M., perfectly 1850. Now I don't know quite what to use it for, since to me shawls of this sort carry with them a curious air of drabness, although they are so bright. On the bed it is less pleasing than my wine

---

15 At art school with Denton. He appears as Gerald in "Sickert at St Peter's" (see 1942, note 2 above), as Gerard Hope in "A Novel Fragment" (see 1942, note 4 above) and as Mark Lynch in *A Voice Through a Cloud*.

velvet eiderdown. Perhaps I must just roll it round me or toss it on the bed when I am ill.

21 April. Ten to eight a.m.

As I have been all this last week — drinking Benger's, savouring all the different qualities of headache, body ache and stomach squeamishness. Every part seems to have been living its own debauched week, not bothering with me at all. High temperatures always turn my thoughts to lovely food — though I can hardly eat at all — to the perfect house I'd like to make — though the thought of doing anything but lying still is horrible. These very material thoughts wind on and on soothingly in me. Perhaps they are bearable and soothing because ideal materialism is a fairy story, a fantasy that charms just when material things cannot be properly enjoyed, either through poverty, prison or illness. One does not necessarily want the delicious food, the beautiful romantic surroundings in reality, one wants to imagine them, spin them out.

Only in a later, more horrible stage is one filled with a churning revulsion by all that has given one pleasure.

7 May. About 3 p.m.

Very windy, sunny, me semi-temperature, in bed.

So Evie has gone at last — after ten years she has gone away to some ladies in Cornwall.[16] She was all dressed up in her new coat and skirt — sort of hot red heather — her maroon masculine slouch cap, her striped scarf.

She came in to say good-bye while I was eating breakfast in bed. I wondered what would happen. She made two little running darts at me. It all melted away. I wanted it to be all drifting away in gaiety.

I ran out afterwards in my cassock to wave them off. The wind blew the skirts of it. Evie was almost hilarious, to cover the good-byes.

Then just after Eric had taken her to the station, a letter came from her brother. We steamed it open to find what we had feared — that he had been a clown and gone to meet her train in London on Thursday! So there was no one there to take her across London, and knowing how lost she is we are still half afraid that she will ring up to say she is stranded.

How strange it is to think that after all this long time she is gone. It is so good for her really that we both hope she will stay some time, though we feel that she is almost certain to return eventually.

How many violent quarrels there have been between her and me. What

16 She went to work at 57 Daniell Road, Truro, falling out with her new employers within a month.

extraordinary behaviour there has been sometimes. Yet I suppose she is what you would call quite devoted. This does not mean that she would in any way comply in small particulars, but that in large issues she would always protect and guard. She has a streak of madness, of course, and that often makes her touching, infuriating and tragic.

12 May, 12.30 p.m.

I know tonight that it is best for me to be alone most of the time — near people who wish me well and like to see me, but alone; for in loneness everything seems to grow into its proper place and there is hardly any waste of spirit. What little there is does not offend, it is one's own fault, one lets it pass.

Thinking back to the times in my life when I have been happy, it has always been when I have been doing almost everything for myself, as when I was at Brixham in 1934,[17] with the house full of other art students, but with me alone — bathing early every morning, making my own breakfast of cornflakes and cream and coffee, bicycling about the country, doing every day a little picture as my work, then gazing at the churches, the ruins and the antique shops, bathing and climbing and bicyling, till I was tired out.

The quiet content came bubbling up, was with me every day then; and I remember how reluctant I was to go back to London and be with my father in Adam Street[18] and Ryder Street, to have to go to Quaglino's and the Monseigneur Grill with him and to his club. Everywhere irked by the bodies and minds jostling one's own. Oh the dirtiness of herding together.

Yet it is most important to have people near one that one need hardly see. Without this consciousness of other human beings I think almost all of us are liable to be swamped by the power of matter. One's strength is not enough to bear this with no other help near.

But the waste that one should do everything to avoid is the pointless, joyless chatter, the dislocations of meeting and parting; worst waste of all, snarlings and irritation.

I do not think that people want love most, they need the settled reverie, the calm testing and tasting of their past and the world's past.

I am talking about "people" when I mean "me".

I have been alone here since Friday evening when Eric went to London to stay with his mother. I took him to the station, then went to Wrotham, where I found in the not very promising shop there a little emery needle-cushion beautifully made in the form of a tiny stool. It was so much a stool and so little a needle cushion that I wanted it at once for the dolls' house. It

17 In Devon, where Denton went on holiday while an art student.
18 Now Robert Adam Street (see 1943, note 16 above).

has minute needlework on top framed in kid leather; the legs of the stool are covered in morocco, with gold trimmings. Where the needles should go is faced in faded rose watered silk.

So much work and love just for a needle-cushion, and quite a usual one at that, I suppose. I like to think of the early-Victorian girls poking their needles in and out to make them glisten.

The little stool makes one think that civilization is fastidiousness.

People will call this missish slop, trivial, shallow; but it is they who are trivial with their blunted coarseness.

If people doted on their needle-cushions more, a great tree of civilization would grow out of them, instead of a wave of bad smells and famine.

I found too in the shop a Regency chair that was only £2 — black with brass mounts and a brass rope handle at the top. This and its unusual shape decided me, although it was worm-eaten in parts. It has a cane seat, and tapering legs, not out-sweeping ones; the back is long and the brass mounts are on the top with the handle, so that one only sees them when one looks down. It is a chair that talks early nineteenth-century to you whenever you glance at it. [*Word illegible*], commercial, rather cheap with the elegance which charms now, but must have grown so tiring, or the fashion could not have changed to "butcher" furniture.

I took it home excitedly and began to clean it. I worked quite a lot and I suppose must have made myself worse, for I had a headache all yesterday and could only lie in bed. Just before I went to bed on Friday, the wireless began its crime book reviewing, extracts striving to create an atmosphere of horror. I did not like it, alone in this house in an orchard; but the qualms did not last long.

Yesterday, when I was ill, but groping in the kitchen to make cocoa, the Adeneys appeared and have been in their studio downstairs ever since.[19] Noël will come and sit on the bed and try to talk disquietingly; but she then remembers that she ought to go, and goes. Perhaps the secret of successful social intercourse is to mask your feelings very little, no more than makes for ordinary politeness. Never make efforts for what you do not want — call out to people you would much rather pass by without a word. Extraordinarily simple advice that I am only just beginning to take.

14 May. About 11 p.m.

The day is messy. I have done some writing, but things are sloppy. I am a melting jelly. It seems that my happiness only comes from being a monk; and when I am not a monk, therefore I cannot be happy. When I am

---

19 When the Adeneys let Middle Orchard to Denton, for £96 a year, it was agreed they should retain use of part of the house for occasional visits.

dammed up and I will not force and break the dam, will not bore through it and will not make the waters flow in however rough a channel, I am not happy. Idleness cannot be happiness for me. It is too heavy a burden. But perhaps half-hearted work is a greater pain. It is like struggling in giants' entrails. To be trapped in the web of unformed work!

With the monk in his dedicated life he may waste some of his time, but he is not distracted, so that even his idleness is dedicated. But when one gives oneself in several directions one is naturally torn to pieces.

15 May, early. Just awake.

Wonderful morning of coldness and sun — frost, only little birds chirping, and my Regency chair standing, silent against the white door, its black glistening, its brass gleaming with the remains of the old lacquer. I am making a squab seat for it out of eight layers of my old rug — rug that I bought with my mother just before going to my prep school.

She said, "That one is nice." It was expensive, with camel hair on one side. I wondered that she could spend so much on a rug; but she said:

"It will keep you warm."

And it kept me warm for years and years until the fire of 1941 spoilt it and pitted it all over.[20]

24 May, 8.30. a.m.

No tea, no breakfast, because of no electric current. Grey about-to-rain morning with cuckoo calling very near me — and with me pleased to have day after long sleepless night, hearing the hours strike until three; horrible, stupid anxieties all those hours — stupid because not for real things, only for imagined slightings, misunderstandings, hatings, maliciousness, all the pin-prick feelings that seem so contemptible in strength and happiness.

Now when it has all gone with the night, only leaving its pale acid taste, I feel freed and worn down, waiting for hot tea. The night was caused by my having to entertain Irene and Hilda Dallas to lunch and tea yesterday. I had cooked the meal the day before, and that made me tired; then having them all day to talk to finished me. They were very charming though and brought lovely salted American pecan nuts, cooking fats and cakes to swell the meal.

When I saw them off at the station, my head was throbbing so much that I could not be still, so I drove first to Wrotham, then up the Gravesend Road, all in the little lanes until at last I came to Ridley Church and I remembered

---

20 In the fire at the Hop Garden Denton also lost all the silver belonging to his mother that he had brought back from China in 1933.

how several years ago I had come across Mrs Hennell tending the churchyard, her very white hair and blue dress staring out against the green.

I stopped and went into the church. The churchyard was not well tended now except for one grave in front.

There was an old wrought-iron door in front of the main door that needed paint sadly.

Inside I noticed chiefly the choir stalls, old altogether or in parts. Always there is the mysterious sleepy feeling in a deserted church, decay, ruthless repair, forgettings, bones, dull dronings, fitful insects. I stayed for a little, standing on the red carpet drugget, half reading the tombs in front of the altar to some Lambes, their coat of arms with all the lambs holding banners in their paws.

Drying arum lilies and some pink flowers in a glass jar on a window ledge.

I went outside and round the west end, where there were large box tombs to Winsoms, till I came to the back of the church, and there I found two other well-tended graves, round with granite crosses laid on them. One was to a woman Bolster and the other to three Hennells, I suppose the father and two sons.

This grave made me think of Tom Hennell, how I'd heard that he'd been reported missing in Indonesia, although the war had long ended.

I decided to go to his house and enquire from the ancient housekeeper. I took what I thought was the wrong lane — because I first wanted to explore it — but after some twisting and turning in the narrowness between the empty fleecy hiding fields and past a most exquisitely cut bird with a cocked tail, all in yew with a red-brown budded sheen, I came upon the house suddenly. It is a very early Victorian workman's cottage that has been modernised and vulgarized with rough-cast and leaded panes. The door had been newly painted in striking, cloying green that unthinking people choose.

I knocked, then was afraid that his mother would be in the house, instead of in her own at Folkestone, and that she would come to the door and burst into tears.

But the nanny-housekeeper, Miss Nangle, came, carefully dressed in her brown dowdiness with her thick loose cotton stockings, her bleared eyes and her satiny, crinkled toupee between the wings of her own hair.

She looked at me without recognition, cold, uninterested. I explained my errand.

She said very mechanically, "Will you come in please", and led me into Tom's narrow living-room.

She still said nothing about him and I thought she was arranging the words, "I'm afraid he is dead."

But when we sat down she expanded all at once, smiled, said, "We've heard nothing since November," then went on to tell me that all was quiet where he was until one day when the citizens began to riot. Tom and the others who were in the hotel with him completely disappeared together with all his possessions. Nothing has come to light, no one knows any more. She said that every day she expects to hear more, to have a letter. She could only live in hopes. She had heard of others who suddenly reappeared after many months.

We sat and talked very easily. I felt that she enjoyed my visit. She explained how very cut off Ridley was — several miles to bus and nearest station, Meopham. Before I left I looked at Tom's Old Master drawings, Parmigianino, Gaspard Poussin, David Wilkie, Gainsborough; then Sickert, Sutherland. I had the greedy person's desire to know what would happen to them, if he did not return.

After I left Tom's I drove on until I got into the middle of a soldier's training camp — leisurely now; but with extraordinary physical training devices like diabolical swing boats, and dummies black and evil crouching on a hillside, as if creeping up it.

When I was free of this I suddenly saw a German prisoner coming out of a farmyard. He looked up almost secretly at me and I was held by the thought of him. He was squat, unstriking except for the prisoner's glance. I turned the car to watch his walk. The great coloured spot sewn to his trousers seemed truly ignominious, and I could understand that an Italian had killed himself because of it. The prisoner went roaming into the field and as he kicked out with his feet disconsolately and tacked to this side and that, he seemed to be the symbol of lost people.

Quarter to eight p.m.

I have just come in from a long drive with the bad headache again, but better now after Eric's fried egg and hot coffee . (At first I thought I could not eat it, but I decided it did me good, not made me sick.)

In the car I lost myself after leaving Malling, where I bought quite a pretty Regency chair, pale wood, streaked, brass mounts; badly re-upholstered over the original slip-in squab seat, ends of the curved back missing, but only £2.5s.

Well, I went down the wrong turning and found myself descending into the arms of a great factory (paper, I think). And there was that painter thing, Peter Bishop, who I knew worked in a paper mill. He had a dolly attaché case and looked unbelievably officey smart Cheshire cat. A peculiar look I can't properly describe. I pretended, of course, that I saw nothing, since we had not met for several years.

But when I'd passed him I found myself at the end of the cul-de-sac and had to turn round. Just in front of me was a dumpy pink little Noah's Ark soldier, endearingly square, but Dutch-doll pig-faced. He kept looking round yearningly, so I made poking signs forward with my finger and he nodded eagerly. He wanted to be taken back to the main road.

I was starting up again to go forward, when Peter turned the corner, and although I didn't look at him, I know that he was mystified, wondering to see me there in the paper mill lane, with the square soldier — wondering to see me at all.

The soldier told me the way to Aylesford, thanked me for my lift and said it was just the ticket, smiling all over his face like a square baby and waving his hand.

I had not seen Aylesford for a long time, perhaps not since I walked through it twelve years ago and stopped in the narrow old street to ask for water or directions. I know I saw the poverty-clean interior and that it was the dim, church-bell, deadened English evening when you remember the dead formless history of country towns, how people have talked and cooked and slept for many hundred years.

I went over the narrow bridge, not being able to go as slowly as I wanted, because an officious policeman kept signalling me on. Leaving the car I climbed up to the church, read the stone plaque saying that the meagre yew was planted in 1708. It looked wasted and worn but with not enough body for two hundred and forty years. I wondered if it were only a shoot; or do yews take three or four or five centuries to thicken and spread and glorify themselves? Wonderful trees of deep black blood and ghosts and skeletons.

In the church the great marble memorial in the chapel next to the chancel hung over me, brooding in its eighteenth-century conceit. What a world of egoism it was in itself!

Family pride sweeping and stinking and swaggering up to God. The marble peruke, the bloated marble bags under the eyes, the marble sneer (I mean a sneer) on the curled lip. The sneer is nothing assumed, not a facial trick; it is just the black look of worldliness solidified. Perhaps sneer is wrong. It is not contempt; it is just preening, puffing of one's gold guineas and fine acres. But I loved its solidity. The medieval things in a church are nearly always ruthlessly repaired, so one flies to the memorials, the eighteenth-century marble worlds for relief.

I poked into the bottom floor of a round turret, where there were mournful degraded brooms and bottles, abandoned and horrible.

I thought that by leaving Aylesford by another road I should eventually come round to the Maidstone road again. I chugged up towards the downs. The wind blew me, freshed me; but my head had begun to buzz its ache, to kill my adventuring.

I stopped the car to feel the wind, see the view, the clothes-peg chimneys sticking out of the ground, the powdered green-blue of the spring-summer fields. In this half rural, half factory land one is continually made sad and happy, aware of life and death in a wearing way.

Why is it all so clear-cut that factories are a threat to a lone human being and green fields an invitation? We seem to be very frightened of our own contrivances and to call them ugly, evil, almost at once. We take what comes from them, hating their faces and breathings all the time. Biscuits please, but a biscuit factory is nearly as evil as a bomb factory to one's heart. I do not mean just ugly visually, I mean wicked atmosphere. The threat the torture-chamber has.

As I looked down from the ridge I tried to find my way towards home. I thought I should thread through the lanes if I continued; so after going over an open space with houses on my right and an old chalk pit, I turned down to the left; and suddenly I was in front of a derelict church, at the end of a farm lane with factory outhouses beyond and the river near. There was a man tending his garden. There was a lot of smoke from somewhere — the evening air and sun round the ruinous church — the feeling of everything passing away — me dying — church crumbling — money-mucked factories choking — man scratching on the chocolate earth for ever. The atmosphere of that church suddenly come upon pricks me.

It was roofed still and with fragments of glass in the windows. From what I could see I guessed that it has been deserted for perhaps fifteen or twenty years; but it may have been longer, for I saw in the porch the pencilled date of a tourist, 1919, and do tourists write their names in unruinous churches?

It is so surprising to see a church not grossly over-restored but quite neglected that I could only stare at it and feel pleased for a little.

When I went in and saw that the silvery, bony beams were there, the walls with their plaster still on them and the marks of arches filled in, I was more pleased.

The church had evidently been larger, with side aisles, several centuries ago. Now it was utterly bare except for some ropes and spades and the framework of a bier. The coffin shape on the ground, discarded — and all over the walls pictures of girls in chalk, enormous breasts, little pants, frizzy hair.

Always the little pants, never naked. And remarks: "Wot, no ghosts!", "Maurice loves" and so on.

Soldiers must have been billeted in the empty church. I pictured the grim dormitory.

Again I guessed that the church had undergone fairly sensible repairs sixty, seventy, eighty years ago.

The tower was good. There were no memorial plaques on the walls and I think the floor had been entirely relaid with some cement.

If the church now could be properly cared for, before it is too late! The roof will crash in soon.

I kept wondering why it had been deserted. When I came out I asked the gardening man its name. "Burnham Old Church," he said; but he could tell me no more.

I shall go back another day.

On my way back I turned into what had been a defence area — notices of punishment for trespassing everywhere, ruined horribleness, mess with no soul.

I had to go over a makeshift bridge, insecure-feeling, with rough wobbling wooden sleepers to drive over. It was near another church that I did not visit, because of my head. But looking back I saw this church, a skeleton of a mill or factory, the hill behind, a waving flag. It was a biting landscape; old-new-heartless, black and clear and ugly beauty like a witch.

5 June, 11 p.m.

Suddenly after writing tonight about exulting and weeping and walking the streets of Broadstairs eleven years ago in the rain and blackness, I was filled with restlessness and, tired as I was, got up, ran down the outside staircase and got on my bike, which I have not ridden for months. Eric had gone out in the car to the Golding Hop.

I had the impulse to ride on the bike to the cottage on the edge of the wood where a dark-eyebrowed youth used to live whom I had known when I lived at Platt. I thought that he might have returned from the wars and we might meet in the garden, just as if it were still five years ago.

To get to his cottage I branched off down the rough lane that leads through heather and broom and dark overhanging trees.

It was very foolish. I was not well enough to be jostled about on the roughness, and the path went straight into the blackness of the wood — the wood that stretched on and on almost to Maidstone.

As I rode over the glimmering white path, pushing sometimes through the cushions of broom, all scented in the night, feeling the crisp crackle of the heather underneath the wheel, I thought, "Can I really be doing this, can I really be making myself worse by hurtling along? And am I really digging into this wood, where I know how easy it is to get lost?"

When I was in tunnels of dark trees I hated it, had the fear that is so often written about; but I was determined to go on and come out at last on Seven Mile Lane. I was still very confident, thinking that I knew the way. The chief thing that worried me was that I was doing a silly thing and making myself worse. I wondered if I would be ill for days afterwards.

I dropped down into a hollow and climbed up the other side. I was already beginning to be very hot in my raincoat and Guernsey sweater.

The path on the other ridge dug straight into much blacker wood; but still I was confident. "If I just follow this path, I'll come to the cottage and the road."

It soon got much wetter and more rutted, and I saw trees felled and flat glimmering trunks, the marks of tractors everywhere.

And these were what really betrayed me. They seemed to trail in all directions over the wood.

I turned a little to the left, imagining that the path branched off thus at this point. I was soon wandering — a little down, a little up, over bushes, with branches being caught in the spokes, through wet soggy spongy mud puddles.

Suddenly I saw a light; it came and went out in a moment. I thought, "It must be on the road," and I went forward. Then I saw a whitish block, as of the side of a white house between the trees. But I couldn't decide that it was a house, and the ground seemed rougher than ever between it and me.

I was sweating very much now from the effort of pushing forward and stumbling and from my thick clothes. I was dismayed by what I had done. I knew now that I was lost, that I probably could not even find my way back. The great caterpillar trails twisted in and out, crossing, re-crossing, rising, falling; of the old path, every sign seemed to have vanished.

I called out once or twice, knowing that nobody would hear me. Then I followed a trail almost hopelessly.

"What if you should wander for hours," I thought, "what if you should be in here all night! You would very probably die. Already you are very strained and knocked about. You who lie in bed for days, will probably not be able to get home now, even if you do find the way, which seems unlikely. And when strangers find you, they'll not know what to do, and you'll have to ask, if you're still capable, to be taken home."

Everything seemed threatening and quite dead. The black threat of a wood at night is fearful. I was filled with fear now, not of wood ghosts and darkness, though ghostliness was there as well, but just with fear of being lost, exposed and stumbling through the wood for hours.

Because of the night I could not stop for a moment, I had always to be forcing forward. Strange that when one is afraid and lost one cannot stop to contemplate for a moment.

The tractor trail that I had begun to follow took one up and down hillocks, over bristling scrub that made me convinced that I was more lost than ever, through deep slush puddles. I fell down once. My face was streaming. I felt, "That you could do this, play this idiocy for a whim! This is how people end themselves all in a moment — a wild impulse that dishes them."

If I had been a strong person the largeness of the wood netted with false trails would have been intimidating; but for me it was appalling. And that it was in the heart of the tame country-side — people and houses and cars all about me — that was horrible.

The trail suddenly wormed round into a larger, more rutted track. This brought a snatch of relief to me and I only hesitated a moment before turning to the right. I felt in some way that it would lead more quickly to a road.

And I was right, for after more ploughing through the soft mud and scrubby bushes I began to see a bigger and bigger hoop of dim light in front of me. The sky was gaining on the threat of the branches and I should soon be on the edge of the wood, if still near no road.

I felt stronger now, able to bear more, because I had been forced to. I could understand that old bustling phrase "I can't afford to be ill." I know that it was false, that you had to afford to be ill, had to take notice; for the moment I had to do nothing but push myself and my bicycle out of the wood.

I came to a sort of shack with hanging piece of canvas, and I seemed to know it. I walked further and knew that I had come out in his very garden, which tailed into the wood with no fence.

I was amazed at this, and wondered what could have brought me to this very spot after all my blind struggling.

I saw the oil lamp in the back window, but I did not stop. Someone was in there moving slowly. I guessed it was his father. No dog barked, but my bicycle made a great rattling in the ruts. I wondered if anyone would come out. I hoped not now because of my exhaustion. I had to get home as soon as possible.

But the relief was so great, to be there, *out of the wood*, close to the road, to people!

And almost at once the horror began to melt away and lose reality. It had been there, but now it was a fantastic shadow.

The grim ordeal was just an escapade. Why does horror melt so quickly? Its reality is sucked away at the first touch of warmth and comfort.

I rode back on the bike with no light. The moon had risen. I had seen it dimly in the wood and felt that at least I would have that. But then it gave me no real comfort. Now it shone for me beautifully. I saw two girls, perhaps returning from the pub, both riding on the same bike, like fishes threaded on a string. They too had no light. We passed each other warily.

My tiredness never really made me feel that I could not get home, although it made the tiny journey arduous.

I saw as I turned at last into the garden that Eric had not come back yet in the car.

Almost at that moment I heard a car on the drive and then saw the lights switching round into the drive.

I flew into the hall, pulled off coat and gloves, climbed the stairs, kicked away the muddy shoes, then got under the eiderdown on the bed and pulled my notebooks and pen up from where I had left them.

He found me writing, just as I had been when he left.

I had the wish to tell no one of my fright and my journey into the black wood.

And though we drank tea and stayed talking for a long time, I said nothing at all about it.

11 June, 10.15 p.m.

On Saturday, the Victory Celebration night, Eric suddenly suggested that we should go out to see the beacons and bonfires.[21]

We had just heard that Evie had lost her job in Cornwall and might be coming back to us, and the upset had made us restless.

We drove in the car through the dark up the hill to Plaxtol, and there was a fire in the grounds of Fairlawne, huge, sullen, flat to the ground, with great boughs crumbling. A few people were gathered round it, staring into the flames, and some boys on a bench were singing sadly' "Oh my darling Clementine". They were nervous of their voices, joking about them. The people stared, there was a great weight of emptiness. I felt that everybody was shamefaced and deadened — dumb, watching, waiting-for-death people.

We went on to Shipbourne Common and there was another larger bonfire with even fewer people about it. From the New Inn, several hundred yards away, the most extraordinary jig and blur of music was coming — demoniac in its clanging, smashing smudge with the crooner's whisper frighteningly magnified.

Over the long bending grass it ran, through the blackness. It was sadder and more damned than a black monkey or man in a stone cell clawing at the bars. The great voice was mourning and jigging and weeping all over the world. The blurs and atmospherics were like stabbing sparks. Eric and I watched the flames and the black shapes of the children running against them. There was a moping man too, who seemed to be searching in the grass, shoulders hunched, head sunk.

When rolls and plumes of sparks swept up out of the fire, then showered themselves down on the moping man and the dancing children, it was a medieval devil scene. The load mechanical wailing, the sullen torpor, the life of the flames were all part of a hell picture.

When we drove on past the New Inn we saw coloured umbrellas, drinkers and singers on the flood-lit grass. It was the only pub that had seemed gay. But its gaiety was like the deafening voice; merciless, made of tin, and mad.

I thought the whole night scene was a gaunt display of desperate failure. The people, for so short a time on the earth, watching their lives' hopelessness, as they stared into the flames.

Evie has quarrelled with her woman in Cornwall and threatened to come back to us; but it has been such calm without her that I shall do all I can to get her some other place. Never, for anything at all, live in a house with brooding blackness and unreason, though the person may have devotion and a hundred other virtues as well. The black bile seeps everywhere in everything.

21 The Japanese surrender.

17 June, 7.45 a.m.

On Thursday, after John Hesketh had left, Eric and I went out in the car and drove up the Gravesend road from Wrotham in the evening sun.

We came again to the huge, almost deserted camp in the woods at the top, where soldiers here and there walked quietly between the trees or entered the long, black corrugated huts — so like giant ribbed toasting loaves cut in half, lengthwise.

The air of calm that now hung about all the useless war contrivances was delightful. It was as if everyone, to stop any more mischief, had been put to sleep. A sort of enchanted wood of soldiers. Some few still walked in their sleep, but the rest lay snoring in rows under the crinkly iron and would lie there for ever.

We turned again down the road where I had seen the German prisoner walking forlornly in the field, and after passing through a cluster of houses — one a little early nineteenth-century wooden one, very pretty pillared porch, windows spoilt with big panes — we swooped down a narrow lane, long, always descending, between two folds of hills.

There were little ugly huts — minute, and sometimes with large well-tended gardens about them — on either side of the road in one part. They turned me against all makeshift, all contriving. I wished that everyone had a good pleasant small house, and I saw how grateful we must be for what we have left in the way of small houses in villages and country towns. I contrasted the least agreeable Victorian labourer's cottage with these horrible little light-hearted slums.

At the end of the long, long descending lane we came to a toughly built mid-Victorian chequered brick school. We turned to the right again and I then saw a notice, "To Luddesdown Church", so we decided to stop the car and explore.

I drove up to the edge of the churchyard and next-door farmyard, and I saw then that the church through the large rich old chestnuts had either been horribly mauled or else completely rebuilt. It was all of glistening blue-black flints, and the stone dressings had relentless hard edges and mouldings. The tower was a little less regular, but even that seemed to have been ruthlessly doctored.

An old, old woman in long draggly tweed skirts and a sort of mushroom hat was trimming the grass verge just by the east window. She had a pair of long-handled shears, and she bent her head down and brought her arms together in queer convulsive movements.

As we approached she looked up and bade us "Good evening" with a pleasant Victorian afternoon-tea smile. I saw then that her face was very lined and leathery and that she had never considered her beauty or any nonsense of that sort. She was clearly the tomboy of the seventies (could it be so long ago?) grown into this ancient woman.

She said, "Go round to the door, you'll find everything open." I realized that she looked on the church almost as her own. Just before we'd turned the corner, there was a sort of screech behind us, rather alarming and mad-sounding. I thought, "She is unbalanced." But the screech quickly formed into the same words, "Go through the little door into the tower and look at the old staircase, that's part of the original building."

We thanked her and entered the porch.

There was an old tombstone carved with a cross on the left of the door, fitted upright into the wall, but as soon as we were in the church I knew that it had all been rebuilt. Perfect early-to-mid-Victorian Gothic interior, breathing out inhumanity and a sort of struggling will to rightness.

Two much older arches had been kept in the building and there was a very low doorway, also old, into the tower. We went in obediently to look at the tower, and it was quite black in there, so Eric lit a match. We then saw the sort of ladder staircase made of rough logs — not at all exceptional.

I wondered why the Victorian rebuilders with their lust for destruction had left this or even some parts of the tower, as they seemed to have done.

We went out again and walked round the tower outside. As we came round to the vestry side again we were confronted once more with the ancient woman.

"Well, have you seen it?" she asked, beaming; then she looked deeper into me and said, "Of course, you know it isn't old, it has been rebuilt. When my father came here in 1856 the place had been allowed to get into such a ruinous state that it had to be all taken down. The man who had the living before was one of the student type and he spent all his time up at the British Museum. He'd ride down every week and ask the clerk if there was anybody ill he ought to see, then he'd do his visits, take the service and be off again back to his books. The church was utterly neglected."

While she was talking, I kept delighting over this link with the past. I had told myself that she might be an ancient parson's daughter; but it seemed too good to be true, when she turned out to be the daughter of the very parson who tore the church down in 1856.

"Eighteen fifty-six, eighteen fifty-six, ninety years ago," I hummed to myself.

She seemed almost to be defending her father from my unspoken comment, for she continued, speaking rapidly, "Of course, you know my father did everything he could, had all sorts of architects and experts down; but they all said that there was nothing else to be done — it wasn't safe."

I imagined those greedy architects and contractors fatly thinking how well the tottering church would pull down — oily beetles fattening with every stone displaced.

"My father saved everything that could be saved — all the stones were numbered and reassembled. You saw the arches inside? And there is the top of this window," she said, pointing. I saw perhaps four old stones at the point of the Gothic arch.

They had indeed been very sparing with their preservation. The pitiful remnants of the old church were gripped and held in a glistening mass of new flint.

But the flint had such a solidity and worth, and the woman was so determined that we should applaud her father, that I had to smile and appear to think that he had done right.

"Have you been in the vestry yet?" she asked. Then she led us over two rubber "kneelers" into the long narrow low room. "We've enlarged it twice," she said.

All the brass handles shone and there were many on chests and cupboards. There was an old memorial, eighteenth-century I think, to a former rector or vicar. "He used to keep a school, I was told, for the sons of the nobility and gentry," the parson's daughter said to us, an almost startling return to past ways of speech.

Her phrase, and the fact that she was discussing an eighteenth-century clergyman as if she had known him, made me feel a little dazed. She did not seem real.

Seeing me look for some moments at the long Latin inscription, she said, "It's very old Latin, I don't know whether you can read it; but I have a copy here if I can find it."

Was this mention of the "oldness" of the Latin just simplicity? Or was it delicate feeling for my probable ignorance of any Latin, "old" or new?

She rummaged in one of the chests, almost frantically emptying envelopes, uncomfortably. The inscription was very complaining.

"A most unfortunate man," the old lady said.

Then she showed me a photograph at the end of the vestry. It was of her father.

"Yes, that's my father," she said, and it seemed to me that she was proud, defiant and also a little shamefaced. Why? Just the anxiety we all feel over the effect our nearest (not dearest) will have on strangers?

I saw a man with a beard — long — on the end of his chin, a lot of the rest of his face shaved. He was smiling serenely, complacently. He looked strong, possibly cruel. Good too in an ungiving, unbreakable way. One admired the face a little, but had a lot of doubts.

"Yes, he's the one who built the church," his daughter said.

She saw me looking again at the one remaining memorial tablet.

"It used to be in the chancel," she said, "but in the alterations it was removed here. My father had such energy. He built two schools as well; and now they've both had to be closed, because the young people leave the parish and only the old ones stay. There used to be fifty children in each. There weren't twelve when they were closed."

"Was the rectory or vicarage also rebuilt with the church?" I asked.

"The rectory was burnt down in 1867(?) and unfortunately all the parish registers with it. But we've managed to patch something up from Lambeth Palace and other sources," she said.

"Aren't you hidden here in the fold of the hills!" I said stupidly.

"Yes, it's all hills, as I know on my bicycle!" We saw then her new bicycle leaning against a bush.

She wanted to know the time, and said, "I'll call to the children in the farmyard."

She called in her slightly crazed way, and the disgusting children — one specially painful little girl in yellow silk — tittered and turned away. The insolence of it made me very angry; but Miss Wigan (I had discovered her name under her father's photograph) seemed to notice nothing and only said, "What slow-coaches!" Again an almost archaic phrase. With her, one really saw slow stage coaches.

Eric at last found the time for her. Then we said good-bye and left her to her industrious border clipping.

I knew that she looked after the churchyard because her father had rebuilt the church. I was dragged by her sense of duty and vivid talking right back to 1856. There was a clear feeling of being present when the asbentee parson rode up on his horse to take the service and ask the clerk about the sick in the parish, and of being present when the new man called in the architects — and the old building was doomed.

We saw one of the deserted schools as we drove away, and then we saw a man we both remarked on. He was bending over, digging in a cottage garden — and he had on sandy, dirty, khaki battledress. His hair was gold, his head beautifully compact and square. His sleeves were rolled up and we could see blue tattoo pictures right up to the shouldets. There was something very complete and perfect about him.

20 June, 10.20 p.m.

Gerald came on Monday and gave me a headache and a temperature. He told us, not well, of his visit to Buckingham Palace to see the Queen about the pictures she is probably commissioning, of some old servants, I think.

He went to the side door; the guardsman did things with rifles, the policeman came forward. He went down long passages and was at last shown into a small library.

15 July, 7.25 p.m.

This evening, after I had come in from a drive alone through Birling and up the steep hill behind, I found that this telegram had come from Edith

Sitwell: "Enchanted to hear of your essay letter in post Edith."[22]

It gave me a glow, a tingle of excitement, and washed away some of the gloom feeling that has been on me today because I am less well; the feeling that I am threatened, that everything is saying good-bye, yet clamped down like me, hopelessly forever, in the wind.

I had written to Edith to ask if she minded my writing a description of our first meeting, for an American magazine, which was bringing out a symposium in her honour. I said that if she did mind I would of course tell them that I couldn't do it. I didn't expect her to say this, but I also didn't expect her to send me a telegram, saying that she was enchanted.

It is so difficult to write this article, for so many things cannot be repeated. Edith said she thought Vita Sackville-West and Rosamund Lehmann poor writers. Dorothy Wellesley also. These names I have to wipe out. There was all the amusing part too about the Dorothy Lady Gerald Duchess of Wellington that is arriving drunk at the poetry reading and not being allowed to recite. I long to travel over this forbidden ground. But all the time I have to think if my words will cause mischief between these people and Edith.

I am reading Fanny Burney's *Journal* and it is just what I want at this moment. I cannot but be very fond of her and hate [*sentence unfinished*]

16 July

I worked at my Sitwell essay, then I drove the car through Wrotham, up the hill, and came at last to Gravesend. I was rather too tired to take in my surroundings properly, but I bought cherries, regretted the ugliness that seemed to fasten on most faces sooner or later, and then found I had lost one of my gloves, coming out of a chemist's shop. I immediately went back, but it was gone. I chased all down the narrow street to the public lavatory and the ferry at the end. I spoke to an old sailor, but he shook his head. Young sailors were scurrying by, running to get on the ferry. One petty officer gazed out over the river, never turning his head. I saw Indians with fuzzy hair and jutting-out teeth.

Another day I went out to Otford, walked in the church, saw the Polhill memorials, beautiful and lumpish, enjoyed the polished brass chandeliers, and investigated the little wooden seventeenth-century porch.

There was a fattish soldier outside, lying on the grass by the war memorial reading some picture paper.

I went towards the ruins of the bishop's palace and gazed in at the hollow tower. The empty fireplaces hung in the air. Children were playing round

22 In May, Denton had been invited to contribute an article on Edith Sitwell to the August number of *Harvard Wake* on the lines of his *Horizon* article about his meeting with Sickert. He called it "A Lunch Appointment". It ran to 7,600 words, Edith Sitwell approved it, but it never appeared in print.

me in the vegetable patches. I saw a bright gleam of sun on yellow flowers through one of the ruined windows. A fat woman tended her potatoes, and two men talked in the farmyard.

I wandered back to the traffic roundabout and then came to a notice on the side gate of the big house next to the war memorial. I had thought at first that this house was barricaded up and unused, but now this notice said "Lettuces for Sale", so I went in and knocked on the back door. I waited some moments. Then I saw through the window an awful woman, low, squat and toadlike in a boudoir-cap and dressing-gown. She had a saucer in her hand and on it an egg cup and a hollow yellow egg shell. She seemed to be snuffling and rooting the air with her nose. I turned and ran before she could see me.

Outside again it really did seem as if the house were uninhabited. The high Georgian front had been changed and spoilt in later times, but it all now looked shut, ivy-grown, silent. I imagined that troops had been billeted there during the war and had helped to ruin it.

Entry undated

On Friday, 19 July I worked all day at my Sitwell article, nearly finishing it; then, as Eric was out in the car, I took the bicycle and, tired as I was, pedalled towards Allington for some change of scene.

It was a very lovely evening and I went into the park, past the Druid stones, then climbed up the narrow road to the church. There were several black glistening bicycles outside, one motor one; then I heard music and saw a light.

I hung in the porch listening to the choirmaster talking to the boys and girls. He was encouraging them with uncomfortable enthusiasm; but they were not uncomfortable. They answered him pipingly; it seemed a happy atmosphere. I wandered all round the church hoping for the practice to finish so that I could go in. But the stops and starts still persisted, then the admonitions.

I lay down in the grass near some old tombstones. The sky was blackening with storm clouds. I wondered if I should be home before the rain fell.

I left the voices in the church. It was a good day for me — busy but placid.

Then on Saturday, 20th, Jack Easton came to see if he could suggest anything to make me better. I had only seen him once before since he had come back from the army in the East, but we flowed easily and he was hopeful, and I felt again the interest that is so rare.

He seemed to like the house and said, as he often does, "You are lucky, how I envy you, being able to live as you like."

What does this mean? Doesn't he live as he likes, and if not, why not? I do not think he only expresses envy to flatter the hearer. He seems to mean it.

He wanted to talk to me too about pictures. The atmosphere seems artificial then, and I want to talk about anything but pictures. He hardly mentions my writing. He brings awkwardness with him, although he is so sympathetic. You can learn from him how bad it is to talk of other people's interests when you do not share them.

He was very brown and well-looking, and when he bent down to look at my eyelids, I saw how big the pores were on his nose.

I made myself ill with the Sitwell article and my first *Vogue* drawing, which was lumpy and dead. So I had to do nothing all Monday; but Peggy Kirkaldy, the "fan" from Colchester, had suddenly sent a letter asking if she could spend Wednesday night with us, while her friend Bob drove on to the races. I decided to say "Yes" in spite of temperature. I did not know what else to say. There comes a time when to plead ill-health any longer seems disgusting.

She came on Wednesday, while I was in the bath and Eric unshaved with only his navy blue shorts on. She had Alan Walton as well as Bob Smith with her. I looked down and saw the two fat men. She had brought food with her and towels and scented soap, the perfect guest. The bed always made, the breakfast things washed up. Eric took her her breakfast in bed. The rest of the meals we picnicked in the garden. I found myself wishing most of the time to be left alone to eat and read in peace.

In my mind I tried to disentangle all the causes of my lack of sociability. There is illness making me anxious and tired. There is work, so easily upset and made more difficult than ever. These two causes make me push away. Then with greater experience comes the cold feeling that most people are vampire bats. Does this condition come because we ourselves grow greedier?

31 July

I was at Peckham Old Church picnicking on cheese sandwiches, tomatoes and gingernuts, then I tried to write up this diary. I had been writing letters all morning and trying to finish my *Vogue* drawing. It was a day of trying.

1 August

Today I posted the *Vogue* drawing and more letters. Then Eric came in and we quarrelled stupidly over the clipping of the hedge, or some such hollowness. So I hastily made another picnic and took it here at the bottom of the downs, behind Trottiscliffe Church, on the Pilgrim's Way. My heart was very heavy, and the air too is weighing-down and thick. I have walked all along the path picking scabious, harebells, cornflowers purple and white and smelling wild thyme — all the flowers purple and mauve except for the two white cornflowers.

There are dummies on low gibbets, set up for the soldiers to rip with their bayonets. There is an engine in a house, all locked, that hums and whirrs everlastingly. High up on the hill was a frilly thin girl and a baby in scarlet.

The buzz of all the insects is like a distant echo of the power-house.

11 p.m.

As I came back this afternoon, about five-thirty, near the Chequers in Crouch I saw a German prisoner, red-brown trousers, green battledress top with the diamond of yellow sewn on the back, so that the whole effect was of a conventionally sad harlequin.

He was standing all alone, which was unusual, and he looked up as I passed, but the eyes expected nothing and had no spark in them. I was reminded of Fanny d'Arblay's meeting with the Spanish prisoners and I saw, perhaps for the first time, that the only quick way to give a prisoner a little enjoyment is to slip a coin to him as you pass. Why should I have to read about early nineteenth-century prisoners before fully realizing this?

I put the car away quickly, then walked back. He was still there. I had the half-crown in my hand, but I did not know whether I would dare to give it.

"Good afternoon", he said to my first murmur. He looked at me, I think obediently, as if I was not to be questioned — or is it that one has this preconceived idea with prisoners?

I could see that his teeth rather jutted out under his mouth, so that the lips stretched over. His pale hair was sparse. He was large-boned — very unprotected and lost there in the long grass and cow-parsley.

I quickly thrust out the coin, only hoping that he would take it as quickly. He stared at it at first, as if not understanding. He seemed almost to draw his hand away; then, with a sort of gulp of surprise, he grasped it and said, "Oh thank you — thank you very much!"

He gazed at me as I was hurrying past. I looked over my shoulder and fluttered my hand in a way that must have been strange. It was meant to welcome, to say good-bye, to wish well. It was the answer brought forth by his "Thank you — thank you ve-ry mooch," the long "e", the long "o". It was jerky and convulsive, and my smile seemed to get fixed and tangled on my face, as if I were trying to express too much sweetness, and the features had rebelled.

I had been extraordinarily elated by his pleasure. I went on, hugging it to me, until I got to the strawberry bed. I had to stay there until the lorry he was waiting for had picked him up; I could not have met him again.

I think you could only give to a prisoner like this — you could not to a tramp, a poor person, a child even.

8 August, 5.45 p.m.

Eric went off this morning to spend about a week in Truro with Evie. Her woman doctor has gone away for a holiday, leaving her the bungalow, so she asked Eric and me to go down for the change of scene. We played with the idea of driving; but I know really that I would find the journey too much for me.

It ended in our deciding that Eric should go alone by train. I took him to the station to catch the 10.19 a.m. It was one of my worst days and my head throbbed. The rain came down soft and warm-cool. The people on the platform looked debased and harrassed. We had packed all the rations and clothes and picnic for the train in Eric's mother's heavy violet leather dressing case. He was taking up my cat picture to the Leicester Galleries too. I had framed it and mounted it on raw silk — pasted the back up, then painted it with terracotta tempera colour.

I thought of all the preparations, and I wished so much that I could go too — longed to enjoy the whole journey as I ought to, instead of avoiding it as too great an endurance test. Eric said, as if it were a new discovery, "Going on a journey with someone else is much better really, isn't it?" Then he added half-seriously, "Couldn't you come too, but I knew you had a headache when I saw you in bed early this morning."

We sat on the seat in the rain on the platform. Then I saw him into the train and he stood in the passage. A woman thrust her hand out of the window, with a sort of flurried grunt to gain the porter's attention. Then she slipped him a tip with her hand cupped and hiding the coin all the time. Eric looked very good. I had trimmed his hair quickly after breakfast, because it was getting shaggy. I had not spoilt it. The train started. I climbed up on the bridge and we waved and waved. A little slither of his arm and his face showed till the last moment.

I could not help thinking, "What if I should never see him again!" My mother had been swept away like that, not in a train, but in a car. I just saw the waving hand, the little corner of face; then they were gone and I never saw them again.

I drove away from the station and went in the rain through Igtham and up between the ferns and woods to Ivy Hatch, then stopped on the hill above Fairlawne.

I stared through the five-barred gate at the clumps of trees in the meadow. The rain dripped through the hood. I tried to find Chessington on the map, where Fanny Burney's Mr Crisp lived in the old house across the wild common. I was surprised to see that, if it were still standing, it would be almost, if not quite, in the suburbs of London.

I thought of Daddy Crisp and how fond Fanny was of him, and this made me think of all fondness. You are fond — the fondness fits all round the person like a cape, a cloak, gloves, socks, velvet shoes. The person goes away dressed all in the fondness, and if he or she never comes back, all those clothes are lost. It is only the greatest friends who raise this fear of disappearance. They sometimes do it even if they go out to post a letter. All the other people in the whole world can post leters, post themselves in the sea or in volcano craters — you are calm. Only the person dressed in the fondness seems to mean anything at all.

I thought of all the people who have written to me and sent me presents, because they have liked my books. I thought of the John Gilmour in Canada who last week, or the week before, sent me olives stuffed with pimento, smoked salmon, cream, lemon juice, orange juice. Then I thought of the John McLellan of Stanford University, California, who sent me a parcel which arrived this Tuesday: boned chicken, plum cake, marzipan fruits of fierce brightness, noodle soup, milk, cocoa, sugar, devilled ham.

I thought of Peggy Kirkaldy's presents, the black Wedgwood jug, the Norwich shawl (which is over me at this moment — orange, black, yellow, mauve, green, blue, spider pattern), the George III teaspoons with their pretty faceting and cutting, the charming old topographical books.

All these presents do make me warm for a moment. There is a jump of pleasure that I am chosen for presents — that I am supposed to have given some pleasure which is being returned in this way.

Then there is the fear of falseness and misunderstanding.

On Tuesday night Eric came back from Tonbridge with Rosemary and Jenny Mundy Castle. I was on the bed, but they both came into the room fluttering affectionately, and Eric made nice sandwiches and coffee. We ate off trays round my bed, slicing chunks from the first cucumber I have had this year.

Then Rose told us of her experiences after putting an advertisement in the paper. She had written something like, "Young gentlewoman seeks interesting secretarial post to do with music and literature."

She received three answers. One from a theatre she did not answer. The others were from private people. One retired K.C., whose name I think was Darcy, took her out to lunch. He was elderly with a rose in his buttonhole. He wanted someone to relieve him at the wheel on his trip down to the south of France — his first holiday for six years. He said he believed in people having a "little flip", and that he was determined to have a "last little flip". He wanted Rose to have nothing but a rosy time. "We must bathe and lie in the sun and enjoy ourselves," he said. "I do like to give a little pleasure to other people. Would your parents mind you coming, my dear? They can trust me absolutely. I think I know a young widow who can come along with us. If only you could drive! You could even bring a boy friend with you."

But Rose couldn't drive, so it came to nothing, and they parted with great friendliness and warmth.

The next man wrote — was it from Gloucestershire, Shropshire? — some more Western county I don't know well. The name of the house was

Dimwell Manor, or something rather like it. Everything is vague because I did not like to stop Rose and make her repeat everything clearly, for fear of making her wary and reluctant to give details.

He said that her mention of literature and music in the advertisement was what had held his interest, since he too was devoted to them. He hoped shortly to be privately printing his own poems, and he had an organ, in the hall of the Manor, which was now being reconstructed or repaired by a young ex-R.A.F. pilot, also devoted to music.

He asked Rose to meet him in Oxford. He would book a room for her.

Rose went, and again she was confronted with an elderly man, this time not so tall or buckish, but dressed "expensively", and also with a flower in his buttonhole.

He took her, I think, to the Randolph to a meal. Then he said, "Let's go back to the caravan and have a long talk."

It appeared that he had arrived in this caravan and was going to spend the night in it. Rose said it was most beautifully appointed, but she did not describe its luxury more than to say that the wide, almost double, bed was turned down and that she was asked to sit on it. She did so, rather reluctantly, right at the end, and the man said to her jauntily, "Now, you know, you're sitting on the cellar."

He pulled out from underneath her gin and other cocktail things, and poured her out a glass.

He wanted to tell her everything. He described the house with its fourteenth-century chapel in the middle of a thousand acres, or was it four thousand? He said, "I have no one to talk to there who would understand my poems, who could share my interests at all. My wife is up in the North and she is going abroad, to Denmark."

There were daughters too, but they also were out of sympathy or married and far away.

He was growing more and more excitable. He said he wanted to share everything with Rosemary at Dimwell Manor. They would have no secrets.

"The only thing, Rosemary, my dear, is that I'm afraid you may be lonely there — away from all other houses."

He was calling her Rosemary and "dear" more and more, and he seemed to be working up the bed, patting it as he moved along. He told her that she had wonderful legs, and that he knew as soon as he saw her that he could share things with her. He told her that "these instincts are given us by God and we should enjoy them".

"But not in this way," Rosemary replied sternly.

(She seemed to grow a little unpleasant as she told her wise, stiff answers to his importunity. I saw her then as completely material and pug-nosed.)

"It is getting late," she said, "and I haven't seen my room in the hotel."

"But I haven't been able to book one," he answered. "Won't you sleep here in the caravan? I promise I won't worry you in any way. I shall sleep in the car. I shall do nothing to disturb you. It shall all be as you like."

Rosemary did not know quite what to do, but she decided at last to go to the station, to find out if the last train had really gone. They told her "yes". But as she waited there, by some great chance, a room in a hotel was offered, I forget by whom. Before this she told the man that she would wait at the station all night rather than go back to the caravan.

"But it is so dismal!" he exclaimed.

"Well, the alternative is not very attractive," she replied. (I did not like the pertness she acted here at all.)

She went to the hotel, but the man said he would meet her the next day after breakfast. He took her again to the Randolph and said that he was glad that she had decided to go to the hotel, he thought it was sensible, but there was one thing she had forgotten. "Yes, there is one thing you have forgotten, Rosemary."

"What is that?"

"That a man in my position can't afford to do wrong."

Again he told her about the acres, the organ, the re-dedication of the chapel by the bishop, the happiness for her if she would share his poems with him there. But she only said she was sorry she couldn't stay any longer to look at the colleges in Oxford with him, as she had to go back that afternoon.

"Of course, you know what I'd like to do," he said.

"What?"

"I'd like to stay the night."

After all her abuse he had come back for more. Rose was amazed. She said at the end with a flash of ugly frankness, "If only he had been young and attractive and unmarried — what heaven!"

Ten to ten p.m.

The telephone rang and I have just been talking to Eric and to Evie. I ran downstairs believing it was Eric, yet wondering if it could be anything else. The bell's ring was in those little gusts, frightening, exciting in an empty house, like a mad doll bouncing.

Then the request, "Hold the line, please," the wait, and at last Eric's voice.

He had just arrived and was still eating his supper. He had been given Dr Wood's bedroom, and they were thinking of going to Land's End tomorrow. He had a delicious ham sandwich in cellophane at Paddington or Victoria. The journey was very easy. Evie met him, timing it perfectly.

I spoke to Evie at the end. She remembered the cat postcard I had sent her, as it lay about for months in my room at Pitt's Folly. I seemed linked with peculiar minute links.

10.25 p.m.

Bernard has just been in, saying that he was rather perturbed, since Noël went on, when they were out for a walk together, but was not at home now. (They are down for some days in their studio and hut.)

He seemed so serious that I immediately thought that *he* was thinking of suicide. He asked to ring up the neighbours they know, and the first two families knew nothing of her. I felt that I would hate to ring up people and wait for their remarks. I wondered why he didn't leave her to return or not to return.

He found her at the Keith Lucases, so there will be no horror story tonight.

She cooked a very good stuffed marrow, some tomatoes and cauliflower, and gave me some for supper, much against my will.

9 August, 7.15 p.m.

Rain now soaking down softly. Noël is still here, although I've made it quite plain that I'd rather be alone.

The naval commander who bought a picture of mine at the Artists' International show now writes again, and I cannot look at it properly, only glance at words, then throw it down.

I wonder if many people have this difficulty and embarrassment over reading letters. Letters from a few friends I want to read at once, and also letters from unknowns; but all the rest I prefer to leave, sometimes for days. Then when their immediacy has worn off, I read them in snatches until I have all their information.

Did I mention that some woman of the *New York Post* wants me to write something for that paper, and that another woman of the *New Yorker* wants me to send her a story, as she so liked my "When I Was Thirteen" story republished in America in a book of *Horizon* stories?

I would like, whenever I am asked for something, to be able to do it; but I cannot, and so I feel confused by requests and wish to be left alone to finish my book. *New Writing* wants me to do some little headings and tailpieces. An adolescents' magazine, *Junior*, wants me to illustrate Katherine Mansfield's *The Voyage*. It would be lovely to have the health and vigour to do all these things one after another smoothly, in the moments that I spared from the book. I have always this tantalizing picture of happy busyness to goad me.

10 August, 12 noon.

Noël has gone back to London, so I am all alone here in the orchard, and the sun is shining after the rain.

Routledge sent me a copy of Maiden Voyage this morning, their third edition, but really some of the second American printing, shipped over here, bound by Routledge and covered with my original dust-jacket.

Maiden Voyage has come out four times here — that is including the six thousand copies printed for Readers' Union Book Club. Twice in America. Once, so far, in Sweden, France, Italy, Germany and Austria (soon).

I used to think in my simplicity that to be published in many countries meant much money for the author. But of course it does not follow. I don't think so far that all the publications of Maiden Voyage have earned me more than £500, certainly not more than £700. But I have not yet heard of its progress in the European countries.

It was the New Yorker yesterday that asked me for a story. Now today I am sent the Sun Bathing Review and told that Bernard Shaw, Laurence Housman, Naomi Mitchison, Vera Brittain, A.E. Coppard, J.C. Flugel, Robert Gibbings and C.E.M. Joad have written for it and will I write too — a likely theme, the value of nudity in schools "as a means of countering the unhealthy practices with which anyone who has been educated at a boarding school is familiar".

I think the only thing I can truthfully say in reply is that I feel that nudity would increase the "unhealthy practices", whatever they may be, perhaps set a fashion through the whole school for them — that is, "nudity" of this magaziny-shiny-photograph sort. The booklet is uncomfortable. I know that if someone came into this room at this moment, I would hurriedly explain that it had been sent to me, and that I had not bought it for my own delight. Why do other people's fetishes seem ugly and improper? I am fond of naked people, but not of a great to-do and business of nakedness. To read this magazine is to be half told that if everyone would suddenly strip off their clothes the world might be made quite wonderful.

The articles are very like the tracts Evie's sister brought me from the Bible and Tract Society. God and Jesus are replaced by Sun and the Naked Body.

Yet, just because I have had my thoughts drawn to nakedness, I think of this high wind battering the house, making it shake and creak, and I am more aware of the air playing on my body as I laze on the bed only in my cotton kimono, the sort that Japanese men wear when they go for their steam baths.

11 August, 10.10 a.m.

Last night, after being on the bed all day, I got up and drove towards Trottiscliffe through the sunset. The moon was large and scabby behind me, growing whiter every moment.

I went up the Vigo, then through the huge army camp, quite deserted, along the ridge of Birling Hill. I came out somehow into the little back streets of Snodland. They were squalid and sociable, like the streets of a northern town.

How different from Malling, my next town! There everything, except the pubs, was dark. The waterfall gushed and tinkled, the pretty houses looked secret, much less amiable. Youths wandered about, whistled, gossiped, stood on tip-toe to peer into the pub windows.

I left and came soon to the Moat Farm near Wrotham. I saw so many cars that I stopped, and there through a big glass door I saw the couples dancing. I could hear the music too. Old tunes of the early nineteen-twenties were being played. The women's dresses seemed very bright scarlet, salmon pink, hot beige, and there seemed to be women dancing together, plump, bobbing, swimming. I can remember no man clearly.

"Yes, we have no bananas" floated out to me, the couples swept across the glass doors.

The pang of sadness shot through me. It is caused so often by the jazz tunes of the jigging jolly sort. Perhaps dancing has a great sadness and regret too.

I looked from the little box of dancers with its one glass window to the fields and trees all round, to the waiting black-beetle cars and the moon high over everything, lording it, queening it, radiantly staring, radiantly insolent.

13 *August. Ten to eleven a.m.*

Last night the wind was whining and sweeping, and I was quite alone here, listening to Ibsen's *John Gabriel Borkman*. In the play there are footsteps overhead, on, on, like muffled hammers. They woke an alarm in me and I wished Eric was back. I wished too, *violently*, that I could be always active, for when I think of day after day slipping by in half-hearted "rest and recuperation" I feel eaten up with waste.

Earlier in the day Mrs Spicer, who cuts the hay in the orchard, came to the back door and wanted to telephone to a farmer called Miles to let him know that she had a horse for sale. I suggested she should go into the drawing-room and telephone herself, but she said, "No, you, please sir, I can't." She smiled anxiously.

She came and stood behind me as I got through to Wormshill. (Where is it? The operator repeated it as if I were joking.)

When I had given the message, she said, "Please, how much is it?" She was screwing a shilling about in her hand.

"Oh, nothing, I expect only a penny or two. It must be a very short call." I felt very uncomfortable and did not of course want her to give me anything.

She was still holding the shilling out dangerously, so I began to lead her back to the kitchen. There she slipped her hand into her basket and brought out a paper bag.

She put it down on the table. "There are two eggs for your tea."

"But you mustn't, eggs are so scarce."

"I brought them specially."

Very carefully she tied the shilling up now in the corner of her handkerchief. Then she screwed the handkerchief round and round.

"What is the matter with you, young man?" she asked rather briskly and suddenly. "Is it a chill or something?"

"Oh no, I'm only supposed to be resting as I keep having high temperatures. I once had an accident."

My constant difficulty — how much to say, how much to leave unsaid.

"Oh, I thought it might be a chill or something." She was looking out of the window, and instead of continuing in the nursing motherly strain, she said, "My, look how the wind has brought down the plums!"

I thought she was like a musical box which suddenly switches to another tune.

This morning I had a letter from Michael Ayrton. The notepaper rather peculiar, or isn't it at all peculiar nowadays? MICHAEL AYRTON in Roman letters,[23] then 4, All Souls Place, W.1. in small type. He wanted me to submit some small pictures to him for a show he is organizing at Heal's. He begins, "So much steam was generated by a chance remark I made on a B.B.C. Brain's Trust about the comparatively low prices at which good pictures by young painters could be bought, that Messrs. Heal & Son have asked me to sponsor and select a small exhibition of pictures below £40. Heal's are to buy one picture outright, the rest to be on sale-or-return basis. In order to make a really good show, only about sixteen artists will be asked to submit work. I very much hope you will be able to co-operate in this venture."

There is a postscript at the bottom, in his own writing (the rest in type): "I hope this will give us an opportunity to meet, as I am an admirer of your work."

Does he mean writing as well as painting? And would I dislike his conversation with me as much as I dislike it on the wireless? I suppose so much of his pleasantness would depend on mine. But on the wireless he seems quite spoilt by a distressing parade of youth and talent. He seems to be insisting rather school-girlishly on his charm, when all the time I feel quite unwilling to give him any credit for any charm at all.

But the wireless must be such a horribly deep vanity probe. One could not hide one's weakness or help slipping into some falsity, or being twisted into it. So really I feel that I would like his true self much more than the wireless voice; but even then, it might not be so very much.

I feel happy that he wrote to me though, it made my breakfast of toast and

23 He meant capital letters.

honey and coffee happy.

E wrote yesterday, two letters from Cornwall. They had gone to Truro Cathedral and seen Archbishop Benson's jewels and then had come home to cook sausages and go to the Daniell Arms.

My naval commander who bought the flower picture also wrote a long letter all about *In Youth is Pleasure*. Very sensible, in his own way, I think. One sentence that is rather strong: "Orvil is, I think, painted in exquisite detail and is, I think, pathetically horrible." He asks, too, "But who do you *want* to read it? There is such greatness of perception and feeling in so much of it, it would be a disaster if it went the wrong way."

Who do I want to read *it*, or anything else I write? It is impossible to answer simply, unless one says "nobody", and then that is not complete. I want nobody known to me, everyone unknown, perhaps that is it. Then the everyone must be qualified by "who can find any food in it".

Why is it shameful to be confronted with the words one has written? Is it just cowardice? The fear of being judged by imperfect expression, of being thought silly or preposterous? Is it the fear that one has changed and can no more agree with the words of a few years ago? It seems to be all these things; but added to them is that curious dislike we all have of things that have lost their flow and become fixed. Though I for one love fixed and settled things more than most people I know.

14 August. Late afternoon in the garden, wind blowing.

Wind blowing coldly, sun appearing and disappearing, only the Norwich shawl over me on the camp bed.

Irene Dallas has just been, appearing round the corner of the house unexpectedly. She reminds me of all my childhood. She had been to Paris to the annual meeting of a group of Christian Scientists. She described in hard details the aeroplane, the hotel, and especially the food and prices.

The mad Connie Piffard had been left in the car with her companion Miss Brown; but she came out afterwards and said to me, "Hullo, darling, shall I give you this plum?" She handed me a burst, split one from the lawn. All her remarks had this tea-time social charm and madness. Her teeth hung over her bottom lip. She was wearing some gaudy puce scarf. She looked like a very ancient fairy half transformed into a toad.

It is going to be a storm, but I don't get up, though my hands are too cold to hold this pen very well.

17 August

Three letters from Eric today, the last saying that he had arrived back in London, gone to the Leicester Galleries and found both my pictures —

"Spirits Above a Flower", and "A Cat Waiting for its Master" — with little red stars on them. My "Woodman's Cottage" one, that had been hung before, was on a chair near by, on exhibition too. The man would not tell him who had bought them, but I shall hear from Brown.[24]

I painted all this afternoon with thick oil paint. I have not used it for a long time, all my pictures lately being pen, chalk, water-colour mixtures, and I loved the soft rich paint. Putting little dabs of it on the canvas board, sitting back in the Victorian mother-of-pearl armchair, I was rested and happy. Outside, the wind raged, and rain whipped across the window panes.

I had two fan letters today from America. One from Syracuse University, from a Lester Grosvenor Wells, the other from Robert B. Platt of Philadelphia.

L.G. Wells says towards the end, "At a little party in New York I met someone who has met you and I do wish that I might recall his name. The bowl was flowing freely — so my memory of the occasion fails me a bit." Who can this be?

30 August

I have been in bed for over a week, and Evie has been, arriving last Wednesday night from Cornwall, and leaving last Friday night. She brought me two old mandarin cups, with no saucers. Why are there so few saucers and so many cups of this type? She brought Eric long cigarettes, Joysticks. She was extraordinarily excited and nervified. She had stopped at several places on the way up, to visit places her mother had described. She visited Summerhouse Hill at Yeovil, at the bottom of which her mother was born, I think in 1851.

"But the house isn't there any more," she said. "The railway came sometime in the 1860s and swept it away." She went on to describe the charming summer-house at the top of the hill. She called it eighteenth-century, said that the woman who lived in it asked her in, seeing her interest.

When Evie cooed over it, the woman said morosely, "It leaks."

Evie said it had strange wooden ceilings and was a curious shape outside. I said I supposed it was the cottage ornee or retreat of some large place, and she agreed, telling me the name of the estate, which I have forgotten.

I was at my worst while she was here and could see her hardly at all; but she had her sister Mildred to stay the night, without telling me, and they talked and laughed and clattered over the box floors till late at night!

Then yesterday she sent me three peaches, a few grapes, Brand's Essence and some peppermint creams.

---

24 Oliver Brown, a director of the Leicester Galleries.

On Sunday, Phyl Ford wanted to come, but Eric put her off, and told me afterwards. She said she felt dreadful and wanted to get out of the house, because she had just heard how much her son Michael hated the army, which had just snapped him up, because he's eighteen.

The telephone rang again on Monday and I heard Eric talking to an unknown. It turned out to be a Keith Vaughan, who had written to me about *Maiden Voyage* when it first came out. He is a painter. We asked him to appear for tea, since he said he was going to be in Sevenoaks and would like to come over.

I didn't really expect him to find the way, but almost exactly at four I heard someone walking up the path to the front door. Eric ran down and said, "Hullo." The next moment he was up here beside the bed — he being Keith Vaughan.

He was fairly small and slight, very smiling, hair a little thinning, dressed in corduroys and a sort of policeman's jacket, which I rather liked. He had an open neck and wore a broad leather belt.

Almost at once it was friendly and easy. I thought that he was one of the pleasantest of my chance guests. He told us that he walked all through the lanes and that at last he had found someone and asked the way to the house only to be told a little vaguely that it was past "Grandad's" house. He found the footpath though and came to us that way.

He talked about his time in Yorkshire guarding German prisoners, how much he liked them. He talked about that part of a house which he and John Minton were trying to get repaired and converted for themselves.[25] At present he is living with his mother in a flat at Hampstead. He began by telling us what an excellent manager she was, but before the end of his visit he had told us more.

Tea, which I had put together quickly on one of my rare visits downstairs, was nice. There were water biscuits, plum jam and butter, dried bananas, almonds, a plum cake Eric's mother had made and two ginger and one chocolate biscuit.

K.V. ate in that way which is not quite discriminating, yet certainly not uninterested. A sort of stolid way of eating.

At six o'clock he jumped up and said he must be going. I let him go, not wanting to make myself tired. But as Eric walked down the drive with him, they came upon our neighbour Mrs Potter and her son cleaning the car.

The son, Ian, mistook both Eric and K.V. for me, one after the other. He then, when he knew that K.V. was going back to London, offered him a lift at eight o'clock. So Vaughan came back again.

I heard the voices and wondered what had happened. Eric hurriedly got together soup, omelette and plums for supper, and we began to talk again.

---

25 John Minton and Denton Welch both contributed decorations for a book called *Contemporary Cooking* by Doris Lytton Toye (Condé-Nast, 1947).

This time we heard how difficult it was for a grown son to live with his mother, how unsuitable it was, how irritating, how bad. There was a lot of this, and it gave me a feeling of sadness. I saw how many people must despise their parents.

Vaughan's mother was a "good manager" and was very fond of him — too fond and doting — but she had no money and he had to keep her. She could share none of his interests. She questioned his movements. Her friends were dreadful. He wished he could admire the wisdom of the old, but he had never known an old person with wisdom. The ideal mother would be someone with a comfortable home and a husband. Someone who had a life of her own. Someone who did not live only in her son (and *on* her son).

Now we were seeing a little more of the leathery side of K.V., the desire for comfort and money, and the greater respect he gave to those with material advantages. He blamed his mother for the lack of them.

I suppose we would all like our relations to be as rich and as comfortable as possible, if we could choose; but we would like riches for the whole world too. I wondered if most people resented supporting their parents — regretted so much their lack of money and importance. I wondered if I often felt pleased with my father whilst he was alive because he was rich enough to promise comfort to me and not responsibility.

Keith Vaughan told me that my last little picture at the Leicester, the "Woodman's Cottage" one, had been bought by John Lehmann.[26]

11 September, 2.15 p.m.

On Mount Ephraim, Tunbridge Wells Common, in the car, with the picnic Eric has made for me — baked-bean-tomato-cheese sandwiches, plum jam ones, digestive biscuits, Supex chocolate, dried prunes, two big not-quite-ripe plums, coffee in which I have melted some of the chocolate — and I am drinking it, looking at the bright beetle cars running down the hill to the Pantiles. Up above, a noble far-away droning of a fleet of aeroplanes. They go so steadily, resignedly, over the new church (pretty early Gothic-revival). The trees blow. A small boy is climbing over the big rock, against which a house is built. Another older boy has firewood tucked under his arm. He is climbing up the hill towards me. Beyond are the hills dotted with woods and houses.

I am thinking of Mount Ephraim and the Pantiles in Fanny Burney's day. Soon I am going to see May in her new house in Church Street.

A child just near the car has shrieked out to another, "Well, you wouldn't like it if everyone said to you, 'You've got fleas!' would yer?"

26 Currently in the collection Mr W. H. Boomgaard of Haarlem, Holland.

This is the day that I should have gone to London to have lunch w̟
Edith Sitwell, and afterwards to be with her at what she called a big te̝
party!

But I could not face going in my precarious state. This is the first day —
except for the dentist on Saturday — that I have been out of my room for
three weeks or a month. I wish I could have gone to Edith Sitwell's.[27]

13 September, 9.20 a.m.

Two Thoughts:

(1) Do not worry too much about the indiscretion, foolishness or
banality of what you write. Leave Time to take care of it all — either to kill it
and hide it for ever, or else to change it in its magical way into something
strange and rare and not silly at all. This diary, if it is read at all, will make no
one blush two hundred years from now. Someone might blush a little in a
hundred years, just as I have squirmed a little after reading some of Keats's
earliest poems this morning.

(2) It becomes more right and acceptable to believe that the other things
in the world were made for us to enjoy, if we think that we were made to be
enjoyed.

These truisms pounced on me in the very early morning, when I was half
in dreamland.

21 September, 7.50 p.m.

We went to Rochester. Saw the gulls on the brown mud, heard the boys
and men singing and droning beautifully in the cathedral. Close to me lump
of the Norman pillar, so massive, it made me think for once of all the weight
in the air above me, round me — every moment pressing down, threatening
century after century.

And the west front with the broken saints, thin in their Romanesque
riches — black, crusted, cruelly restored in some places. It gave me the
feeling of a noble slum. It had been there, I suppose, since the twelfth
century, gathering all the defacements and scourings and mendings to it,
until it seemed toughened to receive almost any outrage.

The old gatehouses, with sash-windowed rooms above the Gothic arches
— we walked under one coming up to the cathedral, then through another
to trespass into the deanery garden. The deanery door was open, and it still
had all the lugubrious, brick quality of the mid-nineteenth century, though

27 The invitation, sent on 30 August, also included a suggestion that Denton should attend a
performance of *Façade* on 9 September. This too he had to miss because of his health.

some of it must have been much older. I expected the deanery to have a comfort about it, a warmth and richness; but it was almost as uncherished as my uncle's vicarage used to be.[28]

When we grew tired we went back to the car and ate oranges, by the river, close to the fat balustrade.

We saw a man with a beard, a yellow-coated wife with sluttish hair, and a small white-haired child. They looked at us several times, and we supposed they were some sorts of artists, who were looking for others.

We found the Guildhall door open so we went up the fine wide staircase, gazed up at the plaster angel's fully modelled stomach, in the middle of the ceiling, admired the wide panels on the walls, then came into the fine room hung with full-length portraits nearly all in early eighteenth or late seventeenth-century clothes. Only one man was in nineteenth-century tail-coat. And he seemed disregarded by all the men of Anne's reign, and Anne herself. Or perhaps it is truer to say that all the whigged people were so busy concentrating on their own consequence that his lesser sort of pomposity looked almost like the sad smiling anxiety of the snubbed.

Coming back, we passed the small house of Tudor or Jacobean brick, which I remembered on the main road. There is a coat of arms and badges above the door (all too defaced to be deciphered) and a very tall arch into the garden, making it seem that this had once been the elaborate lodge attached to some large place — a bishop's palace. I shall try to find out.

When I had seen it before the war, it had been abandoned and almost smothered in ivy. The ivy was there, quite covering walls and roof, but it was dead, the stem having been cut. And there were curtains in the dingy windows.

What had been nearly a ruin was now inhabited.

I forgot to write of Wednesday, when we went to Fairlawne to the auction of some things that had belonged, I think, to Victor Cazalet.[29] It was very rainy, but we took a picnic to eat in the car — devilled ham from America and chocolate and apples.

The auction was held in a marquee outside the old kitchen quarters, where the objects were stored. May was there, sitting next to Cecil Gardener, so we avoided her to begin with.[30] She told us later that Gardener had bought a four-post bed for £100 for his daughter's twenty-first birthday. For some reason this seemed a strange present to me. Is it that one

---

28 At Leigh in Surrey, where Denton's uncle, the Reverend Thomas Kane (see 1942, note 24 above), had been vicar from 1924-38. It was to Leigh that Denton was making his way in 1935 for the Whitsun weekend when he was knocked off his bicycle. The vicarage, in which Denton frequently stayed as a boy and a young man, was destroyed by fire in 1972.

29 Formally Conservative Member of Parliament for Chippenham. He had been killed in an air crash in 1943. Fairlawne was his family home.

30 The husband of Jane Gardener of Pond Farm.

always associates beds with brides, and four-poster ones especially with the Wolf-Grandmother in *Little Red Riding Hood*?

I found that I was allowed into the storeroom, and as I had not been to the view day, I went in with Eric and found there two pairs of lovely eighteenth-century Chinese mirror paintings — exquisite courtesans sitting in pavilions surrounded with flowers and birds and monkeys and cats, all so wonderfully and delicately painted, against the background of old tarnished speckled mirror. One pair was slightly larger and really the most beautiful. I was determined to have both if I could. Only rarely does this absolute decision seize me.

I had an empty feeling, waiting for the pictures to come on to the end of the table, and when they had come I could look at neither of them or the auctioneer. The bidding rose and rose and rose. I reached thirty-one guineas, then fell out. They were knocked down for forty-six. (I have written to ask who bought them, but have had no answer yet.)

When the smaller pair came on I was quite prepared for them to go out of my reach; therefore it was almost with surprise that I found they had been knocked down to me at twenty-four guineas. I found that bidding had made me very hot.

I went round quickly to pay for them, so that I could take them away; in the car with the raindrops dripping through, I looked at the two fairy-like little lady-harlots in their almost transparent clothes, pulling back the gauze curtains of their pavilions. I saw their tiny, pearly bosoms tipped with rose, their rounded arms. Everything about them was to please. And the effort made to please was so strong, so solid, that they succeeded.

They made most modern pictures look as dreary, commercial and slovenly as old newspapers. Why does anyone buy such pictures?

I have had a letter of appreciation from a naval chaplain written in three different coloured inks, in enormous letters on two different coloured papers with different stamped headings (violet, green and scarlet) and little whimsy pieces, such as: "No telephone on purpose." A photograph enclosed too. Is this called exhibitionism or vanity or what?

8 October, 7.15 p.m.

Yesterday we went to Rye. Eric got up early and made the tea, and then the breakfast. I stayed in bed until it was time to dress. We were in the car by nine o'clock. It was a very lovely autumn day — warm sun, spiced chilled wind. We went down Seven Mile Lane, through Hale Street, Paddock Wood, Brenchley, Goudhurst, Northiam. There were so many little houses with delightful details, and the sun made them sparkle. One, I think just in Sussex, had a large curved bow with three windows in it, and then, in front, all the sash-window bars were curved at the top in Gothic arches crossing each other. It was in some ways the most elaborate little house I have seen. The bricks were very red and close-fitting — not white pattern of mortar.

When we reached Rye it was still early, but I was tired. We got out at the medieval town gate and I went down narrow stone steps to the little underground Victorian "convenience". It was attractive to me with the green dankness oozing between the white tiles, discolouring them in some places, and the three curved recesses of heavy porcelain made to resemble red-brown marble. Fronds hung over the twisting stair. It was like a minute grotto.

We drove down the main street, then round until we were back where we began; then we found our way up to the church. There we found an absurd curate standing in front of the church door, showing off to some workmen on a scaffolding and any other parishioners who would stop to listen. He was dressed in grey flannels and very light colourless tweed coat, which made the black silk V of his vest below the dog-collar look peculiarly out of place. He was short and rather boneless. On his head there was a soft black trilby; below that, glasses with dark rims; then a long black mean-looking cigarette-holder with a cigarette hanging down a little drunkenly at the end. He kept fingering the holder with fingers spread out rather as if it had been a flute. It was clear that the dingy and preposterous holder and the cigarette, smoking so boldly in front of the very doors of the church, meant a great deal to him.

The self-assertive, consequential, inquisitive, furtive-brazen bullace eyes fixed on us for a moment as we passed to get into the church. I glanced back at Eric, raising my eyebrows in wonder, and one of the curate's female companions turned and, I think, caught my mockery. Did her face show anything when she turned back to the curate? I almost expected rude words and brawling.

In the church the great gold pendulum swung slowly and threateningly, as if it were a giant's club foot, swinging to and fro idly in the dusk, while he waited, planning some treachery and death.

Just at the door was a lame woman behind a table heaped with apples, marrows, chrysanthemums, wheat and roses. I could see her surgical boot under the heap of fruits and flowers. She wore glasses too, and perhaps these gave me the notion that she was playing at being a schoolmistress who had ordered all her unruly charges up to the desk for punishment. I imagined her beating the fat bare bottoms of the marrows, pulling the shaggy gypsy hair of the chrysanthemums, slapping the already tingling cheeks of the apples. But what she said when she really opened her mouth was, "Thanks, Vera," (or some such name as that) "they'll be an enormous help." Great stress on the "enormous".

Now as I write, I wonder if many of us ever think that, while we are talking, moving about our daily business, some stranger may be near us, listening, watching, melting away to write our words down in his little book at home, there to fix them as long as the ink and paper last, or longer still if they are found, printed and scattered broadcast all over the land.

I was feeling very tired in the church, so I left Eric just by the Mayor's childish emblazoned pew seat and went back to the car. I moved it a little further back in the street where the Town Hall stands, then settled to rest and watch the people passing. I poured out steaming dark cocoa, for we had run out of coffee and left before the milk arrived. Its heat, twining down me, comforted me, and I began to feel better. Without waiting for Eric, I began to eat the cheese, the succulent pink nut-meat and the toast. When he came back, he sat in the back of the car, and we passed things to each other and stood them on the seat next to me.

Suddenly the absurd clergyman appeared round the corner of the Town Hall. He was walking and talking with a most prissy man in pin-striped suit and heavy glasses. They came nearer and nearer until they stood outside the decorating-craft-antique shop almost opposite us. The pin-striped man fumbled in his pocket, then brought out the key. First they stood outside, and pin-stripe's voice rose higher and higher. It was a very Cockney voice with that strange, plaintive, resigned quality in it. Then they went in; but they were soon out again, and this time the curate began to twiddle his black holder more than ever, then to blow down it like a trumpet. I felt that it was almost too easy to disapprove of him, to laugh at his sad little pretensions, that there must be something to redeem it all; but when he left pin-stripe and turned to an older man with the loud exclamation, "Oh, but I'm meeting all the celebrities this morning!" I felt that it was a fitting ending. It did not quite end there, for he took the older man's arm with a sort of strained bonhomie that was clearly not appreciated. Something like this must have been said, rather dourly, I feel: "You are on my deaf side." We saw the curate change from right to left. There was a moment's hesitation, then he decided to be bold and linked arms again with the taller man. They disappeared like that, the little curate clinging tenaciously to the elder, bearish "celebrity".

The naval chaplain of the coloured inks and papers, Richard Blake Brown, has written again, this time on vivid blue paper with a mustard yellow seal. The latter had come just before we left and I had brought it with me; but as I often do not read letters for days or weeks or months, Eric now took it, opened it and began to read it to himself. A busted, toqued and bunion-shoed caricature of the Queen Mother fell out,[31] then a New Year card for 1944, pink board, gold edge.

31 Queen Mary.

"Cheerful petition of 1944

The calm of the cloister calls afresh
To men who are spiritually tireless:
The thirst of the over-rated flesh
To be free from this filthy wireless."

(How is one meant to connect the two lines after the colon? I puzzle and puzzle and of course I shall never know.)

After the poem there is this sentence:

"Mr Richard Blake Brown (who is retiring slowly from excessive cycling) wishes you alertness and teachableness in the New Year."

This is an even stranger performance for a clergyman than the long black holder and the starting eyes, I suppose.

Another enclosure fell out — this time a white page. It turned out to be a letter to R.B.B. from a thing called Granville. I say thing because he/she seemed of such doubtful sex. It told R.B.B. not to go to Liverpool to preach because they were not human. Preach to humans, not animals, it said. I can never believe that they are all God's children, it said, that there is no distinction.

Afterwards we wandered in the town and ended up at the antique shop near the gate by which we entered. A youth was stripping the paintwork off the shop window with a blow-lamp and a scraper. He came down when I went into the shop, and Eric said he quickly smoothed his hair down with the palms of his hands. He was dressed in a navy blue sweater very like the one I was wearing on the day of the accident, and when he began to talk to me interestedly about the things in his shop, which he kept with his older brother, I was reminded even more of an earlier self, and, I suppose because of that, I warmed to him at once.

There was an old dolls' house in the back of the shop, early nineteenth-century, clumsy and formless; but when he opened the doors I saw that things had been collected with care for each room.

"My brother and I have taken a long time and we've spent over £40 on furnishing it," he said simply. "It hadn't anything when we started."

I told him of mine, adding that I wanted fire grates and other things just like the ones he had found for his house.

"I'm afraid we couldn't sell anything out of it. We want to keep it all together."

I looked at the other things in the shop and he came with me, confident and uncertain in turns, explaining things to me in a disarming way. Then I turned and was glad to see Eric had come into the shop. We stood together in the middle of the room in a friendly, rather silent bunch, then Eric saw the old lotto board that had been at the Fairlawne sale and we asked the youth if he had been there himself. "No, it was my brother who went," he said.

Just before we left the shop, I saw by the door a little mirror with tiny Chinese houses and trees painted in one corner. It was exactly of the period of my two mirror paintings, I think — the same shallow bevel and soft blurred mirror — but the little houses were so disappointing and insignificant after my two beautiful women in their pavilions that I could not bother to look at it really seriously; and now I wish I had, for it was only £3.10s. and we left the shop without buying anything. I was sorry to disappoint the youth. He went back to his stripping, we smiled and said good-bye, and I never even found out the name of the shop. It did not meet our eyes above the shop window, because everything was stripped away, leaving only smears and scratches of red, green, black and chalky white; also a sort of filmy pink, striped with the very grain of the wood underneath.

Eric and I dashed quickly down to the sea at Camber; but the surroundings were so disgusting, both in themselves and because they were shelled and bomb-blasted, and the sea was so far away, so monotonously vast and flat, that we sat on the beach for a minute, then scuttled away to the car again.

Driving back was an ordeal, because my head was aching so much. Before Hawkhurst Eric took over. Then I lay back and tried to ease it. We stopped to have tea at Goudhurst and I felt a little better; but after that I got worse and worse.

As soon as we were home, I went upstairs and soaked in a hot bath. I stayed there for a long time, almost falling to sleep at one time. Then I got out of it and went to bed; but as soon as I had settled, I had to jump out again and be violently sick. I repeated this three times. I was so exhausted afterwards that I fell down on the bed and soon floated off to sleep. When I woke, Eric was there too, and he had some hot tea and I was feeling much better. It was a true healing sleep. I have never recovered or rather half-recovered so quickly from a sick headache.

26 October, 8.30 a.m.

I have had a letter from someone called Roderick Walker who signs himself my "fervent admirer". He is twenty and teaches at a prep school called St Bede's, somewhere in Staffordshire. He only does it for bread and butter and hopes to earn his living by writing ultimately. He doesn't like the idea of exposing all his private feelings in his writings, and this is what keeps him from writing novels. Why should Tom, Dick and Harry be privy to my innermost thoughts, he asks. This disinclination to share his secrets and intimacies makes him think that he may devote himself to historical fiction. Certainly it sounds very cold-blooded. But in spite of the fun that can be poked at his letter and out of it, I could not help liking a little something between the lines; and Eric was in agreement with my thoughts, though outwardly we were at variance — he protesting and I uncovering.

I have heard that my "Hand Vase of Flowers" is in the front window of the Leicester Galleries and the "Rabbits in Front of the Coffin House" in the side window.

The three last pictures I sold there were bought, one by John Lehmann (whom I have mentioned already), another by a Mr C.A. Neil who bought another picture some time ago. (We saw a large notice of his in *The Times* to say that he had returned to the teaching.) To the ignorant he seems like a sort of psychologist-manipulator. The last buyer was a Mrs Mann of Mayfield House, Weybridge — a new one to me.[32]

John Lehmann writes this morning to say that he likes so much the "quite enchanting little drawings" that I have done for *New Writing*, and yesterday Keith Vaughan wrote to say that they are "very beautiful indeed".

It is very warming to have these words, because I liked the drawings, but thought other people would not like them so much.

The chaplain has written again, this time with an enormous bishop's mitre, seal of turquoise wax, and red-and-green initial R on the envelope. I have not read the letter yet, because of my strange reluctance to read most letters, but Eric has read it and says that R.B.B. found my letter very refreshing after hearing all the troubles of the seamen over their frigid wives and steaming mothers-in-law.

There was a letter too from a Bob Platt of Philadelphia. He has written before, but this time he encloses a photograph with "This is me" across the back. He is elderly, clearly American, standing on what looks like the steps of a Georgian house. He says that he deals in jewellery. I would like him to send me a very nice jewel.

On Thursday we drove to Greenwich to have lunch with Noël at Croom's Hill. Again it was a very lovely day, and this journey was much shorter than the Rye one. I was hardly tired at all by the time we left Lee[33] and climbed up to Blackheath. How it made me ache a little because I knew it and because it was beautiful! We went first into Blackheath Park and circled amongst the old houses — only one house for sale there, and that one an ugly Edwardian one. The wide quiet road, the old trees, made me think of the evenings I had walked there with John Russell when I was nineteen, how we had fooled and laughed and quarrelled as we took the air on the heath after work — I at the art school, he with his practising on the cor anglais.[34]

---

32 Denton may have been confusing "Mr C.A. Neil" with A.S. Neill, the founder of Summerhill School.

33 Denton's phonetic spelling for Leigh, three miles west of Tonbridge; not the village of Leigh in Surrey.

34 Whom Denton had met while an art student. Russell appears under his own name in "A Novel Fragment" (see 1942, note 4 above).

We came out by the beautiful Paragon, with its colonnades and middle houses half in ruin now. Two houses at least completely bombed away, I think. We got out of the car and looked in at the beautiful long windows under the pillars. The wind rustled the dripping papers, the hanging laths. I had the feeling that things would fall on our heads. Eric picked up an old drop-handle off a dresser.

I think the Paragon was one of the most perfect late eighteenth-century small crescents. The square blocks of semi-detached houses are joined together by colonnades, behind which are only the reception rooms, no upper stories, so that there is the delightful effect of pavilions threaded on a colonnade. And there is the added refinement of the gentle curve with gardens before it.

All the details are very delicate. Adam, they would be called. In front of each door on the pavement is the mounting step to make climbing into the carriage easier.

I am wondering what is to happen to it, if it will be repaired carefully. It is surprising how well some old houses have been repaired by the bomb-damage workmen.

We left the Paragon and drove over the heath and down Croom's Hill. It looked very charming and not at all slummy in the sunlight.

Thirty-four was still unpainted, but when Noël opened the door and showed us the jut-out room and the long dining-room we saw a great difference to that first day when we brought them to their new house. There was a fire in the jut-out room, their pictures on the walls, the floor fairly clean and polished. The long room was even more transformed — china in the delicate mahogany built-in cupboard with its Gothic-window doors, the gas fire roaring the warmth, curtains at the long windows, more pictures, mirrors and books. And the garden was almost in order — the air-raid shelter destroyed, a round bed dug and things planted.

We had a very good lunch of clear vegetable soup and vermicelli, hoarded rice (I have not tasted any for a year), hard-boiled eggs, parsley, buttery milky eggy sauce, grated cheese, steamed scate (if that is how you spell it). Afterwards apples steamed with quince jam and yoghourt, then coffee and cigarettes.

I was getting bored, wanting to go out on my own into the streets of Greenwich, chafing to explore, when suddenly it came about that a visit to the next door house was suggested. It is being repaired for a young architect. It is an early eighteenth-century house, much altered and spoilt, but with a good staircase with curly Cromwellian looking banisters. This has made people call it late seventeenth-century.

On the landing some of the layers of paper pasted on canvas had been torn away, and underneath was the very plain panelling that might have been expected; but because the panels themselves lay back from their framework, the spaces had been filled with rough planks to bring the surfaces level so that the canvas could be stretched over. The paintwork of the panels was the usual pale dove-olive-grey. Why was this colour so much used? Or is it really a white or cream, darkened and stained with dirt and age?

What a pleasure it will be for the man to strip off all the canvas and rough planks and reveal the panelling.

But the main rooms have lost it; also their mantelpieces. The rooms on the second floor retain theirs and it has not been covered up. It is of the very plain unmoulded sort.

We left the house and drove between the hospital and the sparkling white Queen's House, then up Maze Hill and round the park till we came to the Manor House at the top of Croom's Hill. Braxton Sinclair, Evie's brother, has a long lease of this, and it too was being repaired.

We went up to the door and Noël asked the workmen if we could go in.

It is a lovely early eighteenth-century house of the little-big type. A beautiful great shell for a canopy above the door; inside, fine, rich panelling, with bulging mouldings. The whole house resounded to the bangs and shouts of many workmen. We went through to the staircase, then looked in every room. Here there was everything one could wish for. Mantels, mouldings, windows, doors of lovely design. I wanted it so much.

The garden juts out above Croom's Hill. One side is a terraced wall twenty or thirty feet above the road. There is a sunk garden with old walls, and steps from which the iron railings have been stolen, I suppose by the salvage enthusiasts. The balustrade on either side of the door into the garden has been taken too. This door has cupid faces to support its canopy. The windows are tall and narrow. There is a wonderful view over London and the river, and an old broken mulberry tree, dragging some of its branches along the ground. House, garden and position are wonderfully good. There is a little stable yard with fine herring-bone paving, a decorated rainwater tank dated 1815.

The front of the house has not lost its iron railings and pretty archway. There is an old pump too and pillars at each side, topped with balls.

I don't think I know any other smallish house with so many fine things about it inside and outside. It has been built for comfort and beauty, and has not been too spoilt either by past owners or bombs.

Noël gave me a booklet on the Queen's House, and only after reading it did I realize fully that the Deptford-Woolwich road had originally passed right through it. All the next day I kept thinking of this strange conceit, imagining the house as Inigo Jones first designed it, two separate halves, joined only in the middle by the broad bridge which carried a fine room on its back.

I thought of the courtiers and Queen Henrietta Maria watching the pedestrians and coaches from the windows of this bridge room. At night, were they disturbed by the tramping, the horses' hooves, singing and swearing and inquisitive loiterers?

I understood why the Queen's House had been built when I learnt that it took the place of an older gatehouse. It was meant as a belvedere, a gazebo and a magnificent bridge and covered way between the royal palace and gardens by the river and the deer park. It at once became quite reasonable and not almost unbelievably strange to have a public road passing through the middle of a palace.

Now that the road has been diverted since the early eighteenth century, and since the house has been made to look like a solid block by Webb's addition of two more bridges across the original road, carrying two more upper rooms, the house has lost much of its true nature. It looks at first glance like a flat, plain, elegant small mansion of the late eighteenth, or even the early nineteenth century. Any seventeenth-century air it may have had was swept away with the mullioned and transformed casements, with their leaded panes; and now that it has eighteenth-century sashes to all the outward windows, it looks astonishingly precocious.

Have you ever thought that a large harpsichord played by a master or a mistress is like a large very beautiful cat unsheathing its claws, pawing the air, mouthing, miawlling, waving ostrich-plume tail, gnashing white needle teeth? This cat would be smoke-grey with sinews of the toughest leather under the distasteful velvet depths of the fur; and its eyes would be wolfish topazes or burnt sugar. It would be stretching and plucking and striking, calling up some spirit that had never been wakened before.

8 November, afternoon, grey.

Last night in the moonlight I ate a melting white peppermint from America. The moon caught it and made it sparkle. Thin lines of the moon cut across the floor and my bed, and the clouds sailed in the night. We had both been in bed since last Sunday.[35] It has been a strange time of getting out of bed to heat a drink or cook a mouthful, then of falling back into the tousled clothes.

13 November

It is wonderful to feel much better in the early morning, with the traffic humming on the main road far away, and the morning air smelling, and a great red rosebud on my tea-tray. The rosebud is like a cannon's mouth. The crimson hole goes right down to its heart.

---

35 Five days.

4 December, morning.

After almost a month of bed, I got up on a fine day, last Tuesday, and went with Eric to picnic in the car. We were on the way to Maidstone and we stopped in a clearing where hop-poles were to be dipped in creosote. There were logs, poles, palings and twigs all about us — nothing but wood — even soft sawdust instead of earth.

When our picnic was over we drove on to Maidstone to find a christening present for Paul's godchild. To preserve me as much as possible, we only went to one shop, the Malt Shovel, and there I chose a little cream-jug, George II, 1759, £8.10s. It is not really what I would have chosen, if there had been other later jugs; it was too vague — the embossed flowers, the rococo scroll, the three little feet and fat pear shape were strangely perfunctory, as so much mid-eighteenth-century stuff is, really as if the business of decoration were nothing but an exhausting duty.

The jug has its own prettiness and interest though; very good marks on the bottom and three charming old initials with tiny stars scratched between.

We also bought a good tea-pot, but with no lid, of very bright mandarins and ladies; burnt orange, puce, turquoise and lots of gold. 10s.6d.

Driving out of the town, we passed one more junk shop by the County Hall. I had to stop, and there we found a little jug of the same mandarin ware, only more delicate — mountains, pavilions, a garden and people. Under the handle two tiny pig-like creatures chasing each other down the branch of a tree. It was in perfect order, and when I got it home I found I had got a lid of exactly the right size and design for it — off another jug that had been broken. All these jugs originally had tiny lids.

When I was home, I realized too how tired I was. I woke up in the night and felt that my temperature was rising. In the morning I was really ill again — aching all over, but I always prefer this to only aching in the head. I drowsed and lay there all day and the succeeding days, and when the temperature subsided I caught the cold which Eric had had! So I am still here in bed, with nothing done for over a week.

Lying here, able to do nothing, I have realized that all the year has been a sinking into bed and a painful rising out of it, only to be dragged down again before I could breathe or spread my arms. I have realized how half-afraid I have been to do anything because of what comes after. How many hours, days have I had to let swim over my head? And I, who could be busy all day long. The feeling has come over me that I must let everything melt away, that I am no longer in command at all. And in my idleness all I can think of are rich strange dishes wonderfully cooked, amazing little houses in fine gardens, rare and lovely objects for these tiny palaces, and then wills and bequests both fantastic and more down to earth.

I keep wondering if I shall receive anything from my father's estate, and whether Cecil Carpmael intends to leave me anything or not. I wonder what she has to leave. Sometimes I work it out contentedly at anything between £50,000 to £80,000; and I go through her possessions too, remembering the few nice things, the Georgian silver teapots and the Persian rugs.[36]

I see now that day-dreams like these, very material — always of things, wealth, security — crowd in as the chance to finish work recedes. Agitation, fear of all the things that may never be done, is suppressed. One can no longer plan happily to begin or to complete, so only wealth is left to dream about.

This is the reason why people's thoughts, as they grow older, turn more and more to the safety of wealth. Other things cheat them, escape them, are snatched from them, only the fat mountain of wealth remains.

But as this process of decrepitude is so speeded up in me, for that is what invalidism seems, a sort of wicked acceleration of one's life, I feel not happy in dreaming of wealth and security, but curiously fobbed off with wishes that I do not wish for, unconnected with other wishes, that can no longer be entertained. Wealth alone is, I think, everywhere secretly thought of as a second best, a lump of dough that must be lightened with fame, happiness, even rank. It must have some trimming, real or frothy. That is why those only rich faces are so peaked, so cheated and complaining.

I have not said yet that Evie came back on the 18th of November, and has been cooking really delicious meals for us. In spite of bad beginnings over time — everything late and the clock looked upon as a useless ornament — we now feel glad that she is here. She does make life easier, and I have got beyond worrying over her eccentricities.

5 *December, morning.*

Just after I had written yesterday of fortunes, money, inheriting, Cecil Carpmael appeared in the green car, together with mad sister Connie and the companion, Miss Brown.

Cecil can only climb the stairs very slowly now, because of arthritis, I think. She cannot use her hands much, and I cannot look at them for more than a moment; but her expression and her bright, small, clear blue eyes sometimes create a curious impression of youth — the hectic, inquisitive, bright and pig-headed kind. It was as if nothing had been received into her since the age of seventeen or so, and all the things that had happened to her body had only taught her more about grumbling, the art of turning everything to a grumble, of feeling omnipotent and dissatisfied. She seems to squat in her ignorance, passing judgment on all that she knows nothing

---

36 Mrs Carpmael, who disappointed Denton by bequeathing him nothing, left £51,557. 2s. 9d.

she has, cutting across this, a sort of hankering for things outside of If. She talks of what she intends to do in a strange unreal way. One day will read Fielding and Richardson and the other older novelists — she has forgotten the other names for the moment. One day she will find out more about antique furniture (a subject she is perfectly indifferent to). One day she will take her pictures to Australia and have a show there because nobody bothers with "ordinary old-fashioned painting" like hers in England.

It is strange, too, how with her arrogance and limitation she could use those very words about her own pictures. Of course she believes that they are in the right tradition and that others are wandering in the desert, but I am often surprised by flashes of this resentful humility.

When she came yesterday she was in one of her better states, when an unexpected sweetness shows in her face and eyes and almost amazes one. She seems to show then real solicitude and gentleness lightened by gaiety.

17 December, 5.30 p.m.

Biting east wind and powder snow on the ground.

On Thursday I had a letter from Hector Bolitho with the article that he had written about me for *Town and Country*. They had called it "In Welch is Youth"; he explained that it was not his title. He wrote from the Mayflower Inn, Washington, Connecticut, and said that he was lecturing, trying to make enough money to buy a house on the York River.

The article is buttery, and they have reproduced, quite well, my pen-drawing fancy portrait of myself. I also had a Christmas card from Julian Goodman, but with her new name Vinogradoff on it — nothing more. So she is properly remarried. Every time I have a card from her I feel a little piqued, I suppose because I gave her the picture I painted of her instead of selling it and have ever since expected a beautiful present — an eighteenth-century silver-gilt snuff box or a tiny Chinese mirror painting. Don't give pictures away, you will always begrudge them, or feel that they are not properly appreciated.

The most surprising card of all was the one that came on Saturday, forwarded from Pitt's Folly and accompanied by one from Mrs Sloman. This makes me think that Mrs Sloman first peeped at it. It was a long card with a distressing picture of a sort of outhouse and star crosses in a black sky that shaded down into spots and dots and stripes — a sort of madness of cross-hatching. I opened the book card and found on the left page in a rather bulgy, flowing writing: From the Duchess of Wellington (Dorothy Wellesley) Xmas 1946 — just like that, brackets, Xmas and all.

On the other page was a poem of hers, "Caedmon for Children", one of those poems one rather enjoys reading, because it has been sent to one, or is in some way temporarily special to oneself, but which are not really received and eaten up.

The card was a great surprise, because it is three years since that Poetry Reading, the only time I ever saw her; and then she did not seem to make contact with any part of me.[37] She looked at me with recoiling eyes and said, "Well, it's a good thing we got you here at any rate." The eyes seemed anxious to get away from my image back into their lairs, where they would grumble and grouse and brood. They seemed rather to spark and spit at me for keeping them waiting in the cold.

John Turner, whom I first remember as a small boy of fourteen watching the air battles of 1940 and whooping with excitement and delight, came the other day after being in prison for four months, at Birmingham and then Wormwood Scrubs, for refusing to wear the King's uniform. It appears that he went on parade with yellow tie and battle-green corduroys. He has now had his tribunal, and is discharged if he will do welfare work, so he is probably going to the Arctic — is it Finmark? — with the Friends Ambulance Unit.

He looks well and scruffy; only a little, a little wild, and as if he was made of India-rubber. He talks all the time about Anarchy; with Christianity poking its head through the folds every so often.

Everybody, so he says, behaved very well indeed to him, both in the army and in prison. The people who had not seen active service were the most inclined to be hostile, but I haven't heard that before and, perhaps, hasn't he.

He did not mind being locked up. He seems to mind nothing. I was both reassured about human nature and untrusting of John's receptiveness. The Anarchic Christianity seemed to have come between him and all his experiences.

The next time he came he brought a French girl with him, Martine Nathan; she has come from Paris to live with the Turners for three months to perfect her English.

She is dumpy with lots of frizzy dark hair, cherry shaped lips (that is, the bottom one pouts like two black cherries just rising together out of the surface of a fruit salad) and those dark, wet dog's-nose eyes. She often stops to hold the attention before she tells in a restrained way some story of German cruelty in France. It is as if she were giving a lesson to a class; she is too solemn and too rigid to be quite sincere, and there is the awkwardness of having to suit one's face to hers.

---

37 At the King Charles Hall in Tunbridge Wells, on 2 October 1943.

Entry undated

On Christmas Day we had a German prisoner to lunch. His name was Harry Diedz and he was twenty-one.[38] He came from Thuringia where he had been a glass worker. He was little, with a flat face and curly hair. He liked Mozart better than Wagner, and football better than boxing. He ate a great deal and enjoyed it, I think. He was in the Channel Islands when he was captured. His brother was captured by the Americans when he was only sixteen.

We sat by the fire smoking and eating sweets and talking stumblingly, until Harry said that he had to go back to the camp to act in some "drama variété".

His camp is at Mereworth Castle. When we went there I saw again the cedars spreading out flat against the stable buildings, and the castle with its dome in the background, one light on in one of the corner rooms, and the geometrical garden beds spread out in front. It looked very lovely in the evening — the dark colonnade, the squareness set down among the hills. It was the house to wish for, to preserve carefully for ever.

---

38 He appears under his own name in "The Hateful Word" (see 1943, note 35 above).

XV

Journal

1947

28 January

AFTER THREE weeks of bed, able to do nothing, I began to revive again and try to write here first. I have been too sad to want anything, and the snow has been falling for days. It is falling now, there is a great layer on the roof. The wind bites through the apple trees and round the corners of the house. I have just heard this morning that there is a red star on my picture at the Leicester Galleries, and that has made my happy and more alive. I am waiting now to get back to everything; but my head has been swimming too much for me to do anything.

I had a strangely hideous New Year card made by someone called Auger who says he is one of a group of young people who like my books in Hollywood. I have not answered yet, because I have answered no letters. Why do I feel guiltier not answering strangers' letters than those from friends?

I wonder all the time I am ill if I shall be able to earn enough money, since so much time is wasted. I am strangely worried and unworried about it, as if it were only a problem I had set myself. I suppose I feel I shall have the money somehow, that I shall recover in time, that my books will bring me in some more. Then, as I said before, my mind in illness runs to the idea of inheriting; it turns over all the chances and possibilities, and is now hopeful, now despondent. It is all a game to keep one warm and secure-feeling.

In all the illness, I have had the horrible sensation that the tables, chairs, lamps and confusion of books near me were writhing into life and becoming extensions of myself, like new limbs, utterly unwanted, but insisting on living and doing my bidding. All the time I would wish nothing to be done, and yet would give all these things their horrible senseless life. And I even myself grew to a wretched largeness and was invaded too with the activity of nothingness. It was an endless toiling and posturing and living for nothing, so heart-breaking and deadening that I longed and longed to be still, to stop churning and to sleep for a little.

Sight, sound, touch were all distorted. I was living in a twisted stretched world, where I invaded everything and was the horror that I could not escape. There was no self-love left, only an exhausted disgust.

29 January

There were frost flowers thick all over the panes this morning and the milk was frozen. The pipes were frozen too, and the snow thicker than ever.

I have not got out of bed, and will not till I hear the pipes thawing. I have been writing here, then eating chocolate as a reward. The panes are all dripping and splashing in the sunshine now. Eric has gone for a walk in the snow, and I wish I could too. It is the most snow I think I have known in England.

2 February, 6 p.m.

The snow is still thick, and it falls fitfully, the flakes floating down, or driving more firecely mixed with a little rain. As I lie in bed, only getting up twice a day, I feel that I shall never walk about again. The effort seems tremendous. My legs sway and my head swims. In bed I try to write a little and to do something to my latest drawing, but my head and eyes do not seem really clear. Nevertheless I do something, and it makes me feel a little more serene. Eric and Evie read to me and I eat to make up for my fasting. I think of food too — of oysters cooked with creamed turkey, of salmon and potted shrimps, of rice with pimento and chickens' livers and peas.

A poem of mine has come out in *Orion III*, and I wish to have stories and poems in many magazines. I want to finish my story and my book and get them to the publishers. I want to be a sausage machine pouring out good sausages, savoury and toothsome, delightful, desirable. I want pleasure and interest to flow out of me, to feel alive and able to bear a heavy load of work to be done. I want to be able to go out and find old books and objects in the promising dirty shops. I want to go down into the house and make it live again with my interest. I want to go out and see different sights.

How awful Rimsky-Korsakov's music sometimes seems — embarrassing, strident, posturing, sweaty. Why does it? What is it in me that gives it this colouring?

How almost non-existent is my feeling for other people, especially when I am ill! There they are, doing things for me, making life possible, and I am dead to them, hardly even conventionally grateful, almost unable to realize that they have feelings at all. Yet I am dimly worried by them, afraid that they find my illness depressing and gloomy, afraid that there is not enough interest in their lives, that I am dragging them down into despondency.

3 February, 6.30 p.m.

Rain today spattering on the window, yet the snow does not go, and Eric says that a great tide of slush is mounting up in the road. I wrote a fair amount this morning in a contented sort of daze. What can the result be like? Then this afternoon I tried to cover a picture mount with yellow muslin bandage. The pasting was difficult and I suddenly became very tired.

My limbs ache from lying in bed so much, yet I feel I can do nothing else. I wish I had not the weight of my body to support. It seems like a dead asleep thing hanging on me, bearing me down.

13 February, 11.20 a.m.

A few days ago I had a letter, and when I opened it, I found it was from Rose Macaulay, and she had bought my "Coffin House" picture with the rabbits in front.[1] I was very delighted and surprised and wrote back at once. Yesterday I had another letter describing very acutely the spirit that I had wanted my picture to have.

"I find the picture more and more fascinating," she writes, "as I knew I should when I failed to resist it at the Leicester. The detail is so exquisitely mortal and corrupt, the robin singing against it with such brave, larger-than-life protest. I especially like the blind white hare pawing the toadstool; and the clawing tree-trunks, like dendrofied ghosts or dragons reaching for their prey. Your penwork is so beautifully precise and strong; and all the colour so good."

Then later: "The picture almost smells of fungus and a damp wood; I know the smell so well." And later still: "There is some poem of de la Mare's about a wood, that your picture suggests to me. It seems to me unusual to be able to do two things so well as you do, writing and picture-making." At the end: "Anyhow, thank you very much for the Coffin House, and the pleasure and interest it gives me; it is precise yet ghostly, like an odd and beautiful and frightening dream. You really must come and see it when you can.

Yours sincerely,
Rose Macaulay."

I sold the other little woman-faced bird picture too, but I don't yet know who has bought it.

The bitter weather, the snow and ice, never disappear. If there is a thaw, it freezes all the more afterwards to make up for it. All the bathroom taps and plugs are frozen now, in spite of our having the electric fire on all night. And now with the electricity cuts, we have no current between nine and twelve, two and four. Eric is sawing wood in the snow. Evie is bumbling about in the kitchen, waiting for the current to go on so that she can cook lunch. My hands are so cold I can't write smoothly or easily.

Joan Waymark, who used to be at the Art School and whom I haven't seen since 1940, came to tea the other day. Her New Zealand husband has bought a dentist's practice in Tonbridge, and is making money "hand over fist" as she puts it gaily. She has a little boy of five, who is still naughty about

---

1 Reproduced in A *Last Sheaf*.

wetting the bed, and they are going to buy a new Riley car for £800 at the end of the year. But it was not nearly as bad as I have made it sound. Joan was gay and flighty and good-natured, just as I knew her, and we talked of the time when several of us rented a house at Brixham for the summer (we were none of us over twenty) and of all the little things that happened.

Joan's hair has gone prematurely grey in front — she can only be thirty-one — and she is plumper, but these things don't prevent her from looking young and bouncing still; in fact, the grey coxcomb in front I first mistook for one of those blondy wigs that some women favour.

It was strange to have Joan here. When we were very young we saw so much of each other. She was always driving down. Then we would go to the coast or to Windsor or to some other castle, mansion or ruin. We would sometimes take food, sometimes search greedily for the tastiest-looking tea-shop or café. She was always good-natured and gay, so that one forgave her for anything else she lacked. Eric said she seemed silly. Perhaps it is that very birdlike quality I found so easy.

Silly but shrewd, flighty but sane, conventional but unjudging and not to be horrified. There is the mimic in her too — not the professional mimic who embarrasses with too much acting, but the slight imperfect mimic who just, in a fit of levity, lifts a shoulder, twists a lip, tries to produce an accent, so makes one laugh at the sheer grotesqueness of mimicry and mimicked.

24 February, 9.15 a.m.

Today is the coldest day of all; frost feathers, flowers, ferns all over the windows, giving a dim clouded light inside; my pen frozen, so that I could not write with it or fill it.

Then broadest sunlight pouring on to me in bed, warm, melting the frost flowers so that a steam goes up, waving, wreathing its shadow across this page as I write. I have a lot to do. *Junior* has taken my story and wants me to do pictures for it. *Vogue* has written, wanting me to do two pictures of summer foods and drink. I have to finish two pictures and revise my long-short story.[2] I want too to send some poems to John Lehmann.

3 March, 2.25 p.m. Snow all melting, lovely sun.

Cecil Carpmael is dead. I heard this morning from Irene. On Friday night she fell on the studio floor and broke her thigh. She died the next evening, Saturday. It must have been while I was listening alone to Emlyn Williams's

---

2 "Brave and Cruel", the title story of his first collection of short stories, published on 7 January 1949, two days after his funeral.

Welsh play, which has the death-bed ending — the small Welsh boy, the supposed Jesus, dying of cholera after saving the Crimean soldiers in the village hospital.

I felt very gruesome and alone then at night, and I wonder if C.C. was dying then.

Irene did not get down till Sunday morning. She wrote to me in the afternoon. Her letter gave me much more of a shock than I could have imagined. At the bottom of one page were the words, "I am writing now from the Oast House to give you some very sad news.[3] Mrs Carpmael slipped on ...", then the writing stopped and I did not want to turn over. I called out to Eric, who was outside the bathroom door. He waited and I turned over and read the rest, "... the studio floor late on Friday night, and broke her thigh. She passed on on Saturday evening. Hilda and I came down this morning, and I am staying for a few days, at least. There is an awful lot to do. Cecil was so grateful to have her pictures at the Leicester Galleries — you certainly gave her a real pleasure, bless you!"

When I had collected myself a little, I went down to telephone Irene. She told me that Miss Brown helped Cecil to bed on Friday night, but nothing was done (because they were Christian Scientists). In the morning Miss Brown could not move C to make her more comfortable, and it was clear that she was very ill, so she attempted to get the district nurse, but she of course could not come without a doctor's directions. So at last a doctor came. Irene said he was very nice. He took X-rays, found the thigh was fractured and then gave C what Irene rather contemptuously called "dope" — that, at least, was a good thing. He then ordered a nurse who drove over from Tunbridge Wells. Miss Brown took her up to Cecil's room. She opened the door, looked down on the bed, and said, "Oh, but she is gone."

To hear of a death makes you shake a little, makes your head ache and your stomach; and your mind sticks, never moving from the dead person. You talk and talk, as Eric and I have been doing, about C. The whole day has floated and hung heavy, has had no shape, except for the rather distasteful interlude of lunch — well grilled herrings and good blackcurrant tart. It is so curious that Eric is almost as affected as I am, yet she can mean hardly anything to him. I can remember her since I was four — how when I was older, eight or nine, she would ask me to her studio in Cheyne Walk and let me paint with her fat tubes and large brushes. How she took me to Romney's near Harrods and bought me a fine little oak easel. How there were always good things to eat and old things to look at and examine, the things I loved, the famille rose plates, not very good, but charming with their conventionalised flower baskets, the boule clock, quite broken, the springs shivering rustily within — the view from the drawingroom windows

3 Mrs Carpmael's home in Trottiscliffe.

over the grey Thames to the factories, and Soane's monument just below us, and the corner of Chelsea Old Church; all gone, C.C. too, now.

The funeral is on Thursday and I can't decide, if I am well enough, whether to go or not. I have never been to a funeral.

Irene knows nothing definite of her affairs. She has written to Barclay's Bank since they were C's husband's executors.

6 March, 10 a.m.

This was the day fixed for the funeral, but it may have been postponed, because of the public enquiry which sometimes is held on accidents.

All the orchard trees are coated with ice, the twigs all beaded so that they look like stiff crystal necklaces. The blizzard has been blowing for two days. The robin's tail is frozen and he can't walk properly. The birds dance and gobble up the crumbs.

The day I heard of C's death was the day my mother died twenty years ago. C came then in the car with Irene to the school to fetch me away to the Oast House for a few days. I went into the headmaster's drawingroom. I didn't cry. I was very stiff and still and smiling. I held my gloves, straightened my coat and waited to be taken out to the car.

The chauffeur, Garrard, was there holding open the door. We got into the rather old fashioned Humber and lay back on the large, loose, puffy cushions. We swept away from St Michael's down the steep drive, and I was watching, watching all the time the streets, the houses of Uckfield, the people walking, shopping. Then we were in the country — old houses, new ones, fields, the schoolboys at Tonbridge running in their red and white striped football vests, the black and white house near the road before Igtham, then the slum of Borough Green and we were down the narrow road to Trottiscliffe. There was the lovely Elizabethan brickwork of Ford Place, the old sign board with the spelling Trotterscliffe. Now we were at the Oast House with its cerulean front door, and we were breathing the curious Carpmael air of oil stoves, radiators, flower bulbs and woollen wraps.

That night I sat with the earphones on my head — the new loudspeakers were no use to Cecil in her deafness. There was some music on the wireless, romantic music, and I remembered the ancient gramophone in China which had played a record of just such music. Why can I not remember what it was now? It seemed alive to me for ever then. The music floated to me and melted me, and I wanted to listen to it, but Irene saw me there so near to tears, sitting by the stove in the long, low room that had once been the bottom story of the barn, and she smiled and gently put her hand up to take the earphones off my head. I did not want her to, I wanted to listen; but I let her. And then I began to cry and gulp, and she began to tell me Christian Science truisms and words of comfort. She did it very well, with great conviction.

Later, when I went to bed in the little larkspur blue room with its oblong flowery-painted lampshade, I cried and cried again and thought that I was lost.

Another evening, probably the next, I was wandering disconsolate about the upper barn that had been converted into a studio, and Cecil Carpmael found me there and with hardly any words knelt down on the floor near a large board and began to model something in plasticine.

"Come on," she said, "let's make something." And I knelt down too and we made flowers and horses and little doll people. I remember the dull red, green, grey colours and the dull sticky feel and smell of the stuff. Cecil was smiling as we played, a very far-away, sweet, amused smile. She was doing all she could to hold my attention to the present moment.

7 March. Five to nine a.m.

Yesterday the glassed-in-crystal trees were all banging together, jingling, hissing like fire, pattering like rain on the roof, in the blizzard wind; but today the extraordinary sound has stopped and a more wonderful sight has come. The sun glitters through all the iced twigs, as if tiny electric tube lighting ran over every part of the trees, outlining them, making them tingle. The sky is palest blue and the snow has a thick cake crust.

I am not well enough to go [to the funeral]. Miss Brown and sister Connie are to come here while the undertakers do their business; so unless people from the village go to the funeral, the church will be almost empty, and the parson will have no one to address from the lovely tall eighteenth-century pulpit in Trottiscliffe Church.

I want, in some ways, to go to the funeral, but I would want to sit unseen in some gallery away from Irene and whoever else might be there. There are no galleries and I could not go invisibly, and Eric says it's silly of me even to play with the idea.

All last night I was miserable, and it was about money. Resentment welled up like secret water from a rock. I felt, in wave after wave, that, although I was Cecil's only young friend, and in spite of her real feeling for me, a feeling stronger perhaps than that which she had for anyone else, she would leave me no money, not even an object from her house.

There were so many reasons for believing this. There was her utter self-preoccupation, except in rare moments, and this alone would make her oblivious to the needs of others. There was the complication of her mad sister. There was her old association and friendship with Irene. I felt that with an impatient, lazy sweep she would push all responsibility and money into Irene's lap, not because she loved her much, but because she was competent, old and efficient, and had managed sister Connie for so many years.

And as I resented, I knew that it was quite right for Irene to inherit everything; that if I had been C's heir, I would have been horribly uncomfortable in many ways.

27 March

I have not been able to write in this book, have felt an utter distaste for it. I have felt dull and empty and trivial, and this was due partly to being less well, and partly to the news that Cecil Carpmael has left me nothing at all. Her Will was made when I was nineteen. She must have taken it for granted that I would be well provided for by my father. But of course there has been lots of time for her to add a codicil, after learning that I would inherit nothing until my stepmother's death, and perhaps still nothing, even then.

Everything is left to Connie for life, except £500 to Irene, £200 to Joan Sharp (a god-daughter I knew nothing of), £100 each to the two sisters-in-law. After Connie, Carpmael money goes back to Carpmaels, Irene gets two-thirds of the Piffard money, and Joan Sharp the other third. C's paintings are not even mentioned; all goods and chattels are for Connie's use, and after her death they will be sold and the money divided between Irene and Joan.

Before the Will was known, Irene had asked me rather half-heartedly if there was anything I would particularly like of Cecil's. I thought and then wrote firmly to say that I had always been particularly fond of the elaborate late-Georgian tea-pot and cream jug, which came to Cecil from her brother. The surface is all chased and embossed with fruit and flowers and scrolls, and a tiny mandarin perches on top of the tea-pot; a fat ugly cupid's head emerges from the handle of the jug. Its exuberance, its lumpishness and sheer weight, its fine workmanship make the set very attractive to me. It is both frivolous and monumental — surely something rather difficult to achieve.

I knew really, without being told, that Irene would be obstructive. She has that managing, interfering madness that cannot bear to let anything escape its grasp. Even if I had asked for something quite worthless in her eyes, she would have worried and pondered, trying to discover a hidden value, never resting until she had refused my request.

When the Will was known, the wording of it gave her just the authority she was looking for. The silver, together with all the other household things, in trust for Connie. She told me this repressively, when she came to tea last Friday. She never mentioned the tea-pot or my wish; but I was to take the hint. I did, and smiled as if nothing had happened. But after she had left, as always happens, my resentment flowered. I realised more completely the unfriendliness, the stupid suspicion. I wrote a letter to say that I knew it was foolish of me to have taken her words seriously, but I was taking a little time to adjust my ideas. I had always considered myself one of Cecil's closest friends. The fact that she had not even mentioned me in the Will proved quite clearly to everyone that she had no particular interest in my affairs; therefore it was quite right that I should be refused one of her three tea-pots. The letter, I hope, was more gracefully put together than this last jumble!

It brought a reply full of darlings and other endearments, telling me that after Irene herself, I was certainly Cecil's closest friend. I was to let nothing spoil that friendship. I was not to measure love "by a Will". Cecil made her Will at a time when she thought that I would have more than enough from my father. She remembered the god-daughter only from a heavy sense of duty, not a pleasurable one. She had not seen her for years and years, she had just sent her birthday and Christmas presents.

The Will laid it down that everything must be kept till Connie's death, when it would all be sold.

Somehow this wrangling about a teapot depressed me even more than the news that Cecil had not bothered to remember me at all. I was dirtied by it, turned into a vulture on such a tiny scale. I had thought so often of Cecil's Will, when she was alive, hoped so much that she would leave me a cosy fortune. That had been quite simple and natural and friendly. Now there was a sort of pointless resentment that fixed itself round the teapot, but really spread out far and wide.

30 March. Five to eight a.m.

Rain and wind — my washed pyjamas fallen off the rope on to the dirty boards of the veranda; the round flower-beds little round pools with the mock-orange tree and honeysuckle standing in them; forsaken, grey feeling.

Yesterday was my birthday and Evie brought up with my early morning tea a tiny glass urn with square base. In the urn were snowdrops, primroses, flower of winter jasmine and a white crocus with orange clubbed tongue. She had found the little urn in Tunbridge Wells. I think it must be a late eighteenth-century oil or vinegar bottle. It has the smoky blue of some old glass and the cutting is chunky and irregular. I am going to try to find the right sort of pointed stopper for it, then it will be perfect. I have never seen a square-based urn-shaped piece so small. I have sweetmeat dishes, mustard pots, salt cellars, a pepper pot that all look giants beside it.

Soon after I had begun to drink my tea, I heard more rustles outside the door, then Evie threw it open and Eric came in bearing three most lovely hyacinths — mauve-blue, yellow-cream and raspberry pink. They were huge, and he had banked fresh moss round each so that it made a shaggy velvet hump.

A card was on the middle one, and in my early morning, bleary-eyed realising how appropriate my leaning so near to read had been; for Irene always has to do this and the card was in direct initiation of her affectionately worded notes denying me the teapot and asking me to be of service in taking Connie out in the car, or getting Evie to cook her pies. It said, "Many Happy Returns to Denton with much love, Bless you!"

When the breakfast tray came up, there was a lovely bunch of glass-green muscatel grapes from John Bloom. He it was who had also got the hyacinths from Covent Garden for Eric. These are the first hyacinths I have seen since the beginning of the war. I am going to keep the bulbs in sand, year after year. How long will they live?

By the morning post the *Cornhill*, which Julian still sends me, arrived, but no letters from my aunts. My brother Bill had sent me a telegram from Hong Kong the day before. Last year he sent me £100, the year before a telegram; before that, never anything. I cannot help feeling pleased but confused.

Noël Adeney rang up after breakfast to say that someone called Tommy, with a mop of dark hair, was going to spend the week-end in the studio; would we order him some milk? We didn't know when to expect him, but after I had bathed and dressed and gone downstairs, the first time for a week or two, I arranged the lovely hyacinths on the marble topped chess table, then lit the fire, which would not burn at once because of dampness. The room was charming with smiling Venus and Cupid in the cartoon behind me, the glitter of the glass drops and May's little oval silver Dutch funeral plaques before me, and outside the drear wet orchard trees and beaten-down grass.

We had lunch there of egg-cheese-and-potato pie, then plum pastry pie and chocolate.

At about half-past three a very wet, tall, willowy person came to the door. He had hardly any hair at all, but what he did have did stick out and was black and frizzy. He wore a long pale tweed coat and carried a knapsack. He spoke with a slightly foreign accent, and swayed through the door when I asked him in. He had rather tight little cheeks and a flattish broad face with rather a Jewish cast, I thought. I took him round at once to the studio, since he seemed anxious to see it.

Later he came into tea and we discovered that he came from Mauritius and had been in England only a year.

"Then how do you speak English so well?" I asked, wanting to make his face light up.

"Well," he said, a little reluctantly, "my mother is English." And immediately my compliment was turned into a criticism of the English.

"We spoke English at home," he went on to explain, "and French everywhere else."

He told us of the sugar plantations, the bread fruit, the custard apples, the lychees, the mangoes, the mosquitoes, the avocados and the rain.

"Every roof leaks in Mauritius," he said.

I saw now that what at first had seemed Jewish features were really French ones, with somewhere perhaps a suggestion of negro — flat nose, dark eyes, curved, quickly moving lips, frizzy hair.

He was really very tall. He twisted his legs together and cupped his chin in his hands. He was wearing a bright terracotta pullover which matched the carpet. He liked food and looked both lazy and self-sufficient. It was difficult to tell whether he was thirty-eight or twenty-two. But since he said he was a student at the Central School, I suppose he must be nearer the twenty-two.

He was intelligent and easy to get on with, but one did not mind about not seeing him again.

5 April

Irene brought Joan Sharp, Cecil's god-daughter, to tea yesterday. She was fortyish, small, thin, almost pinched looking, rather nice and neat in tweeds. She wore glasses and looks like a real schoolmistress, not just a conventional one; but she works as a secretary in the London University, and she has been in the A.T.S. She told us of her strange feeling on first being called M'am. She was very willing to appreciate and enjoy all she saw or had to eat, and Eric thought she was pleased to get away from the Oast House and come into our atmosphere for a little. She is staying over Easter to help Irene with Connie, while Miss Brown is away for a little rest.

Connie nearly lifted her skirt over her head at tea. She began by playing with her stocking fastenings, and everyone went quiet waiting for the worst; then suddenly she came across the room and took my arm. Eric says she wore a very nice expression as she did this. I did not see; I only saw the tiny fleck of white in the corner of her eye.

John Lehmann sent me the Czechoslovakian edition of *New Writing* with one of my stories in it, and some of my poems back; he is keeping one, which he wants me to decorate for a later number.

I have been doing a water-colour of a big-eyed girl in a large hat for the last two days.[4] I must have begun it some years ago. I suddenly came upon it in a cupboard, and in spite of not feeling well, I was so pleased with it in some way that I began at once to make all sorts of little changes and additions. I want to go on with it all through the day, it would amuse and interest me the whole time; but now I must stop, or I shall have a headache all tonight. If one could have the perfect, untiring head and eyes!

4 "A Beauty Waiting in the Fields", currently in the collection of Mr Geoffrey Parsons; illustrated in *A Last Sheaf*.

We took our lunch out today and ate it near Cobham — cheese and pea-nut butter sandwiches, then marmalade ones, and almonds. Afterwards we went to Cobham Church — all decorated for Easter — and I showed Eric the lovely brasses and the little Persian rug, beautifully mended and preserved, that someone has given. A youth and girl from Chatham were in there too — quietly staring, withheld, serious, sexy; the youth with a satchel slung on his shoulder and grey-blue smoky skin round his eyes, giving him rather a beautiful, made-up look. They were both short, and I thought of them as pleasing, stumpy dolls.

We left them and went round to the little college or hospital behind the church. We went under the arch and then walked rather guiltily across the green courtyard surrounded by tiny Gothic windows, and doors with oval brass name plates on them. We looked into the great hall with its fine table and mantelpiece of stone. It was covered in thick dust and the windows were blacked in parts. One of the pensioners told us afterwards that it hasn't been used for twelve months, and won't be again until some repairs can be done.

He caught hold of us as we emerged on the other side and insisted on repeating to us the whole of an inscription on a ruined gateway.

He too had white flecks at the corners of his eyes. I was reminded at once of the tea yesterday and I thought of Joan and how she had the share of Cecil's money that I might reasonably have thought would come to me. I found that I couldn't believe in money or Wills; I couldn't really feel that she would ever benefit. It was all turmoil and talk. Then my thoughts were switched back to the Almshouses and I thought of the Cobham who had built them as a college for priests to pray for his soul forever; I thought of their conversion into Almshouses at the Reformation, and it seemed to me that this was the very best way of all for a man to commemorate himself and be useful to others century after century. If he had left that money to his sons, it would have been spent and forgotten in a few years; as it is, even the fourteenth-century building is standing almost complete. Any private house of that date would almost certainly have been sold, changed, defaced, restored, pulled down by now.

It comes to this, that things are preserved chiefly by trusts, charities, impersonal bodies, not by descendants. Descendants sell, and trusts preserve carelessly.

As we were walking away I thought of the day eighteen or nineteen years ago when Cecil first took me to Cobham as a little boy. I was staying at the Oast House, and Irene was there too. I had never, until today, been in the courtyard of the college or looked through the glass screen into the great hall. It was all exactly the same. I remembered Cecil's light laugh, a little patronising, a little humble. She was bored with sightseeing and only came to such places to keep me amused and interested, yet at the same time she wished she could enjoy more.

12 June

So many little things have happened and none are written down. I have been in bed nearly all the time. To begin with, Eric was injecting me with penicillin every four hours. We almost got used to the business; only after it was over did I realize what a relief it was not to be pricked. I don't know how he did it so well or so often; surely it must be difficult to bring oneself to push steel needles into human thighs.

Just before I grew worse I had to cut Irene off one Sunday on the telephone, because she was so unbelievably stupid. She had offended and outraged everyone by her ridiculous fussing over the unimportant details of Cecil's Will. Connie's companions both say that she treats them like schoolchildren and that if she doesn't change they will go. They are ordered and managed from morning till night.

Irene is a combination of suspiciousness, greed, calculation, exploitation, religious conviction, moral superiority all knit together, pierced through and soaked in stupidity. And she was the person I admired above all in my schooldays.

After my rudeness on the telephone there was a silence of several weeks; but then she began writing again, telling me that if ever Cecil's Georgian teapot came into her hands I should have it at once, and that it would be so nice to have me understanding and sympathetic again.

The three letters I have written back have all started off so much more warmly than they have finished; somehow, as I wrote, the criticisms formed themselves and mounted in strength. It was as if I started the letter in the spirit of the schoolboy she knew, and ended it in the character of a condemning schoolmaster. But it doesn't seem to matter; she always writes back as if she couldn't tell the difference between praise and blame.

13 June

Last night I had a rather wonderful dream. I was in a lofty dimly lighted old hospital ward; nurses moved about silently and rapidly, sometimes murmuring a word to a patient here and there.

Beside my own bed stood a Roman Catholic priest, and behind him were two other cloudy people, perhaps an attendant priest and a staff nurse or matron. He was a little ferrety man with large rimless glasses and a rapt, tortured expression.

He seemed to bless me with embarrassing depth of feeling; then, still murmuring something, he put his first and second fingers into my mouth and held the points of them against the roof of my mouth very delicately. He was looking up to heaven murmuring faster now. His pale face was beginning to be dewed with sweat.

Gradually a most delicious tingling began to spread through all my body from the point in my mouth which the priest's fingers touched. In spite of

331

this surging pleasure, I was dimly ashamed of being the priest's patient or victim. I felt that he was a man I could not help despising a little. I was in a false position. He must feel that I loved him for the miracle he was performing, whereas I really felt, deep down, only a pale disgust for him and the thing he was doing to me.

After some moments of this uneasy ecstasy, the priest lifted his two fingers to Heaven, then blessed me and left. The nice staff nurse or sister at once came up to me and said, "You are healed, isn't it wonderful! You are healed!"

I could hardly believe it, and kept saying: "Healed for the moment, healed for the moment," to myself. Indeed my whole attitude in the high hospital ward was a grudging and humiliated one; yet I had affection for the nice sister and even felt something like respect for the priest, in spite of my distaste or rather through it.

Now that I was healed, I must have wanted to get away at once from all signs of pain and illness; for I next found myself in the wings of a vast theatre. I had run there deliriously expecting to find all the friends I did. Valerie White (a girl I had known at the art school, who has since become quite a well-known actress) was there. I had never particularly cared for her, but now I was polite and kind and happy, and she was too.

I flitted from group to group of gay friendly people. I explored all the strange heights and depths behind a stage. I danced most of the way, spinning, tumbling, kicking, to exercise my new-found joy in movement to the full. I was singing too, letting the wild excitement ripple off my tongue.

Then just as I was in a low, wide corridor hung with choking draperies of cotton, a sort of dust-sheet decoration, grim and hopeless, just as I was beginning to feel tired and very thirsty, someone appeared dressed as Hamlet in tight black velvet. He carried a wide stumpy crystal goblet frosted with cold. He was rather short, or perhaps the wide shoulders made him look stocky. His face was squarish — lips, nose, eyes, the cut of his dark hair. Although I have never seen anyone like him in real life, he was immediately, I knew, my best friend. He knew it too, and offered me the goblet with a gay flourishing gesture, as if he were laughing at himself.

I took it in both hands and drank the inky purple liquid; it was loganberry juice — something I have not had since I was seventeen. It seemed that I could never have enough of the ice-cold deliciousness. I drank and drank and looked over the rim of the goblet at My Best Friend. Why did he seem to wear this invisible label? He was smiling at me, laughing with me; we seemed in complete accord, yet I could tell at a glance that we were very different types of people. This seemed to make his graciousness all the more precious. I found myself thinking wildly of ways in which I could be of service to *him*. I stretched out my hand to him, he stretched out his hand to me; we were about to do some stamping, strutting, military dance, when he dropped his stage bravado, ran up to me and urged me to leave, in a low serious voice that cut across all our former gaiety.

The dream faded as we both fled on tiptoe, our fingers to our lips. But in spite of this ballet-dancer's ending, there was real regret in both of us. We seemed to be acting this stealth and anxiety to cover up the fact that we must part at the stage door.

The whole dream was extraordinarily vivid and joyful, and remains as a valuable memory.

18 June, 8.30 a.m.

Last Wednesday evening when Eric had taken Evie to Ditchling and I was all alone here attending to the frame of one of my pictures, I suddenly heard my own name in a book talk on the wireless. I had only heard it once before, when my first book was published. The man, Woodrow Wyatt, only mentioned it with those of a few other writers he thought interesting, but it gave me great pleasure — perhaps especially since I was all alone in the house.[5] I hugged it to me, as if my own name were a Christmas or a birthday surprise.

19 June

Last week I had six copies of *Maiden Voyage* in German. So sad it was on its grey lavatory paper on which steel filings seemed to glint. The binding, too, one felt might split in half if one attempted to open the book to read. But I can't read any German.

Then I had a letter from my translator; it was a touching letter. He is sixty years old and was interned on the Isle of Man in the last war. He has written a book about the British and their Empire, and also novels. He says my book arouses great interest in Germany. They have published five thousand. He regrets that they are not allowed to publish another five thousand.

I have two letters and a postcard from readers in America. One of the readers, called Walker Mallam Ellis, has written to me before, but his last letter had one or two obscenities in it — strange since he was not swearing at me — and my answer was a little light, so I did not think I should hear again. This time [*sentence unfinished*]

---

5 Editor of *English Story*. Shortly after the talk, he rejected "Evergreen Seaton-Leverett" (see 1944, note 34 above) and "Leaves From a Young Person's Notebook", published in *Brave and Cruel*.

25 July. Five to eight p.m.

Yesterday the postman called up to me in the morning that there was a parcel for me, but it was too much for him to carry with the letters so he would bring it in the afternoon. This set me wondering, but not very much. I thought it might be food from America or books from Peggy Kirkaldy. But when the afternoon came and I was painting my water-colour flower piece, Eric ran up to me with a parcel that clinked. I grew rather excited, put down my paint brush and began to tear off the paper. I uncovered a biscuit tin. Opening this I came to cotton wool. I pulled it up, and there was the tarnished gleam of silver, and the bright colours of pottery.

I picked one of the tiny little silver utensils up, a tea pot I think. It was obvious at once that it was early eighteenth-century. Excitement and pleasure really flooded over me then. There were four miniature silver objects; one was a tankard embossed with acanthus leaves round the bottom. The lid had a little thumb piece as real ones have. It was fully marked. I felt that it was late seventeenth-century, and as soon as I could look the marks up I found it was 1690.

The other three pieces were made by the same maker. They were only marked with a lion, but everything about them placed them between 1720 and 1730. There was a coffee pot, the only broken piece, the spout needed soldering. It had a lovely little turned ebony handle at the side and was very tall, with a straight spout. The tea pot was gourd shaped, bulging out at the bottom, also straight spouted; the other piece was a mug with delicately twirling handle.

I was so fascinated by these lovely little rarities that I couldn't pay the pottery much attention at first. It was peasanty and bright, rather like the stuff from Brittany. But afterwards I saw that it had its charm and was less usual than I had supposed at first sight. There was also a white blown-glass coffeepot with a cup, saucer and spoon.

Only later did I discover a letter under the cotton wool. This lovely surprise was from Mildred Bosanquet, who had been to tea on Tuesday.

She had given them to me to put in the dolls' house, which of course also came from her.

I am wondering if she realises how valuable the early silver toys are. I myself have never seen them anywhere except in the shop in Albermarle Street, which deals in tiny antique things. There, less attractive things were pounds each. What would they ask for those perfect little pots and tankards? I still keep gazing at them and mumuring, "William and Mary, George the First," to myself.

7 August. Ten to nine p.m.

Yesterday I was in much pain until the evening when Jack Easton came and gave me morphia and atropine. Even the presence of a doctor was comforting; I could feel that, and yet every time I hate calling one just as much.

When he had gone away I floated off, not to sleep but into a pleasant stupor where I heard the infants squawking and screaming outside the cottage at the end of the orchard, heard the birds and the aeroplanes, but didn't care anything about them. The killing pain lost its grip, became playful even, nagging a little, jabbing, dancing, settling down at last to a comfortable thrumming.

Later when Eric came in to me, I opened my eyes and smiled. Something made me pick up a bit of mirror and hold it above my head.

My lips were thick and warm and red, my lids thick and creamy. Underneath, my eyes looked happy and deliciously sleepy. My whole face seemed transformed by my drowse.

11 August, 3.30 p.m.

Last week someone called Style came to tea. I had written to him about the big dolls' house, since he has an antique shop in Maidstone. He was nice, easy, early to middle thirties, and very rich, of course, since his father, the brewer, had died two years ago and left him several hundred thousand pounds and a lot of land. He had sold the place at Boxley and moved to Westeringbury Place (which his great uncle had left in the 1880s, I think). It is rather a fine eighteenth-century house which I have often seen over its high stone wall; but he tells me there is another huge piece behind added in 1862.

He described the things he had bought for this house, two fine Adam mantels of pink terracotta, wall hangings which have been rolled up in a damp cellar for forty years. They originally came from Italy. He had managed too to track down the sofa and the chairs from the Oxon Hoath drawingroom. They are the chief things I remember when I went to tea there in 1939. The chairs are very broad, the backs latticed. The sort of Chippendale that is half Chinese and half Gothic — made for an orangery, he thinks.

The sofa he got in Tonbridge, the chairs he got at last in London; he had to give over £200 for them.

He wants to go over to see the house as soon as he gets back from somewhere in about ten days time. He has also bought a house in Yeoman's Row, and has found a little panelled room.

At Wateringbury there are grapes and peaches and waterfalls and statues — in fact everything a garden needs.

Style told me that in the little ornamental thatched cottage on the other side of the road, Lord Cornwallis had lodged his Indian hostages in the late eighteenth century. Was this something to do with Tippoo Sahib? Then other Italians had had it. Finally a man had gone to live there whose wife had many wonderful jewels which were lodged in London. The man thought that he would go one day to get the jewels, so he took a coach and pair and set off. Neither the man, the jewels, the coach or the horses were ever seen again.

I retell his story so badly, because it was just tossed off to me — I shall try to hear more — but I describe him, his house and the meeting poorly because I feel angry and impatient all the time I am writing. It seems that nothing flows. I have been able to do nothing for four days, and now I want to do nothing, yet hate idleness. I have to push my pen through wads of cotton-wool, and outside the men are emptying the cesspool.

I was sent *New Writing* yesterday. I opened it when I woke, telling myself not to use my eyes at all, only to glance; then I suddenly saw a reproduction of my "Woodman's Cottage", after I had looked at all the other pictures. Before I quite realized it was by me, I felt pleased and thought "that is the nicest picture here". It is one of the few times when I have come unexpectedly on a piece of myself and been given pleasure.

12 *August. Five to five p.m.*

Mildred Bosanquet has just written to say that the little silver pots and tankards came from her husband Geoffrey's family; she found them in a secret drawer in a davenport that had belonged to her sister-in-law. I wonder how long they had been there unknown to anyone?

Last night I was looking idly at a review in the *Times Literary Supplement* of the miscellany *Modern Reading*. I came upon the words "— and there are agreeable verses from Mr Denton Welch and others". "Agreeable verses" sounded so very graceful and delicate. I felt I had produced some pretty trifle for the *Lady's Magazine* of 1808.

18 *August, 7.5. p.m.*

A Mr Edward Dunn, a business friend of Pauls's and Bill's, has just been to tea with a nice red-haired girlfriend, Enid something. He asked himself, saying that he was determined to see and take a report back to my brothers.

They had difficulty in finding the way and turned into the Archdales' bungalow at the end of the orchard. The taxi was long and black and glistening. Eric guessed it was for us. It was confusing going to the hedge and asking them to come round. I busied myself arranging the chairs, so that I should not have too far to walk to meet them.

He was all in white socks, shorts, shirt. The day was very hot. He had brought a hundred turkish cigarettes, two enormous peaches from Holland, five bars of chocolate and a bunch of bananas. I felt rather overwhelmed. He called me Denton at once.

He told me that my brother Bill had just got remarried to someone called Judy Lambert. They had found what he described as a fine Californian-Spanish house outside Hong Kong. It was long and low with garages, a laundry and drying room. (Why did he tell me specially of these?)

He said that he worked in very well with both my brothers; they understood one another. Then he described several concerns in which they were interested. Why does "Business" always sound faintly dishonourable and shifty? The business men are always so bent on presenting it in quite another light. It is that one discounts their rosy stories, swinging over too much to the other side? Or does one just still suffer from the age-old snobbery which considers trade dirty, in spite of the fact that all the kings and grandsons of the past engaged in it as much as anyone else?

He asked me to call him Eddy. The Enid girl called him Ed. She was confused at tea, because he called her "Gutsy" when she liked the tomato sandwiches. She felt he was too intimate, and he made matters worse by turning to me and talking about "where we live in Curzon Street". She laughed and hummed and wanted to stuff her hand-bag down his mouth.

When he got up to give her a cigarette, he contrived somehow to make a little scene, in which he rushed at her and ruffled her hair. I was interested, wondering just what the relationship was. I think he is being her sugar daddy for a little while, while he is in London and she is showing him the sights. He has not been home for ten years. He is forty-four (she told Eric), she about 25.

She resented him a little. There was a definite gentle underground warfare. I thought it was going to be embarrassing at one moment, that they might really argue in front of us, but it smoothed itself out.

He was friendly and easy and unaware. She was friendly, nervous and sensitive. She made my picture of her situation even more complicated at the end by telling me that she was going up to Girton in the autumn to study economics.

When Eric took her into the vegetable garden to pick her a bunch of sweet peas, Ed began to ask me if there was anything he could do for me. What did he mean? I took it that he meant, did I want to send an urgent message to my brothers for money. Somehow money seemed to be lurking in the background. I floundered rather, murmuring that, so far, I had managed by painting and writing to make ends meet fairly well, together with my tiny income. "You should come out to see us sometime, Denton," he said.

I mentioned my peculiar health. He said it only took four days to fly. I asked how much the fare was.

"It's not bad," he said. "About £300."

When they went away I had a happy feeling. An incongruous afternoon had smoothed itself out delicately and well. The man had brought a hard, secure feeling of well-being, the woman a sympathetic, appreciative one. Eric had felt at home and easy. I had been comfortable.

And the meeting rested on nothing but the rather precarious well-wishing by the man.

People that make and spend money quickly, freely, give one the released feeling one has with some priests. Because they are so set and sure, the priest can joke with one about sacred matters. So these people joke and slap their God, money, irrelevantly. One feels that it is not a terrible God, that it flows. One feels that a wave will sweep up to the front door, leaving there all one could want in a neat sealed envelope.

2 September, 6.30 p.m.

I have just heard a talk on Tom Hennell on the wireless, given by Vincent Lines. Although he was seen in a more solemn, reverent light, the talk reminded me so much of him and of that afternoon last year when I called on Miss Nangle and, after first blinking at me, unknowingly, she asked me into his long room, "exactly as he had left it" as she explained to me. There were the brown, slack easy chairs and sofa, and drawings everywhere in large portfolios, "just as he had left them", for him never to come back to. He was mad and smug and narrow, far more interested in the ornamental top-knots on haystacks than in the charming Empire clock which stood on his mantelpiece. The design of the clock interested him so little that he had stuck a hideous little cast statuette of Joan of Arc on top. It offended me so much when I first went to tea that I found myself saying, "What a lovely old clock, but the statue doesn't really belong. Doesn't it look better without it?" Impatiently I stood up and lifted the statue off.

It was only when Tom took the statue from me and replaced it with hard, smiling finality that I realized how self-complacent and set were his ideas. He always knew; the notions of others were usually trivial and wrong-headed. But in spite of all this, in spite of his sudden blusterings and temper, which made me afraid that madness might be descending on him again, hearing of him tonight heartened me, hopened me; I don't know why, since his whole life was thrown away when the head-hunting Indonesians took him into the mountains and left him to roam in the jungle until he died or they killed him. It heartened me, I suppose, because right up to this final pointless waste he was working, scheming, musing, dreaming — not at all in a way I felt whole-hearted sympathy for, but I, who today have not been able to do anything, jumped at the very thought of anyone so interested in doing, so confident (outwardly) in his own productions. For a moment it was encouraging, settling, to think of Tom busy with his stored-up life to the horrible end.

Irene has at last let me have some of Cecil's things. Four family portraits; the earliest a tiny head (monochrome, washes of Indian ink, I suppose). It is of Gerald Piffard, done in 1810 at Versailles by a travelling Swiss artist, when the sitter was thirteen. He never lived to grow up. He looks out, his wind-swept hair, his man's cravat and high-collared coat fixed as long as the ink and paper last — nothing else left to show that he ever was.

The other three are watercolours — the face done with a miniature technique; the biggest, a picture of a child in long pantaloons, blue striped frock, black sash, black bow, huge black hat with ostrich feathers. To the right is a red collie with button eyes and nose. Behind, vague trees and bushes. This is Antoine Piffard, Cecil's uncle, or so Irene tells me. There is another older child in blue-striped smock or frock, but this picture is much less interesting, since there is no background.

The last one is of a serene, rather beautiful woman, with a decided look of Cecil. Perhaps it is her grandmother. She sits on a puce-coloured early-Victorian sofa against the wall, part of the panels of a door on her left, two ancestors in gilt frames on the right. She has sleek, black hair, parted in the middle. She wears a white lace cap. Her dress is very rich and sombre — black satin with stripes of sable reaching from the throat to the ground. She clasps a book and looks straight at you tentatively, smiling. Her teeth show a little, her large eyes are delicately ringed with bluey-green.

On the back of the paper is Whatman's (?) watermark for 1840, and the little boy with no background has the initials I.W. and 1842 at the bottom, so all three are dated fairly certainly.

When I have finished cleaning and re-framing them I want to hang all four in my bedroom, together on one wall. What would they think, all four forgotten people, if they knew that a stranger was at last cherishing their pictures after years of neglect in Cecil's apple room and loft?

13 September, 6.45 p.m.

We have found one more family picture of Cecil's; it was in a drawer of the sideboard that hasn't been opened for years, because it is so heavy and awkward. Everything was covered with thick, brownish dust. The picture is of Cecil's great-grandmother, one of the very same pictures that appear in the painting of her grandmother (on the wall to the right).

I recognise at once the folded hands and the mob-cap. The only difference is that when the painter of the grandmother included the great-grandmother on the wall behind her, he enlarged her picture, making it fit a square instead of its real oval, I suppose because he could not manage to indicate anything in an oval that would be to scale with the rest of the grandmother's picture.

At the same time, in the same drawer, we found the two oval mezzotints that Cecil promised me several years ago, when she gave me the two smaller prints that always hung with them on either side of the Cheyne Walk fireplace. These two are lovely eighteenth-century red-brown prints by Bartolozzi or some other fine engraver. They are of "A Lady in a Turkish Dress" and "The Duchess of Richmond", also in Turkish clothes, near a tambour, with a design on her lap. I think the date on one is 1775, but the painter's and engraver's name can't be seen, because the titles have been cut off the prints and stuck on the back since the eighteenth century, so they are now quite dark, grey and worn.

The pictures are in their original Hogarth frames; both have cracked through at the bottom. I am having to stick them and clean the glass and frames and backing. The backing too is original — a sort of elegant wooden stretcher with canvas and paper on the front. The frames had been opened, renailed and pasted several times. I found one bit of newspaper, three layers down, talking of Lord John Russell and Reform, so I suppose it must date from the early eighteen-thirties.

Last Sunday Eric went to Hadlow Castle. The peculiar parson, Richard Blake Brown, who wrote to me so much last year, had got the key from the caretaker. I didn't go because it would have been too exhausting. R.B.B. brought with him his old Cambridge friend, Norman Hartnell. Eric said Hartnell was good-natured and fat; he sat and watched while Eric and the clergyman climbed the 150 foot tower. He had gold watch, cigarette case and signet ring, giving him a rather prosperous and commercial air; but he wouldn't talk about his dress-designing although pressed by the parson to divulge the cut of Princess Elizabeth's khaki bloomers. R.B.B. is like this all the time; the naughty remark has to be dragged out and flogged whenever there is the slightest opening.

He came to tea on Wednesday to meet me for the first time. He had on one of those sad ties of bright scarlet, decorated with large foxheads. He had stiff, curly, grey hair and rather a nice expression.

14 September, 1.20 p.m. Gover Hill in the rain.

All my hard bones go wild with music notes, here in the rain. The fibres tremble with the whipping leaves. To be alone in the car with sandwiches and coffee and a Turkish cigarette! So snugly alone that the world is the car, and the wood, the road, the view stung with rain, the rest of the universe. I have been reading in the *Times Literary Supplement* about the Portuguese in Asia in the sixteenth century. I have been thinking of my mother who died twenty years ago. In years to come, when I shall be older than she was when she died, it will be as if I were her elder brother; then, later still, her father. It will be as if an old tree had sprung out of a young tree. It will not seem at all suitable. On my handkerchief I have stale eau-de-cologne from Paris which

I sniffed up my nose before I came out, to wake up my eyes and head.

Later

As I was driving home by the Pilgrim's Way above Wrotham Water I came upon a mass of scarlet and red in the corner of a field, that I first mistook for a bright new farm implement. Then as I drew nearer I saw that the mass was soft and not shiny. I then half-explained it to myself as a bundle or folded tent belonging to some very brilliant gypsy. Only when I was almost upon it did I realize that the heap was a man and woman lying in each other's arms on the stiff dried-up grass. They seemed perfectly still, locked and twisted together intricately — the black legs and arms of the man over the vivid scarlet sausage of the girl's dress. I wondered if they would always remember this Sunday, or whether it would be lost in a vast heap of other clinging, clutching, hugging holidays. Below them the cars rushed by on the arterial road; a man got out of a high old-fashioned Morris, clutched up a handful of yellow flowers and thrust them through the top of the almost shut window to fall on the head of an unheeding child.

20 September. Five to eleven p.m.

I heard them singing "Bye bye, Blackbird", "He can go and get another that I hope he will enjoy", while they were walking home from the pub; and one of them had an accordion that lazed and whined and droned and skipped. All their gypsy, hop-picker feet shuffled and danced; their voices rang out in the soft damp air, with large drops falling from the orchard trees. They fell like skeleton feet breaking the night, or robber's feet in a wood. All was still except the drops from the trees and their voices.

23 October, 11 p.m.

As I looked out into the wet dark night, I longed bitterly for my strength and health, nothing more, just the old things I had lost and am almost too ashamed ever to write about. One can lose them for a little; one can wait with beautiful patience; but when it comes to lying day after day, hardly daring to look at anything for fear of restarting the pain in one's head, [*sentence unfinished*]

2 November, morning.

Now, after all those days of waste when Eric did everything for me, so that, even in my dulled inhuman state, I understood the incalculable value of his attention, I can look out a little, think, talk, eat. And all my thoughts are of lovely food and buildings — everything as material, as magnificent as possible.

Now, after breakfast, just after Eric had put the thermometer in my mouth, I was suddenly surprised by a rattle against the wall. On looking up I saw that one of the eighteenth-century Chinese glass pictures I had bought last year at the Victor Cazalet sale at Fairlawne was bouncing on the wall as if pushed from behind. I jumped out of bed to save it, for the picture hook was already twisting on the rail.

I held the picture and called to Eric. We could not understand what had happened till we saw that one of the sides of the frame had become unstuck and sprung back against the wall. We quickly got the precious picture down.

Is this one of the narrowest escapes of the two-hundred-year-old mirror plate with its shallow, silky soft bevelling? I gloat on it now in bed beside me. I shall stick the frame when I'm well. I have a temp. of 99° which makes even writing this a fight, a run uphill, an [*sentence unfinished*]

4 November, 7.0 a.m.

Eric's ducks are quacking in their house. It is early mist, and yellow where the sun has risen. Far away busyness on the main road, humming. My violent headaches in the morning have gone, leaving only their shadows behind. Sweet-peas are pretty by my bed. Oh morning, build up into goodness, so that I can eat, think, work, enjoy.

17 November

Awful days and nights since I last wrote. High fever all the time. The first night of this new attack, I was in so much pain that Eric gave me a morphia injection. Then I floated off wonderfully because the wireless was playing Mendelssohn's violin concerto in E. I floated away on this lovely music. Every day after that I was just drowsy, aching in a high temperature for more than a week.

All through this time the agents were fixing up an agreement with Hamish Hamilton, my new publisher, about my book of new short stories.[6] I spoilt it all by saying that I thought the longest story, "Brave and Cruel," libellous. Hamish Hamilton agreed, and now it all hangs fire, with me still in bed, able to do nothing properly and wondering what to begin on.

I don't want to think of writing any more. It is a deadness and a worry.

---

6 *Brave and Cruel*, which Hamish Hamilton were planning to publish. Edith Sitwell had recommended Denton to her own agents, Pearn, Pollinger and Higham.

18 November

Hamilton writes that he doesn't want to sacrifice "Brave and Cruel" since it is such a good story and adds so to the bulk of the book. He seems to want to get round the libel difficulty somehow. I felt heartened; but I still don't know what he is going to do. If it's libellous to describe Monte's being sent to prison, I suppose it will always remain so. Short of writing a quite new story, I can't really disguise the present one at all.[7]

Brown also asks me to send something new to the New Year show at the Leicester — this in spite of not selling anything of mine this summer. Again I felt heartened. I don't know why because writing and painting both seem impossibly difficult to me at the moment. I feel wrapped in a deadening blanket, just able to eat and think dully. I spell words wrong and muddle them up and feel unbelievably tired after writing one letter.

It is snow today and bitter cold, so that my fingers keep on turning white and numb.

19 November

The snow has gone, but it is still so cold. I had presents of books from Peggy Kirkaldy, and food from Aunt Dolly, jelly, muscatel raisins, crystallized fruits, just what I want. When people are good to me I feel dead, not alive enough to thank them properly.

25 December, Christmas Day. Five to nine a.m. Grey but clear; sun later perhaps.

Eric has given me a lovely glass mustard pot in the shape of an urn with square base. On the sides are cut stars and nicks out of the ribbing. It is quite perfect — no chips anywhere. The cover is very tall and hollow, so that the mustard spoon can fit inside. I keep thinking of it when it was new, in the late eighteenth century. I think of it standing on the white damask, coming down through all the hundred and fifty years safely to me.

On the 19th was the sale of Cecil Carpmael's things at the Oast House. Most of the things I knew at Cheyne Walk are now scattered; the heavy late-Regency sideboard with its large lion head handles, the dog's coffin cellaret. I bought the two ormolu sconces that hung above the sideboard; but now I find that they are too heavy for the walls, too coarse for my room. They have fat cupids, two sleeping, one throwing grapes on top of the other two. Perhaps they are French, Louis Philippe's time. They would look well in a coarse, rich room.

---

7 The story had been taken from events that occured in August 1943. Monte's real name was Bone. He masqueraded as Francis de Montaigne, and Denton called him Micki Beaumont (see 1943, note 23 above).

Eric met Graham Sutherland at the gate and Sutherland was very pleasing and modest, insisting on talking only about my work. I remember him like this too. It made me a little uncomfortable. He told Eric that he had heard someone talking about me to Somerset Maugham, and Somerset Maugham had said that I was a very good writer indeed, or something of that sort. How peculiar it feels to write it down! In wonder what really was said, how many qualifying clauses were added? Sutherland, in an excess of polite flattery, added, "I don't know whether Denton will take this as a compliment or not."

Hamish Hamilton is going to publish my stories after all. I have made slight changes in the offending one, and he now thinks there is no danger.

Eric went to London yesterday with two pictures for the Leicester Galleries. Just to write these plain statements down gives me a feeling that something has been done, some effort made. And yet the book may be a failure, the pictures unnoticed and unsold. Working is stepping into the dark and making each tiny happening into a sign.

26 December

Yesterday after breakfast Eric began to cook the potatoes and our own brussels sprouts. He put the plum pudding to boil on the tiny stove in the studio, and he made delicious, but unorthodox, chestnut stuffing, with sage and onion in it too. I made hard sauce with butter and sugar and almond essence, because there was no brandy.

We had a little tin of turkey from America, and this Eric creamed and turned into turkey à la King.

We arranged the meal upstairs in my room. I pulled the flap of the bureau down and laid it with the new coloured tablecloth from Eric's sister. It is a sort of plaid of mauve, orange, green and pink. On it I placed the old white porcelain crab candlesticks with ormolu mounts, and in them I fitted green candles. There were tangerines and apples in a Kang-shi blue-and-white mortar. Sweets in the Georgian salt-cellars and delicate elaborate old sugar scissors with which to pick them up.

Afterwards we decided to go for a drive, my first time out since October. But the ignition had not been switched off, so we had to get the Redford children to help us push the car till we came to the hill.

At last it started and Eric and I went towards Gover Hill. It was already almost twilight. We circled down to West Peckham, past Yates Court, Mereworth. We saw shadowy German prisoners looking back at us as we passed, wanting some Christmas excitement, but we did not stop or ask any of them back to tea; I had too little energy left for broken English and nervous, straining smiles.

Soon it was quite dark. When at last we reached the main road between East and West Malling, Eric took over the wheel. I sat back tired. The rain began to beat again. I could see nothing out of the wind-screen.

As we turned into Seven Mile Lane, I saw a German sheltering under the railway arch. He, too, looked up expectantly, as if he longed for some slight happening to while away the hours.

The roads were almost deserted. In all our drive we only saw two other cars.

29 December. Ten to eleven a.m.

I have been out every day since Boxing Day. We went to Cobham first, in pale sunlight. We sat in the car and drank maté tea and ate coffee-chocolate. Across the fields we could just see Cobham Hall hidden in the trees. I felt curiously revived and fresh to be out in the world again.

The next day we picnicked in a field between East and West Malling. The rain was pouring down, the wind whistling amazingly through the wires on the hop-poles; and we drank rich mock-turtle soup out of the thermos and gazed through the streaming windows.

Yesterday we went to Goudhurst. It was grey, with the sun showing through the clouds like a watery moon. We saw old houses bowed down with decay, impossibly crooked. Why do these fill one with such a sense of wonder? Their craziness defies common sense and so we are pleased, is that it? I do not mean that I dote on their quaintness; but I stare and stare at the gable that might fall off, the mullioned window that might cave in, the chimney stack that leans like a tree blown by the wind.

31 December, 10.45 a.m.

Hector Bolitho has written to say that he has given my name to the Mayor of Auckland, so that I shall receive one of the Mayor's Christmas parcels. This explains the mysterious letter, telling me to expect two tins of dripping, one tin sheep's tongue, one tin pork luncheon, one tin steak-and-kidney pudding. We had it before Bolitho's letter and could not understand how the Mayor had got my address. The parcel hasn't arrived yet.

The Mayor finished: "I trust sincerely that you have a happy Christmas and that the New Year may bring relief from your present hardships"!

I also had a letter this morning from a Peter Verreker of University Union, Park Place, Edinburgh. He says, "I bought and read your autobiography *Maiden Voyage* the other day. It quite overbalanced me, and I had the sensation similar, I imagine, to that of the traditional shipwreckee who sights a sail after many years of isolation." He says my sensual passages excite him almost too much. *Which are these?* There is a lot more which I am too lazy to write down.

I find, in answering this sort of letter, I feel stiff and dry. How can I flow and glow as he has seemed to do? On first reading, the letter excites my vanity, makes me think, "Well, at least I've pricked one person a little more alive for a moment!" Then I sink back and find I have nothing for the unknown person except a lukewarm gratitude strongly tinged with suspicion and a vague distaste.

1948

RAYNER HEPPENSTALL has written to say that the B.B.C. want me to do some sort of feature programme for the Third Programme. How tremendously dull this plain statement will sound in the years to come! I write it because it is a smooth cover for all the other things that are so difficult to put down — how it comes over me suddenly that my life is really too limited to bear. I can do nothing without fearing the effect on my body. When I see others twice, sometimes almost thrice, my age running to catch buses, gaily digging flower beds, beating mats, painting walls, my eyes go beady and hard. "They've nothing to worry about," I think coldly. I snarl to myself over all the hours I have to waste, lying with my handkerchief over my eyes. I wonder if I am living for an improvement, or if that hope has really died in me and I'm only pretending to do so.

Frustration like this has never come to me before. There is so much sensible, obvious reason for feeling it that I am made helpless. I used to think that encouragement, appreciation could help me to do better and better, could keep me happy and busy all day long. Now they are bitter goads prodding me to impossible tasks. There should be many new words for what I mean, words that don't whine and pity. But now, if one does not use whining or self-pitying words, there is only the dreadfulness of cheerful optimism.

Later

Eric has gone to bed early, the rain flushes and swishes against the wooden walls, the orchard trees sigh and rush — I can see them jiggering, mad black twigs, like mentally defective [*word illegible*] playing "dolls" with their fingers. Nina Milkina plays Chopin's Nocturne in C sharp minor on the wireless. I am a seed here, a worm that must lie in a warm bed. And round me blackness seethes; the lonely roads, the fields, the houses are desolately stewed in it.

1 February, 8 a.m.

Rayner Heppenstall came on Friday to lunch. We had it here in my room. The rain beat down on the panes, the wind shook the walls. He seemed slow, almost drugged; he had the sort of composure that puts one at a disadvantage, if one is afraid of gaps in the conversation. One rushes in with trite things, with anything to break the dreadful, imposed, uneasy Buddha calm.

He was dressed in rough, heatherish tweeds, whose hairiness made him look all the punier and more waspish. The salmon-red tie brought out the yellow paleness of his skin. One felt this skin would match his teeth. The bony fingers of one hand looked scorched, as if he wore a glove which had been in the oven too violently. He smoked nearly all the time, holding his elbow high up, on a level with his mouth, hand and cigarette. His eyelids seemed often to be sliding down, like rather sluggish drops of porridge.

7 February, morning. 7.30.

Yesterday we went to a preview of a sale at the Ponds, Brenchley. It was a day of wild changes; the sun shone brilliantly, then the rain came down mixed with sleet, the sky grew blacker and blacker, there was thunder, and, after the thunder, sun again.

Eric drove, and we had Noël Adeney in the car, since she and Bernard had come down to spend the weekend in the studio. I sat at the back, the fur-lined coat round me, the rug over me and my feet perched up on a cushion on top of the picnic basket. The cold air blew on my face. I felt delightfully comfortable lying there, gazing out at the country. It was strange and wonderful and new to be doing something like this again, to be dressed in my Donegal tweed suit, a new grey roll-neck sweater and a yellow scarf. The only thing that reminded me of illness was the difficulty I had in moving. Ever since Jack's lumbar puncture last year I've had to move about with painful care. If I don't, terrible pains shoot through me. He first said he might have split a cartilage (when he did the puncture) but now he doesn't like to talk about his mistake, and tells me that the aches and pains are probably due to the original accident, when I fractured my spine. Of course they aren't but I say nothing. I only wonder when I shall be able to walk again with comparative ease. I do feel it that the *doctor* has added one more trouble to my list! One resents it specially coming from that quarter. I should feel easier if I thought it was melting away, but it isn't. And of course, to be sick is quite out of the question. One just feels as if one was being torn apart by wild apes. But enough of that health talk; the words always seem ugly and rubbishy when I write of states of health. I don't flow with my words at all, they express so little and that incorrectly.[1]

So I had set out to describe our visit to Brenchley. We came upon the

1 A lumbar puncture is a routine operation, carried out with a local anaesthetic, for the removal of cerebrospinal fluid from the spinal canal, sometimes because too much fluid is being formed and sometimes, as was almost certainly the reason in Denton's case, for diagnosis of the fluid to determine infection. It is also a method of introducing spinal anaesthetics or drugs. It was from progressive uraemia that Denton was suffering his feverish attacks, and his history of urinary infection, and eventually a diagnosis of tuberculosis of the spine, made Dr Easton's decision to perform a lumbar puncture perfectly feasible.

Ponds suddenly; a long line of cars gave us the clue. It was raining so violently at this moment that the car shook and steadied itself like a boat. We stopped at the end of the queue of cars and began to unpack our picnic. Huddled together under the dripping roof we drank scotch broth from the thermos and ate the sandwiches filled with a sort of foie-gras from Australia — very good. I delighted in the barley at the bottom of my bowl, each grain a tiny palish peach with the crack down the centre.

Afterwards we walked up the new drive of the Ponds, I very slowly, leaning on my stick, hoping to come to an end soon. We passed two little ponds, clearly the reason for the name of the house. But they weren't natural ponds, they were funny wriggling shapes, and they had neat cement rims running all round the edge. Water lilies and irises were imprisoned within these ponds.

The house on the bank above suited the ponds perfectly. Strong, naked, subdued brick, with large stone dressings in peculiar places; a sort of twentieth-century flattened-out Tudor, no carving and decoration, no leaded panes in the stone mullions, only blank plate glass. Indeed, so much of the Tudor style and intricacy has been left out that one wonders why the house had been built in that fashion at all. One can only imagine that the architect was unable to rid his mind of past flourishes, although he had tried very hard to build a perfectly *plain* house.

This plainness on top of the whimsical planning gave one an uncomfortable feeling. It was as if a wedding cake had been stripped of all its sugar cupids and flowers and left, an undecorative lump, exposed to cruel eyes.

But inside this flat, bleak, pointless little house bodies were seething in a stew of cigarette smoke, the walls were covered with old engravings, the cabinets were stuffed with Kang-shai blue-and-white or famille verte, the shiny narrow floor-boards hidden under all kinds of oriental rugs.

I sat down in the drawingroom near a pair of satin-wood sidetables. People kept passing and peering and writing in their catalogues.

11 February, 3.30 p.m.

Grey, my feet a little cold in the car, waiting for Eric outside the Ponds. He has gone to buy a little eighteenth-century worktable and a Persian rug, if he can get either of them; but prices are horrible.

I have just been writing to my great-aunt Blanche whom I have not seen for years.[2] She is partly paralysed and lives with her nurse-housekeeper at Beckenham.

---

2 She had married his paternal grandmother's brother.

The housekeeper rang up the other day and asked Eric if I had used the 'phone at two o'clock that morning. Eric said, "Of course not," then gradually the housekeeper told him the whole story.

It appears that someone who calls himself Joe rings up my aunt constantly. He then asks, "What colour knickers are you wearing, or perhaps you're not wearing any knickers today?" Some variation on this theme always. He has worried them so much that both aunt and housekeeper seem to have lost their sense of balance. I suppose my aunt still thinks of me as a boy, capable of preposterous tricks. The housekeeper told Eric that she thought it might be me because I had been so ill. If the telephone was near my bed I might easily do silly things to while away the hours of the night.

I think Eric convinced her at last that I had not been enquiring about her knickers or my aunt's.

I am wondering now how many other friends and relations have been rung up. Surely some elderly men would be quite outraged at such a question! Eric said that the housekeeper sounded a little nervous at first, but soon repeated the knickers questions with a sort of childish simplicity.

12 February. Ten to eleven a.m.

Sun warm on the back of my head.

I have at last heard from Evie with her address on the letter.[3] She is with an outsize Scotch woman of about eighty, who lives at 23, Albany Gardens West, Clacton-on-Sea, Essex.

Evie, who has surprisingly read some Proust while away, describes her in the words of Madame Guermantes. "I saw a herd of cattle wearing a hat and asking how I was, walking across my drawingroom towards me."

There is a parrot, too. Evie has done a peculiar little watercolour of it — speckled grey body, scarlet tip of tail, deep rich purple-brown background. The pictures of people who do not usually paint are always surprising in some tiny part; there is something there to be used and transformed by the professional artist — a starting point he would not have thought of himself.

17 February

This afternoon, with the red sun sinking down into all its coloured cushion clouds — so cold that the people in the streets seem to be ashamed of their faces — and now here, after Russian tea and two fat chocolates sent

---

3 In October the previous year, relations between Denton and Evie had reached breaking point, and Evie had walked out.

by Pocetta, just arrived from America, Chopin pours over me from the wireless box. Nothing but this small picture will be left of the day; many years after, people may be able to read, then say, "He was cold, he watched the sunset, he ate a chocolate," but nothing more will be left to them.

21 February, 8.45 a.m.

The snow is so thick that it has made great balloons and cushions on the roof and on my balcony. It has spotted all the windows to the south and lies snugly on every sash-bar. The orchard trees are burdened as if they were puddings — decorated with too much white of egg. Everything is so lovely that I only regret the lack of water in the bathroom; no tap works, so I have to wash in the enamel kitchen basin. The plug will not pull. What will it be like if the pipes burst? They didn't last year, although we were without water upstairs for about six weeks.

25 February, morning.

I lay yesterday on the camp bed in the bright hot sun on the veranda, the dazzling snow all round me. Now this morning we discover that the tap in the Adeneys' studio has been pouring water all over the floor; it is about an inch deep. Eric has sent for the plumber. Mrs Reffold, the "help", is turning out the furniture and mopping up. The excitement has broken into my work, although I have done a tiny bit of revision which nagged at me all yesterday. Why does the mind go limp and soggy when confronted with two sentences that are not as they should be ? Why can't one shake one's head and begin anew? It is almost as if the words were strangling one.

27 February, 8.40 a.m.

In Gide's Journal I have just read again how he does not wish to write its pages slowly as he would the pages of a novel. He wants to train himself to rapid writing in it. It is just what I have always felt about this journal of mine. Don't ponder, don't grope — just plunge something down, and perhaps more clearness and quickness will come with practice.

29 February

I had a letter yesterday from my agents to say that they had placed one of my long-short stories, "The Trout Stream",[4] with the *Cornhill*; what did I

---

4 Reprinted in *Brave and Cruel*.

think of a fee of about twenty guineas? In the same post was another letter from a Mr O'Higgins, art editor of *Town and Country* in America.

"When I was in England," he says, "during the war, I greatly admired your literary style, and subsequently saw a number of your drawings which pleased me tremendously. If you ever have manuscripts of short stories which you think might interest us, please do not hesitate to send them to us.

"What I should like to do one day is to feature you as an author-illustrator. If you have any novel on hand which is going to be published in England, I should very much like to see it, because we are often given to buying chapters from such novels and publishing them as such. We recently published Christopher Isherwood's *Lions and Shadows*, and we also ran Evelyn Waugh's *Brideshead Revisited*, which will give you some idea of the range of material we like to use.

"If you have any photostat reproductions of your drawings and paintings, I would very much like to see them. Lastly, may I add that we pay for an article between [sic] two hundred dollars which is the equivalent of £50, and for illustrations we pay approximately seventy-five dollars per drawing."

Why do I copy this all out? It is irksome for me; for anyone else it would be boring reading, yet I seem to want to preserve it, if only to impress it on my mind. So many opportunities are offered to me, so much I can't do or don't do.

1 *March, 8.20 p.m.*

A moment ago I heard the telephone bell ring downstairs. Eric went to answer it. I could hear nothing of the conversation because the wireless was on. Then suddenly he had come into the room and was standing by me; I could tell at once that something had happened. I waited till he had gathered his words together. "Denton," he said at last, "May died on Saturday."

May Walbrand-Evans, whom I have known so well, seen so much of for the last ten years. She had gone into the Tonbridge Cottage Hospital some two or three weeks ago for a slight operation — to do with a prolapse, whatever that may be — and we had gone to see her there on Sunday a fortnight ago. She seemed rather miserable still, lying quite flat, looking as if she had been through an ordeal; but she often assumed a suffering expression when she wanted to fix one's attention on her, so I thought little of it. I understood that the operation was not a serious one and that she would be quite well again in two or three weeks' time. We sat with her talking. We had brought books and dates and barley sugar. She gave Eric a few old coins because she had heard that he was interested.

In the high, shiny, bare little room with no outlook, I felt trapped; my legs ached slightly because I could not put them up. I was sitting on a straight-backed wooden chair. There were azaleas in a pot and cut daffodils and tulips. The tap dripped gently into the hand basin. Above May's head hung the sort of gibbet and chain which is used by patients when turning themselves from one side to another.

The sister came in brightly. "She's looking really very well, isn't she?" We both untruthfully agreed. I even went so far as to say that I had been surprised by her look of health when I first saw her.

That was the last we ever saw of May. We meant to go again on Sunday a week ago, but the snow was so thick that we could not move from here.

On Thursday last we were in Tonbridge and Eric suggested going to see her, but I said that I felt I could not sit there uncomfortably on that particular day. Then on Saturday people came here. It was the day May died.

I was ill on Sunday with a temperature but I suggested Eric should go to see her without me; but he was very busy burning dead wood in the orchard.

Even today there was talk of his going again. Until her daughter-in-law Jill rang up to tell us the news we had had no suspicion that May was in any danger. Nobody expected her death. On Saturday she suddenly went unconscious, and was dead in twenty minutes, before either of her sons could get to her.

I think of her now as she must have been forty years ago, when Lavery painted her all in black as an Edwardian beauty. She had pink roses in her hands and was leaning on a grand piano. Then there is his other portrait of her in a pink balldress with pearls in her hair.

Jill said that she has left me her lovely Queen Anne mirror, in two plates, the upper one engraved, and the broad walnut frame shaped in delicate curves at the top, rather like a decorative gable end.

She has left Eric twelve books. We wonder when she made these bequests. What pleasure it gives to be left something in this way! It has never happened to me before.

Cecil Carpmael's little family portraits and bits of china were given to me by Irene, only after endless waiting and difficulty.

May has died almost exactly a year after Cecil. Cecil too died on a Saturday and we knew nothing of it till Monday. We had also planned to go and see her on several of the days just before she died, but never got there.

I think of May in great cartwheel hats with scarves, in crooks' slouch caps jammed over her eyes, in surprising widows' bonnets with streamers. I see her tiger-skin bootees, her mustard-yellow satchel, the coral and olive green of her one-time best afternoon dress. I see her heavy maquillage masking every inch of her real complexion, the vaseline on her eyelids, the mascara on her lashes.

I remember what a cook she was. The first time I ever had lunch with her there was hot-pot with tiny sausages and mushrooms in it.

16 March, 10.5 p.m.

How I am aware of the thinness, the affectation and strain of what I write! Revising, correcting, is hateful, fishy, shaming. I would knock the posturing out of words, bash them into shape, iron out their obstinate awkwardness. Wishing violence means impotence.

On Saturday, I remember the German in Malling, standing on the pavement in his too-romantic, rush-brown cloak ending in graceful points. With a furtive movement he glanced at himself in a shop-window, then drew out a black comb and sleeked back the close-fitting skull-cap of his fair hair. It was thick, horribly smoothed and trained, catching the light and glinting. It seemed a pathetic little triumph and glory — his golden hair cherished in captivity.

Yesterday, Peter Verreker, who wrote me such immoderate letters from Edinburgh, all about my books and his loneliness, came to lunch, and he was quite sober in a dark suit. We talked sweet platitudes all through the spaghetti and the spinach. Just before he left, when we were alone, he said to me, his smooth pale face puckering with awkwardness, "I say, you mustn't think I'm mad. I must have seemed an awful ass. I've been a naughty boy." Surely "naughty" was an odd word to use! "Silly", "rash", "inexperienced", "impulsive", were more to be expected.

23 April, morning.

Yesterday I had a letter from Count Carlo John Russoni who said that he had stayed up till four a.m. reading *Maiden Voyage*. He seemed to think that it exactly mirrored his own experiences as an adolescent. He needed to feel somebody really near him and my book had made him feel it. "Your book was like a rope thrown out to one in the deep waters. I hope you won't disappoint by showing me that the rope was an end in itself. If I follow the rope I must find you. I hope you will forgive my writing in such an exacting manner. The fact is that I need some help very badly, and it may be your help I need. I have been in your country for six months, and I am afraid I have failed entirely in whatever may have been my purpose in coming here."

He gives me his Florence address: Via Leone X, Firenze, Italy, then finished off, "Try to contact me soon, will you, as in a few weeks it may be too late."

I have asked him down to lunch. One can never stop being a little curious about people who write such letters, they are often so strangely unlike their letters; witness Peter Verreker. Another part of one is only pushed into having them because they seem to expect it. This part is always reluctant, "put upon", ill at ease and irritated, because it is so aware of the disappointment in store for them. How outrageous it is of them to expect an oracle, a miracle or some other equally monstrous thing! And that is exactly what they do expect. Is it only the very simple who write such letters?

The other week Eric and I drove towards Wateringbury Church. We had had some difference and were sitting side by side rather sullenly. Seeing the church, I suddenly said I would like to get out. I wanted to relieve the tension and I hadn't been inside it for several years.

We climbed up the steep path and found the Style tomb with the early eighteenth-century ironwork surround, newly painted and weeded. A large sapling pushing up through the flagstones had just been sawn off.

Inside the church we went straight through to the chancel and saw the other Style memorials. I sat on the altar step and gazed for some time at the great Jacobean pavilion, painted and inlaid with marble, the two recumbent figures making "steeples" with their hands for ever.

We went into the vestry, dark and large, and found four late eighteenth-century hall chairs, large and clumsy, thickly daubed with blistering paint, but attractive with their taper legs and shield backs.

My mind was full of Styles so we wandered out and went up to the narrow gate that lead into David's grounds. Wateringbury Place looked lovely, "stately", "impressive" across the wide smooth lawns. It was more beautiful than I had imagined. The garden was ornamental, with early-Victorian gods and goddesses and urns in some sort of pottery or composition. The yew hedges were clipped tightly, mercilessly.

I crept up into the shadow of one where a peacock was crouching disconsolately. The peacock moved its head about, its heavy body close to the ground, but it would not show its tail. A long line of limes, I think, had just been lopped off halfway up. We looked at them and wondered how they had been done, so high they were and dangerous-looking. One unlopped, one still remained, soaring up and up, and at the very top a rook's nest and rooks circling distractedly. A ladder ran half-way up, then a rope that made one sway to look at it.

Suddenly a shot rang out, terrifying us so that we forgot everything and ran back into the churchyard laughing guiltily. We peered back again through the gate and saw David and his sister walking in the garden. David had a gun under his arm and had evidently been taking pot shots at the rooks. He was talking with his head down and could not have seen us.

We went behind the church and climbed up on a heap of rubbish, bomb-damaged old slates and the broken carcasses of radiators. On the very top of the squalid heap I looked down and saw a dead rook with wings bent out crookedly. I looked away over stone walls to where other lawns swept away and away to a distant wall. To the right we found a water garden, a great square pool with waterfall at one end, more statues, and on the far side all the security and cosiness of an old-fashioned kitchen garden, long orange walls, espaliers, greenhouses. I understood the charm of being rich — even the melancholy and the deadness of it.

We turned away, passing an unusual seventeenth-century tomb carved with skulls, hour-glasses and implements that looked like spades, forks, rakes. It was surrounded with large primulas of different pinks and tawny colours.

The rooks were cawing. Then Eric raised the alarm by saying that he thought David was coming into the churchyard. He did not want to meet him because he did not feel properly shaved. My legs were aching, so we made for the car and drove on into Wateringbury.

When he was here last summer, David had said that he had broken up two old statues he did not want. I did not know whether to take him literally or not, because the next moment he said if he could find them I could have them for the orchard. Did he mean that he would piece them together for me? I should like to ask if he still has them; they would make this place. The avenues of apple trees would make the perfect setting.

Gerald was here last week. He came from Eton where he has been living in his lodgings and painting while the other masters are on holiday.[5] He was full of his Christmas trip to Paris, Constantinople and India with the Nizam of Hyderabad's second son Faud (how is it spelt?). On his wrist he wore a large eighteen carat gold Rolex watch with alligator strap, clearly an article of luxury that he had never bought himself. Faud had given it to him for his services as unofficial courier, equerry, jester and companion.

On Saturday night Eric took him to Trottiscliffe where they met Graham Sutherland in the Grove. Gerald looks like a younger, rather debased Sutherland, but he is growing much plumper; his bottom has the fashionable feminine bulge. It continually brings the word "globes" to my mind. I told him rudely that he ought certainly to grow thinner.

He had to be back at Windsor today, because he had been asked to be present at the service in St George's to mark the sexcentenary of the Order of the Garter.

I listened to the commentator's absurd inanities over the wireless and thought of Gerald sitting in a dark corner, wearing the expression of a self-possessed but slightly hostile mouse, drinking in the sights and sounds, silently rolling the names over his tongue: Princess Elizabeth, the Duke of Edinburgh, Montgomery, Portland, Devonshire — to say nothing of the King and Queen.

Tomorrow he goes to stay with the Wavells at Rinwood. Eric says he hopes he makes his bed there instead of leaving it all tousled and frowsty as he did here.

5 Gerald (see 1946, note 15 above) had become an assistant art master at Eton under Wilfred Blunt.

24 April, morning.

Four nights ago, with the moon puring down and the nightingale singing and stopping, singing and stopping unaccountably, I suddenly heard another sound. I thought it was a laugh from some woman in the lane. I imagined her wandering round the fields with her lover after leaving the pub. I heard it again and then again. It was no laugh but extravagant sobbing. It rang out, drowning the nightingale, dirtying the night. I ran into Eric's room and told him. He came into my room and we sat by the open french door. The sobbing was a mechanical repetition of notes falling in a scale from high to low. The light was on in the bungalow through the apple trees. The weeping came from there, where a Hungarian lives with his English wife. They are young, newly married in September or October. There was no hint of comforting, reasoning from the husband, no word from the woman, just the hard boo-hoo crying, louder than any other crying I have ever heard, then a sudden ceasing, the light flicked off and nothing. The nightingale streamed on, the wind grew colder, and the moon milked itself into the grass's hair.

13 May

I dreamt I was at a point on Southborough Common which yet was vaguely like the Green outside the West Door of Westminster Abbey, just where the gate opens into Dean's Yard.[6]

Some tall monument, a sort of pillar clamped with iron to a flat, rather thin base, was about to be demolished by a gang of workmen. I asked a bystander why it was to be destroyed, and he answered in one of those commonplace, indifferent voices: "Oh, it's not very old, only early Victorian, and it was put up by mistake; besides, it's very ugly."

I was angry at the wanton destruction and thought the monument not at all ugly. I wanted to get close it it, so that I could read the inscriptions, in large Roman capitals, on either side of the base. But even as I tried to do this a gorilla of a navvy in very old-fashioned red cap shouted out roughly that the pillar was about to be blown up. He was chewing all the time, and he spat constantly, a very wet saliva, as if his mouth were full of water.

All at once something was placed at the base of the column, the workmen tugged on a rope tied to the top, the pillar both blew up and was slapped down by the men with the rope. I thought that one of the men had been trapped in the collapse, he seemed to be wriggling about in the ruins; then I saw him run out and join the crowd.

I was furious and sorry. I thought, "They've pulled it down now, they've

---

6 The Green is enclosed within the gates of Dean's Yard, on the south side of the Abbey. Denton obviously realised this, but expressed himself badly.

had their imbecile destructive way. What will they start on next?"

Just then I looked up and saw Nancy Brooke — an old childhood friend. She was grown-up now and had her young man with her. They were both very tall and well-made, walking rather loosely and lazily. She hailed me with conventional pleasure, said with conventional feeling. "Yes, isn't it a shame pulling the old thing down! Still, it isn't very old," as if time, ancientness, hundreds and thundreds of years, were the only test for preservation.

"Come with us," she said, "we're just going into the medical school." She indicated the building to the right of the destroyed monument (where the hospital stands in relation to the corner I tried to describe at the beginning).[7]

I went with her, still talking about our past and not regarding my surroundings.

We were in a dark room draped like a tent; there were lamps concealed in the folds. Nancy and her young man were becoming businesslike, about to put on their white coats or something like that.

Suddenly I noticed the high trolley in the middle of the room. On it lay a body with arms and shoulders bare. The flesh was purply dusky white. It was swollen as if filled with air.

I thought, "Good God! I am in a place of horror. They take no notice. I can't any longer."

They moved on to the mouth of what was the children's ward. I saw rows of absurd frilly cots — very small. I knew each baby would have some horror. I could hear them crying. I turned to leave Nancy. She said good-bye preoccupiedly.

I realized now that I had to pass the bloated corpse again. I made a little dash, cringing against the wall; but it inexorably, passionlessly put out its arm and let the great weight of putrefying flesh fall across my face.

It had me there under its bored embrace.

26 May

Count Carlo John Rusconi has been here twice to stay, once for the night because he arrived so late and showed no signs of going to catch a train, and the next time at Whitsun from Saturday to Tuesday night.

He is nice, intelligent, sensitive, dreamy, greedy about his food, and sentimental. He is about thirty, has a fine delicate nose, those Italian eyes with too much white, for me, and some scars at the corner of his eye and mouth. His hair is the thin, rather frizzy sort. He has very white, slightly

7 Presumably a reference to Southborough Common, three miles south of Tonbridge; there is no hospital adjacent to Westminster Abbey.

uneven teeth that look brittle; he bites very carefully. His shoulders are very narrow. He is rather hairy. He once had tuberculosis in one shoulder and had to be in a sanatorium above Montreux for two years.

He lives in Florence with his father, mother and youngest sister. Another married sister in New York. His eldest brother died in the war.

I did not see him much because I was ill, but he told Eric his grandfather was exiled "for being a patriot" and lived in London for twenty years. Carlo himself has only been here for about eight months. Nothing has gone right. He is so lonely, so restless, so all to bits. He can't make up his mind if he is a creative person or not. He *wants* to be a creative person, a writer. How is he to tell if he is a creative person?

Yesterday he wrote us a letter pages, pages long, telling us how much he loves coming here, how much better it is than anywhere else in England! He is happier too because he has fixed himself up working as a monitor for the B.B.C. He lives in a hostel, a "millionaire's" house, with fifteen or twenty others. There are lawns and great trees and a pool.

He wants to come again this weekend. I have been very ill since his last visit. (It wasn't his fault, it was coming.) But talking to a lot of people is a strain, although it used to be a joy of life. He is easy, is fond of Eric, helps with the cooking. If he comes, I must only see him a little in the afternoon. To be ill is to be another person. I have been an inert person, lying all day, eating nothing, but imagining my wonderful dishes. Then I have been imagining the most frightful pustules, like guns or pigs' snouts. I have been beheading them until all the horror and corrupting suppuration has gushed out like a geyser. The release of my illness, I suppose.

Now I have to climb back again, work a little, try to move about. I realise now how easy it is to do things if one has no headache. When I am getting worse but am not yet prostrate, I have this bugbear to fight all the time. I think that I shall never shake it off.

28 May

They have destroyed the Grotto at Oatlands, the one that I wrote about in *In Youth is Pleasure*.[8]

When I was with my father at Oatlands in the nineteen-thirties, how I would love to wander down to the wickedly neglected, enchanted little corner!

Destruction is much more than a negative power. It is an evil force at work every moment. It is just another form of cruelty. The Grotto was condemned as "dangerous". The *Architectural Review* says the great brick

8 Oatlands was one of Queen Elizabeth's palaces, near Weybridge in Surrey. It had been converted into a hotel, and Denton stayed there with his father and brothers in 1930.

piers underneath, the stones, the stalagmites, the shells and other lovely nonsense were utterly strong for much more than another hundred years. It was only some of the ornamentation which was loose. This is exactly what I remember as a child of fifteen. The whole place was left to fall to pieces, but only a few fragments lay about mournfully on the floor covered with its dead leaves and other garden rubbish.

Surely a little cement and good repairing costs less than destroying the whole place with pneumatic drills?

When something beautiful and fantastic that will never be made again is destroyed one feels that the earth is just that bit drearier, less precious, more worthy of its surveyor and urban district councils.

How wonderful it must be to be on the side of the destroyers! Almost everything sooner or later would fall into your lap.

8 June

With a high temperature these last few weeks I can read for long stretches, a thing I have not been able to do for months and months, but I do not seem able to write at all. Through the day I stop and wonder enviously how it is done. I wonder however I have done it in the past. I wonder how I could ever have believed even a little in what I wrote. Such emptiness and rubbish is in my mind that I would have no one ever see it.

I have been reading Mauriac's *Thérèse* page after page all morning and afternoon. It is lovely just to feel able to eat up the printed page with no physical obstacle. Calm, with the page turning and my eye following. He is a writer that it is so easy for me to take and embrace that I find myself enlarging all the little things that grate on me.

May's sale was the Saturday before last. Of course I could not go, but Eric bought her largest Chinese Chippendale lacquer cabinet on stand, which had once cost £80 and which May had paid £49 for at the Mint House, Pevensey. Eric paid £8 for it. We have it downstairs now in the drawingroom, where also is her Regency couch of mahogany and brass inlay, for which he only paid £2. I have her smaller cabinet, all bright with birds and flowers, about 1760-1777, up here. It cost £10. It was her favourite. She bought it cheaply in the first war for £15. A bunch of lovely green ivory-handled little knives and forks, the first used at Gunter's in the eighteenth-century, some three-pronged silver forks with early Dresden handles, a George III silver butter-knife with green handles, all went for 30s.

We were amazed at these low prices — unbelievable after the prices of the near past, when pounds had to be paid for the most ordinary things. I think I shall always regret not being able to get more of May's things. Such a chance will not come again soon. And now I keep picturing all the people who have the things that she collected over so many years.

7 July, morning.

Maurice Cranston was here yesterday bringing titbits from Oxford and other places. He said Lord David Cecil, whom I have never met, asked him to tell me that one of my books, I think *Maiden Voyage*, was one of the only two things that have moved him in the last seven years. When I say "things", I mean of course books. One would not like to think that nothing else at all had affected him. He went on to tell me of two favourable mentions of me in books on modern prose, and the absurd note in Joad's book on *Decadence* about my short story "Narcissus Bay". Joad apparently thinks it decadent, I gathered, because it did not seem to lead one anywhere or point any moral. This is all at second hand, so I may be mangling his words.[9] Maurice even mentioned again his American friend who bought thirty copies of *Maiden Voyage* to distribute to friends. He repeated once more W.H. Auden's remarks and seemed surprised that I knew nothing of the latest notices he had just told me of.

What do all these little bits amount to? Nothing to anyone else but me, of course; but I write them down just because they bring for a moment the hint of comfort that is always slipping away. I will not say that they bring encouragement, for they have hidden in them the absurd portentous fear that one can never hope to please again. Solicitude for one's work must always seem ridiculous to others. It is especially easy for the writer or artist to know this, for half the time he is himself utterly unbeglamoured, ashamed of his own silliness.

Last week there was a wireless programme on Marie Bashkirtseff. As I listened again to some of her preposterous boasts and aspirations, Eric suddenly turned to me and said in one of his comic, assumed voices, "I think this little girl is rather like you." What was it? A condemnation? A compliment? Both? Why did it please since she was, after all, rather contemptible? I think it pleased me because I liked to be likened to someone so conscious, so striving, so unresigned. She had the horrible one-track-mindedness of a successful businessman or a devout missionary. She wasted nothing, or if she wasted, she knew all about it, and was violent with herself afterwards. It is strange why egoists of Marie's sort are not more hated — laughed at they often are, for their antics or vanity; but some people come to love them just because of their belief in themselves.

9 Professor C.E.M. Joad had taken "Narcissus Bay" (see 1944, note 10 above) as an example of decadent fiction on the grounds that it was a work written under the assumption "that any experience is significant and worthy of record, irrespective of the quality of the experience or the nature of the 'object' of which it is an experience". *Decadence: A Philosophical Inquiry* (Faber & Faber, 1948).

1 August, morning.

On Saturday I went out with Eric in the car, the first time for weeks. We were going to see a stable and coach-house, "suitable for conversion", near Matfield.[10] The day was wonderful, hot but with a breeze. We took biscuits and cheese, and peanut butter and chocolates and lime juice. We picnicked on Matfield Green, looking at the heavy Queen Anne house with its cupola'd stable and row of cottages, all beautifully kept. Out of the window it made a stiff little picture to look at, a sampler in needlework.

When we packed up the remains of our food and went to see the stable we found that it was enormous, three floors high, on a blind corner on a hill. In front an orchard full of nettles fell away at once, so that one felt that one was perched on a small brick ledge above a precipice. People talked inside the building. One knew they were at lunch, busily eating round a large table. Dorothy Perkins roses unravelled their indecent pink amongst the weeds at the edge of the coachyard. The place was impossible and strong and lasting — an affront in some way.

Brian Easdale's daughter Josephine was here with her mother Frida to see the Adeneys. Josie came round to us and danced on the lawn in her bare feet. They were narrow and smooth and bread-coloured. When she came nearer I saw that she was quite ugly with the ugliness of eight. Her remarks held surprises. When Eric asked her what she wanted to be, she said, "A teacher." "Why?" he continued, rather taken aback by her unromantic choice. "Because Mummy's going to have a baby and that hurts, so I want to be something that doesn't have to have a baby."

Did she feel that it was impossible for a schoolmistress to have a baby? Or just that she was exempt from the unpleasant task?

3 August

I have just had rather a mad letter from T. Sharpley (who first wrote about *Maiden Voyage* and told me that he remembered me when I first went to Repton as a boy of fourteen. He, I think, had been some sort of temporary master).

Now he writes to say that his mother, who died three years ago, often mentions me when they manage to communicate. She was Mary, Countess of Pembroke, Philip Sidney's sister; I was in literary circles and probably attached to the Court. "Quite a lad", as Sharpley puts it. He wished he could put a name to me, but that hasn't come through yet.

I was suddenly released by the dottiness, warmed by it. It was nice to be of

10 Denton's three-year tenancy agreement on Middle Orchard was due to expire in March 1949.

interest to a ghost who had not even known I had existed when she was alive. It was pleasant to be told that I was "quite a lad" in Elizabethan England. I even did not resent the pamphlet on Spiritual Healing enclosed in the letter. Phrases like "the time of waiting seems endless", "when we are beaten to our knees and God takes over, then we begin to get the hang of things and He can work", "you are accumulating power and being held back for the work you came to do".

Such things, thrown at one suddenly by a stranger, seem to have a punch, almost a momentary newness.

10 August, evening. 7.40

Death seems so far away; it recedes and becomes more and more impossible as one grows iller. It is not that it presents itself as some unattainable goal, rather it appears to take on the character of some specious, shiftless creature for ever sliding behind partitions and smiling weakly. The horrible thing about it is its utter silliness.

I have a new doctor, because of this new National Insurance scheme. Jack is too far away at Tonbridge. I can't say I take to him — wooden, caricaturish face, a sort of sparse-haired, golliwog effect. When I had told him of my accident, he began to examine me rather as if I were a doubtful kipper at the fishmonger's. He seemed to find me just as unappetising as he suspected, for he said suddenly, "Have you been told anything about a tubercular condition or not?" I shook my head. The word had a funny sound; I thought of cows and udders and children with crumbly bones like the ones found in tinned sardines.

18 August

David Carritt was here last week when I had a temperature of 103°. He came from Sissinghurst and brought with him, so he said, messages from Vita Sackville-West and Harold Nicolson.[11] They had heard, perhaps from Edith Sitwell, of my most precarious state. They asked me to go over as soon as I was better. I don't suppose I shall ever get there, but I should like to see the house amongst the castle ruins, the habitable rooms here and there, so that one crosses the courtyard to reach the dining-room or bedroom or retreat in the gate tower. I only imagine it all from a scrappy postcard. Perhaps the reality would disappoint me. I have a little sneaking

11 Sissinghurst Castle, in Kent, the dilapidated estate purchased by Harold Nicolson and Vita Sackville-West in 1930, with the intention of restoring the Tudor and Elizabethan buildings and creating a beautiful garden.

silly hope that there might be some tiny place near there for us, if we have to leave here in March.

Noël was in this afternoon — rather jerky and witch-like. It is clear that she cannot really decide what to do about this place. She would like me to go on living here, would like to sell it for an enomous price, and keep it herself all at the same time. A division of desires in a person's face is curious to watch. The features seem to loose themselves. It is as if the nose, the eyes and mouth were hunting for each other.

A journal should be more of a solace than it is. Half the time one is angry with it for its shoddiness, its inadequacy.

31 August, 10.07 a.m.

I want to write it all down, for it was quite an occasion for me, not leaving my room here from one month's end to another. It so happened that I was well, for me, on Friday, in spite of proofs of my short stories which had arrived to be corrected two days before.[12] But Eric had helped me with these, reading them out to me, so that most of the time I could lie back and rest, merely listening intently.

On Friday itself I tried to do nothing at all, husbanding all my resources for our visit to Sissinghurst in the afternoon. We started rather late, because the realization that we had all day made us dawdle over everything, including lunch and our final dressing. I put on my Pekin grass-cloth shirt, my Donegal tweed suit and old "patinated" shoes with lolling tongues. The back of the car was filled with two velvet cushions, gold and terracotta, and the green-and-black Nairn tartan rug Paul brought back from fighting in Italy. I lay there with my feet up, preserving myself fanatically.

It was a most lovely day, clear, the wind a little cold, the sun hot and seeping. We passed many carts, tractors, horse rakes and other implements on the road. By some chance most of the people driving them were extremely young, hardly more than adolescents. Perhaps they were helpers down from London; or semi-gypsy boys from tents and caravans. They were more picturesque than ordinary country people. One wore a dirty beret, almost as large as a tam-o'-shanter, right on the back of his head. Another had silky bleached hair falling over his face. Another, being shaken to bits on a tractor, had an early stiff growth of beard and slanting, unreliable eyes.

We passed through Paddock Wood, Brenchley, skirted Goudhurst. Because we were a little late, and because I knew the places, I could only glance at them. It seemed a waste that I could not enjoy them more since I came out so rarely. Near Goudhurst we asked a robust, elderly road-

12 *Brave and Cruel.*

sweeper the way to Sissinghurst Castle. He smiled, his little white army moustache lifted. He was pleased to show off his knowledge of the country.

"Go to the main road, turn left, drive on until you come to a little green where they used to keep—" Did he say "prisoners in a cage", or am I making this up? There was some antiquarian interest attaching to the little green. We found it all quite easily, since there were signposts further on.

We had meant to stop in Sissinghurst to post letters and buy coffee, but when we reached it I saw that it was already half-past four, and I had told Vita Sackville-West that we hoped to arrive about four. We passed the inviting grocers' shops; I saw that the main inn was being hideously rough-cast. This dashed me a little. To treat an old building in this way is every bit as bad as tarring and feathering a statue. That is too weak; it is far worse, since so much more permanent and damaging.

I now took out the tiny map that Vita had sent me. We passed the church, which looked to be a rebuilding of the early-to-mid-nineteenth-century. There was time to look at nothing properly. Nervousness at meeting strangers mounted up and was suppressed sternly.

Suddenly there was a little turning to the left, half hidden behind a stationary cart. Eric dipped down it almost before he had asked if it were the turning on the map. We drove down the narrow lane, not quite knowing if we were making a mistake or not. On each side of us were broad fields, bare, sweeping away, "deep country" as one understands it.

I remember nothing on the lane until we saw straight in front a long gaunt line of buildings with an archway in the middle. I knew it was Sissinghurst. I felt disappointed; it was so almost ugly, so featureless and unruinous. It had the quality of a granary, a barracks, or an enormous stable.

We drove into a little gravelled square where another car was just about to depart. A tall woman, whom I took at once to be Vita, was bending down, saying good-bye to the man through the car window. She wore cord riding-breeches which disappeared into tall laced canvas leather boots which were very slim. Above the knees she gradually bulged until she came to some blowsy reddish, jersey thing, I think belted at the waist. This part of her body seemed soft and full. On her head she wore a large straw hat, floppy and flimsy, woven in pink-red checks, the sort of large nondescript hat that might be kept for years to wear in the garden and on the beach.

When she had finished with the man in the car, she did not approach us directly, but paused a moment, trying to decide, I suppose, if we were who we were, or if we were simply sightseers come to look over the gardens. I leant out of the back of the car and she came up half-welcomingly. She had a rather mauvy complexion and less severe features than I had remembered across the length of the hall at the Tunbridge Wells poetry reading in 1943. Bits of hair escaping from the hat seemed rather frizzy and curling and greying.

bright enough to make a first meeting really easy; but, on the other hand, it would be wrong to call it boorish or neglectful. Can I describe it as sluggishly dignified? Her voice was slow and rather sleepy too — almost drawling. She said that it was good of us to come so far, and that I must be certain not to walk too much.

We were under the central archway now, and I looked across a beautifully mown green court to an early Tudor tower,[13] slim, with mullioned windows, the organge soft brickwork in a pleasing condition that bordered on disrepair. It had not been spoilt with harsh pointing.

Vita took us to the right, to a gate in the wall which led us through rose-beds to a seat in a high semi-circle of wall. We were in shade. On the wall behind us were trees heavy with unripe nectarines. We sat on the long wooden seat, and Vita offered us her crumpled cigarettes. They came from a leather case, like a man's note wallet. Conversation was a little turgid. I wanted to know about the remains of the great house, and Vita, familiar with it all since 1930, gave me rather vague answers, as if she felt that I could not really be interested, and was only showing politeness. She did explain, however, that most of the house had been allowed to decay, then had been pulled down some time soon after 1765, when the Government gave up using it as a prison for two or three thousand French prisoners of war.

She said lazily: "I'll tell you whom you might know of — Horace Mann owned it in the middle of the eighteenth century, but he never came here. As you know, he spent all the latter part of his life in Florence; but in 1752 Horace Walpole came to look at it for him and described the court as 'very beautiful' and a 'fine gallery' with 'wainscot pretty and entire'."

I longed to hear more, but descriptions did not flow. The elaborate flower garden all about us was exquisitely kept. At the end of the long grove I saw a shadowy white statue. Gardeners passed once or twice in front of us, but each time I looked away, expecting the next moment to be introduced to some son of the house.

At last Harold Nicolson did approach us. I saw him out of the corner of my eye, took in his white trousers and rather bustling walk. He did not smile at first, seemed in rather a hurry, as if we were keeping tea waiting by lolling on the seat under the nectarines. Standing up to be introduced, I was able to take in the little tufts of white above each ear, the easy-going, almost chubby face. The white trousers were of some coarse silky linen. He wore a black and white "fancy" belt which seemed to be slung under his belly as a sort of support. His jacket was dark, almost nautical. He wore canvas shoes.

"Is tea ready?" Vita asked, with a trace of petulance or anxiety.

"Yes," said Harold, "it is waiting."

Now began the stickiest part of our visit. We had to walk across the

13 The tower is in fact Elizabethan.

garden, down the yew walk, to the Priest's House[14] where tea was laid, and neither Vita nor Harold seemed to be able both to manoeuvre their guests and talk to them easily at the same time. I found myself half walking with Vita, half talking to her, while Eric did the same behind me with Harold. Half-hearted attempts at conversation ended in uncomfortable pauses. I tried to take in the doorway, the window in the wall, the little garden in the remains of the cellar through which the path led. It was strange to me that Vita and Harold Nicolson, after years of experience, should not be better at putting new guests at ease. I felt a little resentful, as if I were being forced to try to make up for their deficiency and when my efforts failed, they were holding me responsible.

As we approached the Priest's House I saw a little woman, quite old, dressed in grey, bending over the blooms in the rose garden, picking off old heads. At first I thought of her as some aunt or other relation, or perhaps some old nurse of Vita's. She carried a stick. I imagined that she would be querulous, detached from the world, not understanding us. But when Vita introduced us, a little bell rang, and my notions transformed themselves with amusing rapidity. I was shaking hands with the Lady Colefax that I had often heard about through my life — only a mention here or there, so that I never had any clear idea of her, only thought of her vaguely as a "hostess".

I saw now that she was very beautifully dressed, and that her jewels were interesting. I could not decide about their age, nationality or value. She wore two large rings, a square of cloudy blue, and a circle of diamonds (?). A delicate openwork bracelet seemed to be made of silver, diamonds and dark sapphires. One of her brooches was a diamond spray holding green leaves (which she had picked in the garden) against her lapel. As I have said, my covert examination of each ornament left me perplexed. Silver, diamonds and sapphires seemed such an unlikely combination, and yet I felt that the metal was not platinum. The cloudy square ring, like blue soap, was the most mysterious of all.

If I had felt, before, the awkwardness of Harold and Vita, I was now made doubly aware of their shortcomings; for Lady Colefax at once began a sprightly conversation about nothing in particular. I warmed to her, admiring her animation, decorativeness, the whole indomitable display.

We had entered the Priest's House now, and I saw a long Spanish table with pointless spikes and curves of wrought iron running along its stretcher close to the floor. The table was only laid with a large farmhouse cake and cucumber sandwiches, but there was an air of richness and profusion. Perhaps this was caused by glasses as well as cups being at each place. There was also a large old silver shell, rather beautiful, holding about half a pound

---

14 A cottage in the grounds where the Nicolsons' two sons, Ben and Nigel, lived. It also contained the family dining room.

of butter patted and spanked nicely with ridged wooden boards. At our approach a manservant retreated behind a curtain. The room had a mullioned window, an arched brick fireplace, brick floor, high beamed ceiling, Oriental rugs, fragment of tapestry behind a little medieval wood carving of a saint. Our chairs were William and Mary with high caned backs. I tried, unthinkingly, to rest my arm along the back of mine.

Harold Nicolson said, "There's cider, tea or water — who wants which?" Eric and Vita chose cider. The rest of us had tea, Lady Colefax and I in thick, large Italian peasant cups, Harold in some smaller straight-sided, less clumsy thing. Tiny flies had got into the keg of cider, and Vita fetched an old silver wine funnel through which to strain it. I was glad that I had chosen tea.

Lady Colefax was saying to me, cosily and platitudinously, "Yes, I always like a cup of tea, too", as if she were siding with me against the cider drinkers. The meal began. Vita was the most silent, but I began to feel that she was becoming easier. She turned to me on her left and held out the box of matches with one poking out, ready to be struck.

"I haven't seen that for years!" she said, explaining that a new manservant had only just arrived, and that this convenient arrangement of the matchboxes was one of his little tricks. It seemed to please both her and Harold, in the way that parents are pleased with the pretty ways of their baby.

Harold had already said, as we were walking into the Priest's House, "I didn't think much of your publicity agent, Vita." The remark seemed irrelevant to me and I took little notice, but now the conversation came back to this unfortunate man who had been to lunch. He it was whom we must have seen getting into the car at the gate just as we arrived. Vita again turned to me and said, "This is a man who is hoping to be agent for the new National Trust scheme for taking over the care of gardens which the owners can no longer afford to keep up. He didn't make a very good impression because he didn't know some of the first facts — things we already knew ourselves about the plan."

She sounded mild, drowsy, not very malicious; but then she suddenly grew more animated, looked at Harold and Lady Colefax, and said, "I'll tell you what I do think;" a little pause, "he's the most terrific snob."

My attention was caught. The poor man was going to be torn to bits. Vita was talking again.

"Yes, there was a story about the Duke of Connaught; that one, you know; and there were others too. Yes." She made a funny little repressive shape with her lips, as if she had enjoyed Mr Ackworth's snobbism, but would keep its wildest manifestations to herself.

Lady Colefax, after several criticisms, said: "In fact he ought to be a sort of major — a major would be just right. Oh, and he ate so slowly; that was the thing I really objected to."

This dismembering of the just departed guest in front of the but lately arrived ones struck me as stimulating but perilous. I waited for someone to overstep the mark; confused by suddenly imagining that Eric or I had taken some arrow to our own bosoms. I thought, "I too hate people to eat very slowly, but I am finding difficulty in getting through this enormous bit of cake which Harold Nicolson has given me."

The talk switched to Lindbergh, and his anti-English sentiments expressed to English people when living in England.

Colefax said, "You let him have your house, Vita; everyone said the Nicolsons were so good to him, and yet he hadn't much gratitude, as far as I can see."[15]

"Let him have it!" Vita exclaimed. "You must remember, Sibyl, that he paid us an extraordinarily good rent. They were really very good tenants, and always appreciative of England personally. It was just that his political sympathies were not with us. His isolationist outlook was very common amongst Americans at the beginning of the war; it was just that he was very outspoken and rather tactless."

"It always seems strange to me when a person in a foreign country goes about criticizing it to the inhabitants," I said.

"I do agree," said Lady Colefax, "one doesn't come to settle in England and then tell English people that their country is rotten or falling to pieces; but then I've heard from someone who used to be one of Lindbergh's greatest friends, but now won't have much to do with him, that he was always rather a twisted person. He had an unhappy childhood, and of course that can be responsible for almost anything."

In writing down our conversation, flatly, quickly and rather clumsily, I am very conscious of its inanity and purposelessness; and yet in reality it had another character. Lady Colefax made it bright, quick-moving; Harold and Vita were beginning to feel at home again in their own house; Eric was enjoying his cider, and I felt warmed and protected by the richness of the room. Almost everything stopped short at the seventeenth century. For once it was refreshing to see nothing from one's own favourite eighteenth and nineteenth. Taste which is not one's own is a sort of holiday. One criticizes but enjoys. I wished I could be left alone to look about me. Even now, as I write, I [sentence unfinished]

[Denton Welch died at two o'clock in the afternoon of 30 December, 1948. He was thirty-three. His funeral service was held at Wateringbury Church on 5 January, 1949, and he was cremated at Charing.]

15 Colonel Charles Lindbergh, who made the first transatlantic solo flight and whose child had been kidnapped and murdered. He had leased the Nicolsons' previous home, Long Barn, near Knole.

INDEX

3/17/43 Horace Walpole on Time

Obelisk

Denton Welch's *Maiden Voyage, A Voice Through a Cloud,*
and *In Youth Is Pleasure* are also available in Obelisk editions.

Obelisk